A YEAR *of* SILENCE

A Year *of* Silence

Solitary Retreat in the New Zealand Wilderness

Kiranada Sterling Benjamin

Up Country Books
2017

First Printing: 2017
Second Printing: 2018

ISBN 978-1-387-40956-3

Up Country Books
24 Second Street
Kingston, New Hampshire 03848

www.kiranada.com
www.kiranadasterlingbenjamin.com

Contents

Dedication vii

Acknowledgements ix

Introduction 1

Chapter 1 July 7

Chapter 2 August 33

Chapter 3 September 77

Chapter 4 October 109

Chapter 5 November 135

Chapter 6 December 167

Chapter 7 January 207

Chapter 8 February 237

Chapter 9 March 261

Chapter 10 April 283

Chapter 11 May 303

Chapter 12 June 327

Epilogue 343

Glossary 357

References 363

Dedication

To those who went before,
And to those who will follow.

"To let go, be purged, purified, washed by the night rain, seen-through by the full moon; to be liberated, freed, let loose from all the samsaric bonds of suffering. To see with fresh eyes. To be aware of the deep silence that supports us. To return to source, drink there, be renewed and step out again. To let that compassionate heart flow and spill over. All these things I have learned over twelve months."

Acknowledgements

This book comes from a year of silence on the Coromandel Peninsula of New Zealand and the six handwritten journals I carried out of that retreat full of daily observations, reflections, and introspections; insights from those 360 days alone. I did not plan to produce a book while on retreat but my desire to do this silent retreat "for others," encouraged me to find a way of sharing that experience in a more tangible way.

What is here comes from the gifts of so many including those who led the way, who sought solitude, for both secular and spiritual reasons, following a path of silence; and their writings that inspired me to do this; and those who supported me through the long time alone, with their trust and confidence that I would/could come through for them.

In reviewing this potential book, some recommended that I drop the journal format completely saying, "journal writing is a difficult genre." But there were others who saw what I wanted to do—to take the reader with me through each day, so I could be their eyes and ears; to channel my experience, with all the joys, struggles and suffering that comes from long retreat. Thank you.

It was Kristi Graham who suggested that my journals might, potentially, have value beyond something to share with family and Buddhist friends. With some serious work, she said, this could be something of interest to a wider audience IF I was willing to put in long hours rewriting, deleting, and explaining my experience in language accessible to a non-Buddhist. She offered to help as editor. Succumbing to a second concussion at the beginning of the editing process was most unfortunate since my cognition and ability to work effectively suffered, but Kristi persevered. We went through three edits over ten months, honing and polishing. Deep appreciation goes to this noble woman of Ubud, Bali, for having a vision and for sharing her expertise to whip this into something that might truly benefit others.

The support of so many friends was there though this daunting task, sustaining me though editing, proofing, and formatting this volume. I extend gratitude to those transcribers of the original long-hand notebooks, including Janet Kawada, Peri Onipede, Eileen Clifford, Meredith Fitzherbert, Saddhamala, Joan Walsh and Carolyn Gregsak who told me she cried when the typing of her chapter was completed because she would have to wait to read more.

A number of wonderful people helped me with the onerous process of proofreading. Gratitude to Joan Walsh, Susan Carragher, Bettye Pruitt, Neil Harvey, Bob Guaraldi, Adam Roberts, and the finally the wonderful pro in the UK, Vidyadevi. Despite great efforts, any mistakes or errors that still exist are my own.

Early readers who gave me feedback and encouragement include Victoria Fahey, David Keller, Beverly Russell, Neil Harvey, and Maclean Barker. It was Beverly who spoke of a "modern-day Thoreau." When I needed help with Buddhist references, Amala and Karunadevi came to my aid. Thank you.

Feeling some urgency to get this published soon and knowing the long delays of the publishing business, I was advised to produce it myself. I received expert help from Dale Moyer with the formatting and printing process. Dale worked through the idiocrasies of Lulu publishing with equanimity, coming up with all the answers and polishing the work. Many, many thanks for his effort. And when a cover was needed I first thought of an Order member in the UK, Dhammarati, whose work I had admired for years in books published by Triratna's Windhorse Publishing Company. He agreed to work with me, coming up with an evocative cover combining a view of the moon and fiber work I created on-site in New Zealand. A very pleased Dhammarati realized the fiber piece was titled "Reaching for Silence" only after he juxtaposition it reaching up to the moon image.

And my gratitude spills over for all of those people who helped me accomplish this long year in seclusion. Deep gratitude to Triratna's Abhayaratna Trust and to new friends in New Zealand who were there in numerous ways throughout my stay: in Thames and at Sudarshanaloka: Kate Ewing, Nityadana, Steve Howe, Tony Shaw, Caroline Chambers, Dharmamudra and Satyananda at Lotus Realm. In Auckland, thank you very much to Malini for her kind on-going support throughout my retreat, as well as Akampiya, Vikasani, Purna and Ratnavyuha in addition to Vajrajyoti, chair of the Auckland Buddhist Centre who wrote to me in the USA offering to help in any way, even to walking through my visa extension with the New Zealand Embassy while I was in seclusion. Without the help of all these on-site friends my retreat could not have happened.

For amazing generosity and enthusiasm, I thank many individuals including the gracious Bunny Bowen who offered to set up a website for the purpose of answering the many questions including how, and why I was to doing this retreat. "Make it easy", she said, "and people will want to support you," creating a button to press. And they did, donating food for my belly, the roof over my head, clothing for the winter, and feathers to finance my flight home. Grateful thanks go to the many: Amala, Amy Nguyen, Suzanne Woodland, Dharmottara, Chris Shorey , Ann Wessmann, Sue Winski, Brinda Callahan, Steve Bruce, Lois Sans, Carolyn Gregsak, Viradhamma, Dayalocana, Dayanandi, Danielle Genovese, Diane Worth, Diane Palaces, Nora Judd, Elizabeth Constable, Lark Hammond, David Buehler, Shantikirika, Jennifer Pitre, Karunasara, Vidhuma, Kamala Masters, Janet Kawada, Jim Hagen, Jay Rich, Meredith Fitzherbert, Joan La Moure, Judith Leeman, Kami Kanetsuka, Sekiko Yamade, Kety Bagwalla, Karunadevi, Khemavassika, Shirley Stewart, Luana Coonen, Martha Andreatos, Rhonda Mann, Neil Harvey, Nancy Nicolazzo, Kristine Cummings, Saaraliisa Ylitalo, Samayadevi, Kerstin Gleim, Lilasiddhi, Stephen Cardwell and Vikasasri, Sunada, Susan and Dale Moyer, Setsuko Ries, Mary Schaefer, David Keller, Vidyasara, Vimalasara, Viryagita, Sandra Sirois, Myra Bicknell, Linda Phillips, Tanya Prather, Merridee Smith, Gail Valtz Mecklen, Ardys Roemmelt, Marney Roemmelt, Singhatara, Sudaya, Cynthia Troup, Dharmasuri, Wendy Allard, Jean Emmons, Linda Lisciarelli, Susan Carragher, Lisa Paiva, Eileen Clifford , Evelyn Pieydell, Mary Jane Keys, Lisa Reily, Gail Yahwak, Paul Dupre, Mark Gillis, Anastra Madden, Steffanie Schwan , Erin Robertson, Corey Doherty, Kamalasiri, Inga Strause-Godejord, San Miguel Meditation Group, Kingston Community Library group and many more.

To those who held down the fort at home and dealt with moving money from the USA to New Zealand in my absence, booking flights I could not make a year in advance, forwarding documents for visa needs and making sure that my websites did not crash with 10,000 messages, a big thank you goes to my daughter Amanda Benjamin-Murray and friends Bunny Bowen, and Dayalocana.

Finally, I am grateful to my community at Aryaloka Buddhist Center, to my friends and teachers, and to Urgyen Sangharakshita, who founded this Triratna Buddhist Order where I could seek ordination as a western woman, giving me a clear, liberating path to freedom. Gassho.   May all beings be happy!

***

I am grateful for permission to use material from publishers whose works have inspired and guided my solitary retreat. Every effort has been made to seek out all copyright holders. If there has been an omission or error, please contact the author for prompt rectification.

Excerpts from the following work published by Windhorse Publications, are used with permission: Kamalashila. ©1992, *Meditation: The Buddhist Way of Tranquility and Insight*; and the following by Sangharakshita, © 2001, *Dhammapada*; ©1993, *Drama of Cosmic Enlightenment;* © 1993, *What is the Dharma?;* © 1998, *The Essential Teachings of the Buddha* ;© 2003, *Living with Awareness* and ©1995 , *Ritual and Devotion in Buddhism.*

Excerpts from following work published by Bloomsbury Publishing Plc. are used with permission: Vicki Mackenzie, copyright © *1999, Cave in the Snow: A Western Woman's Quest for Enlightenment.*

Excerpts from the following work published by University of Hawai'i Press are used with permission: Sally McAra, Sally, copyright © 2007. *Land of Beautiful Vision: Making a Buddhist Sacred Place in New Zealand.*

Excerpts from the following work published by Open Court Publishers are used permission: Philip Koch, copyright © 1994, *Solitude: A Philosophical Encounter.*

Selections from the following work published by Shambhala Publications, are used with permission; Ryōkan, copyright ©*1997, One Robe, One Bowl: The Zen Poetry of Ryōkan.* Translated and introduced by John Stevens. First edition. 1977. Protected by copyright under the terms of the international Copyright Union. Reprinted by arrangement with the Permissions Company Inc., on behalf of Shambhala Publications Inc., Boulder Colorado. www.shambhala.com.

Excerpts from the following work published by Wisdom Publications are used with permission: Bhikkhu Bodhi, © copyright 1995, *The Middle Length Discourses of the Buddha (Majjhima Nikaya)*; Bhikkhu Bodhi, © 2000, *The Connected Discourses of the Buddha (Samyutta Nikaya);* and Ajahn Brahm, copyright © 2006, Mindfulness, *Bliss and Beyond; Shaila* Catherine, © copyright 2008, Focused *and Fearless;* Jane Dobisz. Copyright © 2008, One *Hundred Days of Solitude* and Bhante Henepola Gunaratana. copyright © 2009, *Beyond Mindfulness in Plain English.*

Introduction

I fly out of a New England summer of lake swimming, watermelon, tomatoes and fields of corn, across the United States, through San Francisco, where I board a second plane that will take me around the world, to Auckland, New Zealand, 13,000 miles and fourteen hours away in the Southern Hemisphere. It's a long, long flight over the Pacific, yet it feels quite familiar, for I lived in Japan for eighteen years and made yearly travels back home. It was in Japan that I found Buddhism, seeing a monk walking the back streets of Kyoto with such a glowing face that I wanted to know what he knew, and how it could make him so happy. It was there that I started the daily meditation practice that has been part of my life for thirty-five years. Japan was also a time of raising children, ending relationships, pursuing my art, multiple exhibitions, and producing a book on the Japanese wax-resist that I researched and practiced. My Soto Zen studies were important too, but with my limited language facility, it was difficult to move further. And the idea of Buddhist ordination, as a western woman in Japan at that time, seemed unattainable.

Upon return to the Unites States, I found Triratna, a western Buddhist Order, where I could study the Dharma in English, have the support of a vibrant community, and undergo the training I needed for the next step. In June of 2009, I received ordination in the mountains of Spain with an international group of seventeen women. I became Kiranada.

Now I'm on an airplane, at 36,000 feet, flying across the Pacific to a year of silence in the New Zealand bush while others snooze all around me. I look at what brought me here to this time in my life and many things come up. I have always been a searcher with an adventurous spirit, curious about nature, about people and their stories, about my own internal story and what motivates me. After multiple short solitaries, two to four weeks in length, the idea of a full year of solitary retreat intrigued me.

But why now? A little over two years ago, I returned from a winter in Mexico with overwhelming responsibilities: preparation for a large solo exhibition, a new commission request, a car that was breaking down, and a computer that had stopped dead. It was the computer and car that did me in and had me thinking it was time to reassess this busy

1

life and go. I'd just come from a month's solitary retreat in Mexico. It had been disturbing, but held much promise of future illumination.

I sat down, looked at my life, and saw a new decade beginning in just two years. I knew that it would take me that long, with careful planning, to make it happen. Checking with family and work colleagues, I made a plan to be off by July of 2014 for that long retreat—to focus on my meditation practice, watch the birds, deal with any demons that came up, and be silent for a year. What would come of it? Work colleagues worried I might never come back. Family and friends worried if I would be safe. What I wanted was time for something that had been intriguing me since I was a child.

It's 5:20 AM when the plane lands on a clear July day. It's deep winter, I'm told, but a mild, rainy one rather than the snowy chill of home. In Auckland I spend two nights in a Buddhist women's community getting over jet lag, gathering supplies, and seeing an old friend, before I disappear for a year.

The drive out of the city takes me through suburbs and a landscape of flat farmland. In an hour, I enter the Coromandel Peninsula. Its jagged peaks form a backdrop to the small town of Thames, formerly a gold mining village, now sleepy and quiet. At first, the road hugs the Firth of Thames, but soon we turn off eastwards and up for twenty minutes between steep, overlapping spurs covered in a craggy deep green, overlooking the dark valley that I will call home for a year.

We're unable to cross the river onto the Sudarshanaloka Buddhist Retreat Center's land because of a swift current from heavy rain. It's a typical occurrence here, I'm told. But a four-wheel drive vehicle is there to pick me up with my supplies. We drive across and up, up, along a rugged gravel road for twenty minutes to the small hut in the bush that I'll use as a hermitage. I feel like Alice slipping through the looking glass. Again, I'm reminded by a local supporter, "it's for a year" and "ALONE." Who will I be when I come out? Will there be insights? Will there be troubles? I have no idea how hard it will be, but I'm ready.

I've asked for this solitary confinement at Abhaya Hut, whose name means Fearlessness. I put my right hand up, palm facing forward, fingers rising to the sky in the mudra of fearlessness, and step off the transport to walk that last quarter mile in.

I step into the darkness of overhanging growth: tree ferns, perching lilies dangling above, kauri, rata and puriri trees, and bamboo tangles of supplejack. This is a land I'm so unfamiliar with.

I walk into the dark of the bush. And then, around a corner, a small green hut appears, perched on a precipice, open to the grand valley below, sitting in the sun. Home!

I'm committed. I've been drawn since childhood to do this year alone, eager and curious to learn what might be presented to me. I'm looking for answers to the simple question: what would happen if I sat in the high bush by myself for twelve months without the support of everyday distractions? Other more profound questions come up: would I survive, would I go mad, would I continue to create, would I discover new things, who would be my teachers, would my Buddhist studies and meditation support and ground me? Would my solitude allow me to find what that Japanese monk with the glow knew?

I'm guided by words from my elders and carry these words with me into the silence.

"I went to the woods, to live deliberately."   — *Henry David Thoreau*

"When you realize how rare and how precious your life is, and how completely you are responsible for how you live it, how you manifest it, it's such a big responsibility that naturally such a person sits down for a while." — *Kobun Chino Roshi*

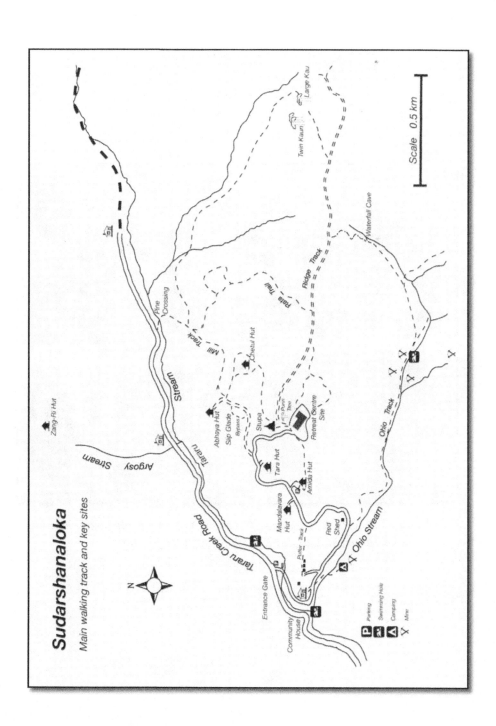

Sudarshanaloka
Main walking track and key sites

Scale 0.5 km

Zang-Ri Hut

Argosy Stream

Stream

Taranu

Taranu Creek Road

Pine Crossing

Mill Track

Rata Trail

Ridge Track

Abhaya Hut
Slip Glade
Bypass

Chetul Hut

Twin Kauri
Large Kauri

Stupa
Puriri Tree
Retreat Centre Site

Waterfall Cave

Tara Hut
Amida Hut

Mandalavara Hut

Putfur Track

Red Shed

Ohio Track

↓ Ohio Stream

Entrance Gate

Community House

N

Parking
Swimming Hole
Camping
Mine

P
Swimming
Camping
X

5

Abhaya hut with netting covering the porch vegetable boxes, hanging pansy pot, and the outdoor bath to the right.

Chapter 1   July

Abhaya Hut
Sudarshanaloka Buddhist Retreat Centre
New Zealand

July 19, 2014

This morning I slept late in this small hermitage with the deep cold around me—waking at exactly 7:38 AM and up for twenty minutes of exercise while water boiled and tea steeped on top of the gas heater. This little heater takes hours to really warm the room here on a ridge of the Coromandel wilderness, when it starts at 36ºF/2ºC outside and 43ºF/6ºC inside, but exercising helps to warm me up. It's been a week of many "firsts" since arrival, but I finally feel settled enough to open a new notebook and start this New Zealand journal in earnest.

It's good to be here on my seventh full day alone, writing on the porch in the winter sun with gloves on, a hat and a blanket. It's not quite the New England July I'm used to. I'm delighted that I did have a good six to seven weeks of summer weather before coming to the Southern Hemisphere and winter.

My first night on the Sudarshanaloka land, July 12th, it began raining and went on for twenty-four hours. Arriving at the entrance, the staff helped me over the river ford, which was soon running over three feet, or one meter high. It became impassable soon after I arrived on the land, and half of the women's retreat members who were coming a few hours after me were stuck on the other side for the night, unable to get to the Community House for the start of their week's retreat.

I'm indeed remote and cut off, yet I feel secure and confident in my choice to come here. I have been given Abhaya Hut, at the far end from the river crossing and high above the entrance to the property—about two kilometers and a thirty to forty minute walk downhill. Abhaya is one of five solitary abodes on this land.

After solitary retreats in Thailand, Wales, Mexico and Indonesia I have chosen New Zealand and Sudarshanaloka as the site of this long year retreat because of the expected mild climate, the support team here, and what I thought was a lower housing cost. What I later learned was that the small rustic hut would be one of the most expensive places I have rented in my life, and that includes the eight-room house in Japan where I lived for eighteen years. But I have always been blessed, and my needs are simple, and the support and weekly food delivery service I have paid for will be worth the price. Others have helped me with this cost and my gratitude to all of them overflows. This is an opportunity I have dreamed of for years.

Today was the second day of morning frost. It would have snowed, I believe, had there been any precipitation. The forest on the far side of the ravine has two steep hillside fields or pastures, and they appeared snowy white this morning as the sun crested the valley wall to the east. Now, at 10 AM, they're back to pale green. The roar of the Tararu River, heading west to the Firth of Thames, is strong down below, but no longer the urgent deluge of a week ago when I arrived. The waterfall I can see with binoculars across the valley is barely visible, unlike the tumbling white of last week when it ran gloriously for a few days—a source of hydropower for a farmhouse in the valley below me.

I hear a "cheet cheet" sound and am visited regularly by a friendly fantail the size of a sparrow, called a piwakawaka bird in the native Maori language. He chirps and cartwheels a greeting many times during the day. When I hacked my way through the dense bush, down twenty feet to the base of the big pine tree below the hut, he flew within two feet of me, quite tame and curious as I sat there on the steep slope, part of the landscape.

I'm watching and learning from all that's around me, my eyes wide open to see this quiet land. Could that have been a New Zealand quail or koreke couple I saw at the edge of the front clearing at noon? One had facial marks and was scratching and digging; the other seemed a common brown. But they had a topknot, so my local bird book tells me they had to be California quails.

Besides blessing my living space and the surroundings, and doing a dedication to this long retreat, it was important for me to do a few things during those first few days here. This included a visit to the Sudarshanaloka stupa, investigating that roaring river I hear but cannot

8

see, and a climb down to the one lovely pine whose top I can just see from the hut porch. I wanted to touch that trunk reverently, and connect through the 13,000 miles to my New Hampshire home of pine trees. I expect I'll climb down there often to say hello and smell the pine sap and needles, one of numerous ways to ground me in this strange new land.

Another grounding place is the stupa hill. It's a spiritual focal point here on the 250-acre retreat land. It was the first thing built when a group of Triratna Buddhists purchased this land back in the 90s, and one of the first places I ventured out to experience. The walk took me through the dark bush of Slipglade Track, and up Dharma Road to the high plain of the stupa. Standing almost thirty feet tall, it glows in the changing light.

A stupa looks like a spherical structure but is actually a sacred monument that embodies the qualities of enlightenment. Most stupas contain the ashes or relics of a Buddhist monk or teacher, and the Sudarshanaloka stupa is no different. It houses the relics of the Tibetan high lama Dhardo Rinpoche, who died in Kalimpong, India in 1990. Dhardo was a close friend of our Triratna founder and teacher. On this land, the stupa hill is a place of deep inspiration, a place for festivals and gatherings, and a quiet space to sit and meditate. I have come to this hill with my senses open, absorbing the atmosphere, feeling the energy, knowing that it could be a place of deep comfort and support during my long stay.

Today I did one of the traditional practices in my Triratna Buddhist Order—the Refuge Tree and Prostration practice. I began this over ten years ago as a regular daily practice, and did it for over two years before my ordination as a means to draw me closer to Buddha. I felt that the familiar visualization as well as the physicality of full prostrations could help to ground me in this dense wilderness. In this practice, I imagine the Buddhas and Bodhisattvas, Sangharakshita, our Triratna founder, and the Teachers of present and past, and sit quietly with all of them, taking in that energy. Next, I mentally welcome my parents, family and friends, and bring them into this small hut hung on a precipice above the river. The nights here are a deep, dark black and the bush is quite dense, so it is reassuring to feel all those Buddhas, teachers, friends and family present with me.

I feel blessed, secure and welcomed. The welcome extends even to the moon phases, and I wait each night for that moon to rise in the east, often about 1 AM.

And it was a gloriously full moon my first night here, when I glimpsed it during a break in the rain—a "super moon." The next morning, I gasped when I opened my door and saw a huge yellow moon disc setting in the west. I've clocked its set, size and location each day as if I were Admiral Byrd doing meteorological reports in the Antarctic. He's one of several solitaries I've been reading about with great interest, feeling they will be supporters for my retreat.

I'm happy, content, and exceedingly grateful to all those here and at home who have helped me arrive for this special year. I'm aware of so many beings here with me including some on the roof (are those birds?) and in the eaves. The silver tree ferns that the New Zealanders call ponga are full of little feathered friends cheeping their support. I feel it. Blessed be.

And today, along with all the other "firsts" of the week, I decided I should try out the outdoor tub installed for my use. An hour and a half later the burners under the tub had made the water warm enough for an Epsom salt bath. The air temperature wasn't more than 55ºF/12ºC, yet there I was, out under the sky, soaking in a tub with a view of the vast valley before me. It felt exhilarating. Afterwards, I hustled inside quickly and dressed. My late lunch was some o-chazuka (or Japanese rice porridge) with a sweet piece of kinoko mochi (pounded rice) for dessert. After eighteen years in Japan, I was delighted to find a Japanese/Asian food store in Auckland to stock up on these delicacies for this time in the remote bush. How exotic!

July 20, 2014

A tremendous windy rainstorm kept me awake last night. Rattling windows and blowing gusts surrounded this exposed little hut. I read until 11 PM, turned out the light, but soon turned it back on to read some more, too unsettled and disturbed by the gale to fall asleep easily.

Over this first week here in the bush, I have found that my dreams are surprisingly vivid. I know that I'm stepping out of an old life and perhaps decompressing from a busy time full of schedules. Why would I be surprised that my dreams are slow to catch up and have me still stressed and rushing to meetings? Two nights ago, a particularly anxious dream had me accidentally locked in a car in a parking garage for the night with my niece Jenn and her five kids.

However, last night's dream was sweeter. The Refuge Tree/Prostration Practice, the chanting, and even planting some little seedlings may have helped with the deep grounding I feel I need to truly "arrive." I woke this morning from that sweet dream with Terry, my young sister, and Jerry, her husband, present—as they were thirty years ago, young and happy with each other, before illnesses filled their Christmas letters with doctor's reports. Terry has been gone ten years now, and her kids are 24, 25 and 26, with children of their own. However, a different dream . . . one of banana pancakes . . . was the one that clearly woke me up.

It's Sunday and I'm sitting in a small hermitage on a ledge above the Tararu Stream. It's a cold, overcast day, with everything slowly drying out from a raucous, rainy night. I'm still bundled up and wearing gloves inside the hut, trying to conserve propane heating gas, but I feel less stiff and somewhat stronger after my fifteen to twenty minutes of morning yoga. I follow that exercise with forty-five to sixty minutes of meditation, and then breakfast, writing and study.

Today is the end of the women's retreat down below at the Community House, so I'll walk down to the Center to visit the small library there, pick up some fitted bottom sheets, and drop off my camera and phone to be recharged on their equipment. Telephone reception here is on and off with only one to two bars, depending on cloud cover, but perhaps there will be enough in the future for a text message or emergency call. Again and again, I come to the realization that I am here, remote, in New Zealand alone.

This week I'm reading a lot of poems, pujas and articles on Amitabha, the red Buddha of the West, and feeling his warm love here in Sudarshanaloka, "the land of beautiful vision." I am comforted to remember that Amitabha shines in the top-knot crown of Kuan Yin. She was born of a ray of light from his eye, a manifestation of his compassion in the world, and is bonded by a vow to comfort and save all sentient beings. Kuan Yin is a Bodhisattva very close to me. I received her path at ordination along with my name, "Kiranada," as a manifestation of who I am or what I aspire to, part of my practice for the future.

Along with words on Amitabha, I'm reading of Dilgo Khyentse Rinpoche, a Tibetan master who speaks of devotion as the essence of the path. To have nothing in mind but the Bodhisattva, to feel only fervent devotion, means that whatever happens in life can be perceived as the Bodhisattva's blessing. He says that "to simply practice with this constant present devotion, this is prayer itself." I'm listening. To invite the Bodhisattva to live within me, to walk in her robes, to see the world through her eyes, to manifest her compassion, these are some of my wishes for this solitary retreat. Some.

But echoing through my mind, I hear the sentence "Not I, not I—but the wind that blows through me." Where did that come from, and who said it? It seems to fit as I lose myself here on this precipice and flow easily into this wind that will be with me for twelve months.

July 21, 2014

At 6 AM, it's really cold inside this hut (45ºF/6ºC). It's lovely to open a book I've brought with me and find the photo of my friend Diane, with me in New Hampshire sunshine, our foreheads touching, transmitting our love and best wishes to each other. On the back of the photo she prepared as a gift are quotations on how friendship can deepen in absence.

I get the heater going early, but it goes out and I worry that the propane tank, replaced when I arrived, is already empty. I relight it and it keeps going this time. Good. I'm slowly learning the ins and outs of life in this hut. Lighting the cook stove with a lighter takes some finesse—getting some gas flowing first and snapping the lighter for a scary swoosh of heat and flame. I need to keep the burners turned low, however, even though Tony cleaned the stove when I arrived; if the flame is high, it burns orange and fills the room with a bad smell.

I have a true yoga mat now and roll it out first thing do my Moon Salutations. Every other day it's the full Refuge Tree Prostration Practice. I'm not doing the prescribed three hundred sets of full prostrations but allowing myself to slip back into the vigorous practice slowly, pleased to be on my knees, then on my belly, forehead down and touching the floor—all to honor the Buddha and the potential for enlightenment in all of us.

I've been happy to have a session of meditation outside almost every day, either first thing in the morning when the moon is setting in the west, or in late afternoon as the sun disappears over the canyon wall and the night chill begins. I try to be outside much of each day, connecting to this land of tree ferns, pines and lilies, watching and listening.

But by early evening today, I'm struggling. I come to this retreat with a brain injury, a severe concussion twenty-one months ago that still troubles me with recurring symptoms. I fell while carrying a thirteen-foot ladder and it landed right between my eyes. Yikes! There's still some brain fog and a slight headache daily upon waking—even now, so many months later, and I still have dizziness and nausea when I read too much and use my glasses. But the debilitating headaches have abated. Only six months ago, at six thousand feet altitude in Mexico, they came daily. There, I struggled to function, to travel through airports, and even to hold simple conversations. I did minimal work on computer screens since that seemed to irritate the symptoms. A visual Skype call could put me to bed for hours. Now I'm trying to alternate reading with time outside watching clouds.

Excitingly, just now as I was reading a chapter, I saw the moment when, in the past, I'd have to put down the book and do something simpler rather than concentrate on complicated concepts, but . . . I could go on! What a thrill to see my brain wrap around some things that were beyond me six months ago! After almost ten days of quiet, no computer screens, no TV or telephone calls, I've found that cognitive edge and stepped over it. Hallelujah!!! Amazing to find some mental function still being restored, after 21 months. As my neurologist predicted, "This year retreat will be the best thing you could do for your healing brain. Go off and be well. Come back healed." I'm beginning to feel that further healing clearly today, and I'm so grateful.

I did a Kuan Yin Puja ceremony tonight and felt so fortunate to have her with me. Kuan Yin, the Bodhisattva of Compassion, is my yidam. In our Order, we each chose a yidam, often a deity associated with tantric or Vajrayana Buddhism said to be a manifestation of Buddhahood or the enlightened mind. When we do a regular personal meditation (sādhana) practice, we identify ourselves, our attributes and mind, with those of the yidam for the purpose of transformation. Kuan Yin is my personal deity, here with me for this long haul, guiding, protecting and inspiring.

In my mind, I saw a six-foot tall, white robed Kuan Yin standing near the door of my room and wanted paper to draw her. Will I do it? Can someone help me get a roll of white paper, I wonder?

Despite trying to bring everything I might need for a year, every day additional needs come up. I am trying to keep my "needs" to a minimum and just manage but the staff and near-by Buddhist communities want to support us long-term retreatants. Bless them! Just this morning, after leaving a message last week in a "drop-box," new friends in Auckland helped me get some "seed syllable" images, the research I wanted for mani rock painting. These seed syllables don't always have a precise meaning, but each deity has one associated with him/her. Kuan Yin carries the seed syllable "hrih" and I'm delighted that I can soon start painting some of those Tibetan letters on rocks to disperse energy throughout the land in the next few months.

This week, as I walked the paths, I looked for rocks with appropriate flat surfaces. However, I know that I need to focus on walking the paths more and not rock hunting. I'm compulsive here. The art, the creative side of me, is eager to flow and be expressed but it is late and time for bed. May I be well. May all beings be well.

July 22, 2014

Just a bit of moon showed about two o'clock this morning, in the eastern sky, over the Tararu Sanctuary. Now, at 7:50 the sun is cresting the eastern ridges and shining across the peaks. It's the first morning of sunshine in three days. I woke at 4:30 AM, cold and chilly after a modern version of a "hell realms" dream, one I'd never had before. My sympathies and desire to help others in my dream, with kindness and compassion, seemed to come to no avail, and I had to awake and let go.

This morning I wrote up my first weekly food list. The arrangement is that Steve will pick it up from the box today, and tomorrow make the trip to Thames, shopping for all the retreat huts that are occupied. I saw him briefly on Sunday and passed my phone and camera to him for recharging. Coming from town he had some welcomed mail to hand me and offered a lift back up the hill on his four-wheel off-road vehicle. At the hut, he stopped to write out a list of what still needs doing when he drops the groceries. He asked when I would go into silence and I said—from now—today! But it cannot be quite yet. I'm eager to begin, to step into this new quiet space and see what will come up with no human contact and no distractions from outside. But this will need to wait until the work on the hut is completed.

I see a difference in the two great "bush" men who form the support team for the huts. I worked with quiet Tony when he dropped me off some days ago, installed a smoke alarm, and explained how the water and solar electricity worked. He showed some surprise when I pulled out my own voltage checker from the States. Steve, the white-bearded, gregarious one, told me today, "I'll be here often. You'll need a lot of help—because you're a woman." I raised my eyebrows, surprised. Although I do get some help from neighbors in New Hampshire, I live alone and do much of the maintenance work on the house myself. I rarely hear such comments from other Buddhist men—but I work mostly with the women's community.

At noon I suffered dizziness and nausea as I came down the Chetul Track after sketching on the hillside at the stupa today—those lingering concussion symptoms. Stepping inside the hut, I was happy to be home, able to make a nourishing lunch, rest, and read some of Henry David Thoreau's solitary writings. Looking at his views on poverty and getting by with less, I remembered that food list I had left out in the pick-up box, scampered out there and crossed off five things. Then I added two more!

It's cold outside, down to 44ºF/7ºC with high winds by late afternoon. The seedlings and pansies I purchased early for some porch color are covered for another chilly night. Locals have told me they're pleased I arrived during the worst season because from now on the weather will just get better.

I've realized that to stay in one locale, one hut, for a full year is truly unusual for me. This is the first year since early childhood that I won't be traveling. Even as a little child under four, I remember taking a Greyhound bus with family up to Quechee Gorge in Vermont. And every weekend, from spring through fall, we went to New Hampshire from our home in Lynn, a Boston suburb, to work on the camp where Dad hoped to retire. In summer, we had two weeks camping on sand dunes in Montauk, Long Island to visit our grandmother in Easthampton. In my teens, I traveled with the Girl Scouts to encampments in the Midwest and Canada and took Greyhound buses on my own to visit childhood friends in New York City and Montreal. My adult years found me living in Japan, Iceland, Mexico, and Indonesia, and traveling extensively through Asia, Europe, and the Americas. Travel, always. I wonder . . . what it will be like to stay in one place, on my cushion, for a year?

I am open to new experiences and deeper realizations. One thing I especially want is to become more mindful, and connect more strongly with nature. Thinking of this in New Hampshire, I thought I would document the changes in the pine trees: when the needles dropped, when new growth started, when the pine cones developed, and sap ran. But here I am placed in a landscape with few pines, surrounded by trees that I don't know. I realize that "waking up" and true awareness can come in any landscape. I want very much to drop self and just "be" in the universe, even in this small patch of land.

July 23, 2014

Unhappy news: there's a rat in the poop house. Not just in the house but in the hole, running around. Maybe at first he was enjoying my vegetable scraps, since that's where I've been told to dispose of compost, but now he's frantic. How did he get in, and how will he get out? I wrote a note to leave for Steve, asking for help with this when he stops to drop groceries, and a new gas cylinder.

At 1 PM the rat was still in there when Steve and a helper, Nityadana, arrived. I was all packed up ready to walk down to Pine Crossing before they arrived to work so that I could stay in silence, but seeing Nityadana, I stopped to speak with him of the devotional practice we share. He's another Kuan Yin practitioner.

While we chatted, Steve found my rat note, managed to get the baby out, and then used some plastic bags to push into the one-inch space at the top of the container barrel where the six-inch rat slipped through. He really was trapped. The guys were rushed and did little more than drop my food, leaving a number of other jobs for later. We both hope to be done with all these move-in chores, so that visits end and I can go completely into silence, and Steve can go on with the maintenance work at the other four huts he manages, but not today.

I finally got down to the Pine Crossing, taking a good forty-five minutes on the way, clearing as much windfall and debris from the path as I could without a saw. I moved slowly, watching my footing—not wanting to take a tumble. After a day and a half of nausea and dizziness, I felt better being outside. I did some serious tree-hugging also, and that may have helped with my needed grounding. At the river, I sat way out on a flat river rock (a good test of my Merrell waterproof shoes—yes, they work), lost a work glove in the rapids and scooped the other one out as it swooped in an eddy. Surrounded by all that moving water, it felt good to have so much solid ground nearby.

I was happy to come home and dip into some cauliflower and vegan sausage soup. Happy to be here. Happy to be warm some of the time. Happy to have a hot water bottle, especially when the night time temperature goes to 41ºF/5ºC inside. The guys had asked me if I ran the gas heater all night long. No, no, I said! Yet it seems I went through a whole tank of propane in eight days. They felt that the tank was not functioning well and quickly changed a valve attachment. While he was here Nityadana showed me how to change tanks and get the valve really tight with a damp hand towel—even with my limited muscle power. I'm learning how to manage here alone as I do at home and looking forward to the challenge.

Looking over my day I see that I am moving into four hours a day of meditation, I hope for five to six hours once all is settled and quiet. But with the distractions of visitors and caring for hut needs during this extended arrival period, I'm just able to hold mindfulness. Morning visualization and two or three sits during the day is what I can do. I'm reminded of my New Hampshire friend Karunasara, who advised me to just take a good month to settle in, but my mind buzzes with many things including art projects. After a lifetime as a visual artist, ideas for art projects just bubble up. I had a wonderful inspiration this morning to wrap drawing paper around the upper wall with marks each day recording weather, rainfall amounts, the moon phases, etc. Will it happen? It's brewing. Is it on paper or cloth? Hmmm.

17

July 24, 2014

Another morning waking to a headache (6 on a scale of 10). I function—changing the gas tank again, preparing tea and oatmeal, cleaning up spilt chia seeds and washing my bean sprouts, but my mind is foggy. Meditation is always difficult in this condition, but I try. Chanting, doing some visualization, pulling Kuan Yin down for help, blessings, and compassion—all help.

When I woke last night at midnight, the sky was heavy with stars—possible the deepest night sky I've ever seen other than on the beach in Mexico and a few places in Bali. It was in the low 40s, so I thought twice about going outside to explore with my night sky charts, but I will. I don't know this Southern Hemisphere sky at all, but I have a year to become familiar with it. I wish I had someone to introduce it to me (as well as introduce the birds and trees) but this is my year of silence, so I will do it alone. This solitary retreat throws me back onto myself, to what I can find within and from the written words I've brought with me. While reading, I discover amazing things that I might have missed in another context, such as the fact that more than 90 percent of the world's population lives in the Northern Hemisphere. The Southern Hemisphere is truly sparse. I wonder why? Is there less habitable landmass here?

The headache keeps me from contemplation. I ask myself why I don't want to take pain medication. I've had so many months of medication for these concussion symptoms that I'm just reluctant. It's a bit better after eating breakfast. And it's always better when I can be outside, so I try that too. Although I just want to lie down, my "doer mode" has me reading, studying and note-taking instead. I put that aside and look out at the ridges, watching the smoke that's coming from a far-off homestead chimney, and revel in the piwakawaka fantails who are cartwheeling in the sun in my front yard.

I notice and write down such small things, inconsequential to others but seemingly important to my life here: the sky is clear blue, a small plane goes over like it did yesterday afternoon, and the temperature is a cool 51ºF/11ºC at 11 AM.

I've brought many other solitary recluses with me to this ridge through their writings, including Admiral Byrd in the Antarctic 83 years

18

ago, Milarepa in his cave in eighth-century Tibet, the Desert Fathers, and Mothers, of the third century Christian era, and the more recent solitary Bob Kull, who used a year of rugged survival alone on an island off Chile in 2001 to examine solitude, the topic of his PhD thesis.

I learn from all of them. Being on solitary, I'm retreating from society, community, and social responsibilities. And yet the natural result of retreat is return: the coming back, sharing the observations, sharing feelings of complete quiet. To not return, or to not share in some way, would feel incomplete—only half of the whole. Yet I understand the yearning for solitude even as I know I will return.

Peter France, author of *Hermits: The Insights of Solitude*, writes that the monastic Thomas Merton felt the need for solitude to escape the "artificial self" created to satisfy other people's expectations. Echoes of that come forward as I remember the comments of two senior Order members who told me others "would want a piece of you." A piece of me? What does this mean? Is it connected to others' expectations or wishes about what might come from a year alone?

My earliest inspiration for a solitary life, the first time I knew I had a yearning to do something like this, was in my teen years when I saw the film *The Birdman of Alcatraz*, with its solitary confinement and sensory deprivation. Even at that young age, I was curious; if all the usual societal connections and stimulation that we respond to are taken away, what would be left? What would develop? I know some people fear madness, and this can happen, yet here I am. I see myself surrounded by books and art materials, and wonder if these are indulgences to keep me connected, sane. Perhaps. The life I have here isn't the deprivation of prison, nor a bare minimum for life. Perhaps I HAVE brought distractions with me. I read that food too can be a retreat distraction. I do get excited occasionally, thinking about what's for lunch. I realize I'm spending far too long creating meals, and promise to watch that, and see it as the possible diversion it is.

I watch; I listen. By afternoon this house starts talking: creaking and popping as the wood in the roof expands, I guess. I first thought birds were on the roof dropping things, but no. The hut creaks and pops with warming sunlight. It happens only in the afternoon, never in the night or morning. During an afternoon nap, I find myself dreaming that

19

someone is throwing things at the house. It's loud enough to wake me from sleep. But I am alone on this hill.

Alone! In all my walks, over the thirteen days I've been here, I haven't seen one person on a woodland track or the Dharma Road. It's a big space—240 acres—and remote. I guess I really could be here a year without seeing a soul. Amazing!

July 25, 2014

I woke early under a star-filled sky. Light comes slowly to these winter mornings. I meditated in bed, chanting mantras and counting breaths, and found myself slowly drifting back into a dream. Buddha and Kuan Yin, as little statues/rupas, sit on the window sill above my bed doing guard duty so that all my dreams lately are easy ones, not the strange, disturbing ones that came last week.

Rain clouds clung to the peaks across the valley and lifted as the sun tried to pierce the gray for a new day. It's delightful to have it somewhat warmer outside. It's easier to get up and start.

At 9 AM a shower slides into the valley, bringing pelting rain. "Watching the mountain with my ears, hearing the stream with open eyes," says Shutaku, the Zen poet of Nanzen-ji from the 14th century. I listened to his words and am present to the day, turning each moment in my fingers—aware and awake as I always should be, but am too often not. I heard the deep silence after the noisy rainstorm, as if the whole valley was taking a breath and the wind was listening for what might come next.

Rain showers continued off and on throughout the day. Steve came in between them to bring some new attachments for the propane baffle, and netting hoops to go over the small planter. I helped him lift that big, 100 lb plastic compost barrel and shove wood under it so it would meet the loo seat better and keep the little guys from hopping over the edge and getting stuck in the trough like three days ago. We worked together easily, and I was happy to carry his tool box. It reminded me of times in my childhood when I worked with my dad on our New Hampshire summer house.

With this last bit of fix-it help, I may be able to cut the cord and have my quiet retreat begin. I've had two weeks of visits by Steve, Tony, and Nityadana as they worked to get the building troubles solved and help me to have a fully functioning hut. Steve says it seems I've been here a long time. I think so too. I feel quite at home on this windy precipice watching the weather swoop down the Tararu Valley. Home!

July 26, 2014

Am I really just now waking up to the realization that I'm in this one room for the next eleven and a half months? Wow! I share some feeling for those incarcerated in 6'x10' cells . . . but unlike them, I have a whole wilderness to wander through if I want. And, I chose this. I have the wilderness of my mind to consider. With my returning headaches comes a fuzzy brain. There's much I want to do and contemplate, but not the ability right now to do it. So for now, I just watch birds fly on the opposite forest wall and work at being present to this moment—not past, not future.

Ugh! There's nothing like the smell of a couple of rotten eggs to bring someone down from the realms of nirvana to samsara in a whoosh! The new food delivery Steve dropped had a box of six organic, free-range eggs. It says, "use before July 30" but at least two were black and definitely off already. The shells must have gotten cracked. They were certainly potent. A sampling of Turkish dates took the memory away, but my hands will smell "iffy" for a while.

My rotten-egg spirits benefitted from some mantra chanting. I included "Om Mani Padme Hum" and the one hundred syllable Vajrasattva mantra as well as the Shakyamuni mantra before I did the Prostration Practice. This ritual seems to reinforce, ground, and open my heart. I salute a day of rotten eggs and all that helps us take the lumps with the joys. I'm now cloud gazing and sky watching while my day's wash dries over the heater. Bless.

Today, I walked up a new trail, through gorse and tall manuka trees to the stupa. It's a very different forest from the wet, dark ponga wood around my hut, where giant tree fern droppings make Slipglade Track so damp. The new track was almost civilized and refined, though the map calls it an overgrown farm road. It's now only two feet wide, but

21

perhaps once, fifty or seventy-five years ago, it was a road for settlers. Who would they have been?

At dusk, with my eyes glued to the peaks on the horizon, it seems I'm watching the most engrossing TV program of the week: clouds. I'll be waking tomorrow to my birthday, the first of my eighth decade, with a new moon that night. The nuns of Buddha's time asked to be filled with all good things, like the moon on the fifteenth day which is completely full of wisdom in the massive dark. I sing this song with them asking for that wisdom, that deep quiet in a cloudless sky, that new moon of wisdom.[1]

July 27, 2014

Wonderful morning sun crested the eastern hills amid clinging clouds—a Chinese mountain landscape that turned into a New Zealand bush birthday morning. At 46ºF/7ºC outside, it's the coldest birthday I've ever experienced.

I prepared a special breakfast: blueberry and walnut pancakes with some chopped dates thrown in. While I was working on breakfast, I came across a special present that I didn't know I had—a new bag of peanut M&Ms hiding behind the sultanas. I placed them on my shrine. And soon I imagined that I was joined for a birthday breakfast with Amoghasiddhi, the Buddha of the north, here on the North island of New Zealand. He's the Buddha of abhaya, for which this hut is named. "Fearlessness." I needed this, here alone on a clear day of quiet reflection.

And what a lovely day it became! I went very slowly and didn't even have my blueberry pancake breakfast until after 10:30 AM. That's what happens when winter has the sun coming up so late. I had meditation, writing, yoga, and reading to do before breakfast. I did much of my meditation facing the glass window, where I chant to the mountains and the mist.

I'm pleased to find my solitary friend Bob Kull sharing discoveries on his July birthday in cold Patagonia thirteen years ago. He writes of the stories or myths that we remember, especially while on solitary retreat:

Personal myth is a real risk. We tell stories about the past and forget that these stories are our own creations, built on selected aspects of experience. The stories describe a self-identity we come to believe in: "I did this or I thought that." Once we believe the myth we've created to be literally true, we become—in our own mind—the character in the myth. Then the problems begin. We must live up to our expectation.[2]

I do love stories. I ask myself: Do I make them into myth? I've had a lifetime of sharing adventures and travels through stories. The family story of a very independent "tricycle takeoff" down Hollingsworth Street on my third or fourth birthday has become something of a myth. Do I believe that because I showed a strong independent streak at an early age I must live up to this story? Are stories of the past markers? Am I influenced by them? Do they give some insight into who is sitting here in the present? All this focus on self today must come from this silly idea of birthday—a day once a year that is somehow special. Yet I'm pleased, and reminded of all those others who are waking up around the world to a birthday on the 27th of July.

I brewed a cup of kukicha tea that I've been saving for something special, and continued to marvel that I'm here. After two years of planning, I'm here to manage with what I've packed and what I forgot, which includes wool socks, long underwear, and New Hampshire maple syrup, all set out to come, that somehow didn't find their way into my luggage. I was so fearful of New Zealand customs and the stringent regulations I read about online that I questioned everything that was in my luggage, especially food items. But customs was a breeze. There was no delay or request to look in my luggage even though I'd unlocked my bags expecting a thorough search.

The day had a cloudy start but I did get an outdoor bath prepared. While it takes about thirty minutes to siphon that water down the mountain, and almost forty minutes of gas burners running under the metal tub to heat that chilly rainwater, it's a delight to be warmly submersed under a blue sky. It was only 50ºF/10ºC and steam rose off the water for ten minutes before it got too cool. It will be lovely to have it warm enough soon to bathe under a moon, and my moon-friend will start waxing into full in the next two weeks. I was thinking of sending a card to my daughter and close friends saying, "I am very, very happy!"

Yes—even with rats in the loo and temperatures just above freezing. Who could believe that's possible?

The morepork owl is hooting tonight, but so far—no dancing possums on my roof. Perhaps it was my friend Morrie the Rat who got my parsley and radishes that first night rather than a possum as I supposed. The netting on both planters is working nicely to protect the little green shoots of beet and the parsley transplants. It's wonderful to watch things grow each day, even as the frosty nights are producing dead fronds on the fern trees. The past few nights, I haven't covered the pansy basket and planters as the temperature has hovered at 39ºF/4-5ºC, though I do check the thermometer about 4 AM as a precaution. When it gets close to zero, I'm out there with towels to cover everything.

Solitude—a life alone for a year. I wonder what it will be like? It seems completely normal to me in some ways—meditating, cooking, cleanup, washing, reading and note taking, a trek every few days, and lots and lots of cloud and tree watching. Entertainment is minimal and I'm sensitive to every small change in the environment. For the second Sunday I heard a motorcycle flying along unseen roads in that green wall of forest that faces me across the valley.

July 28, 2014

There's frost on the grass and the far fields, though it's not as heavy as six days ago when I scratched "FROZEN" on my deck's crust. I'm glad that I did a wash two days ago since I'm wearing every bit of my warmest clothing today. I really should have packed that long underwear, those wool socks, and a flannel nightshirt, but the news that the New Zealand winter was mild confused me. Bringing the fleece vest and jacket was smart. And I send blessings for the British tradition of hot water bottles. I'm a convert, at last.

I had cocoa again this morning with soy milk and a little manuka (tea tree) honey. I'd be worried about putting on pounds with these sweet indulgences, but here I think I don't need to worry. I'm eating only two meals a day, and that's all I have the appetite for. An evening meal seems unnecessary. A cup of soy milk suffices, and maybe a sesame cracker or piece of banana.

I spend an hour or more each morning on the porch in the sun, watching the distant forest wall across the valley and tearing up used cardboard into quarter-size pieces for composting. Today while I was watching that valley, a brilliant blue kingfisher suddenly flew directly through the garden. Whoa! It didn't slow down or perch for me to see it well, (no pole or wire nearby), but with its large protruding yellow beak it seems to be the only brilliantly clear blue bird that size possible here, the bird book says. Birds are the local entertainment, I find, and I am learning to identify many species new to me. I had a New Zealand pigeon scolding me from the big puriri tree near the stupa on my first outing here, but near the hut only the piwakawaka fantail visits me regularly. She's a show-off, and so curious and very friendly. Once she fluttered just two feet away and almost landed on my shoulder. I got some wild bird food in my grocery order, but haven't yet established a feeding center so I can visit with the local feathered ones on a regular basis. Soon I will be accepted and they will come.

July 29, 2014

A small prop plane goes over from southwest to northeast on its regular run, and I'm reminded that there is an outside world somewhere off this mountain. It seems to fly across the Coromandel to the Pacific side in a regular pattern. It's not a fire-searching plane as I see in New Hampshire forest—nor one surveying, but perhaps one delivering to some airport up Whitianga way.

Thinking of this North Island, I'm reminded of Maclean, my first contact with a Kiwi and housemate in Japan in the 1980s. She grew up in Gisborne, not so far from here. When I came to New Zealand for my first time in 1992 to lecture on Japanese textiles and visit her, the country I saw reminded me of the USA in the 50s: lace curtains in the windows, women in skirts pushing prams, a quiet, gentle country. When she arrived in Kyoto in 1986, she needed a safe haven, and Amanda and I were happy to include her in our small traditional home for two years, a vivacious, enthusiastic young woman—spiritually-bent, but with other things to complete before a dedication to that path. We renewed our relationship when I arrived here earlier this month. Now she's the mother of a grown son at university in Dunedin. Knowing that this dear friend from thirty years ago is on this island someplace helps me to settle in this first month.

It's o-chazuke with quinoa rather than rice for lunch with Swiss chard, or "silver beet" as they call it here. I cut my first lettuce leaf from the planter and it tasted exquisite. Eating so much local chard has me lusting for lettuce or kale but it is silver beet that grows best here in winter. I have the two planters full of it and the plants seem quite happy on this high porch with their leaves fluttering in the wind. The parsley and chives will take root soon and I have my fingers crossed that my arugula, planted ten days ago as seed, will break ground before long. A bee swings by each morning to check them out (and me) but none of us are flowering this week so she's soon off.

I walked up to the drop-box on Slipglade Track at noon, left my grocery list and my weekly trash bag, then went on to gather some leaves for the compost hole as advised. There was noise last night and when I saw many, many hoof prints there in the mud—quite large ones, 3-4" across, I wondered if it was animal movement that disturbed me. They seem to be wild pig prints and perhaps even a wild goat, with two-point hoof marks as well as some four-pointed pig ones. I wish I could research this, but I'll just need to let go of my insatiable desire "to know." It's a desire to learn, but also a habit of grasping that could be lessened. Yes, I'm here to watch my habits and to wake up.

That "wanting to know" carries through to the equipment I brought with me. When I told Tony what the inside/outside temperatures were on my first day here, he asked me how I knew. I showed him my L.L. Bean Weather Station with its solar powered battery. A typical New Zealand bushman, he told me that when he wants to know the temperature, he just sticks his head out the door. I check my gadget four or five times a day. Somewhat obsessive, I agree but this is what happens on solitary the first month. It's a fascinating toy, but sticking my head out the door would help me develop other assessment skills.

It was so very cold this afternoon with the sun behind clouds that I chose to do an afternoon sit inside, at the glass door. I sat in meditation and, putting aside distractions, easily fell into a familiar space of joy, or dhyana, not allowing any thoughts to stick or dwell in my mind. As I've been trained, I then moved into the deeper meditation states of second and third dhyana and dwelled there until something pulled me back, and I lapsed into thinking that my back needed more support. In another ten minutes I was back with piti (ecstasy they call it) and joy, moving

26

into contentment and stillness, the signals of further dhyanic states. It was a lovely sit and gave me reinforcement that deep meditation is possible here. I'm also happy to notice that despite some dizziness in the afternoon and a headache last evening, my brain is feeling less foggy. It seems I may be growing back to where I was in my meditation practice two years ago. What a long lapse it's been! And yet I've learned from that miserable concussion.

At 7:30 PM I'm in my bed, in hat and gloves with a flannel shirt over my night-shirt, socks, and a hot water bottle at my feet. I see that the poet May Sarton, whom I'm re-reading, was at her home in Nelson, New Hampshire in January with her thermostat set at 80ºF. In her journal, she fusses when she finds the room where her parrot sleeps is below 70ºF, and immediately builds a fire to warm it up. If the hut here gets to 58ºF/14ºC, I feel it's luxurious, and turn off the heater to conserve propane. Such contrast. But I don't have a tropical parrot to keep warm.

July 30, 2014

The sky has opened and is pouring down heavy rain with great force. It's lovely to be inside. With the temperature a bit warmer today, I woke and could actually see out the windows clearly and watch the rain-soaked landscape, rather than hunting for a towel to wipe down windows fogged up with condensation. After mopping up four window panes and two door panels, I must wring out the towel twice. The clouds are clinging to the rugged ridges and falling into the creek valley, defining the landscape in new ways. I do love these weather changes. They call this the land of four seasons in one day—something like New England.

The Japanese restaurant in Abhaya hut continues to serve up special lunches. Today it was organic cha-soba noodles and mentsuyu dipping sauce with shitake mushrooms, backpacked in dry from the Auckland Asian food store a month ago. My stash will soon run out, but meanwhile I'm enjoying the indulgence. When friends asked what I'd miss in the bush, with no refrigerator and only one weekly local food store drop-off, I thought—Japanese food. So I stocked up on what I could: miso, shoyu, mirin, nori, sembai crackers, dried noodles and shitake mushrooms. A further food thrill today was a small cupcake with butter frosting, a candle and a little New Zealand pennant in my drop-box in the woods. Steve had sent belated birthday wishes. Such treats and kindness are so very special out here on a precipice over the roaring Tararu River.

"Won't you be scared?" someone asked before I came. "Scared of what?" I said. Fear didn't cross my mind before I came. Yet earlier, hearing strange sounds in the night, I sat wondering exactly how safe I was. Was it the sound of wild pigs moving down the road in the dark hours that spooked me, or rumbles from the troubled man I've been told of in the hut high above me in this wilderness? Am I really safe here? I realized I could lock my door if that would make me feel more secure, but I didn't. I had been told that there has never been an "incident" in the twenty years of this retreat land. New Zealand and the Thames are quiet, gentle places, not like some inner cities where I've lived.

What also brought up fear and thoughts of security today was reading, "Why do We Take Refuge?", an article in my Buddhist magazine by Yongey Mingyur Rinpoche. Refuge—security, safety, trust, comfort—is a precise Buddhist term but can transfer to the vernacular. Some of us take refuge in relationships, or the stock market, or even anger or helplessness. We expect someone outside to rescue us, and are then often let down or betrayed. When we're tired of being disappointed, we turn to another source, or to what we find within us. I did. It brought me to Buddhism thirty years ago. Mingyur Rinpoche says:

> We take refuge to be happier, to be free from suffering and to feel more secure and stable—we never accept suffering as the normal or natural human condition. Whatever the degree of our unhappiness, this longing arises to be free of it . . . we intuitively know that our unhappiness is off balance, that it's not our true self, and that it can be alleviated.[3]

I carry this belief with me, brought here to a land as far away as possible from my New England home, to a hut called Abhaya—fearlessness, clothed in confidence and trust that I will be okay. Was I born with confidence? Perhaps. Did conditions and family further encourage this trust in the world? Most definitely. Do I expect goodness and positivity? Ahhh. And am I rewarded with the same? Yes. And yet there are worries. When that New Zealand honeybee visits my porch every morning in search of blossoms and finds only me, the one with two EpiPens my doctor sent to counteract the anaphylactic shock I could drop into if I'm stung, does it cross my mind that I could be in danger? Perhaps. But mostly I trust that I will be okay until I'm not. Watching the busy bee, I just drop out of self, become curious, and fall into being a bee myself, flying from spot to spot, checking the lettuce and the hanging pot of pansies, the paper torn up for compost, and the quiet energy this human puts out. I'm okay in this rugged land—for now.

Ah... sunset on distant trees.

July 31, 2014

It's another morning when clouds cling to the peaks. Yesterday I spent a long time bundled up in hat and gloves, contemplating them, taking them in, wanting to record them in paint. So far I've just been "watching the mountains with my ears, hearing the stream with open eyes." There will be time for painting soon, after I "become" the misty clouds.

The possum guys visited last night, stomping up the steps, clattering across the deck and around to the front porch, huffing and puffing to view the netted seedlings. Their assessment was that the job was well done, so this patrol departed for other young sucklings elsewhere. They already got the plantings that Nityadana put in to welcome me three weeks ago. With NZ$40 worth of netting installed, a possum breakfast was not so easily available at Abhaya Hut today.

This morning I realized how wonderful it was to be warm all night. I got a second wool blanket yesterday from the empty Amida Hut, where I found four in the storage closet. Warmth in a chilly, damp winter is wonderful.

And just to reassure me, today has been the warmest day yet. The sun overtook those wispy morning clouds as I quickly did two small watercolors, feeling this weather might change and I wouldn't have those wonderful misty mountains to paint again. And then at noon, as I prepared a parmesan gratin cauliflower dish in my newly discovered broiler and started filling the outdoor tub, the temperature rose to 63ºF/17ºC! I didn't even see steam rising as I slipped under the water. What a joy to be clean. It feels like a real life here—I'm at home and comfortable, not missing much. I want to send that first postcard to friends in the next few days, but I cannot wrap my head around it. As I slow down, I disconnect more and more. I just want to be on my cushion meditating. Blessed be.

In the evening, I was so happy to see the moon as the sky was darkening for dusk that I shouted aloud, "Here you are!" It's been five or six days of new moon and overcast skies. Today, the moon is straight across from my door—a place in the sky where the sun often disappears in the late afternoon. Earlier this month I didn't see the moon in that spot until early morning. This is all a mystery to me, but I have a year to figure it out and "plot the moon." It's become one of my regular friends—along with the honey bee and the fantail sparrow. Happiness.

*Daffodils stand in the field below the stupa, unharmed
by night-time wild pig digging.*

Chapter 2 August

This morning I did my sadhana practice, manifesting Kuan Yin with all her compassion for others as she "hears the cries of the world" and adding phrases, including *May all beings enjoy happiness and the causes of happiness.*

Afterwards, I sat on my sheltered porch relishing the green, watching the world of bees and birds, awake to the overwhelming and fortuitous conditions that have allowed me to be here. Shaila Catherine's *Intention* poem came to mind:

Today I have a fortunate opportunity,
 not easily come by,
 supported by the sacrifice, trust and generosity
 of many benefactors.
Let me not waste this precious chance to free the mind
 from habitual obstructions,
 to unclog the conditional tendencies of judging, selfing,
 craving and distraction.
May my practice this day be energetic and bright,
 earnest,
 steadfast in the face of all difficulty.
Concentrated, focused, unwavering.
 Happily, I apply myself with vigor,
 Until this mind is utterly freed
 Beyond the range of grasping,
 Having willfully done,
 What needs to be done.[4]

I'm watching many things with care, including my moods and emotions. On days when it's overcast, I notice that the day is less joyous and fulfilling. As I sat in the beautiful sun this morning with visor, sunglasses and UV 15 on, the sun disappeared twenty minutes into my meditation. I sat through a visit by a wasp—perhaps the same one who came by yesterday, brushing my hands. I knew that even with his visit I wouldn't move, knew that even if it began to rain, I could not get up from that sit—so sweet and deep. Moving for any reason was not possible.

After an hour, I was ready to come out of the sit and move inside to prepare lunch. I'm scribbling these notes and preparing a cheese sandwich between meditation sits. I don't have an evening meal so other than breakfast, this sandwich, some cottage cheese, nasu-dengaku (eggplant with miso) and braised Swiss chard will be my food for the day.

I've finished reading May Sarton's *Journal of a Solitude* and find her sadness at living alone echoing with her knowledge that this may be necessary for her writing. She's easily overwhelmed by occasional visitors and their expectations. When others intrude on her solitude, she struggles to keep her anger and depression at bay.

I'm studying that solitude here, and look to others for experiences and realizations that duplicate/reinforce what I'm observing. Anthony Storr writes in *Solitude: A Return to the Self*:

> . . .the capacity to be alone is a valuable resource. It enables men and women to get in touch with their deepest feelings; to come to terms with loss; to sort out their ideas; to change attitudes.[5]

And maybe Sarton knew this even as she struggled.

I'm again overwhelmed with the wonder of how long I've waited for this retreat to come to fruition. I'm here for a year, with gratitude to so many benefactors who've supported my dream.

August 2, 2014

"Red sky at dawn, sailors take warning!" An old mariners' saying.

Red clouds and a morning star shining at the eastern horizon welcomed a quiet day after a ferocious night of howling winds. The roots of the trees on this peninsula shook as the wind screamed up the valley for hours last night. They say the worst storms come from the south, where Antarctica sits, and I'm protected from this by the ridge and stupa behind me, but the angry gods in the west across Auckland Bay and the Firth of Thames roared last night.

The possum patrol stomped across the deck and circled the house last night but found everything in order and went elsewhere for dinner. The garden netting seemed to prevent them from having their expected meal. I've read they'll even scratch at a glass door for a handout if a light is on, but not here.

Soon the winds picked up again. Trees were bending, whipped by high winds and misty rain. This harsh weather is coming from the east or southeast. As I finished my lunch preparation, I processed emotional storms of equal intensity, issues from years ago, a relationship of mis-understanding and criticism. Deep hurt has allowed me to carry this so many years without resolution despite efforts to untangle it. I expect this will raise its head again during this retreat. It may be months from now, but I'm committed to being finished with this hurt.

Difficult times are always a base for growth and I take all criticism seriously, as I'm eager to be more skillful and aware in my interactions with others. As uncomfortable as it is, this time of solitude allows deep wounds to show their face and be dealt with. Here there are no inter-ruptions or distractions, no other expectations of me, only space and time to work on the hard stuff through reflection and meditation.

His Holiness the Dalai Lama says that we learn and grow when times are the most challenging and difficult. He tells us that, "We should meet our broken heart with the great broken heart of the world—this is the first Noble Truth." I listen.

The weather is echoing my emotional state, or is it the other way around? The gale force winds and unusually high temperatures (60ºF/16ºC) feel heavy, like a tropical storm from the Pacific.

I made my first walnut-date scones in the little camp oven on top of my gas burner and didn't burn down the house. I couldn't get the tem-perature up to the desired 425ºF, but at 350ºF they cooked, and didn't burn. What a lovely treat! If Tenzin Palmo could cook sourdough bread on retreat in her Himalayan cave at 13,000 feet, I'm good for walnut scones in a New Zealand hurricane. A happy scone day, even with things yet to be resolved.

August 3, 2014

The wind has quieted down and the howling has stopped, but I had to give up on sleeping this early morning with all this weather-worry. There were too many nightmares of houses taking off and flying through Oz to land in the Firth of Thames rather than Kansas. I kept contemplating sending a text message to Steve to ask if this was the usual August weather. It felt like the US hurricane season had arrived. Then I remembered my vow and affirmation to take whatever comes my way. *If I am sick, I am sick—if I die, I die*: the Tibetan solitary retreat oath. And for the first time, I found myself envying Tenzin Palmo's cave—solid and part of a stone mountain wall rather than an uninsulated wooden hut hanging on a precipice over the Tararu River.

I'm still working to get into a happy meditation schedule. I've been doing my Refuge Tree visualization practice every other day between a Bodhicitta and sadhana visualization practice. I do *pujas* ceremonies two or three times a week, and always one to my yidam, Kuan Yin, on Sunday. I've done that weekly for the past five years. I've pushed myself to start a regular mindful walking meditation also. Today, I did it in boots and a long raincoat. I've done one hundred counted breaths to settle myself down at times and have gone into *dhyana* states of deep meditation a few times, but am still a long way away from where I was before my accident twenty months ago. The depth of my meditation comes from continued, dedicated, daily practice.

Rain is now sheeting down but there's less wind. I reflect on the poignant blessing from Santideva's *A Guide to the Bodhisattva Way of Life* that echoes this storm:

> May I be a haven in the storm . . .
> A boat, a bridge,
> And a ship for those who wish to cross over. . .
> A harbor for those who need shelter.
>
> A lamp for those who seek light . . .a port for those who seek rest.
> A light for those who are lost.
> Like the earth and the water; like the fire and the air . . .
> May I be a servant to all beings on Earth . . .
> Until the world is made whole.[6]

These are good aspirations for life on a stormy day in New Zealand.

August 4, 2014

At last the wind dropped, and the night brought more seasonal temperatures in the mid-40s. Blue sky arrived with the welcomed sunrise.

There was possum activity on the roof and deck again between 7 and 11 PM. When they visit, it can sound as if they're dragging jump ropes across the roof. At other times the sounds are light and scampering, as if a rat or two has also arrived. I'm happy that I'm inside with doors closed, and I have no need to know exactly what is going on up on the roof. Soon the season will change and then I hope to be meditating on the deck under stars. Then, I imagine the possums will wait out their time in the bush until the deck is free.

Ah—my creative mind jumps. To meditate on the roof! Could I? I do have a ladder. What an enticing thought, to be up above this bush! It's true that I have been looking for a tree to climb up into, but so far have not been able to find a welcoming pine with boughs low enough to get my 70-year old bones up into its arms. I climbed trees in my childhood, and even on my Ordination Retreat five years ago I was up in trees hanging tarps and meditation flags. I have a strong yearning to be back up there where I spent so many wonderful childhood hours. Who was the Zen Master who meditated in trees? Does it help with insight and enlightenment to be a little closer to the stars?

Stepping back, I look at what I'm writing in this journal, other than silly possum stories and plans for roof-sitting. I realize that this "reporting in" has four parts to it. A main theme is that of **Solitude**. I did a lot of internal questioning when I was anticipating this year, such as: What is it like to be in solitude? How will I manage with no one to talk to?

And my departure from home into this silence; I knew that some very famous hermits and reclusives have slipped off quietly, without a goodbye—but I couldn't do that. I couldn't step into a year solitary without letting my loved ones, students, and friends know what I was doing, and helping them be included in some way. To just leave would harm them, perhaps harm me, and harm our relationship.

Solitude draws me strongly, yet there is still that part of me that re-
lates to others and need to be accessible and available for support. This
may come from the desire for spiritual friendship that has been part of
my life for years. So, I look at Solitude and my interest in it, researching
its meaning, drawbacks, benefits and history. I ask questions such as,
Why has it drawn others? How is it received/perceived by the outside
world? What benefit might come from it? All these questions have a basis in spirituality. I research and consider.

Another journal theme is the **Practicality** of a year alone in the
semi-wilderness. When I was anticipating this year, people wanted to
know where I'd get my food, what I'd eat, how I'd keep warm, what I'd
miss, why New Zealand, what if I needed a tooth pulled, got sick? These
are the practical dimensions of a year in the bush that focus on "the
how."

A third aspect that I share here is **Organization** or Schedule, answering those questions I was asked again and again. How will I
organize my time? What will I do for a whole year without internet, Facebook, TV, or phone calls? How will I keep from falling into the
morass?

And then I write **Why** I am doing this, which is revealed more and
more each day as I examine the search and inspiration that brought me
here.

All four areas carry much food for contemplation. They're what I
call the externals and the internals. These journals will be full of investi-
gations into solitude, explorations of the inner self and "no self," as well
as the practicalities of a hermit's life in the New Zealand bush, aware of
all that surrounds and inspires. I know that surprising joys and deep
realizations will come.

I've had many surprises even in this first month. I've found that
stepping into a New Zealand winter means 14+ hours of darkness, and
with that is the challenge of how to keep warm with the limited clothing
I brought with me. My walking meditation is not so easy in rainy wind-
storms. Study, reading, even writing, encourage the concussion
symptoms I arrived with. And I've discovered that I came here deeply
exhausted, not only from the long hours of preparation and traveling in,

but also from emotional exhaustion. I had much settling in to do, and found myself thinking again and again—Wow! I'm here! It was almost a waking up to that. Now, three weeks into the retreat, a rhythm has developed. I notice that I've simplified my needs and my desires for specific foods, and even my beloved novel reading.

I continue to watch my grasping, my delusions, and my judgments as I walk into this time of silence with only the sounds of feathered friends for company.

This morning, a little riro-riro (grey warbler) visited the tree fern that shades my water cisterns. He perched long enough for me to identify him—unlike the frantic fantails, who are always in motion. The riro-riro isn't piping yet. His call in early spring is the signal for the Maori to start planting. I've read that this call is so fast that the human ear can only appreciate its complexity when it's recorded and slowed down. He fluttered under the fronds, hovering almost like a large hummingbird, tossing the leaves and grabbing insects. Later I saw a tui, a kind of honeyeater, in my favorite pine tree below the clearing, and identified him by the beautiful blue/green sheen on his black back feathers. He's around here often, but moves so frenetically that I really identify him by his unusual piping call. I also caught sight of a redpoll two days ago, hopping about on a log near my clearing, looking for insects. His bright red breast gave him away, reminding me of the red-breasted robins that used to nest in the hemlock next to my New Hampshire porch.

Although I've never been a "birder," I'm becoming one, connecting with and appreciating them in this rarified environment with no people to distract me. I expect they'll become regular companions, but this first month I'm observing them from a distance. I'm learning to come out of the hut slowly and quietly so as not to disturb their activities. With no squirrels or chipmunks and very few mammals in New Zealand other than the nocturnal rats and possums, the birds are the best show in town.

And then there's the weather—the amazing, ever-changing weather on this ridge. Along with the birds and the few mammals, the weather is a constantly entertaining companion. With the sun shining brightly, a bank of dense fog from the Firth moved into the valley today and then —in ten minutes—dissipated. It's strange weather for me, lowland fog but with high sun. My noon porch meditation was done in a chilly 51ºF/11ºC.

This late afternoon I went out along Slipglade Track to do some work trenching its muddy surface, hoping to create some water run-off. There I saw Steve and a lad also working the road, dumping rocks in the potholes. I expect it's always wet on that track, not just in this rainy winter season, and that some spring coming down Chetul Hill feeds the sizeable mudholes wet year-round. Malini in Auckland, who has agreed to be my local retreat-supporter, was looking out for me early on. She wanted to be sure that my food drop-box was placed on the hut-side of the biggest mud hole to make it easier for me. As I carried out an empty (but still heavy and awkward) propane tank to leave for a refill at the box today, I was happy that I didn't need to go slipping through standing water, tire holes, and squishy yellow gradients. There's a steep bush by-pass below that I occasionally use to keep from sloshing through mud—and yet I take it in stride, still a kid that loves mud.

There was a clear half-moon at 5:30 this afternoon right at the zenith of the sky, and then rain—huge drops—at 6 PM. I expect a cold night.

August 5, 2014

I've had nausea moving into dizziness and headache the past two afternoons and evenings. I've relied on the aspirin combo my neurologist suggested. Sometimes it takes three hours to work, but without medication the pain can go on all night, keeping me rocking and rolling and not sleeping much, just hanging onto the sides of the mattress. I notice my habit of analyzing how to avoid this pain rather than accepting what is. I've truly been so much better here, away from other stresses, but my great wish (and the doctor's as well) is for the end, the cure of this miserable brain injury. May all beings be free from suffering and the causes of suffering, I say again and again.

I fell asleep last evening reading Tsangnyön's *The Life of Milarepa* and woke with mantras repeating in my mind. *Om Mani Padme Hum*, the praise sung to the Jewel in the Lotus throughout the Buddhist world, hasn't been far from my consciousness all day. I've found that in times of fear or pain—when the airplane is going down, or the doctor says, "This will only hurt for a little while,"—this mantra is always there, repeating under the surface. I first realized this in Japan, six years ago when I was on my belly and a doctor was stitching up my foot following a small operation to remove a cyst. After the "only hurts a little" message, I immediately dropped into mumbling something. He stopped to ask, in Japanese, what language it was I was speaking. Not English, he said. I was surprised to realize I was repeating a Sanskrit mantra to manage the pain. It isn't cognitive—rather a reflex, and it works. So waking to morning mantras reminds me that they are just below the surface of my consciousness, much of the time. "Better than cuss words," Steve and Tony would say.

In *The Life of Milarepa* I found reference to a hero of mine, Atisha (958-1005 CE), a great Bengali monk. After spending time in Indonesia, he carried a second wave of Buddhism to Tibet, a revival of its introduction in the eighth century, when Milarepa was born. They're both on my Triratna Refuge Tree as Teachers of the Past, but I first connected to Atisha ten years ago when I realized he'd traveled to Indonesia early in the 11th century to find the only teacher still sharing a Bodhisattva Path—Serlingpa. Atisha stayed there twelve years and carried that teaching of the Bodhisattva Path back to the grand Nalanda University in India and from there to Tibet. In my studies, I've found few references to Indonesian Buddhism, so after ten winters there, I was delighted to hear of Atisha and Serlingpa and these teachings on the Bodhisattva Vow, to help all beings. It's so wonderful when things start interrelating and gelling.

I am so in awe of the tenacious, dedicated Milarepa that I decided to do a "commitment sit" in honor of this great sage. But, wouldn't you know, just seven minutes into my Milarepa meditation I found my mind in the grocery aisle looking for classic potato chips, not the vinegar and salt or sour cream and chive ones that were delivered last week to my box. As they say, it's a moment of insight when you find your mind has wandered away. Just scoop it back to the cushion with gentle kindness, the way you'd scoop up a wayward puppy in training. It's twenty-nine years since I started meditating and sometimes I'm still scooping and leading that puppy back.

Today I made pasta and mentally ate with my Ordination friends gathered in Penas Rojas in Spain, where we were ordained together five years ago. I remember that time as an extraordinary three months. We were seventeen women from five countries invited to be ordained in the Order that spring. The three months included study, training, and devotional practices as well as daily living challenges in a rugged mountain terrain three hours from Barcelona. I chose to live outdoors in a borrowed igloo tent and I loved it, even as temperatures varied from from 39ºF/4ºC in April when we arrived to 108ºF/43ºC in July when we left for home. And now the big sky of New Zealand is over me and it's winter, and I have three wool blankets, a duvet and a hot water bottle. And it is just fine.

Stepping outside at 7 PM tonight, a half-moon is shining near the zenith, but there's still heavy cloud cover. It's a wonderfully dark wilderness. I can see only two lights in my 180 degree visual check; they're on the ridge across the river, far over to the east where Tararu Sanctuary offers homestay weeks. Yesterday I thought I saw a cow over there, but it was hard to focus my binoculars. I hear a moo every few days towards 5 PM, which I associate with milking time, but not on a regular basis. I wonder if the sound might come from the Wass homestead, which is just below me and across the river. The terrain is so deep that although I know they're down there with their boys and dogs (as my hand-drawn map of the area tells me), all I can see is a geo-waterfall that runs heavy during rainstorms and is a mere slash in the wall of green at other times. It's dark and deep here, and quiet except for the running river, and everything a solitary retreat should be.

August 6, 2014

I'm "feeling poorly" this morning, as my New England grandmother would say. I went to bed with nausea and dizziness, and by early morning it had gone to headache. I tried pressing on some neck pressure points, saying some mantras and imaging Amoghasiddhi, the Buddha of the North, whose hands display the abhaya mudra of fearlessness. Then I called for Kuan Yin's compassion. I knew I could try medication, but I hoped the headache would pass. I'm trying some food now as I limp through late breakfast preparation.

While I chew, I'm saying a meal gatha, sending blessings to all who labored to prepare this food: blessings to those who gathered the oats and chia seeds, hulled the walnuts, pumpkin seeds and pine nuts, raised the organic soy beans and processed them into milk, dug the ginger root, ground the cinnamon, and raised and picked the apples. "May they be peaceful and happy. May they find blessings from their labor." I chew, sending loving-kindness to all beings, with gratitude for the rain, the sun, and the glorious wind that wake me up to nature all around. If I don't listen to the subtleties of that wind, then a roaring freight train of gusts coming from the Antarctic catches my attention, raising my blood pressure and saying, "Wake Up and be Aware!" Okay, I'm here and doing better.

August 7, 2014

Last night the moon was waxing into full, enough to cast moon shadows on the deck. I was reminded of my son singing Cat Stevens, *Moonshadow, Moonshadow* with the wholehearted gusto of a three-year old in his pre-school class to the accompaniment of his teacher's guitar forty years ago. Such a sweet, loving child at that moment!

I tried a day with very little reading and am feeling better tonight. Earlier, I walked up to the stupa when I thought the weather had cleared, but five minutes out it started raining again. I continued on, and got to the upper Retreat Center porch to wait out the squall. I was shocked to see all the fields around the center completely dug up, the earth turned topsy-turvy by wild pigs desperate for winter roots to eat. Yet near the graves of two Order members was a stand of daffodils: seven sunny faces in the rain. The destructive pig-digging had left a three-foot ring around them. Obviously, daffodils are not on the wild pig diet. Bless them for leaving this hint of yellow sunshine for us on a rainy day.

Milarepa's trials have been much on my mind today. He lost his father when he was only seven, and had the family fortune confiscated by greedy relatives. With no help from the community, he was forced, along with his mother and sister, to become household servants to those relatives. Later, his mother urged him to study black magic and gain revenge on all those who hadn't helped them. He was overwhelmingly successful in his black studies, unleashing a tide of destruction, destroying crops, and killing many in the community. Later, regretting his actions and realizing the enormous bad karma he had built up, Milarepa apprenticed himself to Marpa, a trusted Tantric teacher, hoping to purify himself and attain enlightenment in this lifetime. For years Marpa forced Milarepa to build up and then tear down stone towers before he could receive the instruction he desired. In pain, he wailed that the human body had no use, since without the Dharma, it could only collect misdeeds.[7] The teachings finally came and he retired to a cave, where he dealt with his own demons and mistakes, becoming enlightened in one lifetime, a true symbol of tenacity, diligence, and commitment to the Buddhist world.

I spent a lot of time on the cushion meditating today and now I'm tearing up cardboard boxes into coin-size pieces for compost with great happiness. This undemanding work brings Milarepa and his endless tower building to dissolve past karma to mind. His struggles carrying those heavy tower rocks on his back were far harder on the body than the swollen arthritic finger joints I'm developing from tearing paper. And my work is far more pleasant. But thinking of Milarepa's towers, I asked myself if I too could be doing this to wipe out some of my past unskillfulness, such as moving too fast, not being mindful, or even not being careful of materials? Ah, how the mind works in solitude.

And then this evening the lovely teapot lid landed on the floor and broke into six pieces. A year without a teapot lid! I sit facing a vast wall of green vegetation, tearing up cardboard, reflecting on my own misgivings and that broken teapot lid.

August 8, 2014

Another cold day but, remembering Milarepa's dedication and commitment to practice, I am out of my warm bed and onto my cushion. "Abandon the frivolous distractions of the eight worldly concerns," he says. "Renounce food, clothing and conversation. Wander in isolated places. And above all, practice with fierce intention to renounce this life." He says that by doing so, I'll not only bring about happiness in this life but happiness to those few people who come in contact with me, everlasting happiness. He goes on to say, "Since the time of death is uncertain, I have given up actions focused on this life and arrogance of worldly concerns."[8]

Wow!

It's been two weeks since work on the hut finished and the door completely closed, and one month since I arrived in this wonderful, gentle New Zealand. I'm finally quieting into this retreat. My meditations are deeper and less distracted. In my mind, I've invited Kuan Yin to do the morning sit with me and my imagination confirms that she's a strong meditator and good support.

44

This morning a very clear message came through: "You have all you need—you have all you need to accomplish your yearning." I'll remember this and rely on it when doubts arise, as they are sure to come. I hope for a clear mind and the deep understanding to enter the Dharma and see it in my life, accepting change and transcending. I need to disappear—to remember that in truth "I don't exist," and all that is connected with I, me, mine, those preferences, emotions, and possessions, don't exist as mine. To let these all go, this is the work I am here to do.

I'm looking today at the "fire of urgency" that has brought me to this one-year retreat on my 70th birthday. While others say slow down, relax, lighten up, and just be present to the moment, I've been driven, perhaps since childhood, to live a life of intention. Henry David Thoreau was an early influence on my thinking and his words resonate here:

> I went to the woods because I wished to live deliberately, to find
> only the essential facts of life, and see if I could learn what it had to
> teach, and not, when I came to die, discover that I had not lived.[9]

This deep intentionality is imbedded in my history, learned from my father, who died just a few months after his 53rd birthday. He was an inspiration, a gregarious, deeply generous man who loved his family and was proud of his daughters. However, I was raised hearing of his regret that he didn't apply himself well in school, and so missed the opportunity for higher education, which might have resulted in an easier life, providing more for his children. Listening to my dad's regrets again and again, I felt urged at a young age to live my life fully and intentionally.

I remember coming to the Buddhist Center in New Hampshire after twenty years in Japan and saying that I needed to practice "like my hair was on fire." Years of relationships, raising children, getting an education, developing my career in art, traveling, and living abroad had brought me to my late 50s with still much work to do.

What is it that feeds this fire of urgency, I ask? Often, marana-sati, the Buddhist practice of meditating on the nature of death, can do this, as can an unwelcome medical diagnosis or a close brush with death.

These encounters can wake us up to the fact that the next moment is promised to no one. All of this contributes to this urgency I've carried through life—the commitment to take advantage of every moment as if this day might be the last. It brought me to the door of the Buddhist Center.

This week my writing and meditations have all been done inside, because of the wind and low temperatures. Time within for nesting . . . and cooking, such as blueberry muffins, in the new camp oven. This oven, a gift from a meditation friend, is promising to be a special treat in the bush, as she hoped it would be. When I cooked date scones in this aluminum prefab box that sits on top of the stove burners, they came out okay despite not getting to the prescribed temperature. Today my efforts were less successful: the muffins burned. But I'm encouraged. Perhaps with a little more experimentation with the burner flame, I may solve the problem.

To add to the fun of baking on top of a stove in an aluminum box, I'm challenged by the oven door handle, which pops off each time the box gets hot. At that point I have an oven door that won't latch closed. Today I used tongs to keep it semi-closed but now I have used a long screw to attach the door knob and latch. We'll see how this works. The Coleman Camp Stove Company should get a small note a year from now with a re-design suggestion.

Truthfully, I'm familiar with cooking on a two-burner counter top gas stove since this is what I used in Japan, but the difficulties of this kitchen continue in a comic vein. It seems the newly installed ceiling smoke alarm goes off every time I fry, toast, or do any serious cooking. So, in the midst of keeping the oven door closed, I must open two outside doors, fan the alarm fixture, and hit the alarm "Hush" button with a chopstick. It's like standing on one foot, and rubbing your belly at the same time. The directions do say to not install smoke alarms in kitchen areas, since normal cooking can cause "nuisance" alarms. However, this 12' x 16' hut has cooking, sleeping and meditating areas all in one. It's a perfect cell for a renunciant, but not so advantageous for cooking with smoke alarms. I wonder if my neighbor up in Chetul Hut or the one down at the bottom of the valley hears this intermittent alarm and wonders who has arrived.

I expect that the tui bird, who is so good at learning new calls (including the truck back-up beep), will be echoing the smoke alarm call at one second intervals within the month. My bird book tells me that a tui can "imitate the call of every bird in the forest, as well as turkeys, geese, roosters, cats, barking dogs, the cough of an old man, and a child's laughter." I learn that the Maori kept tui in manuka (tea tree) twig cages and trained them to memorize welcome speeches of up to seventy words. Far more interesting than the sound of the smoke alarm.

August 9, 2014

A cold, rough night. I was awake much of it—mostly going over past history, but a little future planning also. Slowing down, slowing down. This fingering of past events, conversations, etc. is unfinished business. Some of it needs forgiving: the perceived unkindness of others, my own unmindful missteps. I spend much time just sorting out—what year was that?—where was I that winter? And then asking how I packed so much travel, art and teaching into one year.

Bob Kull writes of solitude and these conundrums as the problems of being lost in past and future when we should just be settled into the present moment.[10] Yes, yes, I know this. But I think these thoughts are truly my need to file away a busy life. After three weeks, here physically, I'm mentally still "arriving."

Today I did a big wash and wrung out seventeen pieces of wet laundry by hand. I was with this activity, feeling/sensing/relishing the muscle it took. I felt the cold on my hands, the sensation of pegging each piece to the line, hearing the grand roar of water over rocks at the bottom of the ravine. I'm taking note of all aspects of my new life here, and being present.

I stopped to observe the green on the hillside and realized things have changed since I arrived. Some areas have thinned, with frost-curled leaves and fronds showing bush below that I couldn't see before. The landscape is a collection of greens, from dark to chartreuse, with dusty grey limbs interspersed. In my clearing, the manuka is flowering more, wanting spring. On my walk to the stupa two days ago, I saw many kinds of grass filling in, some with spiky yellow blossoms. Their spiny branches kept me from bringing them home for the altar. Instead I picked the delicate manuka blossoms for that space, enjoying that my honey is from manuka blossom pollen too.

This evening I watched the 5 PM dance of the piwakawaka, which is deeply enjoyable. Three or four little birds cavorted at the edge of the clearing, doing their dusk insect supper gathering. They leapt and jumped like baby puppies chasing soap bubbles. One lit on a branch and spread its snowy tail feathers three to four times, telling me of its fantail name. What great sunset entertainment!

And I'm reminded to be present to this world, to leave the past back there where it is. And to remember too that the future is yet to be. The 12th century Chinese poet Wu-men tells me:

> Ten thousand flowers in spring,
> the moon in autumn,
> cool breeze in summer,
> snow in winter.
> If your mind is not clouded by unnecessary things,
> this is the best season of your life. [11]

I'm coming to a deeper understanding of the rhythm of hibernating bears in this dark winter season. My natural sleep cycle is certainly following it. Without the sound of neighbors going off to work at 5 AM as in New Hampshire, I'm sleeping in until 7:30 or even 8:00 o'clock. It's dark and cold in the evenings as well, and I'm conservative with my solar lights and heating, so I'm often asleep by 8:30 PM. This comes out to almost eleven hours of sleep.

In New England, we'd call this a mild winter, but it's bitter without a wood-burning stove and an insulated floor and ceiling. Trying to use less than an hour of propane each evening and only a little more in the morning makes for a chilly existence.

I wonder why the temperature interests me so. With so much else removed, does this information give me focus and an awareness of the present? Does it help to "place" me in this somewhat alien land? There's Dharma to study, Milarepa's austerities to read of, and a cushion to meditate on. And once it's warm enough in this hut, this gimpy New Englander can get on with it.

This morning, I was moved to go to the stupa to replace a mani stone that I'd borrowed for its Tibetan letter reference, and saw, from a distance, someone else meditating there. It's my first time encountering anyone on this vast 250-acre land. I slipped over to the Puriri Tree path rather than intrude, and passed an hour there under its wide canopy, taking in all the life it supports. This was my second visit to the puriri tree, but this time it was indeed different since I had slowed down in many ways. I approached quietly, found my seat, and waited, remembering words of an elder Order member, Taranatha, who in 2002 described his love of the land and this tree specifically:

> Near to the prospective retreat center building was a noble puriri tree, whose dense evergreen foliage cast so deep a shade that little grew in the filtered green light beneath it. Under its protection was a natural clearing some 25 meters across (about 82'), carpeted with dead leaves and surrounded by a wall of tree ferns and hanging vines. A place of peace and reverence, whose silence was disturbed only by the song of the many birds that gathered to feast on the tree's abundant berries. This was more than just a forest tree. Here was a presence that evoked from all who encountered it, responses of respect, reverence and a sense of the sacred.[12]

August 11, 2014

The moon was dazzling last night at midnight—almost daylight outside. Because of the intermittent cloud cover that moves in, I'm not able to see it at dawn or dusk, which is a shame. I'll look for the predicted super moon tonight.

Possums passed through last night, but only stayed ten minutes or so. I'm not serving any tasty veggies this week, and either they haven't discovered or have no interest in the birdseed I've put out at a feeding block near the tub. The birds also seem to have no interest. I'm sure they're not familiar with human beings purposefully putting out food for them, so it may take a few more weeks before one of them discovers this feeding station and broadcasts the news. Maybe my selection of wild bird formula, which includes maize, sorghum, barley, oats, wheat, white French millet and hulled oats, is not to their liking. These aren't the seeds I serve in New Hampshire. There, sunflower seeds are a big hit with the cardinals, but I'm clueless in New Zealand. Most of these birds seem to be insect eaters, some catching them on the wing.

I sit in the sun tearing paper boxes with my mindful hands and watching the landscape. A flash of red nearby tells me a redpoll or goldfinch has flown through. This morning I gathered up some loose bark from the manuka and now I'm boiling it up to see if there might be some red there for dyeing, but no luck yet. I'm also making a veggie stew on the other burner with potatoes, celery, carrots, onion, eggplant, shitake mushrooms and some TVP (texturized veggie protein). The veggie pot holds good possibilities, but not the natural dye pot.

I place all of my veggie scraps into the loo barrel as I've been instructed, along with leaf litter, cardboard, and what I produce. Some exotic Auckland worms arrived on Friday to go into the mix and help break it down into compost. I wonder where this "night soil" compost will go once the black plastic barrel gets full. At least we've solved the problem of Morrie the Rat jumping into the barrel and not being able to get out. I was indeed sorry for the frightened little guy. He became Morrie after I discovered a penciled note on the hut floor, circling the opening for the hose to the heater, scratched by some humorous past Abhaya Hut retreatant. There's a cute drawing of ears and nose and a note that says: "Hi there! I'm Morris the Mouse. If you take this out (the gas hose I presume), I will move into your house." I don't know how many years this penciled note has been there, but when the rat fell into the loo compost barrel he became Morrie to me by rodent association. I actually have not seen mice around at all, only the rat. For that, I am happy.

On the subject of toilets, I wondered what peeing in a bucket at night for a year would be like. We take so much for granted, including toilets. However, the bucket is handy and saves me from going out at night across the deck to the outhouse, especially when it's windy and rainy. And squatting is good exercise for leg muscles.

August 12, 2014

Last night should have been our super moon, but a storm rolled in, raining and blowing all through the night. Not a bit of moon. The blowing stopped about 5 AM but the valley filled with clouds from the southwest, and by 8 AM it was pelting down again. I wonder if each full moon will bring strong winds and storms from the south.

Still connected to tracking time, I note that it's one month since I arrived. I've been looking at the distractions that are prevalent in this rarified existence. Although I don't have a teaching and travel schedule, meetings and center activities to help with, friends for lunch or dinner, family to see, or the internet, I can still come up with distractions to entertain my busy mind. This morning, I took down the curtain next to my bed with plans to cut and hem it. First, it needed washing, and then other things got thrown into the mounting hand-washing load. Distractions. And today was the day to bring my food list to the drop-box and my morning to make blueberry pancakes. I watched myself spending many hours over this food list. Distractions. I can spend much time day-dreaming about a "creamy polenta with greens" recipe, and thinking about my next day for making walnut date scones with orange peel. Also, on the "to do" list are mani rocks to paint, teapot lids to repair, and plans for mantras on the deck eaves. It goes on and on.

So this morning I decided it is time to put all these distractions onto the back burner and get on the cushion to meditate every other hour throughout the morning. I decided that breakfast, cooking, washing, journaling, study, etc. need to fit in a one-hour slot before or after the next meditation. The 8:30, 10:30 and 12:30 meditations went well. With meditating after lunch at 3:30, and then again at 5:30, it was soon time to prepare for bed and do some journaling. That schedule gives me five hours of seated and some walking meditation as a core practice. I know there will be benefits.

I found even further distractions, however, and some really exciting news!!!—four brown, white-faced cows have appeared on the hillside pasture across the valley. Wow! They don't seem to be milking cows and one seems younger than the other three. Ah, they are new friends in my mountain valley, along with the skittish piwakawaka birds! To my cushion I go with a happy heart. May all beings be happy— may all cows prosper.

August 13, 2014

I'm again reflecting on questions others asked me before departure, such as would I be afraid, all alone out here. This hadn't really crossed my mind. Although I'm in the habit of prudently locking my door even in the rice fields of Bali, I haven't thought to worry here in the remote New Zealand bush. Yet last night I locked my two doors for the first time, after getting spooked with strange shouts and arguing in the night. I put on my boots and jacket and stomped down the path in the dark to see if I could hear what was being shouted, but it was gibberish. I'm unsure where these sounds were coming from, but someone, some-place, was very agitated. I was reminded of the death of Suzuki Roshi's first wife in Japan in 1952, when a deranged monk whom Suzuki had allowed to stay at the temple despite his family's misgivings had a psychotic episode and murdered her.

This might have just been a tragic occurrence in Japan, with no influence on my stay here, if I hadn't been told before I arrived that a "troubled, agitated, and stressed-out" fellow retreatant was staying for a year at a nearby hut. The retreat staff were trying to help him. The email told me he'd settled down considerably after a few months in the hut, and that I should be reassured. But I'm alone on a mountainside with little help available if something goes wrong. And so, troubled by those shouts in the dark, I mentally went to the resources I carry with me: trust in the universe, positive thoughts, the sending of metta (loving-kindness), and my dear Kuan Yin, who is known for "hearing the cries of the world" and so is always reassuring in times of trouble. I'm here and trust that all will be well. And I'm reminded of Tenzin Palmo, who faced down five wolves that stopped at her retreat cave while she was outside getting some sun. She just smiled and sent good wishes to them, setting a great example of how to handle adversity alone on a mountain. Fear is not helpful. It only cripples, creating suffering. It's better to send loving-kindness and accept what comes along. Ah, to my cushion, to my cushion I go with positivity and enthusiasm.

August 14, 2014

Rain for two days now, with short times of glorious sunshine. When the sun is shining, I meditate on the porch; however, it seems that every hour there's another shower. I know there's benefit from all this rain, though I worry about the forest critters and birds that need drier weather to hunt for food. Unlike the birds, I'm fortunate to have my stock replenished weekly by Tony and Steve and the rest of the great Sudarshanaloka team. They've set up a superb system of solitary retreat support.

I left an empty propane tank next to my drop-box yesterday, and this evening, while I was on my cushion meditating, a four-wheeler came down the track, looped by my hut, dropped a full tank, and departed in ten seconds. Swift and beautiful. Tomorrow I'll walk up to the drop-box with my backpack and carry back my sixteen items for the week. I've watched my food list total out at $60-63 New Zealand dollars each week. Though many foods are double the cost in the USA, I'm on-target with my budget. To be doing hourly meditation sits in the New Zealand bush and yet be able to have sesame bagels with veggie bacon at breakfast instead of cold porridge is a great boon. I'm reminded of Tenzin Palmo's one meal a day in her cave, the same meal day after day: rice, dhal (lentils) and vegetables brewed up together in a pressure cooker, with sourdough bread which she baked, *tsampa*, tea with powdered milk, and half an apple a day. For twelve years she had no variation, no culinary treats like bagels, scones or chocolates.

Meals and food choices can be real distractions and I can see myself simplifying already, eating less and adding fewer nuts and fruit to my morning oatmeal. However, I've brought in some wonderful Japanese food stocks. The sembai cracker stock is dwindling, but yesterday I enjoyed some superb dried soba noodles. After eighteen years in Japan, this is soul food for me. Since the wind was blowing ferociously and there were intermittent showers, I decided today was not the day to walk down that rough Dharma Road to the Community House to return some books. The hut was so cold inside that I needed to wear my gloves and hat to be at all comfortable. I looked at the alternatives of turning on the heater, turning on the stove to cook, or using the heat from both for warmth and moved to prepare corn chowder, using some of that precious propane gas to boil down the manuka dye. Both activities warmed my small abode and my heart.

This morning my mind was especially creative. A whole series of art pieces were bubbling up as well as the dye and the chowder. No matter where I am or what materials or lack of materials I have, creative ideas come bursting forth. Maybe I will awaken or find enlightenment not on my cushion but with needle or brush in hand.

These thoughts brought to mind a time in Thailand when my teen-age daughter and I hiked through jungle and rode elephants up to visit a

Karen hill tribe for a few days. After we both got settled, we took off on our own to explore the small village. I discovered the open-air pavilion with benches and a blackboard, obviously the humble village school. Following the path back to our hut, I came across Amanda with a group of kindergarten age Karen children, all on their hands and knees in the red dirt. They were tracing lines into the vivid, iron-rich earth and carefully placing vibrant green leaves in patterns on the ground, forming an extraordinary abstract mandala—working together without a shared language and creating art with available materials. I often remember those vivid green leaves, those children, and my daughter, when I think of the inborn urge to create and communicate.

It's 7:30 PM now and the wind is howling. The rain is coming in horizontally, battering this small hut. I'm cold, cold. Winter is not for the faint of heart. Thank goodness for a hot water bottle.

August 15, 2014

I must write about last night—which was indeed horrific. Yesterday it rained off and on all day but by nightfall the wind began to blow at gale force strength. The rain was horizontal and the winds so high that the metal chairs blew off the porch. I rescued the swinging pansy pot, and even brought in the LL Bean Weather Station for fear it too would become airborne and never be seen again.

I'm here in New Zealand but that heavy, howling wind reminded me of my time in Iceland in the 70s. They say there's never any litter on the ground in Iceland because anything dropped is off the island in twenty minutes. During our two years there, the power of those winds meant that Amanda was never able to touch the ground, even as a toddler, because she was too light. She couldn't stand up to the wind force. Sean, my hefty 40 lb three-year-old, did walk, but was occasionally lifted off the ground in a gale with me holding onto his hand for dear life.

Last night was reminiscent of Iceland with that banging and howling wind. Early in the night I kept falling into dreams with this hut becoming the bow of a ship, and the howling Tararu Valley below, a turbulent sea. In and out of my dreams, I worked on "disaster-preparedness" and planned the spot I'd slip into when the big karaka tree behind the house came down. I chose a wedge at the foot of the bed that abuts the 4' kitchen wall, assuming it was the safest place if the roof

54

came down. In Japan, a land of daily tremors and many earthquakes, we were trained to have a designated place to stand (ideally, an interior doorframe) when the earthquake came and the clay-roof house tumbled down.

For some reason, when storms hit New England and we hear they're coming from Canada, they almost seem tame. In Japan, when the winter storms came down from Siberia, we took notice. Knowing that the worst storms here come from the south, from dark and cold Antarctica, puts a new twist on the word ferocity. The winds yesterday would have been a serious hurricane in the US or a Japanese typhoon, but here it seems that everything that is going to come down has already blown down, so the tree fern fronds just bounce and flap, the karaka tree nods, and the pine leans a bit. On this steep wall of winter green that I hang over, Abhaya Hut—Fearless Hut—rocks and rolls and is aptly named.

I kept waking in the night and finally decided to weather that storm with a warming cup of cocoa. By midnight the wind actually stopped, and it was dead quiet. I slept for a few hours and woke to the miracle of a brilliant, bright three-quarters waning moon lighting up the backyard so that I thought there was an outdoor light on. Moonlight poured through a window curtain, illuminating my meditation cushion in front of the shrine like a spotlight. Dazzled by it all, I was outside on the deck in my sleeping clothes at 3 AM in 40ºF weather, singing gratitude to the purifying, pacifying moon.

I've moon-bathed in Bali next to rice fields, in Kyoto under cherry trees, in Mexico on a balcony overlooking Las Monjas nunnery, and in my kitchen in New Hampshire where the moon pours through two skylights, all silvery blue at 1 AM. Moon bathing—purification, transformation, gratitude. Last night I had a beautiful image of the boiling demons blowing down the valley, being pacified by that wonderful moon. Awake much of the night, first with the wind and then with the moon, I slept-in this morning until almost 9 AM, when I thought I heard a knock on the door. Of course, no one comes knocking here—but it woke me to a gloriously quiet, windless, sunny day. Though it was barely 54ºF, it felt like spring. I got dressed, opened the hut, put tea water on, exercised, and was on my meditation cushion in less than thirty minutes. I did an hour of meditation, had a breakfast of bagels, eggs, and veggie bacon with tomato, and was ready to trek down to the retreat house by 11 AM, got the books returned, borrowed others, and then spent time tasting leaves in the small herb garden at the top of the stone steps there. Some were that peppery roquette or arugula that I love, and some a red leaf chard that tasted peppery as well. I helped myself to a few leaves to add to the sprouted lentil salad I'd planned for lunch.

Though the hand-drawn map I have says it's thirty minutes from the lower retreat house to the stupa above me, my hut is a bit further down Slipglade Track. It takes me 45 minutes. My hip joints were not so happy with that long upward hike. The trip home was longer than planned since I also detoured further down to see the crossing where I entered this land one month ago. This time I stood in deep silence, without others asking me questions about my homeland, bustling to help, and transporting gear. My whole trip was quiet, with no encounters, though there are two men working on the property and three folks in solitary huts.

I was home just before 2 PM to make lunch and start an outdoor bath to soak my aching hips and back. Glorious! Sitting out under a blue, blue sky after so much stormy weather made me really appreciate calm weather. And yes, the weather really does affect my mood tremendously, especially as I move more deeply into silence and solitude, where all is intensified and sensitivities heightened.

I'll remember this day as quite extraordinary. The contrast of that tremendous storm in the night, the wonderful moon-bathing, and then a quiet, sunny day of walking through the bush all felt precious, like a step out of time and space.

August 16, 2014

This morning I sat a "moon-setting" meditation as that glorious friend slipped behind the steep valley hills to the west, below the wall of green. Later, barking dogs at the bottom of the valley disturbed me, sending me off to the stupa where Dhardo Rinpoche is enshrined to discuss this silly irritation with him. Tromping through the high bush, I realized how very much I love being in the woods, looking and listening, and being quiet in nature. That love was birthed as a young child in New Hampshire on the land Dad bought for a summer house. I found it renewed in Japan in the forest surrounding Kyoto, and when I chose to walk the Hachiju-hachi-dera (88 Temple) Pilgrimage. Here in New Zealand, I stood and witnessed the quiet, the precious earth, the moving boughs, the deep tangle of forest growth and huge trees, and connected with the words describing Buddha's enlightenment:

> Oh Tree of wisdom, tree of knowledge unsearchable
> Tree where under, the worlds deliverance was attained—
> Through all the rain of years between our sight and thee,
> Shall we not look back and behold the veil and our faces?
> For beneath this tree was wisdom perfect.[13]

The stupa always takes my breath away, especially when I come the back way through the bush, stepping from deep undergrowth instead of approaching from the road. The glowing white symbol stands on a steep plane of green with a view down to the sea. With its head up in the blue, blue sky, it's grounded and commanding. It brings the kind, wise Dhardo Rinpoche to mind.

As I sat on the hillside in meditation, I remembered hearing of the 1997 dedication of this stupa and the enshrinement of Dhardo's ashes. Dhardo was one of Bhante Sangharakshita's closest teachers in India. He founded a Tibetan school and orphanage there following the Chinese invasion of the late 50s. Bhante Sangharakshita was already living in Kalimpong. He took initiation and became a close friend of Dhardo. After Bhante moved back to England in 1964 and founded our Triratna Order almost fifty years ago, they continued their friendship until Rinpoche's death in 1990. It was Bhante who came from England to dedicate this stupa in New Zealand and ask that Dhardo have a speedy rebirth saying, movingly, "May you swiftly come as a peerless lion."

Around the stupa on three sides are Dhardo's guiding words: "Live United," "Cherish the Dharma," and "Radiate Love." And he did radiate love and kindness throughout his life. Here, almost twenty-five years after his death, that love is still tangible, still guiding, inspiring, and calming, alleviating any irritation I carried with me this morning.

The sun is down now, the sky glowing a soft blue, but pink and gray in the west. Again I feel this has been a most wonderful day... I've had a smile on my face through the last two meditation sits and wonder if I am indeed imbued with Dhardo's blessings. Much gratitude.

August 17, 2014

It's been a very lovely Sunday. I woke up late after a long night caught up in reading. I did a Sunday sadhana practice for Kuan Yin and my usual Kuan Yin puja. As often happens, I came to a spot in that recitation where I just weep. Ah!

> May the sick be made whole again.
> Those in bondage be freed,
> May the weak become strong,
> And may all beings act lovingly towards each other.
> May the gods protect the helpless,
> The young and the old, the stupid and deranged,
> The heedless and the insane
> From all disease and distress.[14]

The young and the old in my birth family and among my friends came to mind—and for the first time I am not repelled by the words of protection for the heedless and the insane. I used to think it was an awkward translation from Santideva's Sanskrit language. Yet today I thought about a dear friend in Japan, who is remembered by many people for her poetry. She's now close to a hundred years old, is suffering from Alzheimer's, and barely recognizes me. When I return to Japan every two years, I go to her and hold her hand, and we weep together and smile. "May the gods protect the helpless. May the sick be made whole again." Those words were on my lips this morning.

Later, during my meditation break, I went into the bush around the hut with a blade I had found. I pulled out piles of dead ferns and wood for an hour or more before lunch. After my work, I decided that a meditation outside was needed on such a gloriously sunny day. Although it's now a cool 55ºF/12ºC, the temperature got up to almost 70ºF/21ºC in the sun today. And this is the New Zealand winter!

Coming from my evening meditation, I'm reminded how much of my starting time on the cushion I spend focusing on the air entering and exiting my nostrils. If I hang there, all thoughts go. What shows up doesn't stick. I can't or don't want to string it together to make any thoughts. It just melts away.

And on the mundane level, I'm pleased that the baked apricot date walnut scones from my stovetop oven came out beautifully, as if they were made in a real oven, lightly browned on top and exquisite. I'll munch on these as a treat for several days with delight.

August 18, 2014

I awoke from a dream or a half-sleeping reflection in which I was preparing a lecture on my art work, all in the format of the six paramitas:

> *dana*—generosity
> *sila*—ethics
> *kshanti*—patience
> *virya*—energy
> *dhyana*—meditation
> *prajna*—wisdom

Once really awake, I questioned how that works out—art and the paramitas. What was I contemplating? It's evidence of how deeply the teachings are penetrating, and how, even in my dreams, I'm working on integrating them into my life as an artist. I've had artwork much on my mind the past few days, thinking how I might accomplish some with the limited materials I have here. Creativity is a language, my language, a way for me to investigate and process my life and to communicate what I'm not able to articulate in other ways.

A wonderfully warm, sunny day had me meditating on the porch throughout the morning.

August 19, 2014

Oh, Rain

Quiet rain.
Soft wet drops on my face;
My vision goes to source:
Sky—white with textures of blue.

Rain falls and meets the earth
Nourishing responsive seeds,
Making leaves shine,

Refreshing tall pines and karaka.

And below, the earth is renewed.
Worms in their busy work
Take moisture for transforming.
Little possums in their dens
Sleep cozied in dry havens.

Birds snuggle together
In nooks among trees
Waiting their moment, using this
Time for rest, for dreams,
Knowing that soon there will be time
for gathering.

And I too am refreshed, reflective, nourished.
Gentle rain, quiet rain.
Alone on this mountain
You are a friend of the morning.
Connecting, reminding that I am not self
I do not own anything—
I am just part of the
kind natural world.

Responding to weather named "rain"
Responding to elements,
Receiving and manifesting,
Gratitude for all of this.

— Kiranada

August 20, 2014

The rain stopped this early morning, leaving the valley under a blanket of morning clouds. And the sun cleared out those clouds by 10 AM. The lines flap with my array of colorful sheets out drying after a big wash.

I noticed this morning that even in my dreams I'm in silence—in the world, but in silence. Some friends asked what it would be like not to speak for a year, but I do use my voice every day. It's a little raspy—like "morning voice"—but it works. I find, however, that more and more

I'm saying prayers at the beginning of every meditation and dedications at the end in whispers. Soon I'll not be able to even do that, as I sink further into silence.

> May all beings enjoy happiness, and the causes of happiness.
> May all beings be free from suffering and the causes of suffering.
> Whatever happiness, free from suffering, they enjoy,
> may it never end.
> May their minds dwell in immeasurable equanimity.[15]

And Kamalashila's words on the void (*sunyata*) were very real this morning:

> Imagine that in every direction, to infinity, you see nothing but the deepest, most transparent blue sky. You also experience yourself as a void and empty of the same nature as that infinite blue. The emptiness, and that infinity, invests you with a sense of wonder and profound inspiration. You are experiencing your own mind in its greatest clarity and calmness; at the same time you are contemplating the ultimate voidness that is its true nature.[16]

His words hit an appreciative ambiance here in this damp, sunlit hut and brought me into a deep, lovely Kuan Yin presence.

August 22, 2014

A bitterly cold morning—only 35ºF/2ºC outside at 6 AM and 39Fº/4ºC inside. After three hours of sun, it was still only 44ºF/7ºC outside, but the sun was glorious, so I bundled up in blankets, shawls, gloves and hat and ate my porridge on the porch, reveling in the green hills across the valley and the few birds searching for food in the cold.

One worry I had about this retreat was how to manage on my vegetarian diet with someone else shopping for me. It's wonderful to have a food drop every week and someone who'll buy whatever I ask for, but not being in the market myself, not seeing what's in season or what the costs are in New Zealand, I'm in some ways at a loss.

I received a food drop on Wednesday with 1½ kg of frozen blueberries in it. Though I've enjoyed blueberry pancakes and a healthy scoop of blueberries on my oatmeal these past mornings, without refrigeration the contents of that plastic bag are now close to soup. I asked for these frozen blueberries, knowing full well that I had no freezer, not even a refrigerator; but not quite expecting a bag to feed 50, as the label says. I come from New Hampshire, "blueberry country," where I've picked wild, high-bush blueberries in the forest throughout the summer since childhood. It's been a yearly ritual to take my kayak out on the lake the morning of my July birthday and pick from low-hanging blueberry bushes in remote places along the shore, still lush with berries because no one has found them. I wash and freeze those berries, and even this past May enjoyed the last "birthday blueberries" on my morning oatmeal. They're one of the fruits highest in antioxidants and vitamin C so I eat them whenever they're available, fresh, frozen or dried.

Of course, I went looking for blueberries during my one shopping trip in New Zealand before seclusion. No blueberries. No berries of any kind. "Maybe in summer," I was told, and for New Zealand that's January or February. But in one of my first food lists I asked for "dried" blueberries. They did arrive—less than a cup, costing NZ$6.75, and produced by Sunsweet in the USA. Ahh. Well, I moved on. I remembered that at home I got bags of frozen berries even through the winter—12 oz or 1 lb for US$1.49—so after a few weeks I asked for frozen blueberries. This three pound 1-1/2kl bag soon became blue soup. I've been considering whether this is an issue of grasping, ignorance, or both. It has turned into "The Blueberry Saga," and I'm sure my food support person is either scratching his head or laughing—perhaps both. I'm on to blueberry yogurt shakes and losing my taste for them rapidly. Coincidentally, these three pounds of blueberries were NZ$9.99, my most expensive food item yet. Blueberries may be joining walnuts on my list of things I cannot have for a year.

However, the kiwi fruit here are the most delicious I've ever tasted. Maybe I should stick with kiwi for fruit. I'm working towards a "same old—same old" diet so that I'm not spending so much meditation time contemplating what should be on the food list, and what needs to be prepared next because it's about to "go off."

A second new awakening today. I fell in love. I've been more conscientious about doing my second meditation session as a one hour outdoor walking meditation, weather permitting. Sometimes the first pass down the walk is a "clearing the path" round, picking up what has blown down in the nighttime storms, but usually it's quite pleasant. I walk slowly and mindfully, with eyes cast down as I've been taught. I don't take this as a morning nature walk or as exercise, but as a meditation practice. In the Theravadin sect it's a strong part of practice, perhaps equal in time to that on the cushion, and for some monks it's their major practice.

At the end of my thirty-five paces this morning, as I made my turn, I saw an oval leaf, shiny green, serrated on one side, and with some insect holes scattered on the opposite side. With every pass, I saw it there, at first highlighted in sunlight, and later in shade. Each time it became more interesting. Oh, those insect bites, that lovely shape! I passed by it thirty or forty times in that hour. It reminded me of the saying that whatever you focus on you'll fall in love with. That leaf became a practice in mindfulness, awareness, and focus. I look forward to seeing it tomorrow morning and trust it will still be there, sunning itself inconspicuously at the end of my path. Nobody else would be grabbed by its beauty, but with my withdrawal from other stimulation, with my silence and deep focus, I've fallen in love. I'm fortunate to have an opportunity to really see.

May Sarton, that poet of New England, writes of this too, says, citing Simone Weil, "absolute attention is prayer." She uses this phrase often when teaching, to suggest that:

> if one looks long enough at almost anything, looks with absolute attention, at a flower, a stone, the bark of a tree, grass, snow, a cloud—something of a revelation takes place . . . we cease to be aware of ourselves . . . losing self in admiration and joy.[17]

August 23, 2014

I was awake from 3:45 AM, when the possum patrol came by. I'd put some of my refrigerator items in a bucket with a little cold water and placed it outside my door to get the nighttime chill. I placed a metal lid on top of the bucket, but woke worrying what the possums would make of it. They seemed curious, banging around in that area, but seemed to not touch the bucket or the lid. With all the anxiety of wondering if they might go scampering off with my precious food items, I pulled in the bucket and decided not to do that again.

Possums are new to me, and their increasing numbers have become a real problem in New Zealand. There are only four million New Zealanders here and a population of over 70 million possums! Unlike in the USA, this is an introduced species with no predators. Without dogs, coyotes, wolves, or even roads, producing road-kill, in the outback, the population has thrived. The possums eat birds' eggs and any tender forest growth. They were introduced to encourage a fur trade business in the late 1800s, but those fuzzy, omnivorous bushtails with big, bulbous eyes are now considered a major "pest'" by the Department of Conservation (DOC), which is in charge of protecting native plants and birdlife. Hunting as a form of "eradication" (their term) hasn't been successful, so pest control programs have been developed.

Sudarshanaloka, which borders DOC land, elected to participate in these programs, a move that differs from the views of other Buddhist groups. Buddhist precepts include a vow not to kill or cause harm to any living thing. This often creates ethical problems and here is one of them—what to do when one thing is out of sync with another and survival is threatened. While the Sudarshanaloka Trust writes that it regrets having to kill the possums, they've found it necessary for the survival of the native ecosystem. A hard decision; but a response seen more and more often in this land where invasive species have proliferated over the past 200 years.

All of this I learned from books I found in the hut. My personal experience has filled it out. When I first arrived, and had the small seedlings on my porch chomped off at the roots, one of my helpers said they needed to get a "feed station" in place. At the next visit, a white plastic dispenser was screwed onto the lovely old karaka tree just above the Buddha shrine at the entrance to the Abhaya Hut ground and one-inch blue pellets were placed inside. A large jar of these pellets was left for me to replenish those that disappeared. Although I've encountered these white plastic dispensers throughout the bush in my remote area, during treks up to the stupa or down to the river, I see few near the entrance to the Sudarshanaloka property and the Community House. The garden down there seems to thrive without netting but with the barrier of a low metal fence. The possum population seems to be up here.

I'm not happy to be the purveyor of death pellets for Peri the Possum and his friends Paul, Penelope and Pru. My choice would be to come up with a way to reduce their fertility as they've done with pigeons in New York City, but that's not what the pellets are for. They just kill. Yikes! So, I've stopped dispensing death.

Friends sometimes ask what I "can and cannot do" as if the Buddhist precepts are in some way "Thou shalt not . . ." commandments. In Buddhism, we call them areas of practice or training. *Panatipata veramani sikhapadam samadiyami* translates as: "I undertake to abstain from taking life." I'm not "forbidden" to take life. Instead, I aspire to practice not doing it. But there may be times when a Buddhist may feel that taking a life is necessary.

I've found that when I follow the precepts, the guidelines of not killing, not lying or stealing, not resorting to unkind speech, slander or unmindfulness through intoxication, I feel more in harmony, "right with the world." Refraining from unethical actions seems to inevitably lead me to happier states of mind, a calmer, more relaxed demeanor, and clearer meditation, because I'm more in harmony with all beings. So I try my best not to kill in any circumstance. The principle of *ahimsa*, non-violence, means doing what is of benefit to both ourselves and others and not causing harm.

Earlier, I mentioned to one of the staff that I'd be willing to *share* my small plantings with the possum population but, it seems that the little guys are gluttons. I spent time this afternoon thinking of this situation from the possum point of view. I "listened" to their story and came up with an exchange—a children's book with Peri, the New Zealand possum, writing to his USA possum cousin Harvey about the situation. I had it illustrated and everyone named (and there were hordes of possum names) before I dropped off for an afternoon nap. I've decided not to leave tempting things outside and to take in the bird food at night so as not to encourage nighttime foraging, but I wish I had a better solution. Again and again I say, *May all beings be happy*—including Peri the Possum, Morrie the Rat and the lovely bird population. *Om shanti shanti shanti*, I mumble, *peace.*

It was another cold night, but since it feels so like spring with this glorious sunshine, I decided to make two batches of scones (savory and sweet, with blueberries!) after a rice and soup lunch. The last batch is in my camp oven on the stove and should be coming out soon as I write. This "sure to rise" scone mix could do better on the rising side, but maybe my technique is wanting, spreading them a bit too thin on my tinfoil sheet. Ah, mundane troubles in paradise.

August 24, 2014

I was overwhelmed this morning with gratitude for all I've been given. This includes an extraordinarily beautiful view of changing greens, the grand sky clear and blue, morning cloud formations, rising mist, changing weather, and the sound of rushing water down below flowing over boulders. I'm grateful for the sweet tui birds that wake me with their calls, for the season slowly changing, for mornings coming earlier, and for being alive to this life.

More than anything, I'm aware of this opportunity to look and really see—to slow down, sit, relish what is in front of me, and be aware of the present moment and all the wonder I'm offered that at home I barely notice. Yesterday the piwakawakas did their late afternoon dance with swoops and hoots, gathering the gnats hovering over the pollinating pine trees, and an hour later, a little round-eyed silvereye came through. Last evening a covey of quail came to my lower clearing and scampered about looking for seeds and insects. Why did I never take time before to watch, to learn their names, relish their lives, and think of the hardships possums face when they are too many?

I've decided that with so much time "sitting" I need to put my feet on the ground and try some serious walking meditation: only the walking. Moving slowly along my bush path, I remember what Ajahn Brahm wrote of his deep meditations in the Forest Refuge in Thailand, during his years as a novice monk; how he fell into beautiful *samadhi* states doing walking meditation. As he moved into that deepening space, he lost track of time and was soon expected at an important ceremony. When a monk was sent to get him, Brahm was a thousand miles away, completely absorbed in his walking meditation. He writes that it took him more than a minute to lift his eyes from the ground and focus on what was being said to him. He recalls that the beautiful meditative space he was pulled out of was "so cool and so peaceful and so still."[18]

66

When I first read this account, I thought it an exaggeration, taking a full minute to focus on what was being asked. Yet today I had a clear perception of the space he was coming from. I understand more. Peaceful, calm, serene.

August 25, 2014

This was a morning of great remorse, of things not finished. I'd been counseled that if there was any unfinished business in my life outside retreat, it would grow to plague me and could interfere with meditation. We're advised to patch up quarrels, clarify misunderstandings, handle any unfinished business, before stepping into retreat, as those in solitude become so very sensitive.

I know this well and did my best to clear relationships and look at any misunderstandings that I could work on before departure. Yet here I am doing a morning reflection on the porch, and coming up with three issues that need resolution. They each call for my forgiveness. All are friendships that are not in tune and need looking at. In one case I simply was not able to give as much as my friend needed or expected, and in the end, I have someone who is no longer in contact with me. A friendship of fifty years. Another one is a complex relationship that resulted in tremendous miscommunication repeatedly, so that every conversation had to be followed up with clarification of what was meant or intended in the last communication—two people on two roads with no intersecting parts, assuming they knew what the other was saying through their own narrow lenses. I've tried, and she has as well, to clarify our relationship numerous times, but past miscommunications and ill feelings are rearing their heads once more on retreat. At home I would call some confidante and look at this with another. And even on solitary, Order friends suggested I arrange a way to telephone a support person if issues came up and I needed someone to talk them through with. Wanting to stay in silence, I was resistant to this suggestion.

The third issue of remorse centers around my "quick" personality: thinking quickly, speaking quickly, and acting quickly when I should slow down and practice more patience and reflection, especially in group interactions. I own this one for sure.

Ratnaguna reminds us that we often harm others unintentionally due to insensitivity or fear, and that holding onto resentment or anger when we've been hurt only creates suffering. Santideva spoke of this in the eighth century. "It's hard to sleep with a dart of hatred stuck in your heart. Realize that hatred is an enemy—strike it down—be happy in this world and the next." Forgiving, apologizing, letting go of pride and limited self-views are all suggested for the growth needed.

Such clear wisdom is very helpful to me, as I sit on the other side of the world without a kind and wise friend to chat with and choose to deal with this myself. To ask for forgiveness and to forgive is part of maturing. It's not easy to let go of the hurt and extend good will to those we feel are opposed to us, have offended us, hurt us, or just don't like us. It means giving up self-centeredness and moving toward others with loving-kindness. Forgiveness is an act of self-transformation. Harboring resentment and retaliation is immature.

Three friends, three good people, three people I would like to be in better contact with. The clear need to heal this rupture in our relationships.

And so, three notecards are lying out on the small desk in this hut in the mountains and I have ten months to compose my "I'm sorry," to ask for forgiveness and to forgive these dear friends. *May all beings be well.* Oh, the hard work of solitary retreats—who would guess?

August 26, 2014

It was sunny early in the morning and I wanted to get some wash out while the weather held, since another few days of stormy rain could be around the corner. But the clouds came quickly and now I have a hermitage hut strung up with wet laundry, hoping it might dry in the night.

Tonight it's quiet, drop dead quiet. Not a peep. There was little bird activity at all today. A soft rain has just begun to fall so and my heavy sky of stars is hidden. A dark cocoon on a mountain ridge. Quiet.

August 27, 2014

Another cold day, 36°F/2°C in this uninsulated hut exposed to the winds. I could still see my breath inside at 8:45 AM. These inside temperatures are much lower than I've ever felt even in my small New

Hampshire cottage during the ice storm of December 2008, when both the electricity and the heat were off for eight days.

Well, if this is the worst that can happen, it will be a good retreat. When I asked Kamalashila for advice on a long solitary, asking about conditions and what to bring, he said, "A head torch (flashlight) and a tooth repair kit." I have both. And what to expect? "You will be at your very best and your very worst." I remember his story of slipping off the planks into the hole of his woodland john (loo) and the cussing that came out. For me, it was dropping the egg/milk mixture that I was pre-paring to add to my pancake batter this morning. What a mess! What a sad loss of ingredients! My last egg. With some dexterity I scooped up much of the liquid and continued on, making some decent pancakes with the last of my unfrozen blueberries. There was no cussing from me, but some heavy chastisement at not being more mindful.

I'm learning to manage in this small, makeshift kitchenette and I'm actually feeling quite at home. I've had a hot breakfast of oatmeal with half an apple, chopped ginger and walnuts for years, but here I've been trying to eat a few more eggs for protein, so I've expanded to French toast and pancakes once a week.

I got into the pattern of only one or two meals a day on my first sol-itary at a Theravadin monastery in Thailand eight years ago. One of the Theravadin Vinaya rules is no meals after noon, so I expected an early breakfast after my first sit and then a heavy lunch between eleven and twelve. But what I found was even more challenging. A tasty three-tier tiffin of soup, rice and steamed vegetables was delivered to my door at 9 AM, and that was it. I adjusted to this, especially when a cup of filling soy milk was offered at 5 PM; I was never really hungry and am not now. I eat more than I normally would at lunch. Having fewer meals a day saves a lot of preparation and clean-up time, giving more time to medi-tation or writing. Oh, a gentle retreat schedule.

I was aware of a loud, argumentative conversation outside that car-ried on for more than three hours this afternoon. It seemed to come from the upper hut. The voices were hot and shouty, but I couldn't iden-tify the language. I was told that the neighbor above me is Singaporean-Chinese but what I could hear was neither English nor Chinese. Talking in tongues? What could this be? Should I be concerned? Is someone having trouble?

The thinnest sliver of a moon hangs just above the horizon in the west now: a grin with a faint outline of the remaining moon. I see headlights passing below on the far side of the valley, the first car lights I've seen. I seem so alone up here on the bluff, and then there are headlights glimpsed through the bush.

August 28, 2014

I took some time off yesterday, not feeling well, to read something lighter than my Dharma books. I delved into J.B. West's *Upstairs at the White House,* about the logistics of running that grand house in D.C. It reminded me of that day in 1963 when Kennedy went to Dallas and came back to Washington in a coffin. A young president, only two and a half years into his first term. It was part of my childhood, and is part of my present life, bringing awareness of impermanence. I lost my own young father from a heart attack only six weeks after Kennedy's death. Both events have encouraged me to live thoroughly in this moment because the next moment is not promised.

And later in the day I was again questioning why I've been dwelling on conversations and events of forty years ago, wondering if it was just an indulgence of solitary life, when I came across a validating quote this morning in Storr's chapter on prayer.

> The capacity to be alone and meditation (both) facilitate integration by allowing time for previously unrelated thoughts and feelings to interact. Being able to get in touch with one's deepest thoughts and feelings and providing time for them to regroup themselves into new formations and combinations are important aspects of the creative process (as well as a way of relieving tension and promoting mental health).[19]

This integration (as well as insight into the true nature of things) may be one reason why people often come out of retreat transformed and full of smiles.

August 29, 2014

Yesterday was a busy day of cleaning the hut, beating and brushing rugs, and dealing with the huge amount of dust that falls with gas heating. I've noticed there's a tremendous gas smell in the hut whenever I turn on the heater. I imagine it's a warning that the tank is close to empty, but I wonder if it can also do some respiratory harm. Maybe not. I wish I had someone to ask, but this is what I've taken on—dealing with everything alone. I try putting the dial at different numbers, hoping that will make a difference. I air the hut regularly, but it's hard to heat the room and then open the doors to the cold. Hmmm. I try to spend as much time as possible outside in the good air, bundled up, knowing the season will change soon. And then there will be gnats and mosquitoes. Ah, nothing is permanent, even me.

I did a long walking meditation on my path this morning, then tramped up to the stupa in light rain. I spent early afternoon making a tea cozy cover from fabric scraps and painting Tibetan letters on three mani rocks. I'm painting seed syllables and also the mantra *Om Mani Padme Hum.* I remember the twenty-three rocks I painted at my Ordination Retreat in Spain five years ago, and how satisfying it felt to move paint over the surface, then place the rocks in the wilderness as messages to those that would find them, and so, I continue here. By 2 PM it turned into the warmest day yet: 18ºC or 65ºF. A joy. I dipped into the outdoor bath and luxuriated in being clean and warm all at the same time.

I'm pleased to see the radish and arugula seeds I planted breaking ground these past two days. I'm already enjoying some lettuce greens (three different types in this mix) but am using restraint harvesting any silver beets, though they're filling out and getting quite showy, I'm hoping to let them grow larger before I start using them. The parsley—cut off with early possum consumption—is struggling back and looking promising, and though my red beets are small, the leaves are doubling. But the little chive seedlings are failing.

The sun has just burst through the misty rain, and a rainbow has appeared, arching high over the stupa and down into the Tararu Valley in the west. What a delight! As I was riding into Thames 48 days ago in light rain and sun, I anticipated a rainbow, but didn't see one. Now, I just stepped out onto the porch and said "Ah, here you are!"

Again, my mind goes back to the angry voices I heard coming down the ridge the day before yesterday. Strange. Should I be fearful? While I try not to dwell on this, it is present.

While scalloped potatoes cook on the stove, I'm reading Zen poetry about solitude and small huts in dense forests, and hear Ryōkan saying "If you want to find the meaning, stop chasing after so many things." Good counsel.

August 30, 2014

A cold, rainy morning but the light is coming earlier each day. I've been feeling remorse for the past today, and reflecting on where I am in my time here on earth. There are so many people from the past that I'm no longer in touch with. I think of them and wish them well. I think now of other roads I could have taken—more emphasis on art including exhibitions and sharing in that way; more focus on the children, their development and their lives now. And yet I was called to something else because of a father dying young, a love I could not be with, and the Dharma entering my life with answers for which I'd been searching. I fell in love with Buddha—that's what I tell people.

So the remorse of turning seventy and considering what I haven't done needs to be set aside. With my focus on the mountain, shrouded this morning in misty rain, I listen.

> Do not pursue the past.
> Do not love yourself in the future.
> The past no longer is.
> The future has not yet come.
> Looking deeply at life as it is
> In the very here and now,
> The practitioner swells
> In stability and freedom.
> — The Buddha

I look at these words and take them in. Do not pursue the past— look deeply at life as it is.

Today, however, I'm awake to something that keeps coming up and needs resolution. It's surprising what shows its head after lurking under the surface for years. I realized this morning that it's time to forgive a number of people; to put down my anger at losing things to those who hold what once was mine, things that were taken, not given. Our second precept, in the positive version, speaks of giving "with open-handed generosity," as opposed to taking what is not given. It's a more positive way of looking at what could be called stealing. We may steal many things from others in our lives, including goods, time, and attention. This precept makes us aware of the need to work on this. I've done my share of "taking the not given." Today, I need to set aside my feelings and reactions and do a ritual to give away all those things that were once mine but walked out of my house in the arms of another person. It's time.

I can't remember one thing being taken from my house in Japan over eighteen years, even with more than thirteen different people subletting my home during that time. Bless them for not coveting what they saw. Perhaps they were less greedy. And I never harbored anger for the camera, shoes and clothes that were taken from my backpack in Thailand or the break-in during my first stay in Bali. I expect any money from those thefts went to buy rice for families that really needed it. My heart is light concerning those incidents. But during five years in the military, with household moves from Massachusetts, Florida, Iceland and Arizona, others were hired to do the packing and shipping, and a number of pieces of furniture walked away as well as some clothing. Did someone need these, or only covet them? And as I was packing up my own goods in Arizona, my grandfather's Victorian mirror with candle sconces disappeared from the back of the moving van parked in our carport between midnight and early morning. Furniture and clothing left my home in New Hampshire while remodeling work was being done and I was in Japan. (I'm getting this all down so I can really be done with it at last.) And personal wax tools and videos from classrooms as well as some art have all walked away. The anger has certainly dissipated over the years, but some sense of violation or injustice still lingers. I need to transform those incidents and be done with them too. I've decided that today it will be over.

I say to myself out loud, "Those things are yours now. Today I'm giving to you what you took. Those things were never "mine" really, I was only a caretaker. So, from today, please consider all these things as gifts from me. May they make you happy and well; may you enjoy their use. Truly, from my heart, I send this wish: May they make your life more beautiful. They were things that pleased me, that my family enjoyed for eighty years in some cases, and now they are yours. I set aside my feelings of anger and violation. I give up any ownership. With a candle, incense, and a bow, they are yours."

August 31, 2014

Rain all through the night. After twenty-four hours, it seems to be waning a little, though the wind is still high and blowing strongly from the east. I'm taking some time off from this journal to do some deep meditation and reflection on non-self and will be back in four or five days.

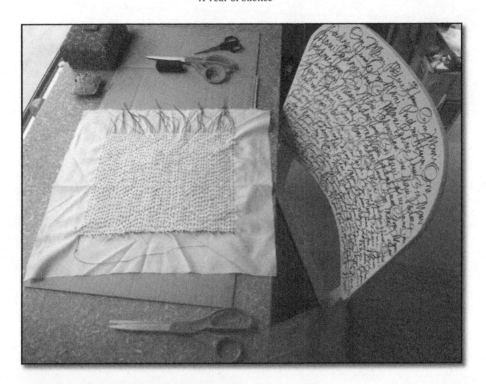

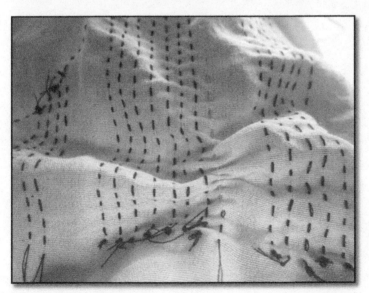

Art table with mantra chair and stitched Shibori in progress.

Chapter 3 September

It rained for three days at the beginning of this month, cooling me inside and out. I became happier and lighter with each day. The experience of giving up past grievances, those that concern both relationships and the "not given," resting and reflecting on them, sincerely delving into the emotion surrounding them, helped to illuminate and transform. The anger and remorse is no longer there.

The past day or two, I've spent more time considering non-self. I know that grasping after self only creates suffering. As Buddha said: "In the seeing only the seen, in the hearing only the heard." When there is no doer, we are light. If "you" are not there and there's only seeing, hearing and so on, how can there be someone to suffer and be discontented? Might this be exactly what Buddha is pointing to as the freedom of awakening?

> There is a place at the table for each of the many beings who show up. Fear sits beside hope, which sits beside sadness, which sits across from joy, which is next to anger, which is next to love . . . They visit and hang around for as long as they do, then are back on their way as long as "I" am not there to block their journey. When there is just this, then the host of awareness and the guest of whatever is passing through are in complete harmony. That is the end of suffering.[20]

As a visual person, this image of fear and hope, sadness and joy sitting down together really appeals to me. I can see them visiting with each other here in this small hermitage. As long as "I" does not appear and get tangled in the reactive web, they manifest, let go, and move on. I'm the host, but they don't become permanent residents.

September 5, 2014

The moon was at three-quarter last night, but rain moved in close to dawn and covered any view. I've noticed that severe weather comes at the full moon each month here. Heavy rain pelting down woke me from a dream I was deeply engaged with. I realized I haven't had a conversation with anyone for over two months but I'm enjoying chatting in my busy dreams.

I'm happy that my digital clock shows not only the date, but also the day of the week. Otherwise, it would be easy to lose track. Twice I almost missed my one "date of the week"—the food list drop-off on Tuesday afternoon. If my list doesn't show up in the box, one of the staff will drive up to see if I'm here and still alive. It's my only health and safety check. I did pass Tony and Steve on the road yesterday as they came to repair the water hose on the outdoor tub, which seems to fault with each storm. We did a gassho bow to each other, but didn't speak. Yet it was good to see some human faces, if only in passing.

I notice my food preferences are easing off the further I go into re-treat. More and more I know it doesn't matter what tea I have or what I have for lunch. Having very defined preferences only creates suffering when we don't get what we want. It's great when what we want shows up, but too often it's not available, and we end up in a funk. Through my meditation practice, I've watched preferences for all things ease, but with food it's very obvious when there's no corner store to replenish my stock. I've developed appreciation for whatever I can get up here on this wet, rainy mountain. Tea is just tea, and hot water only would do also. I watched myself sprinkle a tablespoon of black pepper on my oatmeal yesterday by accident, instead of cinnamon. Now, that's a real "no thank you" choice. I managed to wash most of it off and ate it anyway. No waste here.

I enjoy sharing this morning with four quail who are feeding along the lower clearing near my hut—two males with beautiful gray-blue breasts and fine black top knots, and two duller brown females. They feed on fallen seeds, leaves, and small insects. I've learned they can lay up to 22 eggs at a time and live to be 11 years old. Watching these sweet birds has definitely turned me away from eating those little quail eggs I get in Japan, and I certainly couldn't ever eat squab (the food version of quail).

September 6, 2014

Three days ago, along with the usual food drop, I received a woven bag full of goodies that someone in Auckland thought to send. What a joy: a chocolate bar, a beautiful blue hot water bottle with blue knit ca-ble covering, a blue wool scarf, some incense, a kaleidoscope, and two tea cozies. Someone knew I needed these in my chilly hut and thought that at least one of the two cozies would fit the teapot. I was overwhelmed with gratitude. Little things mean so very much when we're in solitude. I wrapped the scarf around my neck, put the bag on my head (silly), hugged the kaleidoscope and chocolate to my chest, and wept quietly. Kindness and thoughtfulness abound.

This morning, after meditation and breakfast, I walked through misty rain down Mill Track, through dense forests, over and under twenty-foot tall young manuka (tea trees) that had fallen in storms across the path, and over water run-off bubbling down the mountains to the river. The river itself was roaring with so much rain. I sat in my poncho with that roar, watched the rushing water moving to the Firth, and thought of all that is impermanent—this self included.

The past two nights I've enjoyed waking to watch the waxing moon give off so much silvery light that there were shadows on the deck. Tonight, it was surrounded by green and pink halos in a starry sky, then soon lost in the clouds. It will be full in another four days, the last of three super moons this year. August was so very stormy that I never had a clear sky to see that full moon. This month I hope the sky will be clearer.

I stepped out onto the deck this evening and did my obeisance and a bit of moon bathing as I usually do. The moon has always been very special to me, especially since I was given the name Kiranada at ordination. *Kirana* means moonlight in Sanskrit and *da* is a shortened version of *dana*, generosity or giving, so I'm "she who gives or radiates moonlight" and I'm charged with sharing the light of the Bodhi (enlightened) moon with all.

September 7, 2014

I awoke on a sunny, cold morning from a dream that must have gotten mixed up with the mind-stream of another person. In the dream, I was receiving an honor as Teacher of the Year in Washington, D.C., and I was black with shoulder length hair, and wearing stiletto heels. The only part of the dream that seemed to connect with this white, short-haired renunciant were the bolts of ethnic textiles that I gathered up from some office to carry out the back door, avoiding the press at the front. I awoke thinking I'd been to Saturday Night at the Movies. Amazing entertainment.

This morning I was re-reading Suvajra's book on Dhardo Rinpoche, *The Wheel and the Diamond,* and being inspired once again by his compassion and devotion. Each day, if I don't walk to the stupa, I stand on tiptoes in the front clearing and look for the stupa's spire. I can just see it above a ridge of trees to the southwest. His presence is there, and his compassion—a true Bodhisattva in our times. In 2007, my Order friend Amala and I visited his school and Tibetan orphanage in Kalimpong, India. His disciples are now aging and the children who knew him well so many years ago are grown, but his spirit is still vivid and vital in that place too.

I spent a quiet time on the porch after meditation and a Bodhicitta Puja, just stitching and singing a mantra with each stitch. I'm working on loose weave Ahimsa non-harm cloth from the tribal weavers of India. Without any of the wax resist materials I've worked with for 40 years, I'm using a stitch resist process, Shibori, a technique I learned in Japan, to place pattern in the cloth. I've gathered some natural dye materials and hope that I can get some alum locally to use as a mordant to make the dye bite into the cloth for permanency. Soon I'll be sliding these rows of stitches up against their knot and tying them off. Next they'll go into a dye bath and each stitch will be recorded as a resist mark on the fabric. It's a good contemplative process, very meditative, involving lots of mindfulness and patience. And it will be a record of my time off the cushion: one hour of stitching, one hour of meditation, on a lovely, quiet Sunday morning.

While I stitched, a young chaffinch, or pahirini, visited three or four times, feeding in the sunny clearing. Chaffinches have beautiful blue-gray heads and red breasts, and backs with showy black and white wings. While these little birds are new to me (not found in the USA), Brits, Europeans, and even Africans know them well. I've learned from my reading that they're called "bachelor birds" because they delight in traveling in flocks of the same sex. We're moving into spring and mating time, so I expect their colors are even brighter than usual, to attract mates. I delight in learning curious things about these birds who rub individual ants into their feathers as an insecticide to control feather lice and mites. I'm becoming more and more aware of the difficult lives of the birds in the wild, and my heart opens to them. They too suffer, if not from grasping and aversion, from fear and feather lice. *May they be well.* They're lovely, smart little creatures and good company on a Sunday morning.

September 8, 2014

I'm struggling with cold symptoms, or perhaps it's an allergic reaction to the pollen of early spring and the damp mold I live with. I was told conditions here would be damp in every season and I just have to deal with this. I slept in late, unable to move, but with troubling dreams of an angry sister. Today I will just take it slowly—as my good friend Karunasara advises. She's such a good reminder for this over-achieving renunciant.

I find even more advice on the renunciate life: "Genuine renunciation is giving up fond thoughts, all our delight in memories, hopes and day dreams, our mental chatter. To renounce that and stay naked in the present, that is renunciation."[21] I've posted this at my door as another reminder.

The quail are becoming quite accustomed to my presence, coming up on the porch when I'm inside, and regularly scratching and pecking their way through the front yard in late afternoon. Yesterday, two females were doing their work while I quietly stitched the mantra cloth on the deck. Soon there was a rustle and a male appeared four feet up in a bush, vocalizing for more than five minutes. "Macwerta, macwerta, macwerta, chi chi chi" —on and on it went. Soon the others in the group of five were around feeding as well. I've given up on putting my birdseed on a platform since wind often scatters it among the grass and fallen logs. The quail and chaffinches are happy to find it where ever it falls.

Every night I'm serenaded by a morepork owl. I've never seen her, but her home is definitely on the path out back since just about every evening I hear her call. I've wondered how owls can find any game with all the alerts they give, but maybe this is the call for the owl community to assemble. They hunt small birds (like the chaffinch) as well as mice, rats and lizards, and will even silently swoop in for large moths and flying beetles attracted to an outside light. The Maoris call them ruru, which sounds more like their call to me, but "morepork" is what early settlers heard and the name has stuck. I'm learning so much here about what is just outside my door since I'm not distracted by TV news, newspapers, or the regular delivery of my Time magazine.

September 9, 2014

Something has been brewing here in Bushland. The moon is very close to full and at 8:30 PM last night it lit up the valley landscape as if daylight had arrived. Already in bed with the lights out and covers up tight, I again heard yelling and loud, angry voices outside on my upper path. It wasn't the morepork owl this time, but something far more human. Pulling on a jacket, I stepped out onto the deck to listen more clearly and realized that my fellow solitary retreatant, a man I've never met who lives about seven minutes' walk uphill from me through the bush, was in trouble. He was shouting and yelling—I guess in response to the moon or demons, but who could tell? In the heavy bush, it was dark and spooky except for shafts of moonlight illuminating some groves.

With my heart opening to this poor man and his struggles, I reflected on all that I've read recently about the problems of long solitary retreats—the downside of the wonderful benefits. Jack Kornfield, a well-respected Dharma teacher, has strong concerns about the advisability of long retreats for Westerners. He feels that a few months on and a few months off retreat is far healthier than uninterrupted years in an isolated place. Tenzin Palmo (a woman of the West, though an ordained Tibetan Buddhist nun) did twelve years in her cave in Lahoul with joy, including three years of continuous solitary retreat. However, Kornfield argues "that prolonged periods of solitary life" can make it very difficult "to integrate back into society."[22] Jack's experience as a Theravadin monk in Thailand for seven years, and his PhD in psychology, give him an interesting perspective on the topic saying that ". . . the western psyche is unsuitable for such austere practices . . . as many who were beginning to try it on their own home soil had found out. Prolonged solitary retreat is causing psychosis and alienation."[23] Whoops! Is this what I hear?

Stephen Batchelor also wrote about solitary retreats and Tenzin Palmo's cave, and questioned if the retreat she did made sense for the average person. "Knowing Tenzin Palmo, it has obviously been an experience of enormous value, something which has its knock-on effect afterwards . . . I can think of other instances where people are not so psychologically solid and where prolonged periods of meditation in complete solitude can lead to psychotic states."[24] Again, is this what I was hearing?

"People go into retreat looking for answers for their insecurity and alienation and can get locked into their neurotic perceptions rather than going beyond them," Batchelor says, "you have to be wired in such a way to be able to cope with severe isolation." As a monk, he once did a retreat using a model of three months in, three months out, over a period of three years, and is familiar with the kind of damage isolation can give rise to. "You do confront your own demons (if you have any), which is of enormous value. You come up against yourself and you have to respond to your reality using the tools you have been given."[25]

I've heard a number of times of retreatants who arrive without these tools, even here at Sudarshanaloka. I was told of a Tibetan nun who planned a year and left after only three months, and a newly ordained lad who wanted to do at least two weeks and lasted two days. I often share the story of the American who wanted to do a solitary retreat after a year of meditation practice and was encouraged by his teacher, Chogyam Trungpa. On the fourth day he came running out of the woods in his slippers at 3 AM and departed in his car. Forty years later he's a respected teacher with many solitary retreats under his belt, but years ago he lacked the practice tools and stability to do it.

Hearing my frightening neighbor and reading these references, I wonder how can I expect to pull this off myself? I ask if I have the base and the structure to hold myself together and benefit. I was lucky to get some practical experience in Thailand, where I did my first two-week solitary retreat eight years ago. Though I was alone, I had my one meal delivered to my door at 9 AM, seeing no one else throughout the day and night. I heard the rhythm of the monastery schedule as I woke at 4 AM and meditated in two sessions before the sun rose at six. I did my yoga, cleaned, and had my meal before walking slowly and mindfully to a garden area where there was a walking meditation circuit under low trees. I sat there for a one-hour meditation and then did one hour of walking meditation. I remember not being able to shower until after noon, when the pipes warmed up enough to take the January chill off the water. I followed the monks' rhythm, meditating on my porch, watching the sun sink into a nearby pond, and doing a puja in my room by candlelight. It was joyous and grounding.

At one low point in Thailand when my meditation was not going well and my concentration wavered, I mentally asked our teacher, Bhante Sangharakshita, then eighty-two years old and living in the UK, to come sit with me, and I felt a real presence beside me as he did. A year later, when I met him for the first time, I told him of this experience and thanked him for coming. He said, "I did?", considered for a second, and then said, "Well, that's possible."

So I had support on that first solitary along with twenty-two years of previous meditation practice and study. I've gone on and done solitary retreats in Wales, Mexico, Java, Bali, and the USA nearly each year since 2006. There's a romance to the idea for some people. They don't realize how very hard such retreats can be. You're really thrown back on yourself, and if you're not strong and solid, problems can easily arise.

With the moon coming up, almost full, I send metta—loving-kindness—to my screaming neighbor and hope that tonight will be peaceful, tranquil and equanimous. For my sake, too. I didn't get much sleep last night as I considered what to do about this situation. I ended up sending a text message in the night, asking to meet with someone from the support team today to discuss this. I was reluctant to break silence, but felt I needed to look seriously at the situation.

When Tony arrived, at first I couldn't even croak out a "Good afternoon," having hardly used my voice in two months. It was good to share my concerns. I was happy for the chance to ask questions, some I had been been holding for weeks. Hopefully, a resolution will come in the next few days. *May all be well.* My door is locked for the second time.

September 10, 2014

While an undercurrent of anxiety remains, my life in the bush goes on. This retreat is a grand opportunity for me to watch my emotions. It's also a chance to participate more closely with nature, including this dazzling sky that I'm part of. At home in New Hampshire, I'm surrounded by old growth pine and hemlock next to deliciously prolific swampground. My sky views are between the branches and in small snatches of open space. If I want to see a moonrise, I walk to the shore at the end of my road and sometimes even take the kayak out to connect with the night sky. But here, it's all at my doorstep. I perch high on this 250 acres, facing west-northwest, so I'm fully present for the weather that broils and blows through the valley.

I woke at 5:35 to see the wonderful September super moon I'd heard of setting in the west under stratifying stratus clouds. In July, as I arrived, a local newspaper carried news of this unusual "three super moon" occurrence when earth's celestial neighbor comes a little closer to us thanks to its elliptical orbit and I at last have time to read it in more depth. According to the article, July's moon looked around 30% brighter and 15% larger, while August's moon appeared even bigger, and September's would be the last super moon of the year. Astronomers, new lovers, those named for moonlight, and devotees of Kuan Yin would all be taking note of these.

I remember, on my first morning in this hut, waking to that first super moon, but the next one, in August, was completely obliterated by a storm that went on for days. As September's wonderful glow poured into my hermitage, washing the room in gray-blue light and silvering the atmosphere, I recalled a reference to the Hazy Moon of Enlightenment from Zen poetry. With my curtains open, I lay in bed, warm and covered, and watched the dazzling show as the moon descended behind the ridge, and receiving its blessing, absolution and purification. It's better than any blessing from mortal man—though that gassho from Tony as he left yesterday, hands together, head down with a small bow, was a similar benediction. In minutes, the sky went from royal blue to Wedgewood blue to powder puff white. The day had begun.

My cup of gratitude is so full it spills over.

Later, doing a body scan at the start of my meditation, I got to my shoulders and stopped, flooded with memories of that whack on my shoulder last April in a Zen temple in Kyoto and the kind, elderly Roshi at the other end of the kyosaku (wake-up stick). I was in Kyoto with a small group of Buddhist practitioners, and we'd been looking for a meditation sit at a Zen temple. Others were closed for remodeling, so I called the small Ryozen-an Temple in the huge Daitoku-ji Zen precincts.

"No, no, I can't accept any foreigners for zazen anymore. I'm old, I have cancer, and I had an operation on my hip. I'm not well," said the Roshi. "You are friend of Tom-san, a Dharma brother? Well—maybe. But zazen is at 7 AM and that's too early for Westerners," he went on. "Well, if you come, you must be on time and I can do no teaching. I'm doing this because Ruth Fuller Sasaki-sama lived at this temple in the 30s or 40s. Or was it the 60s? You know her? She's American too, and did a lot for the Dharma."

We were there, nine of us at the gate at 6:40 AM, all prepared with pointers in Zen shrine room etiquette. What I remembered was the sound of his footsteps on the tatami mat behind me. For the first time—after eighteen years in Japan and twenty-eight years of meditation—I was willing to accept the kyosaku that so frightened me as an early student. With hands together in gassho, I bowed, knowing that he was walking behind with stick aloft. I knew he was noticing my movement and would stop behind me. He, too, was bowing to me. I moved my head to the right and "whack" —a strike on my left shoulder. I moved my head to the left and "whack" —a strike on my right shoulder. We both bowed again, him behind me, me to the open temple window on a cold April morning. Why was I so moved by this? He later had his five Zen students, who come every morning, join us in the garden for tea and to hear where we'd come from and what we were doing in north Kyoto. A poem by Chase Twichell always comes to mind when I think of that morning and the Roshi's footsteps on the tatami. Reading it, I'm brought right back to that moment, with tears in my eyes. Bless him.

Weightless like a River

I heard of a teacher and I went to him,
In the monastery. I studied his words
And the way he moved his body
He seemed weightless, like a river
Both in his words and his body
Dawn Zazen. The window
The light—I heard
His bare feet on the sanded floor
And the slow fish of ignorance turned
toward the sound.[26]

My slow fish of ignorance, turning. How poignant! This morning that Roshi is with me in this hut, and at the end of the sit I chant the White Tara mantra for long life, and pray that he's still in this world, for a little while longer, at least.

And as Roshi mentioned, Ruth Fuller Sasaki was somewhat familiar to me. Later, I read how she came to Japan in the 1930s looking for a replacement priest for the American Buddhist Center in New York City, and ended up staying many years. After returning to the USA during WWII, she married the elderly, ill Sasaki Roshi in 1944 to get him out of a California detention center. He died the following year. She returned to Kyoto and lived for more than twenty years at the small temple where we meditated that Sunday morning. There she helped translate Buddhist teachings into English until her death in 1967. And as Roshi said, she was significant in opening the door of Buddhism to many, including a small group of British, Australian, and American Buddhist practitioners looking for a zazen sit in Kyoto in 2013. Yes, I must have known her in some life.

But I've fallen into fear tonight. I'll be glad when the problems with my neighbor are resolved and I'm able to feel more comfortable in the dark. Meanwhile, in my mind I'll manifest my husky son to stand guard at my door through the dark hours. He'd enjoy that with his warrior nature and desire—down deep—to protect his self-sufficient mom. "Here's your job, Sean, for the next few weeks, " I say. Thanks.

September 11, 2014

A lovely full moon set this morning. I was up at 4:30 to look for it and saw it slip out below a range of clouds for an hour. Looking at it with binoculars for the first time, I noticed a different pattern from the one I'm used to. I've drawn and stitched the moon into Ahimsa silk, so I've become familiar with the craters and the white and dark lines, and the Northern and Southern Hemisphere moon faces ARE different.

When I went to Japan, I noticed that the familiar east coast USA moon was somewhat different there, but was told, "The moon is always the same around the world." Not so. What we see depends on region and culture. The Japanese see a rabbit pounding mochi rice with a huge mortar and pestle to make rice cakes. I saw that. My childhood "man in the moon" persists in the USA, while those in Europe see an old man

87

carrying a bag of sticks. In Hawaii, there's a gracious banyan tree and myth tells of a woman called Hina who uses bark from this tree to make cloth for the gods. Mahina is Hawaiian for moon. In India, they see two hand prints. All these are Northern Hemisphere views, while in the Southern Hemisphere, the moon is flipped, upside down. Here in New Zealand, mythology tells of the woman in the moon, a Maori maiden called Rona who "disrespected the moon" (how do you do that?) and spends eternity on the moon's surface as penance. She lies on her back with one hand raised and a jug behind her right shoulder. Not too comfortable, I think.

Humans have picked out patterns on the moon for eons. I read that what we are seeing, a planetary geologist says, are light areas (anorthosite moon highlands), and dark areas which are basaltic plains from meteorite impacts and volcanic eruptions. I was delighted to find a full page of "Moon Faces" and an explanation of what different cultures see in the full moon's face in an issue of National Geographic magazine and carried it with me to see if the Southern Hemisphere moon really was different.[27] Sure is. What fun!

Tony has reported back to me that the man would not move out, and had requested the standard one-month notice. I was asked if that was alright and replied, "No, not really." I was concerned with the mental health of this retreatant as well as my own safety, I asked if the retreat center could guarantee our safety, knowing the answer is, no guarantee. However, in the end I knew that I had to rely on the staff's knowledge and judgement and just trust that all would be okay. And then I slid back into my life of silence to wait it out.

September 12, 2014

I woke to a fine mist of rain blowing in from the east and a waning moon covered by clouds. A little blue-capped chaffinch was on the wet grass out front, trying to find some breakfast—poor, wet baby.

Happily, the fear has abated. I worked yesterday to access what I'm actually afraid of, and to reflect deeply on the implications and how this makes me suffer. I realized that, among other things, I fear anger in others that may manifest as erratic, unpredictable behavior, and violence that may threaten my well-being physically and emotionally. This is the fear that predominates today, and it's with me here in the bush. Some of this fear comes from being born female and also from growing up in the typical dysfunctional family. It's up to me as an adult to transcend and transform this conditioning, to function in this world and work towards enlightenment.

Kamalashila writes that ". . . all fear derives from our own unconscious anxiety about death, from a fear of the existentially unknown." To realize our own enlightened consciousness and overcome this fear and acknowledgment our impermanence, this will set us free.[28]

He is very right. I fear what might happen in the night so very far from any other humans, with an irrational neighbor shouting at the moon. I'm on my own. And yet, with morning reflection and meditation, I'm able to do an "exchange with other" and send metta and purification to him, who is the source of what I fear. I walk the room and mentally chant, clearing and cleaning each corner of my hut, and then later walk the path and chant again. I bless this troubled soul, and send compassion and empathy to him. He's struggling with so much pain and suffering. And I'm here—here for the duration—and I'll accept what comes. Accepting unpredictability and impermanence, ending in death, frees me from fear, and from the suffering that comes with it. My doors aren't locked and I don't need Sean to stand guard duty now. The sun breaks through the rain and I'm outside looking for rainbows. How significant!

So here, once more, is a real opportunity to work on some inner insecurity that may never have come up without this catalyst. I look upon my neighbor as my personal Bengali water boy, and remember Atisha's story of dealing with adversity. When Atisha went off to Tibet to reintroduce Buddhism to a harsh land ruled by demons and magic, he chose to take a grumpy, disagreeable Bengali with him because the young monk challenged his practice and gave him grounds to work on his compassion and negative mental states. The story goes that Atisha sent the lad back to India after two years because the Tibetans themselves were enough of a challenge to his equanimity. I've always enjoyed this teaching and think of it when adversity arrives in my life and I wish it gone. Transforming such troubles into opportunities for growth makes us welcome the difficult times as teaching tools.

Kull writes that ". . . the dark times I experience in solitude do not simply arise from my own neuroses but are manifestations of the difficulties faced by anyone who turns their mind inward."[29] And Father Henri Nouwen also talks of solitude, the troubles, and fears as well as losing the false self that can happen, in *The Way of the Heart*.

> In solitude I get rid of my scaffolding: no friends to talk with, no telephone calls to make, no meetings to attend, no music to entertain, no books to distract, just me—naked, vulnerable, weak, sinful, deprived. Broken—nothing. It is this nothingness that I have to face in my solitude, a nothingness so dreadful that everything in me wants to run to my friends, my work, my distractions, so I can forget my nothingness and make myself believe I am worth something . . . thus I try again and again to run from the dark abyss of my nothingness and . . . restore my false self in all its glory...and that is the struggle. It is a struggle to die to the false self.[30]

September 14, 2014

The sweet bell tones of a tui bird welcomed a dawn shrouded in clouds. The wind was moving some of those clouds off the mountain, but they wanted to cling on this overcast morning.

The leaves in the planters seem to tremble with this gusting wind. Two nights ago I brought in the big pot of pansies since the wind was blowing so hard. It's produced fifteen to twenty beautiful pansy faces in six colors, and the fragile petals take quite a beating from a night of winds. Today the wind is blowing from the northwest and I have trouble holding out the opened door without it slamming in my face. What dynamic, changeable weather! Very rugged and primal, in so many ways.

Yesterday, I took a day off from journaling to be quiet, think and reflect. A walk down the mountain to the Community House library for my monthly book drop and pick up helped. After getting home, I discovered once again that there was air in the pipes and water wasn't running to the outdoor tub. Is this the fifth time? The guys must be getting tired of working on this problem for me. They're so sincere and caring that I never sense any annoyance at re-doing something that isn't functioning, but it must be frustrating even for them.

In the afternoon I spent more time looking at fear, its nature and how it creates obstacles in our life. Fear can be a tremendous obstacle to our growth, stunting our learning and cramping our life. With it, I couldn't travel or stay alone on a ridge for a year. Speaking with others before departing, I was asked again and again how I was able to do this. How could I not fear a toothache, ill-health, the death of a family member? People spoke of fearing that their own personal demons would show up and not having the support of loved ones they depend on.

The fear of rats trapped in a hole and being unable to help them. The fear of an angry, irrational neighbor with a past history of agitation and abnormal behavior (shouting again tonight). I sit here, fearful in this deep forest. These fears could be obstacles that freeze me, stopping practice. Fear could send me running out of here in my slippers at 3 AM as that first year meditator did. Or they could be opportunities to look deeply and work with it.

So I look for guidance and protection, purification and loving-kindness in the practices I've learned, and I take this on with my hand up in the fearlessness mudra of Amoghasiddhi, the abhaya mudra that this strong, stable hut was named for. And I recite the Lojong verses every morning and make them part of me:

> By the truth of the ultimate mind of enlightenment,
> Generated by the mighty and sublime Avalokitesvara
> And all the Buddhas and Bodhisattvas,
> May supreme Bodhicitta be born
> In myself and in all beings under the sky.
>
> May the cause of suffering, and the anger of all beings
> And its results, the heat and cold of the hells,
> Come to me! Dissolve into me!
> I give to all beings under the sky
> All the merit of my loving-kindness
> And my freedom from anger.
>
> Thus may all anger's realms, the hells, be emptied.
> May all well-beings become Avalokitesvara of the Vajra family,
> And realize sublime mirror-like wisdom.

May attachment and aggression,
Which arise from constant focus on the self,
And lead to perceiving everything as a threat,
Come to me! Dissolve into me!
I give to all beings under the sky
All my merit form of the four boundless thoughts.

May their minds be filled with kindness, compassion
Sympathetic joy, and equanimity![31]
          — Jamgon Kondtrul Lodrö Thaye

September 15, 2014

How wonderful to be able to open my home up and meditate on the porch in the sun after a walking meditation on the path. I'm more and more aware that spring is coming. Many bushes have buds starting, and some are dropping seed fruit. With so many ferns around, including the majestic 20' tree ferns, it's the fiddleheads I notice first, some as big as my fist. I watch them develop stage by stage, from brown hairy nodules to long fiddleheads covered with fur, to the slow unfurling that shows green, quarter-size medallions inside the disc. These medallions slowly mature, and as the fern gets taller, they unfurl gloriously and become multi-leaf segments on the developing frond. Unfurl is the word. It all takes over a month, and I watch each stage with delight. Even the small ferns on the forest floor that I'm familiar with from New Hampshire and Japan follow the same unfurling stages that the grand tree ferns demonstrate.

I opened my eyes from meditation on the porch and realized how much more blue there was in the landscape than before, when much was chartreuse green. The cold doesn't kill off the plants here, but it does stunt and frost the tip ends, creating a lot of straggly dead fronds, covered in brown and gray.

I was pleased to see the four young bullocks feeding in the high pastures across the valley again today, but I'm aware how very quiet it is here with limited bird life around. I take note of every little winged being, but there should be many more. I learn that once New Zealand was a land of birds, with no mammals at all until Cook arrived in 1769. The Maori, who came from Polynesia in double-hulled canoes between

1200 and1300 CE, brought kumara (sweet potato) and taro, and relied on these along with birds and berries for their diet. It was Cook who released pigs for a future food source on his expected return visits. Some dogs and rats came too, followed by possums, rabbits, ferrets, stoats, weasels, and rats. More dogs and cats showed up on future ships. With the arrival of these predators, more than 43 indigenous bird species have become extinct, and New Zealand now accounts for 11% of the world's endangered bird species.[32] Only the USA, with 35 times the bird species, has more that are ranked endangered.

Today I'm remembering the lovely plum tree just coming into blossom down at the Community House two days ago. Ryōkan's Zen poem of spring coming to Japan appears:

> Spring flows gently—
> The plum trees have bloomed.
> Now the petals fall, mingling with the sound of an uguisu.[33]

But there was more screaming in the night yesterday.

September 16, 2014

Chilled and cold, I sit in front of the heater reading, taking notes on suffering from the Pali Canon. Milarepa and Tenzin Palmo are on my mind. They weathered much hardship on their solitary cave retreats. Alexandra David-Neel, who traveled for fourteen years in the early twentieth century in Nepal and Tibet, often disguised as a male monastic, shares the benefits and joys:

> I know the hardship of that life. But I also remember the perfect silence, the delightful aloofness and the wonderful peace in which my hermitage was bathed and I do not think those who spend their days in such wise ways need to be pitied. I would rather say they are to be envied.[34]

September 17, 2014

I woke to wind, and a dream of installing a museum exhibition of textiles and artifacts in Japan. After living there eighteen years, it seems I'll always carry Japan with me—another life. Perhaps it was seeing those delicate pink blossoms at the Community House that brought spring in the Kyoto mountains back to me, when much of the green is interspersed with pink wild cherries. It's a magical time of year, when the rivers run pink with reflected light.

A cup of tea, some wash in to soak, some yoga, and then to my meditation cushion, remembering how I woke in the early hours, and in half-sleep found myself reciting prayers I've been memorizing. With the years, memorization has become more difficult for me, yet I love being able to recall phrases that inspire me. I spend time each day reciting *May my wisdom grow as vast as the ocean.*

I started re-reading Lama Govinda's *The Way of the White Clouds* last night and am interested in his thoughts on prayer and intention: "Prayers in the Buddhist sense are not requests to a power outside ourselves and for personal advantages but the calling up of the forces that dwell within ourselves and that can only be effective if we are free from selfish desires."[35] Govinda tells us that Buddhists put their faith and belief in the power of motive, purity of faith, and purity of intention.

All the hours I chant, do pujas, and repeat my 108 mantras of *Om Mani Padme Hum* daily, lift me up, create positive emotion, and move me toward that plane of transcendence. When I read of a simple peasant creating a mantra water wheel that spins mantras as a blessing to the brook and all humans, animals, insects and plants who might use the water, I'm lifted up. It's not far from the Christian priest blessing congregants with holy water. As Lama Govinda says, whatever helps us to concentrate our minds or achieve that "inner turning about" in the deepest recesses of our consciousness—whatever puts us into a creative or intuitively receptive mode (emotional equanimity) is worthy of our attention—weather, prayer wheels, mala bead recitations, puja ceremonies with candles or reciting mantras. Some Westerners may consider these mumbo jumbo, and secular Buddhists just want the clean Dharma without the candles and incense, but my artistic soul responds to more.

September 18, 2014

What drama on the porch as I finished my lunch! I heard a thud, and from the corner of my eye saw something small hit the edge of the glass door. Looking out, I saw a small bird crumpled over, slowly pulling his olive head up, showing his right eye tightly closed—a small silvereye. They're sparrow-sized and only weigh about 13 grams. He fell on his side, rolled to his feet, shook some feathers, and dropped again— dazed or dead? It was so painful to watch. I stood looking through the window, sending loving-kindness—*May you be well*. All these mantra recitations descended on him. I left him alone for five minutes, then returned to look. He was right against the sill of the door, head down. Oh me! But he did seem to be more himself, and I soon heard a few soft chirps. Then he turned and flew off to the manuka grove. Hurray! Wanting to know more of these little silvereyes, I read that the ancestors of these little guys came here from Australia 150 years ago. They're great flower pollinators who build cup-shaped nests suspended hammock-like between twigs, and return to feed their young 250 times in a 14-hour day. What hard workers! I'm glad this one made it and is well.

This week the white blooms that I saw through binoculars two or three weeks ago, growing among the trees on the far ridges, have finally appeared on this side. On the other side of the valley it looked like a bush of full, white petals. On a walk back from the stupa, I saw some bright white poinsettia-like flowers high up in a riwa (scaly pine) tree. Checking my plant book, I found they're a type of clematis (puawananga in Maori), and that the Maori made elegant headdresses and flowering wreaths of these flowers. Clematis came to the UK in 1840 as well as the USA, and surprisingly, a plant in Massachusetts is said to have produced 7,000 open flowers at one time. It's so strange to see a tree covered high up with heavy snow white petals, just as spring begins.[36]

A note from the guys tells me it wasn't a plum tree that I saw blooming down in the Community House garden, or even my beloved cherry blossom, but a peach tree! Okay, a peach tree.

September 19, 2014

Papa Possum and a couple of the kids dragged their bushy-tail jump ropes across the deck about 9:30 last night looking for choice tidbits, but found none. They don't even bother with the roof anymore, and only stop by for ten minutes or so on their rounds.

I woke again at 11:00 PM and read stories of Tibet in the 1930-1940s—extraordinary times—in Govinda's *White Clouds*. He has some interesting observations on weather and dreams. He said that in the rarified atmosphere of high Tibet, rain brings dreams of the past. Curious?

I'm not sure if atmospheric pressure influences dream content, but I know that the lessening of distractions in a solitary retreat gives us access to our dream life in far deeper ways. I was delighted to chat with my Dad, who passed away fifty years ago now, during a dream in a retreat in Bali a few years ago. My Mom is also often present, and she's been gone eight years. Last night in a dream, I was introducing my dear friends and supporters from a stage. Too often, lately, I'm doing some public thing—a talk or lecture, or receiving recognition—which is extremely uncomfortable for me. While I'm not a shy person, I shrink from being center stage, and will only do a public talk if I feel it might benefit others in some way. But in last night's dream I could connect with friends from a very far distance.

And of course, there was rain today—it's New Zealand and still winter for a few more days. While four inches is average in September in Auckland, I think we had at least half of that last night alone. This morning I hear the difference in the rapid's flow coming down the valley from the easement above. In 2002 a tremendous rainfall brought a flood that destroyed two caravans (camping trailers) down near the land entrance and ripped up the steel and concrete bridge entering the property at a cost of NZ$30,000. Luckily, there were no deaths, though visitors had just stepped out of those caravans thirty minutes before the flash flood.

So we have rain here, and whether that's helping me connect with my past through dreams, or whether it's just the nature of solitary retreats, this life review is quite real. This is one of the first times I've had unimpeded time to sit and reflect on all that's transpired in my life and sort it through. There has to be some benefit from this, some integration as well as insights. This opportunity feels like the time just before death when we look back before the end. It's a true opportunity to do this in health, supported by meditation and a clear mind.

At 11:00 AM the skies opened and rain poured down again. The valley was a complete "white-out" of dense clouds moving to the east. I managed to slip in a 30-minute walking meditation just before it started, then on to my cushion. Is this the fourth day of rain? I got some wash done three days ago by hanging it and taking it down and up three times between vertical rain clouds blowing on sprinkler mode. Now we're into serious rain, not showers. Ah, impermanence and changeability. Good practice.

September 21, 2014

Today the temperature was the lowest it's been in twenty days. It's also the fifth day of rain in a row. It should get me down, but I'm just grateful to have a dry roof and an outstanding view. I keep dropping in and out of meditation, falling into second and third dhyana (the meditative absorptions they are called) easily with the sound of the rain. Between sits I read, reflect, tear up cardboard for compost, and pull up the last threads on a shibori art piece. I spent three hours yesterday and another two hours today on this. I will await some alum mordant and some natural dyes to put coloring on these pieces later next month.

Between downpours, the little chaffinch came out and searched for the birdseed I sprinkle for him in a protected place. Yesterday, I had a short visit from a silvereye, possibly the "knock-out lad" that came four days ago. He must have some affinity for the location now, so I leave some seed on the top step in case. Both of these little birds are dazzlers, one with a grey-blue cap and red breast, and the other an olive green cap and white ringed eyes. Both are obviously the more colorful male of the species.

I cooked some creative chocolate cookies from leftover muffin mix, butter and cocoa. They came out quite well after twelve minutes in a 300F camp oven. And the Tofu Scramble recipe on the packaged tofu box that I cooked for lunch came out extraordinarily well, good enough that I've included my own adaptation here with additions:

Tofu Scramble—makes 2 servings

1 package firm tofu crumbled
2t. butter
½ c. green onions, chopped
¾ c. red and green peppers, julienne strips
1 c. mushrooms, sliced
1-1/2 medium potato
½ t. turmeric

97

3 T. picante sauce
some chopped parsley

1. Peel and rough cut the potato and cook for 10 minutes until just soft. Cool and slice thin.
2. Put crumbled tofu in skillet with butter. Add turmeric and cook on high for 5 minutes.
3. Add vegetables and potato and cook for 5 minutes more or until vegetables are tender crisp.
4. Stir in picante sauce (if you have it).
Serve on a cold, rainy day on solitary retreat. A sure pick-me-up!

So life in the rain is not bad at all. And we know that all is impermanent—especially the weather. These are the days that Kamalashila spoke of, the hardest and the best. And with spring officially arriving in 24 hours, clothed in all her splendor, life has to get better and better.

September 22, 2014

It's the first day of spring in the Southern Hemisphere, but the temperature never got above 40F°/5°C. I'd dreaming of doing a meditation at the stupa on this equinox day, but the roaring storm with lashing winds cancelled that idea. Actually, I was ready to "toss in the towel" and just cancel the day. I woke early with such a pain at the top of my head (my concussion headache area) that I lay in bed until 8 AM not moving, hoping it might pass as it sometimes does. I got up and limped through breakfast, and washed my hair in the sink since I couldn't stand another day of this hair. I was up and down to bed all day—not meditating until 11 AM, but finding some solace in dear, sweet Suzuki Roshi's *Zen Mind, Beginner's Mind*.

I was amazed that a small chaffinch could make it to the porch door for some seed in this blowing gale—so I shook some out and he tentatively returned two or three times. It's rewarding to sit at the glass door and observe him so very close.

In the Northern Hemisphere this weather would correspond to our March. I'm reminded of the old adage "March comes in like a lion and goes out like a lamb." This wind is very lion-like, for sure. Tony calls it a "big blow," but it's similar to New England hurricane weather. This is such a mild, temperate climate, with winter and summer average temperatures not varying ten degrees, yet I live so much out of doors, hanging wash, bathing, and meditating, that many, many days of rain and 40 degree temperatures make life hard. But those Kiwis I met in July said how lovely that I was coming in with the worst of the weather, and it would get better each month, up to mid-summer in January. I'm waiting. Patiently?

Meanwhile, the ache in my head continues and I feel as if I've been beaten-up. It slows me down, upsets my stomach and makes me focus on the external world more. And then the rain stopped, the wind died just a bit, and the afternoon sun came out. I picked up the metal furniture that was blown off the porch again when the glass door was whipped from my hands, and once again, I delighted in being in this diverse land.

September 24, 2014

The evening before last we had a wonderful clear night with stars twinkling across the heavens, the first time I've seen stars in almost two weeks with all these storms. That next morning turned out to be one of the coldest this month—back down into the 30s/2ºC, but today is milder.

I awoke to another hard headache. The pain slows me down and my meditations are less clear. I've read that after twelve years at 13,000', Tenzin Palmo suffered debilitating headaches and altitude sickness when she returned to Mount Kailas in the mid-90s. I'd have expected her to be well acclimatized to high altitudes after all that time in the Himalayas, but no. Every time I've gone to 12,000' I've been sick—Mexico, Japan, Colorado. And with this concussion injury, even 6,000' brought daily headaches last spring in Mexico, where I'd been fine before the accident. Dhardo Rinpoche, who is so very present on this land, left Tibet in 1947 to seek help from the medical profession in India for continuous headaches, dizziness and weight loss. It sounds like me. He was under tremendous stress—finishing his post-Geshe studies, anxious about money, and living under harsh monastery conditions. He prospered in India, both in Bodhgaya and Kalimpong, where he lived to be 73. So I dance between my headaches and trying to watch what contributes to them: hormonal changes, alcohol, and caffeine in the past, and my concussion, chocolate, and a malfunctioning gas heater at present. Then I accept them as learning tools.

The joy is to slow down and have a somewhat stress-free life here so I can watch my mind and see what I create. I'm a goal-setting, accomplishment-driven soul, and have been since I was a child. It's resulted in a full and interesting life, with many travels and experiences, but I do wonder why I came out so driven, with so much intention imbedded in me. I've always felt I had much to learn. I called it "places to go and things to see," but it was actually a deep desire to learn about the world, and about others. From a young age it's seemed I have many lives to complete in this one lifetime. And now I'm on what is probably the last one, with a year set aside to look at all of it. I'm driven, intentional, intense about life, wanting to use my time and opportunities to the highest, but it's been the spiritual life that has pulled and attracted me most, never material gain or recognition. I haven't had much ambition to be successful either career-wise or financially. I've had another drum I was dancing to—always.

September 25, 2014

I'm happy and well on this "dark of the moon" day. It's somewhat overcast, but with breaking sun. I've been watching the sun come up earlier each day (along with me!) and the lovely light evenings grow longer. I let go of the pain of my headache, telling myself that it is my choice whether I suffered with it or not—and it went. The little chaffinches are coming to my doorstep to eat birdseed and I'm sketching their antics. Life is good on solitary retreat.

This driven, goal setting individual is interested in what Santideva and Tenzin Palmo have to say about pride and self-confidence, and how they work with the ego-mind. It seems that pride can come in different guises and degrees, but these all connect to the ego and are the anathema of non-duality. There's pride in one's achievements, possessions, wealth, looks, and abilities. There's consciousness of one's own dignity. The hard one is having an excessively high opinion of one's own importance, and that's a difficult view to break. I see many modern parents, worried about poor self-esteem in their children, inflate childhood egos in an extraordinary manner. The downfall comes later, when these self-important beings meet the world. Ajahn Brahm writes that pride corrupts our wisdom, making us think our precious "views" are the true ones and missing out on what truly is.[37] ". . . deep insights based on such experiences of profound letting go are incapable of leading to pride . . . these are realizations that undermine the very illusion of a self from which arrogance arises. Wherever no self is seen, pride cannot stand."[38]

We have the pride of extreme self-importance, but also the pride of comparison. There is even pride in feeling inferior to others. We know of people who insist on telling all their problems, their feelings and the horrible things that have happened to them. In my studies I learn that pride arises not only from thinking that we're wonderful, but also from thinking we're awful and taking *pride* in that. "All these aspects of pride are expressions of the ego," Tenzin Palmo says. "Whatever comparison we make expresses duality between ourselves and others. An open, spacious mind does not compare."[39]

And then we have self-confidence and fearlessness, which some people who have low self-esteem see as examples of pride in others. Santideva says there's a huge difference between self-confidence and arrogance. Self-confidence is essential on the spiritual path. We have to believe in ourselves. Tenzin Palmo says we need to believe in our potential: ". . . we have to cooperate with ourselves, and encourage ourselves, and not be obstacles on our own path."[40] Cherishing others beyond ourselves requires an enormous amount of self-confidence and fearlessness. Two sources reflect this thinking: Santideva's *Bodhicaryavatara* (Chapt. VIII) and Geshe Sonam Rinchen's *Eight Verses for Training the Mind.*

> May I always cherish all beings
> With the resolve to accomplish for them
> The highest good that is more precious
> Than any wishful filling jewel.   Vs #1

Knowing that HH the Dalai Lama, with all his humility, kindness, generosity and wisdom, recites the Eight Training Verses every day to help him stay focused on Bodhicitta and his Bodhisattva Path encourages me. I've added this to my practice.

I look at myself for instances of self-cherishing or an inflated sense of self-importance. The antidote to pride is putting others before ourselves, and the tonglen (giving and receiving) practice which I do often is a great antidote to self-cherishing. More and more, as my practice grows, I find myself visualizing a difficult person with their problems, going around behind them, and stepping into their shoes. This could be a family member, a disturbed neighbor, or even the troublesome possums or desperate birds in a cold, wet bushland. I consider what the world might look like through their eyes, what their troubles or pain might feel like, how their anger or acting out may result from their view. And then I wash them in metta—loving-kindness. I'm not trying to change them, but to understand them, knowing that they're like me, the same as me. There is no "us and them," no duality. For me, this practice is transforming. It takes away any anger or ill-ease that I have, and makes me relax. Let go. They're now my friends, even if their behavior continues. Amazingly, I often perceive a change in them as I manifest this change in me.

While I no longer retaliate, I do walk away. One otherwise loving and generous family member carries a shadow side that can enjoy putting others down, implying that they're stupid or inept. When this shadow side focused on me, I saw my daughter raise her eyebrows in amazement and mumble under her breath, "This is not the way you speak to my mother." It's true, I don't hang around for even verbal abuse. But when once I might have gotten angry, now I just laugh in amazement with my daughter and think, wow, what am I mirroring here?

> When I see ill-natured people,
> Overwhelmed by wrong deeds and pain,
> May I cherish them as something rare,
> As though I had found a treasure-trove. Vs #4

> This sounds like Atisha speaking about his Bengali water boy.
> When someone out of envy does me wrong,
> By insulting me and the like,
> May I accept defeat
> And offer the victory to them. Vs #5

Here is my beloved but misguided family member. I offer him victory. I don't take this on. I work at just loving him. And another note on pride, this time from Isidorus the Preacher: "If you find yourself feeling proud of your self-denial (as a vegetarian)—eat meat immediately! It is far better to eat meat than to have inflated ideas about yourself."[41] Love it!

September 26, 2014

A quiet, cool dawn with the hush broken occasionally by eloquent, ringing bell tones, sometimes similar to a flute, from the bellbird the New Zealanders call korimako. He truly is a jewel. When the wind isn't blowing on this ridge it can be "dead silent" and then this poetic call sings above the tree ferns.

I'm noticing more signs of spring as bushes and trees put out new growth in this delightful sun after days and days of rain. Many trees have clusters of berries and the karaka tree behind the hut is carrying a heavy, musty smell from its new growth.

It's spring here, yet I'm constantly surprised at how few ants and other insects are hiding in the damp undergrowth and the discarded tree fern branches that look like large black tubes. In Indonesia, they'd be crawling with insects. The tile floor of my house in Bali can have ants in four different sizes and colors at any one time, yet here there's but one ant species for the two islands. The undergrowth is wet, but not crawling with biters. I know this from extended time on my knees yesterday, raking with gloved fingers, and picking up a tremendous amount of leaves and forest litter that has been there for ten years or more. It felt good to be tidying in the dirt. All my gardening friends were on my mind.

I've been meditating three hours or more at a time out on the porch the past two days, and sometimes I'm joined by my chaffinch friend, whose call I now recognize easily. Often, too, the quiet is broken by Yipper and Woof, the two dogs at the farmhouse down below my hermitage. Last week I finally caught sight of them through binoculars, out for a late afternoon walk with their human in the cow pasture up from the river. They now have names (mine). Yipper is a small white terrier, identified by his energetic bark. Woof is twice his size and a lovely tawny brown. When I first arrived and their barking would start in late afternoon during meditation, I was somewhat annoyed. Soon, that annoyance changed to acceptance, and now I welcome their voices and always wish them well. I sense that they are good dogs and they

103

bring me awareness of the world outside this ridge. I experience so little of that on this cloistered precipice.

September 28, 2014

I'm at Day 78 and I've hit a low that I knew would come. It's a challenge to keep my spirits up and stay positive. It's interesting to watch my mind, see this happen, and just let it be. I think of my solitary inspirations, including Jane Dobisz, who spent a hundred days in the Maine woods, up every morning at 3 AM to do 300 prostration vows and an hour of chanting before breakfast. And Tenzin Palmo, who also was up at 3 AM for her first three-hour meditation sit, one of four she did each day for three years. Bob Kull, on solitary for a year, was rarely up at 3 AM—more likely he had yet to go to bed. He did much of his journaling in the night hours, burning solar and wind-generated lights. This man worked every day to maintain, repair, and troubleshoot his solitary existence, building his own hut and managing on the supplies he'd brought in with him for a year with the help of a Chilean Navy ship.

Knowing of their hard, solitary lives, I laugh at myself getting out of sorts with the monotony of doing the same things every day—the same chants, the same meditation practices, the same dishes to wash and plants to water. I know myself enough to know that I look for variety, even needing a different route to work occasionally. The "same" can get tedious for me.

Nobody writes about Milarepa's low times in the cave, when he'd "had it." I do know that this will pass, and I'll learn from it. Tenzin Palmo's advice to be patient and persevere helps. I know I need to return to my intention, bring all those who are expecting me to be present, to mind, and do this long retreat in their name because they cannot.

Dear Atisha tells me, "Until you have attained stability, distractions harm your practice. Dwell in forest or mountain solitudes, free of upsetting activities. Practice the Dharma and you will have no regrets at the time of death." I'm listening, Atisha. And then he goes on . . . ". . .go to a solitary place. Turn your mind inward, identify your defects, rid yourself of them and develop all your inherent good qualities. Be content with just enough food for sustenance, just enough clothing to protect yourself and your practice will progress from day to day, month to month, year to year."

And here is another hero of mine, Dilgo Khyentse Rinpoche, who translated Gyalse Thogme's verses, also cheering me on:

> In a solitary place
> There are no enemies to defeat
> No relatives to protect
> No superiors to look up to
> No servants to look after.
> So, apart from taming your mind
> What else will you have to do there?[42]

So, that "extraordinary energy and vigor" that I'm known for occasionally wanes too. Yet I know I'll be back, curious, enthusiastic, delighting in small things and appreciating this unique opportunity to look at myself and develop my good qualities

September 30, 2014

It's 12:30 and gray clouds are moving in, but it's been a lovely, sunny, blue sky morning, only in the high 50s/14ºC but warm in the sun. I'm still wearing three layers, but if I was outside working rather than sitting meditating and stitching, I'd be happy with one long-sleeved shirt.

While I was doing some morning sky watching between meditation sits, I noticed someone has been eating the porch planters. Four or five lettuce leaves that protruded outside a small gap in the protective netting have been nibbled. It's very little damage and I'd not even notice it if I wasn't being mindful. I think it could be Morrie the Rat rather than a possum, but who knows? I've not heard any possum activity in four or five days, but did hear some small scampering on the roof and porch last night. Morrie, I bet.

Today is a much happier day. I woke early, exercised, meditated, and prepared breakfast with a smile on my face, feeling extremely content and even serene during my sit. Whatever cloud I was under a few days ago has passed, and I'm happy to watch these moods rise and fall like the weather. Reflecting on this, I realize that I can set up an expectation or a schedule for myself that seems kind and luxurious, but in reality is creating stress, and my enthusiasm wanes. This retreat is to help me know myself better and identify my defects, and it's good at that if I pay attention.

I'm excited to see a tui bird, only ten feet away at the edge of my grove at last, rather than high above me among camouflaging branches. This is the bird that can mimic so much and produces the lovely songs I hear. He has a black face and a dangling snow-white wattle under his chin and eye-stopping green/black iridescent wings. I can see why these feathers were used for women's hats in the 1800s, but what a shame to destroy such a glorious bird for hat plumage! The species has been protected since 1873. New Zealand has made me quite a "birder" and I'm now eager to connect more with my US birds on return. Bless my friend Maclean for the great New Zealand bird book she thought to present to me when I arrived. I've received so much from it.

I realize these last two weeks of severe weather have meant that my nights have been quiet. Though there's still a brewing black cloud of angst that hangs over this end of the retreat land, the screaming and agitated voices have stopped. When the weather keeps me in my hut, it also keeps my unsettled, confused neighbor inside with his demons and not out on the porch or stomping through the bush unleashing his anger. For this, I'm exceedingly grateful.

*Young fern tree frond unfurling as a fiddle head
with medallions.*

Chapter 4 October

One of my goals for this solitary retreat is to become more attuned to nature (and less to the internet!) and it's happening daily. When I first arrived in this southern winter, sunlight barely touched the far ridge across the river by eight in the morning. It was hard to get out of bed without an alarm clock. But now, three months later, the ridge is in golden light soon after six. What glory! The pine tree has lost the 3" golden spikes that held nodules of green seeds. These have fallen, been eaten by birds, and spread to other places, and 6" spikes of new growth have replaced them. Fern fiddleheads continue to pop up everywhere, sometimes three to a tree—glorious fronds that turn from chartreuse to new green as they unfurl, while the small woodland ferns turn from russet to pink to orange-green in a month. I'm connected and part of it all.

> A half-smile unfolds on every leaf.
> There is a forest here
> Because I am here.
> But mind has followed the forest,
> And clothed itself in green.[43]
>
> — Thich Nhat Hanh

Rain came last night, accompanied by some painful howling from my neighbor. But now it's a quiet day with chilly, misty rain, and clouds clinging to high ridges.

I woke once more with a headache, as if the top of my head had been blown off. This does keep me from happily jumping out of bed in the morning to do yoga and meditate. I'm tentative and slow moving. But it's become familiar enough that I just continue quietly and hope it will pass, and often it does. As more than one doctor has told me, if I see some—any—improvement over each six month period—that im-provement will continue. This teaches me patience and an understanding of the suffering of others, and I learn not to take this on as some punishment of "me," but just a function of this bodily shell I'm presently inhabiting. It just "is" and I let it go.

I've been digging out under the lily patches that line the path I use for walking meditation. With so many leaves and other forest debris around them, I could really use a rake, but not wishing to ask for one more thing from the staff, I decided to make do. I put on my work gloves, put a foam mat on the wet ground, and started digging them out with my fingers. I cut what grass there is with scissors and a knife. It works and I've spent some satisfying hours loading many buckets. The pile of debris was waist high when I carried it off to the bush. In the process, I discovered two pieces of plastic twine 3' long that perhaps were once used to hang prayer flags. Remembering Buddha's words to his monks "Be frugal and diligent," I soaked the twine, washed it and coiled it up for later use.

Saving this plastic twine reminds me of all the balls of twine and string that I found at my grandparents' house, products of a depression-era lifestyle. Nothing was ever thrown away. As a child, I loved exploring the cellar of the three-family house that my great-grandfather built in the working-class town of Lynn, outside of Boston, where I was raised. The cellar was full of goodies—Fairy-brand soap curled at the edges, preserves labeled 1920, and wonderful black coal bins with a working furnace for each floor of the tall house.

Growing up on that street was great fun in the 1950s, especially when milk or bakery trucks delivered and all the neighborhood kids followed them around. We followed the postman too. However, our number one excitement was the coal truck arrival. We young ones all lived on the streets in those days, and we gathered in a gang to watch the coal delivery man open a basement window and slide in a wooden chute. What a thrill to watch chunks of noisy black coal tumble from truck to cellar bin! We don't see this now. Here I coil my string, get soy milk and bread delivered to my food box, and heat not with coal but with heavy propane tanks that I maneuver to attach to the house. And I'm making do with what I have, learning to happily rake with my fingers, cut grass with scissors, and pick up leaves on my hands and knees—a mindfulness practice done with pleasure and gratitude.

I had many visits yesterday from the increasing bird life, and for the first time I saw three chaffinches in my grove at the same time, investigating dropped seed. They're the most common bird I see, along with the silvereyes. I've not seen my friendly quail or a redpoll in over a week. I was startled last week to hear the haunting cry of wild geese as five flew over to the northeast, honking all the way. It reminded me of home, where we often hear Canadian geese flying over. They're around more now, even in the coldest months, since climate change has warmed our frigid winters.

October 4, 2014

Today a severe western "blow" started, so strong that buckets flew off the porch and a tree came down in the backyard. This is the third and largest manuka sapling to fall since I've been here. Tall, thin and scraggly, they occasionally die and dry out. At 25'-30' high, they're formidable to haul off the back walking path. They sometimes come down over the woodland trails too, and hang suspended three or four feet above the ground so I have to crawl under them. A gas-powered chainsaw would make quick work of them but I don't even have a hand saw, so I just drag them into the deep bush when possible.

It's hard to do concentration meditation when the wind is howling outside and things are falling, but I try, with three sits this morning and advice from sixth century Chi-I: To keep your mind under control you must realize the "true nature of all things" and not dwell upon them. Let them go.[44] And that includes high winds and falling trees. Thanks for the reminder.

Whoops! There goes the metal chair off the porch again!

October 5, 2014

Another cold, rainy day, but without the heavy winds of yesterday.

The birds get desperate in this weather. I notice that if it's not pouring rain, they're out hunting seeds and insects. A big female pheasant walked through yesterday afternoon, and today two little silvereye sparrows investigated the fallen manuka and the white clematis vines that came down with it to see if there was anything edible on them.

111

These silvereyes are the clowns of the New Zealand birds, scampering in the grass looking for bugs. When a tuft of grass looks promising, they pounce and nose-dive into it, and little fuzzy bottoms come up like ducktails in water. A delight.

I've solved one more mystery this weekend: the motorcycle whine that revs up and down ravines across the river, but only on Sundays. My binoculars show it's a vehicle that belongs to my cow-raising neighbors at the farm where the Tararu River and Argosy Creek meet, the parents of Yipper and Woof. What I'm hearing is a small off-road vehicle, sometimes towing a cart, and often with Woof in hot pursuit, rather that the sound of weekend motorcycle enthusiasts from Thames or Auckland zipping around the Coromandel ridges. Neighbor at work.

October 8, 2014

What a difference the lack of wind makes! The wind here can be ferocious, making lunch on the porch a challenge. Lettuce leaves and popcorn fly out of my bowl. Even the metal plug blew out of the outdoor tub one day, landing fifteen feet away on the grass. I was lucky to find it. But now there's delicious quiet and sun. For the first time in weeks, I can power up my Kindle with solar energy and not worry that it will blow down Mill Track in the next gust.

Last night at midnight, the moon's purifying light poured through my curtains again, landing on my meditation pillow and spotlighting it in the dark hut. It pulled me to go and sit there and say prayers for its monthly grace. My moon almanac promises a full lunar eclipse tonight, visible in North America, East Asia, Australia and New Zealand. We've moved into daylight-saving time, and with the passing of the Vernal Equinox we're having lovely light late evenings with fiery sunsets. I feel as if I sit at the peak of the world, viewing this splendor, displayed all the way from southwest to east. With the angle of the hut, only the southeast is behind me, hidden by bush and a high ridge.

It seems I've trained one or two chaffinches to expect morning seed on the porch. If I sleep beyond 6:45, a little guy is out there, chip-chip vocalizing. If that doesn't bring the food train, he starts pecking on the wooden porch. It works and I'm well trained.

And now, with house cleaning done, floors swept, rugs shaken outside, and the room reassembled, I sit with tea and a date nut scone to get some thoughts down that have been percolating for days.

I've spent much of the week reflecting on what drives me and pushes me to accomplish all I do. I've looked at the conditions I was raised with, and what became "truths" for me, and perhaps wrong views. I've looked at the eight worldly concerns (or worldly winds) and how we respond to changes when unfavorable conditions arise in our life.

I think of these eight "worldly winds" that have us in their grasp and keep us spinning, revolving in a circle of birth and death because we cannot wake up to them. Tenzin Palmo speaks of the dynamic motivation of desire, aversion, hope, and fear, which keep our ordinary, egotistic preoccupation going. We think everyone wants pleasure, praise, fame and gain. It's expected. And yet grasping at desire and hope, and wanting to push away unfavorable conditions, creates so much suffering.

I realize how uncomfortable I am with praise and what we call fame. A bit of appreciation is grand, but the praise I sometimes receive for my artwork at an exhibition puts me at a distance. The more praise, the more separate from others I become. Is it their projections? It's not me, but some pedestal others place me upon. I feel objectified, and placed somewhere I don't want to be. And fame may bring more money, but again, it's not comfortable. To be recognized is lovely, to not be overlooked—but fame is a no-thank you. I often say I would much rather be infamous. That sounds like more fun. To be not attached to this praise and fame—to loosen this self—let go of ego and focus instead on others, that is what's important to me. The last two verses of the Mind Training Prayer I say each morning speak to this.

> And so directly or indirectly
> May I give all help and joy to those who were my mothers.
> And may I take all their harm and pain
> Secretly upon myself.
> May none of this ever be sullied
> By thoughts of the eight worldly concerns
> May I see all things as illusions,

And without attachment gain freedom
from bondage.[45]

Praise and its downside, blame, are just words. We're willing to take credit when people say good things. Why not equal acceptance when people criticize?

> If someone praises us, look to see if it is valid. If so, that's nice. If not, the praising is their own projection. If someone insults us/blames us, see if it's true. If so, the criticism may actually be helping us to see faults we might not be conscious of. Feel grateful. If it's not true, what's the problem?[46]

Tenzin Palmo advises us to just let it go. The only time we should make some effort to defend ourselves is if the defamation or criticism might create problems, especially for others. False rumors could create obstacles or harm for an organization we're connected with, and in this case it would be important to clarify the issue. In other cases, just let it go. It's all impermanent.

It's a challenge to see insults, envy, and betrayal as opportunities for spiritual practice, but falling into anger and enmity is not the way to go. I remember dear Atisha and his obnoxious water boy (I read recently actually was a disgruntled monk whom everyone disliked) and spend more time with tonglen, taking on other people's angst and exchanging it with some purifying white moonlight. What a joy to have this time to reflect on these points I've long considered. I notice how my understanding has grown over the years, but still I need to focus on letting go and recognizing the impermanence of gain/loss, praise/blame, fame/shame, pleasure/pain that keep us spinning—all impermanent and illusion.

October 9, 2014

An eerily quiet morning, no wind and overcast. My neighbor was having trouble again last night. It's the second time this week of howling, screaming, and shouting in the early evening. You'd think it was an altercation between two people, but he's alone up there with only his demons, and no one for support. The team here has been very good to him and helpful, but last month he was asked to leave. He'll be going in ten days, I'm told. I'll truthfully rest more easily. It's been a challenge but I've had to set aside my anxiety about his unpredictability and just send daily metta and tonglen to him. My heart deeply opens to his troubles, and I hope help will be available in the outside world. This has provided me with some real practice points and challenges which, while not welcome, are helpful. Tomorrow is my 90th day here and I am good.

I'm re-reading Byrd's book *Alone*, about his four and a half months in the dark Antarctic winter in 1935. That all-pervasive darkness must have been one of the most difficult things for him. To not see any other people around, even at a distance, would seem difficult to me. Byrd did have daily radio contact with his Little American Base 123 miles away, while I watch the birds, and listen to rats and possums on my roof. I do envy Byrd the classical record collection he brought along, though he says listening to it only increased his suffering. He mentions meditating, ONCE, though it's obvious he didn't have a solid practice to rely on. He almost died from carbon monoxide poisoning during his time alone, and the fact that he needed to be rescued was deeply humiliating, though he writes that the experience did give him a new view on life and his relationships, and some understanding of his tremendous ego.

October 11, 2014

It happened last night. A cloud has lifted, the air feels different, and spring has come.

News came yesterday in cryptic ways—small snatches on the wind and an actual note. My neighbor is gone—gone with the full moon, always a hard time for some. I learned that the police were called in to help after he had an altercation down at the Community House. He's been taken to Auckland for residential treatment of multiple personalities, a dissociative disorder, psychosis, and a mental breakdown. A cloud has lifted. It's palpable. That tight worry and fear, struggling and anxiety is no longer rolling down the hill. For me, it's a letting go. I walked to the stupa yesterday and did some purification and a blessing for the land and for him. I hope that intelligent, compassionate help is there for him. He tried so very hard. We tried so very hard. After I heard the news, I sat and wept.

October 12, 2014

Yesterday was an extraordinarily warm sunny day. By noon the temperature had risen to the 60s (20ºC) and it topped at 23ºC. I ate lunch on the porch after a second meditation and a walk in the bush. The cows were in the upper pastures for the first time and the birds at last discovered my bird feeder next to the tub. After having the more adventurous ones eating off my porch, it was the next step, letting the birds now know that no monsters live in this Fearless Hut. I was so pleased to see some smaller chaffinches arrive without the red chests—the females, at last. The boys have been enjoying free food here for a month or more. In the early evening, as the sun went down, I was out front crawling on the ground, cutting grass with my 3" scissors and humming mantras.

The waning moon was delicious last night, casting moon shadows on the deck and coming in my window to light up a long square on my floor. I continue to be amazed at this porous, clear blue light that flows down on us in the deep dark of the night. It's a treasure to be on this precipice, out from under the canopy of pines I have in New Hampshire, and to be able to appreciate the phases of the moon so completely.

I'm in robes around the hut now that it's warm enough. I have no winter robes, but someday I'll work on that. Our Order wears western clothing out in the world, but on retreat the wrap of blue is a good reminding form. When I did solo retreats in Asia, I was asked to please wear robes if possible, since with my blue eyes and fair hair, I could be mistaken for a visiting tourist and my silence might be interrupted. Since my ordination, I'm always in blue by choice. The robes with their wrap skirt and shoulder drape make it difficult to tramp the bush, but around the hut they work well. As a textile artist, dyer and colorist, giving up color on my three-month Ordination Retreat was a challenge, but to be with a sea of women in blue with no pattern and no other color was so affirming that I took on the retreat directive as part of my full-time renunciation. So everything matches. I no longer worry if my socks match my earrings or if this scarlet is too yellowish to wear with purple. It's just blue and it's a relief. I mourn occasionally for that lovely fuchsia shirt, but that's mundane samsara speaking.

It's natural for me to come up with an outlet for my creative energies, but I really didn't know what artwork I'd do here before I came. I was ready to just respond to the environment. Today I got the last fern image shibori stitch piece finished, pulling up all the threads to make a tight resist, knotted and ready for the alum mordant and natural dyes. This makes six pieces I've been working on over the past three months with many, many meditative hours on each piece, and they're but half-done. After dyeing and drying, I'll pick out all the stitches and knots, wash them, and decide on color embellishments with the threads I've brought along. Many artists, myself included, would do art if no one ever saw the results. It's very much like a spiritual practice. Having a sangha or community to practice with can be very supportive, but even alone on a ridge in New Zealand I'm on my pillow, singing mantras, and practicing my art.

October 13, 2014

I realize that even with all my positive energy, placing my focus on all the auspicious parts of this retreat, and with the support of the staff, still I've been rattled to the core by my fellow retreatant's behavior. I'm struggling to regain my quiet. Preparing for this retreat, I spoke to Kamalashila, a senior order member with wide experience in solitary retreat. His advice, other than the practical—a head torch or flashlight and a tooth repair kit—was to define my physical boundaries and stay within them. He also said that any disruption or change in schedule (for example, a visitor to my hut) would put me back a week. In retreat one is very sensitive to subtle energies and even small things can disrupt the flow. The usual weather and gale force winds we must learn to take in our stride.

The Vajrasattva Retreat Procedure advises "staying in a place pleasing to the mind." I thought I had accomplished that. It goes on to advise choosing a place:
    (1) that has been blessed by previous meditators;
    (2) that is without harmful humans or non-humans;
    (3) that has clear, cool water and beautiful trees in which all
    the necessities of Dharma practice are easily found; and
    (4) that it is far away from noise and the clamor of people."

In brief, it should be a place harmonious to the mind. I thought I was coming to this.

I'm now trying to re-settle my mind and find my psychic safe spot after my neighbor's breakdown. Sitting on this beautiful sunny porch listening to the chatter of late afternoon birds, I know I'm in a wonderfully lush Eden and have all that I need to practice. If I were back in the city and a neighbor in the next apartment had a psychiatric episode, and had to be restrained and taken away for care, I would manifest compassion and positive energy for his/her recovery. Here, those aspects are present, yet my situation is different. I'm remote, have very limited access to help, and knew little of what was happening, or what measures were being taken for my safety and that of others. I was entirely on my own. And at night my neighbor was howling.

Now he's gone, I'm living down that residual energy and trying to come up with all my resources to clear my mind. I walked up to his deserted hut today to try to diffuse whatever unreasonable fears might still remain, see where he was staying, and discharge my feelings. There was no energy left there of his struggles—only sadness.

It was a favorite hut of one of our founders, well-loved and treasured. It is no more. I know the staff will be working to reclaim it. I sat in that sooty, cobweb-covered space with bubble wrap coverings on every window, burned some incense, chanted 108 mantras, and walked the outside land, but I came home to my hermitage nauseous and dizzy.

Now I have to settle again into Abhaya Hut, re-establish my boundaries, call in my protectors and encourage the joy and aspirations I came here with. There's no one to talk to about this, no one to give me a hug. I try to remember ways to be kind to myself, and to honor my feelings and sensitivities. I'm here for the duration. May there be peace and harmony.

October 14, 2014

The waning three-quarter moon worked its way through low clouds and flooded my room through a gap in the curtains, so much bigger and brighter even than the past full moon. I awoke and knew I was slowly rebuilding. My meditation on metta—loving-kindness for myself—was full of beautiful, silvery blue light from inside a quiet womb. I sent kindness, protection and love to myself, knowing I need to be strong, grounded and joyful to be of service to the outside world.

Wrapped in the flowing robes of Kuan Yin, I was comforted and restored.

With tea water coming to a boil, I looked to my notebooks for quotations on "self" and found references I wrote three months ago that resonate now as I rebuild, restore, and remember that the "I" is not necessary.

If "I" and "you" are not there, and there is only seeing, hearing and so on, what happens to suffering, to discontent? Buddha said this might well be the freedom of awakening we look for. I remember reading of all those beings at the table: fear sitting next to hope, beside sadness, and joy and anger across from each other. I remember that they just hang around for a while, and then are off if "I" is not there to block their journey. Reading these notes now encourages and inspires me, and shows me the way to end some of this suffering.

And I do love thinking of fear sitting at this table next to hope. I awake to just letting it all go. Opening my blue curtains to the day, to breakfast on the porch, welcoming the world in once more, I think of confidence and joy. Ah, another breath, another day.

October 16, 2014

Morning dew makes the grass in front of the hut and in the pastures across the valley silvery gray, but the sun is up and the warmth soon dries it. I'm eating breakfast on the porch, watching low cloud fingers pour around high pine peaks, and reach into valleys. The clouds are moving quickly out of the north, sliding down the pastures quietly. And spring is truly here. One of the tree ferns near my deck has many new fuzzy brown fiddleheads coming up, and a lily on the other side has unfurled three stalks of green blossom heads.

I woke early from a dream of disappointment and have been fingering dependability, expectation, and that disappointment like worry beads in my mind's fingers. Reflecting on my history, I wonder where this comes from—this need to be dependable, and to expect it of others. I worked hard as a young mother a few years out of art school. Spontaneous, joyful, and perhaps erratic—I worked to be dependable for those two little ones under two. I knew that if they felt they could depend on me, knew that I would come through regularly for them, they would

119

grow to be confident and trusting of other adults. I remembered, from my own childhood, the dear Girl Scout leader who took us all camping and forgot the tent poles (undependable, but so kind and generous). But also the dad who would step through the door in my teen years at 5:22 PM every day after work and start supper. His birthday would be tomorrow. He's been gone fifty years now. He built trust in me, and gave me tremendous confidence in the world. It's one of the reasons I'm able to be here now.

Along with these people, I recognize, with sadness, those who don't come through for others. I extend some tonglen to them (exchanging self with others) and think about life from their side, realizing how very much may be clouding their minds and complicating their busy lives. I read that our suffering doesn't depend on what is happening out there. It really depends on our own mind, and our reaction to what is happening. Happiness or unhappiness, in the end, depends on the mind. It's the companion that is with us day and night. A mind focused on criticism is hard to please, impatient. I tell myself to let go and enjoy this moment of changing misty mountains, impermanence, transition. I tell myself to be the mountains, smell the damp, feel the wetness in my hair, the white billows flowing around me. Be the clouds and feel myself bubbling with energy, moving over trees, sliding down as if I'm on a toboggan, down, wet, cool, bird-like, with wings penetrating a white chiffon nightgown that disappears in the air.

This is what happens when you're on a retreat too long.

October 18, 2015

I seem to be taking a day off from journaling every so often and that feels good. I started doing a daily journal seriously sixteen years ago and have found it very beneficial for processing and even venting, but sometimes I need spaces in even this. It's also great to have that resource to go back to. It's been my habit to spend New Year's morning re-reading the previous year's writing, and noticing, with that distance, the themes as well as the traumas that arose and disappeared, and the growth that came. When I began this retreat, I was writing in pencil, but my lead was so light that re-reading was difficult. A month ago I went back to all those fifty pages and re-did them in ink. It was interesting, even then, to see my initial reactions, and how things had changed in just two months. I'm being much more reflective now, and have truly settled in. With the departure of my neighbor, a soft, peaceful feeling has descended. It surprises me that I can feel this. Even when there was as much as a week without any agitated outburst rolling down the ridge, there was a tension in the atmosphere. I'm grateful to all those who helped both of us with their metta practice throughout those days. I continue to send goodwill to him.

I woke this morning again considering what I am actually afraid of in this world. I started a mental list as I got up and prepared to meditate. Other than physical harm, most of those fears are on that eight worldly winds list and include the four unfavorable conditions: pain, loss, shame, and blame. If I can remember to apply the understanding of impermanence that I've learned about in my sutra studies to both favorable and unfavorable conditions, I'll realize the world is so much easier without fear. Equanimity is something I thirst for.

In my early childhood, my number one big fear was the tonsil man who invaded my dreams night after night. The second fear was the wicked witch who was going to take my new baby sister away if I couldn't be tough and save her. I had to wrestle that witch every night for months. I succeeded, since Terry was there each morning. My dad eliminated the tonsil man after I woke up too many times screaming. He told me he'd thrown the monster over the back porch and seen him run away. I think those childhood terrors were much influenced by those poignant Grimms' Fairy Tales of good and evil that we read. Maybe every culture has their own evil spirit stories, even those saved from the grim Grimms.

People deal with fear, somehow.

October 19, 2014

Rain began yesterday evening and continued through the night. Early this morning the valley was a complete white-out, but gradually the wall of clouds began to lift, and by 9 AM there were just wispy beards clinging to the top ridges. It's the first rain in ten days, and needed.

October 20, 2014

One hundred days. When others asked how I could do a year alone, I told them it seemed possible by dividing it into three retreats, each a hundred days long. Today, I complete my first hundred days. I sit with contentment and stillness, happy in my small hut with almost all I need (though the staff keep getting weekly notes asking for some book or pen or detergent). I feel at home here and content. That's the word, content. The weather has eased up, the cold abated. I no longer need my heater every morning to get out of bed. I no longer wear a hat and gloves inside and out, and only use my teacups to warm my chilly fingers. I do look forward to weather changes for the variety. But I love that sun, especially when it dries a wash, or recharges my Kindle reader so I can finish my Thoreau. I also have my daily visitors who come by for a chat, though they all have wings and beaks. Life is good at Abhaya Hut. Yet I honor the ups and downs and know they will come. Only two nights ago I wrote, "I can't believe I'm here for a year, seeing no one, going nowhere, left to my own devices and my own mind. What in the world am I doing here? Who thought this was a good idea? Beam me up, Scottie." And the next morning I woke up satisfied, content, and serene.

With my one hundred days, I've let go of binding myself to schedules and clock watching. If I sleep later, my day is just later. If I get five hours or just four hours on the cushion, I don't berate myself that I am failing in some way. My days are free, created each morning when I wake. The weather dictates whether I get the wash done or delay another day or two. Living without a refrigerator, the condition and deterioration of the vegetables dictates what I have for my afternoon meal. Going with the flow of life above the Tararu Valley often leads me back to the cushion and the quiet life of solitude.

There seem to be few Buddhists who have written of solitude, which is unfortunate. I'm appreciative of all those who have written of solitary life since they encourage and inspire my time here. Perhaps I'm writing for those who come after me.

I go back again and again to Bob Kull's *Solitude: Seeking Wisdom in Extremes*. Like Admiral Byrd, he lived alone for scientific reasons rather than as a spiritual pursuit, but he's astute in his observations, and there is much spiritual inquiry in his book. ". . . Once we surrender the idea of who we think we are" —solidity, doubt and insecurity disappear and we feel cradled and cared for. "Individuals on a spiritual quest may go into solitude exactly because it is an intense catalyst for such transformation."[47]

This morning I enjoyed reading Thomas Merton as he alludes to the presence of God. "The hermit's whole life is a life of silent adoration," Merton says. "His very solitude keeps him ever in the presence of God . . . His whole day, in the silence of his cell, or his garden looking out upon the forest, is prolonged communion."[48] It's true that Merton yearned for solitude, but he couldn't live it. He romanticized what life in a cell day in, day out, might be, yet he had little time or opportunity to experience it. Merton is one of the best-known hermits in America other than Thoreau.

It comes to me that the union with God, to live dwelling in "His" presence in the way that the Christian Desert Fathers and Mothers and Merton strived for, is perhaps a basic dropping of duality, dropping the "self" that causes so much suffering as we try to preserve it, guard it, or promote it. Its loss may well be what Christians yearn for in surrender and union with God. To listen for, or to, the voice of God and surrender speaks strongly of dropping self, rising above duality, identifying one with all, and finding Buddha-nature. But in the middle of writing about union with God, I must stop, pull in the Kindle, and take down the newly washed sheets as a rainy squall comes down the valley. Mundane existence and responding to nature.

October 21, 2014

I'm doing fairly well health-wise, though my nose still drips a lot and I use up tissues rapidly. I cough and clear my throat, especially at night. Conditions here are wet, damp, and conducive to mold, and I'm responding to that. My headaches are far fewer since the stove has been off. Occasionally I have a daytime headache, but usually it comes when I lie down at night. I can have no pain at all, then feel it rolling in so that in ten minutes the top of my head wants to blow off. If it wanes, I can drop off to sleep, but then I'll wake in the morning and be afraid to move for the head pain. I've found that instead of waiting for it to pass, if I get up, it goes. This is very strange for me. I feel it's not tension or stress related. I thought that the headaches could come from neck constriction and the raised pillow I need to sleep with draining sinuses, but it comes on so quickly. Perhaps it's a leftover from my concussion.

123

I was pleased to find a recipe for those Anzac cookies on the oatmeal bag yesterday and have worked to adjust to my own version. It seems they're a famous local delicacy. Who would have known? After I had a bag bought for me a month ago and used a hammer to break them up, I concluded they were a biscuit left over from the First World War ANZAC invasion. But when I dipped one in tea to soften it, I found it was like a hard biscotti with hints of coconut and oats. Now they're a favorite.

Anzac Cookies

2 c. all-purpose flour
2 c. rolled oats
2 c. sugar or 1 c. honey
1 c. desiccated coconut
2 sticks unsalted butter
2T. golden syrup or honey
3/4 t. baking soda
1/4 c. boiling water

1, Preheat the oven to 350 F. Grease baking sheets or line them with parchment paper. In a large bowl, combine flour, oats, sugar, and coconut. Set aside.

2, Melt butter with syrup in a small saucepan over medium heat. Dissolve baking soda in boiling water, and add to butter mixture. Stir to combine.

3. Add butter mixture to dry ingredients, and stir to combine. Scoop out a 1-½" spoonful of batter and drop onto prepared baking sheets, about 2" apart. Flatten cookies slightly with the heel of your hand.

4. Bake until golden brown and firm but not hard, about 15 minutes. Transfer to wire racks to cool.

Cookies in New Zealand are called biscuits, as green onions are spring onions, and bell peppers are capsicums. I translate my food list for the guys who do my shopping but they're learning some Americanisms as well. So much of my usual food shopping is responding to what is ripe at the moment or on "special" that writing a list for someone else is a real challenge and a true practice for me. The guys do an amazing job trying to find the specifics I list.

And further on the mundane level, I'm tickled by the Kiwi advertising style—so very down home and fresh. It seems that many companies here are family owned and working "not just for profits." My crackers arrived today from the Huntley & Palmer Company, which uses both unusual kibbled red and kibbled purple wheat as well as linseed oil and sesame seeds. But it's the advertising on the side of the box that got me. It spoke of their love-affair with things savory, how the company started back in 1822 in an English village, and how "madly passionate, head-over heels in love" they are with crackers; "proudly crackers about crackers." Who wrote this copy? I love their enthusiasm. And they're terrific crackers, too.

October 22, 2014

I find myself stepping through a new door of awareness on this sunny morning as I look at solitude more deeply, exploring the container, feeling the corners, and trying to understand and learn more. There is so much to learn! I'm reminded of my surprise when I arrived in Japan over thirty years ago and realized that my understanding of reality relied on skills that were inaccessible with my limited language ability. The experience felt like being in a black box, cut off from all my usual resources, not unlike this solitary experience. At that time, I realized how much I depended on verbal and written cues for understanding. When those were cut off, I went to another, nonverbal level. I watched intensely to pick up any clues to tell me what was happening or expected. It was like watching TV with the sound off and trying to guess the story. That experience honed these nonverbal skills and awareness of my surroundings. And here I am using all of those skills to understand what I'm experiencing alone for a year.

Through my dreams and reflections, I'm coming up with past experiences that don't always show me in my best light. These characteristics don't agree with my image of self and are embarrassing to reveal. The Desert Fathers say a person who lives among others cannot see his/her own sins because of "turbulence," yet when one lives alone in the desert, without the distractions of others, one can see one's failings clearly.[49] And Dilgo Khyentse Rinpoche says go to a solitary place, turn your mind inward, identify your defects, rid yourself of them and develop all your inherent good qualities.

So despite remorse at some of my behavior, including incidents from thirty years ago, I'm grateful to have this time to recognize that I'm capable of such unskillful actions and to resolve to hone my awareness and compassion and effect some change. A solitary hut is not unlike a confessional booth where all the nasties show up eventually. It's nice to know that I can admit to this, forgive myself, and move on. We need to forgive ourselves as we forgive others. One of the verses that I repeat each morning speaks of watching my mind:

> "and, as soon as disturbing emotions arise, forcefully
> stop them;
> since they hurt both yourself as well as others."[50]

It's wonderful to have the time to see and reflect on such things.

October 24, 2014

It seems that I've become an every-other-day journaler rather than a daily one. I've decided to write when it moves me, and to not let journaling become a distraction to my practice. Unlike Admiral Byrd, I have no report to turn in, nor a dissertation on personality and wilderness to prepare like Bob Kull.

Steve came by with a heavy load of groceries two days ago, and chose to drive them up to the hut rather than leave them at the drop-box. It was kind and considerate of him. I was in the path doing my morning walking meditation, and just stepped aside and waited in the bush for his departure with eyes averted. Holding silence and watching distraction has been this week's work.

With the groceries, I received some Order newsletters which spur me on. One brings news of another member on solitary in Spain and his observations of the bird life there—so I'm not the only one with winged friends in silence. Our Order member mentioned some of the painful hierarchy displayed among the birds. As we sometimes see in human life, there are those that seem to be naturally aggressive bullies, and those low in the pecking order, nervous, agitated, and constantly alert to potential danger. I'd been observing this last week, and even re-searched local predators to see who might be frightening these jumpy little beings. I came up with a list of six birds that eat little ones: the harrier, falcon, long tail cuckoo, weka, kea, and the morepork owl. I didn't realize at the time that the fears some of these birds show are for each other, not bigger bird-eaters. The male chaffinches can be quite aggressive, and have moved the fantails and silvereyes right off my porch since I've been feeding them. Where does this aggression come from? What is the benefit?

I'm reminded of the temple dogs at the Thailand monastery who ate my rubber sandals and tore my sarong off the clothesline. The biggest, loudest bully was the size of a little Scottie dog, and had everyone, including me, hiding in fear. Why? And I remember those Bali monastery roosters who took to scolding me for walking in their area. At least here the birds don't harass me although I get some sharp birdcalls every time I pass by doing walking meditation. Ah, life in the wilds—not as kind and serene as we romanticize. I found some tufts of soft brown fur on the walking path yesterday from an encounter during the night. Possum fur, likely.

For two months now, I've been eating only greens from the porch garden and not including any on my food list. I was pleased to be able to pull some long white radishes from my porch planter yesterday, grown from seed. There is such satisfaction from being able grow my own. I've just finished a fresh chopped salad using my grated radish, sprouted lentils, green onions and parsley, to which I added some grated carrots and red and green peppers. Delicious, and such fun to have so much coming from an early spring garden on the porch. One of my other big hits has been a polenta recipe I found from *Vegetable Dishes I Can't Live Without* by Mollie Katzen on my Kindle. I've been making it almost every week using Swiss chard, red beet and lettuce greens from the garden. Here's the recipe:

Bright Greens on a Bed of Creamy Polenta

4 c. of water
1 c. of polenta/coarse corn meal (I use 1 cup of water and 1/3 cup polenta for one person)
1 c. of grated cheese (fontina, sharp cheddar or parmesan)
2 T. extra virgin oil
5-8 c. (packed) of small greens, about 3/4lb, stemmed and chopped as necessary

1 t. minced garlic
Salt to taste

1. Pour 3 cups of water into a medium size saucepan. Add ½ teaspoon of salt, bring to boil. Meanwhile, place the polenta in a bowl of cold water and stir until completely moist.

2. When the water boils, turn down the heat to simmer, spoon in wet polenta and blend instantly. Cool over medium-low heat, stirring slowly and often until it turns creamy-thick (20 minutes or less). Remove from heat, stir in cheese, add salt to taste.

3. Place a large, deep skillet over medium heat. After about a minute, add the oil and swirl to coat the pan. Toss in the greens and a dash or two of salt, turn up the heat to medium-high, stir-fry, turning with tongs for about 30 seconds. Sprinkle in the garlic and cook, turning with tongs, for another minute or so, until just slightly wilted and very bright green. Divide polenta and place freshly cooked greens on top.

Serve immediately; serves 4-5[51]

This is so satisfying, a nutritious simple meal. I'm including these recipes for Thomas Merton and my daughter. Merton wrote in the 1960s that he couldn't live in a remote hermitage because he didn't know how to cook, and my daughter is still learning. Not being able to feed yourself might be a good reason for not doing a solitary retreat, but I wondered if I might have misunderstood Merton. I searched for the reference, since it sounds unbelievable, and found it quoted in Peter France's book *Solitary* in a letter from Merton to his old friend Robert Lax.[52] So, recipes for Thomas and Amanda, with love.

October 25, 2014

I thought spring was here, and then, with the dark of the new moon, I woke to 38ºF (4ºC) outside and a chilly 46ºF (9ºC) inside. I'd put away my heavy jacket, but now I return to wool blankets, a down duvet, and the blue hot water bottle again.

I was exploring the meaning of silence under a vastly clear Wedgewood blue sky during a walking meditation. How to define silence? Is it enclosed? Is it the space between sound? Is it sound that defines silence? Is silence in the morning different from silence in the afternoon? I listened: a dog barked way up the valley, barely perceptible; a light wind moved the manukas; there was the rustle of dried leaves; my footfall crackled leaf litter on the path; my breath exited my nostrils. There was the insistent buzz of a searching fly, so different from the gentle buzz of the bee, and I heard that difference. Silence. The space between. A year without human voices, conversation, music— only listening to the space between birdcalls and flapping laundry. Awakening in the morning from a night of silence to the space between the sounds of chaffinches pecking on the porch wood.

What color is silence? What does it look like? Ten years ago I was an Artist-in-Residence at a Quaker village in the cloud forest of Costa Rica. Every Sunday I sat in silence at the Quaker Meeting. Then, too, I asked—What does silence look like? Is it absence? Emptiness? The color of the dark sky? The indigo black of Kuan Yin's hair? *The Song of Silence*, a hanging scroll I made from this time, includes a shaft of clear black in a green cloud forest tangle, blue with a verdant green climbing up from below. Would I show silence differently now? The space—the expectant pregnant moment? The contented meditation sit? The stillness between the breath?

October 26, 2014

A realization: what I thought was a dazzling olive-green thrush with a vivid orange cap and beak is actually a greenfinch who'd been dipping its beak into the pollen-laden lily flowers. With every dip for nectar, his head and beak were dusted with more and more orange pollen; after he'd drunk from three stalks with multiple blooms, his head was radiantly orange. Then I caught sight of the little beastie when he first arrived with his clean black mask and beautiful olive green feathered head and body. He's become more confident with me nearby and I can even make slow movements to photograph him from three feet away without frightening him. That nectar must be delicious. He's back every day.

October 29, 2014

Last night I sat with my kitchen cardboard (tea, crackers, and pudding boxes, mushroom, and egg cartons) and joyfully spent almost an hour tearing them into dime size pieces. It's extraordinary how satisfying this project is, and how happy it makes me. I realize that whatever we focus on wholeheartedly can bring us joy, even tearing up cardboard. What a revelation! A Harvard study states, "It's not so much what you're doing that makes you happy. It's whether you are mindful of what you are doing—to be in a direct state—attending to the here and now."

It reminds me of the research I did into Csikszentmihalyi's "flow" thinking, and how, when artists drop into their work, they lose self; there's only the white surface with no "self" interfering or even observing the process—no duality—a oneness. The judgmental, critical mind might come in later, but for minutes or hours there's only the process. This flow is immensely blissful and nourishing. Sogyal Rinpoche calls it "pure presence." It pulls those who work with art or in another creative realm back to the process again and again. Athletes too, drop "into the zone." Arthur Ashe, the tennis player, once reported feeling this altered state for a two-week period, which might be possible under special conditions. Also, there seems to be some correlation with meditative states, although Joseph Goldstein writes that losing yourself in an activity such as sports doesn't lead to spiritual growth. What I know is that when I first came to meditation in my thirties, it was already familiar from my fifteen years of working with art—an altered state, immediately blissful. Flow may be activity-based, but the loss of any recognizable self echoes the non-duality of deep meditative states, and is where I hope to dwell permanently.

This morning, I was up to exercise and do my before-breakfast sit when rain began. Remembering the glorious place I'm in, the wonderful opportunity to be with nature, and the uniqueness of having no necessary schedule, I decided to stop and take it in. I listened as the rain slid down the tin roof into the collection buckets: the pinging of water, the splash of gutter puddles. Watching the clouds slide down mountain ridges, I felt the washing, cleansing, and nourishment of this rain. Feeling it in my body, I said, "Come to me. Dissolve into me."

Soon the chaffinches descended, and Officer Finch, the boss, fluttered down the porch stairs, back to the food, across the porch, back to the food. He hardly had time to eat since he had to ensure that no one else got seed this morning. I put out another food spot to eliminate conflict as the rain went into a roar and I was on to "rain-gathering" chores, out in my rain slicker, placing buckets under the eaves and plugging up the tub to see if I might gather enough water to heat later for an outdoor bath. My water source for the tub has stopped completely, and a staff note asks me not to use water from the retaining tanks for the tub. They worry that summer is coming, and perhaps drought, so we are already conserving water. But this manna from the open skies means a bath.

I'm good with water conservation, since I live in a summer house in New Hampshire with only a 2,500-gallon holding tank to take my used water away. I have plenty of water from my well, but must pay ten cents a gallon to have it removed. As a result, I gather and reuse as much as possible, water my porch plants with dishwater, and have a bucket in the shower, so not much goes down the drain. When the holding tank was installed ten years ago, they told me I'd need it pumped out monthly, but it has turned out to be only a yearly cost with my water conservation.

The valley is soaked in cloud cover for now, and this is where I dwell on Wednesday at 2:10 PM.

October 30, 2014

Heavy winds and rain lash my hermitage. A roar as the wind tears through the larger trees on the ridge behind me.

October 31, 2014

More rain. It has been raining off and on for two weeks. Most afternoons it clears enough for me to get some solar energy, but that's it.

I find that life on solitary retreat is very precious. What might never bother me in contemporary life is earth-shattering when contact is so limited. I was having some frustrating hours last night with no one to fuss to. Some people handle ups and downs quietly on their own while some go into depression. It's been my history to talk through the rough spots, the frustrations, anger, and misunderstandings with a friend. And here I am with no one to chat with. Left to my own devices, I write, occasionally weep (only very occasionally) and meditate. As I sat this morning, I was overwhelmed with waves of metta, loving-kindness coming to me from all those who've sent good wishes and brought me to mind as I remember them. I felt surrounded and held by all those who feel I'm doing this long, rough year in part as their surrogate. What benefit may come from this is not mine, but goes out into the world in many, many ways.

As I prepared for this retreat, I reflected on how it should not just be about "me on a cushion in a hut for a year." I considered how it could help and benefit others. Sharing the experience afterwards was one way, but far off. Involving others in the planning and preparation was another. Carrying those people with me, bringing them to mind again and again throughout the year, is a third. In preparation, I worked on a website that a techie friend generously prepared to share information and answer some of the myriad questions I was receiving—like how are you going to eat, and what about a doctor? I prepared a postcard to hand out with links to this website, and did four talks with slides about my plans. To some, it may have looked as if these were all efforts to raise money to finance this year, but to me, they were ways to involve others, share the idea and the benefits, and open the door of possibility for many who are thirsty for such a retreat. Some said, "There's no way I could or would want to do such a thing . . . but go for it." With others, I could see in their eyes how they yearned for a time of silence. In some way I've modeled for them as inspiration, and with others they can live through me vicariously.

I'm grateful to the many who helped pay for meals for a week or a month, financed the roof over my head, or helped pay for part of my air-fare to get home. I'm equally grateful to others who gave me books, donated web services, and repaired my New Hampshire back porch for free. Others gave me good wishes and continue to send those, even to-day. I feel those wishes strongly right now. We humans are all interconnected in so many ways. The good that people do and the ef-forts they extend echo all the way around the world, benefitting all. So hiding out in New Zealand is not frivolous or shirking the responsibility of helping others. Hopefully, we all benefit from my efforts to keep it together here on this quiet precipice of mountain ridges. *May you be well.*

A New Zealand brushtail possum.

Chapter 5 November

Misty clouds are pulling away from the ridges in the east and the sun breaks through by 10AM. How wonderful to see some patches of clear blue sky! The wind has been down for two days now and it makes a noticeable difference in my emotions and meditation. It's great to hear real silence and not howling, but I do appreciate this changeable weather.

The tui bird's tu-tu-twoee-tu chimes in so often that he marks time like a cuckoo clock. With the clear sky and weekend upon us, light airplanes are making passes over to the other side of the peninsula. A few days ago I thought I heard a plane coming right over this ridge, but it was the roar of wind in high pines. I've sometimes mistaken that wind for organ music as well.

October was a rough month. It's good to have a new waxing moon in the sky and know that a full moon will be coming in time for my son's birthday. He's on my mind, and was in an early morning dream. I miss my friends and extended family, but I've spent so much of my life away from them—almost twenty years in Japan, and in recent years at least three winter months each year in Asia or Mexico. But I expect that they're all well and prospering, and that is good.

I awoke at five this morning, made myself some cocoa, and took it to bed to reflect on the coming month. I'm working hard to put aside the unsettling events and interruptions of October. This week I've focused on deepening my concentration and meditation on my cushion. I've gone back to basics, examining any hindrances, looking at those things that could be distracting me, and sending myself loving-kindness. I'm focusing more on connecting to this body I've been given, and have started a new meditation log. All of this has begun to pay off in the last few days.

This morning, I was so pleased to drop immediately into a deep meditative space within minutes of sitting on my pillow. This beginning, grounded sensation takes me beyond counted breaths, sending loving-kindness, or visualizing Kuan Yin and compassion, and puts me in a space where I just blissfully "hang" with no thought. I'm aware of my surroundings, but they're muted, as if at a distance or in another room. Thoughts may enter my mind but they appear as unfinished sentences. I don't allow myself to follow or complete them. They just melt away without being investigated, continued or developed into a favorite story line. Discursive thinking is dropped. My term for this process is a feeling of "Teflon" —where nothing sticks in my mind. I have an active mind with much ado, and it's a delight to drop into these absorptions and rest there in bliss and joy. This is the work I was doing in meditation when I had the brain injury. I've been struggling ever since to come back. I hope that this morning is the start of real healing and progress.

Some thought I was ill-advised to come on solitary retreat after such an injury. But both the neurologist and my physical therapist felt that the visual symptoms and headaches would wane with this seclusion. It's been more than three months since I've seen a screen—no computer or TV or movie screens—and the headaches precipitated by such exposure are now gone. When I first arrived, I was still getting dizzy and nauseous, even during walking meditation (almost motion sickness—from *walking*, no less) and needed to focus my eyes on a distant point to stop my brain from spinning. I realized yesterday that it's been more than a month since movement has set off those symptoms.

To pull someone out of contemporary "screen culture" and expect them not to use a computer for a week or a month is extremely hard— unless you send them on a solitary retreat with just twelve volts of electricity, no internet connection, and no electric plug. This forced seclusion may be just what I need to heal completely. While some youngsters seem to bounce back from head injuries, older folks may be slower. I also feel that getting hit in the front of the head, as opposed to the more usual, back-of-the-head injuries, has different parameters, but this is just my guess. The experience has given me a real awareness of my brain, and great respect for all it does that we take so much for granted. May this be a month of deeper concentration and access to the work on the cushion.

November 2, 2014

This is a delicious day. Sweet, quiet, and warm with a light breeze. After meditation, breakfast and clean up, I got out my walking stick and headed off for the stupa in the sunlight through the quiet forest. What a glorious day it was up there, with the stupa's gleaming white surface, deep shadows, and a view of the sea as a bonus—I guess it's Auckland I saw on a distant shore.

This day has a quality of preciousness, the feeling of a secret jewel. The hut is snuggled into the bush overlooking the valley, witnessing the movement of the sun, birds, and bees. It's a Sunday, so occasionally I hear the distant crunch of a vehicle passing on the gravel road far below as visitors come out for the day to picnic, explore, or visit the few farmhouses on that track.

I've discovered the source of my honeybees. With my binoculars, I can just pick out a distant farm up the eastern valley with a jumble of small white and colored boxes that I take to be beehives. The four or five bees that come daily to drink nectar from my lily blooms have a long fly-time.

I'm home to read Thoreau's chapter on Solitude in *Walden Pond*, written 150 years ago. He writes that, like me, he has "never felt lonesome, or in the least oppressed by a sense of solitude." Though there was an hour or so, after he'd been in his wood for a few weeks, when he thought that "a neighbor might make for a more serene and healthy life," he gave up the idea. We can be so very lonely in the midst of others, and perfectly comfortable by ourselves. Thoreau says:

> I am no more lonely than the loon in the pond that laughs so loud, or than Walden Pond itself . . . no more lonely than a single dandelion in a pasture or a bean leaf, or sorrel, or a horsefly, or a bumble bee . . . or the first spider in a new house.[53]

No loneliness here, just quiet. A treasure.

November 3, 2014

It was a warm night, in the low 60s (15°-16° C) with light from a three-quarter moon. The Possum Patrol decided to make a midnight visit—a little later than usual, but I guess they're not on daylight-saving time. Crashing and banging on the roof, they sound like they've put on weight and are getting more clumsy as spring progresses. There's nothing much of interest up there other than my solar panel, but I guess it's as good a meeting place as any. I've envisioned waking some early morning and finding mom and pop possum sitting on my porch chairs having tea and surveying the valley. I'd be happy to serve tea and have a chat, but they're very nocturnal and are heading for their fern tree nests by the time I wake.

It was a lovely dream night. The last dream this morning had me enjoying a visit with friends in Japan at a Hachi-man Festival. I noticed that it was November 15 or 16 there, so I'm a bit ahead of myself. My friends were surprised to see me in Kyoto in November since it's usually April when I visit, but what a great chance to see old friends, and a wonderful way to travel off this solitary ridge in New Zealand. Dream time.

The barometer spins and a new weather front moves in. While I meditated this morning, the room turned a yellowish green with reflected light from the sky outside. Soon the wind picked up and big drops started. After two days of wonderful sun, sheets of vertical rain are blowing from east to west through the valley, diaphanous curtains of precipitation. Amazing!

November 4, 2014

It seems that the lily-like plant next to my porch, which is attracting a lot of visitors with its nectar-rich blooms, could actually be common New Zealand flax. Yesterday afternoon, a young tui visited this plant, and I was dazzled yet again by the beauty of this exotic bird. Its head carries a hooded black mask with a long, curved orange beak for extracting nectar, but it's the intense color and pattern of the feathers that leaves me in awe. I hear its voice nearby from morning to night, but it's a high-bush bird unless hunting nectar. This time I was only three or four feet away, and I could at last see the exquisitely patterned black lines on its gray neck. It carries a wagging white feather tuft under its chin—almost a turkey wattle—snowy white against its black markings. The wings are iridescent blue-green and show so well with the black background. A truly exquisite bird.

And then last night after dark, the roof banging started again. I got my flashlight out and saw a brown, bush-tailed possum slide down the porch posts to check on the flax flowers. He was the size of a very large, well-fed house cat, sporting little rounded ears, big starry eyes, a rubbery black nose, and a huge fourteen to sixteen-inch fluffy round tail. He wasn't shy or frightened in the least to have a flashlight shone on him and just went about his business, checking out the flowers. I always think that it would be much more convenient for the possums to reach the front of my house, where the planters and blossoms are, by walking around the building rather than climbing up the water cisterns and going over the top of the roof and down the supports, but that's how it's done in possum-land. I guess the roof is like a jungle gym and this is their exercise. He was back again at 4AM, but a little less noisy.

November 5, 2014

Awake early, with the weather in the cold mid-forties (7ºC) again. Where did spring go? Dawn is arriving but the stars are still out in a deep indigo sky. The moon has long gone over the western mountains to shine in India, Africa, and on to Europe. These days it's visible in the late afternoon sky, and later it shines brightly at my window between 9 PM and midnight.

At 5:15 I'm up making tea, doing morning chores, and enjoying a few pages of *Touching the Void*, Joe Simpson's writing of mountaineering in the Andes, where he nearly lost his life twenty-five years ago. He too experienced this solitude I'm living. Simpson writes:

> the camp below disappeared . . . and I immediately became aware
> of the silence and the solitude. For the first time in my life I knew
> what it meant to be isolated from people and society. It was
> wonderfully calming and tranquil. I became aware of a feeling
> of complete freedom . . . no responsibilities to anyone and no one
> to intrude . . . or come to our rescue. [54]

I think of Simpson on a ridge in the Andes, experiencing that freedom, and me on a yoga mat here in New Zealand feeling something similar. I'm soon wrapped in wool shawls, with a cap and gloves on, a blanket across my back and another around my legs, ready to start my first meditation sit just as the sun crests the hills and hits the valley ridges. And the temperature drops another two degrees! With Simpson's conditions on my mind—climbing with ice picks and Arctic gear— I don't turn on the heater, but rely on inner warmth, even though my nose is colder than that of any healthy dog. I ring my bell, chant my Refuges and Precepts, and bring to mind my intention and Bhante Gunaratana's guiding verses:

> Let me clear my mind of all resentments, anger and hatred. Let me banish all want, need and agitation. Let my mind be bright, awake and aware. Let my mind be clear and concentrated. Let it be filled with friendly feeling and compassion ... May all benefit.[55]

Warmth fills my body as I think of all those beings who are interconnected with me throughout the world. A smile comes to my lips and my chest and body are filled with happiness and joy.

Yesterday, after starting my second meditation sit, I suddenly thought of olive oil. Where did that thought come from? The week's grocery list was already up at the drop-box with my week's bag of trash. But I'd been squeaking through with the very last of my oil and had less than a teaspoon left. There would be none for eight more days if it wasn't on the list.

Without coming out of meditation, my body stood, bowed, hands picked up a pen, glasses, and shoes, and walked the path up to that box. "Olive oil—BIG bottle," got written on that paper, the cupboard was closed, the lock dropped, and I walked back to the hut, realigned myself on my cushion, and dropped back in, mind clear, with very little interruption. How is that possible? Focus? I didn't feel as if I was in my body, but somebody knew how to move and act, without any disturbing discursive thought coming to the surface. The doer seemed to be completely gone—no actual thought, no clear decision, no process. Interesting.

November 7, 2014

The grand full moon appeared in all its silver glory about 11:30 last night, waking me as it filled my hut with white light. I got up, wrapped myself in a wool shawl, and sat at my altar facing the east window, letting that bluish white light pour in, penetrating and purifying me and others. Such a cleansing and inspiring practice!

Another cold morning in the mid-40s (6-7ºC). I realize that my family and friends in New England might well be happy with these temperatures as they move into their cold time. Occasionally, they even get snow at this time of year. But it's spring here, and next month is the summer solstice, so, I am waiting to not need a heater, hat, and gloves in the morning. I hope the weather god wakes up soon.

I do count my blessings, however. When a light rain started in the night I was indeed thankful for this wonderful, dry, cozy hermitage. It stands on this crest like fearless Amoghasiddhi, the archetypal Buddha of the North, strong and stalwart, meeting this valley weather.

The sun is out brightly today—a rare morning occurrence—so I finished a hand wash of kitchen towels, handkerchiefs, and underwear. Not a cloud in this blue sky. Yes! Perhaps if the sun warms up the day, I may get an outdoor bath this afternoon. If not—tomorrow.

I noticed this morning, on my meditation cushion, that I'm feeling more settled and serene. Finally, finally . . . yet I know that it is a continuous process, and troubles may rise again. However, it's wonderful to have this quiet, reaffirming month, after the last one. I realize that some of that fear and anxiety I held came from being female and on retreat. We daughters are raised in a society that's not always kind and caring. Those of us who come through unscathed, and who want to be out in the world, independent and actualized, need to carry the intuition of the vulnerable.

I can remember too many times in my life when I was asked, "Where's your husband?" with the implication "Where is your protector?" —the expectation that women do not/cannot go out on their own. Wariness, that uncomfortable feeling of potential danger, is often high for women. Even when we're walking through life with confidence and assurance, we're conditioned by society to always be alert to difficult situations that could materialize.

I can remember teaching my daughter skills, at a young age, that perhaps boy-children never need to learn. I expected she would be out in the world like me, so she was taught about riding subways, arriving in new countries, and traversing strange neighborhoods after the sun goes down. And taught to always trust her intuition.

November 8, 2014

I woke at 4:30 to see the moon moving slowly west. By six, with the sky turning blue, it had slipped behind the tree-fringed ridges far to the west. I think about that moon shining over Asia, over wide continents and deep seas, arriving amid the pines in New England. My Kuan Yin moon friends in England see it, my good friends in America notice it, my dear one in Japan sees it and perhaps thinks of me. All of us, interconnected around the world, lift our heads to watch this miracle of purifying light.

I've photographed the full moon from so many different places: over rice fields in Bali, above temple roofs in Japan, and one super moon rising above the Indian plain in Delhi, silhouetting a small, open shrine as I passed by in a rickshaw on my way home. What do I do with all these moon photos? Ah, the moon.

I'm reading in Koch's *Solitude: A Philosophical Encounter* about attunement to nature, and my moon-viewing is reinforced. Koch defines three areas that resonate in solitude which I'm noticing more and more:

1. Clear, undistracted, sensitized perception
2. Symbolic perception: perceiving nature as signifying or symbolizing other things
3. Fusion/Interfusion: the loss of the sense of barriers between oneself and nature, the sense of flowing out into it as it simultaneously flows through oneself.[56]

This attunement is one of the realities of solitude. "Fusion with nature can launch the spirit upon the mystical flight towards union with the all," says Koch.[57] I think of John Muir in the wilderness, Thoreau on his pond, Byrd in his Antarctic night; all expressing that desire to see, experience, merge. Koch writes of the German Romantics, who clambered to rocky heights during storms, binding themselves to the trunks of "tossing trees in order to merge with the storm" —to experience nature in its wild wholeness.[58]

I too, have stepped out into storms—once taking my young son to experience a blowing storm on a black beach ridge in Iceland, where that howling wind lashed us to each other. I watched his young face— fearful at first as I held him in my arms— (was he not yet two?) —until he saw my enthusiastic, fearless joy. Then he too smiled, and howled to the wind along with me. Is this how we teach our children to be fearless?

Onto my meditation cushion and later—more reflection. My son's birthday today.

November 9, 2014

Another beautiful, sunny morning, and I bow, tapping my forehead to the floor three times in gratitude.

I feel as if I've stepped through a new door, into a new phase in this retreat today. I feel settled and content, and yet engaged. This morning I felt that I was sinking into a container, a deep hole or cave—a cell no bigger than four foot by four foot meditation mat. I could feel the narrow walls as I reached out, walking my fingers along them with my eyes closed. It wasn't dark. It was a hole of aloneness, holding me, and I was comfortable, wrapped in cloth and at peace—completely at home. I am here to learn, to sit until a door opens or something is illuminated.

Milarepa and Robert Stroud come to mind—an ancient Tibetan sage and the Birdman of Alcatraz, both sitting alone for years, paying for past karma, for killing other human beings. I wonder if my plate of karma has such things on it. Am I sitting in response to past actions? I see my ego on that plate—no violent deaths, but ego which has puffed me up with pride, the pride of survival. Pride that may have made me appear haughty in the past. Here is my plate of karma, in front of me, from which to learn.

Yet, I'm surrounded by soft, kind beings. The birds are with me always. Yesterday morning, I heard squabbles in the distance, down the valley, Yipper carrying on with his sharp bark, and then there were two gun shots. For now, I am glad for the birds and no barking dogs or territorial squabbles other than wing flaps and peeps.

Later I heard a thud against my west wall, the third or fourth time this has happened, and looked out to see a very small dazed silvereye sitting on the deck. For more than twenty-five minutes I watched him come to, open his eyes, fluff out his feathers, void on the deck, turn his head, and become aware of his surroundings. I wonder why it's these

143

small silvereyes who seem to crash into my windows, walls, and glass doors. They're usually in twos, and, as I expected, soon another silver-eye came and perched on the fern bough three feet away, watching. These little guys always delight me, hanging on a twig, swinging back and forth, rolling over to hang upside down while they eat whatever insects they can find, twirling like acrobats. The little one on the porch eventually flew off to a high branch to figure out what happened. I was left with only a little puddle on the deck.

Why are contemplatives so connected with birds? Although it's not always birds. Nien Cheng, a Shanghai woman incarcerated in solitude for six years during the Cultural Revolution, was held in horrendous conditions, experiencing brainwashing and torture. She survived with the help of a tiny spider who built a web on the prison window bars. Every morning and evening she watched, learning its habits, admiring its skill, and relieving her own deep isolation.[59]

But birds show up so often for those with solitary lives: I think of St. Francis, and the Birdman of Alcatraz, Robert Stroud. Perhaps contemplatives sit quietly and allow these little beings to come more easily. Contemplatives focus, and notice even the smallest creatures, and the lives of feathered ones come alive. Though I wonder what St. Francis was doing preaching God's love to the birds, and telling them to remember God with gratitude for the streams and mountains, and the feathers that clothe them because they know not how to spin or sew. His words, "Beware of the sin of ingratitude", may be lost on the birds.

The Birdman of Alcatraz comes to mind. Perhaps no one is better known for solitary confinement than Robert Stroud who, in strange ways, inspired me as a teenager to be here on this cushion fifty years later. Watching that Burt Lancaster movie in the 60s, I was intrigued and deeply curious about what might come from being alone, from sensory deprivation. With a life so steeped in stimulation: art, color and pattern, as well as a deep interest in others and their lives, this curiosity seems to be the flip-side. I think it could be my deep interest in "knowing," in understanding, in experiencing all, that has brought me here.

November 10, 2014

Last night found me giggling at an absurd thought that came to mind: "They don't know where I am. If they did, they would come, and ask me to please come help." Who "they" were, I'm not sure, but I felt very much like a kid hiding out in my container or up a tree, free from responsibility for a few hours. The freedom of solitude, again.

I realize that I've been helping since a young age. A responsible, sensitive, intuitive, dependable kid raised in a disorganized, dysfunctional family with an angry mom, overwhelmed by all that needed doing. Parts of that childhood were hell, and I responded by going into helping-mode as often and as much as possible.

I've grown into this role of helping where I see a need, with a willing set of hands or a welcoming smile. I've been a befriender of strangers, reaching out and lightening loads where I could. I didn't do it for praise or recognition. There's no "I" involved. It comes from a heart that loves others, sees need, and responds easily and happily (most of the time). So here I am, for a year, not helping! No one has expectations of me. I must let go of that helper role, step into this interior house, and see what inner work needs doing. I find lots of sweeping up the past, folding the laundry of unfinished thoughts, taking pride off the picture hooks on the walls, and making a breakfast of joy and appreciation.

November 11, 2014

A new week begins. The squeaking male chaffinch is out there, fussing on the porch, reminding me to put out seed.

It's a morning of precious light and green. I'll step out of my sweet container here on this precipice to walk the two miles down to the Community House today and return books (*A Buddhist Bible, White Lotus Sutra, Touching the Void*) so that others might use them. A schedule on the wall there tells me that in the next two months there will be retreats every weekend, so I'll have to judge my time to slip in and out when no one else is around.

It's good physical exercise, the walk down and the slow crawl back up. I do it with great mindfulness, and without the delicious abandonment of youth when my ankles were strong, my balance better, and I had more feeling in my feet. Peripheral neuropathy has been with me for ten years now, and is perhaps responsible for my three ankle breaks. It slows me down, but doesn't stop me walking; I'm just more cautious and step mindfully. I'm not one of those contemplatives who include a five-mile tramp in their daily solitude. I remember well the advice of experienced meditators: set your boundaries physically as well as emotionally. The once-a-month trek down to the Community House is my one outing, and may stop completely soon.

I had a voracious appetite for books in my earlier months here, but have now settled nicely. I'm re-reading, rediscovering, and doing more reflection about what I do read, enjoying cross-referencing the writings of contemplatives who have walked this path of solitude before me. I love it when Bob Kull refers to Phil Koch, who refers to May Sarton. Such a wealth of observation and reflection.

5 PM. Two more silvereyes just hit the window wall. One was up and off quickly, but the second is going through the painful throes of coming-to and seeing if everything will work again. It's so painful to witness. These little guys must be new hatchlings who missed out on some part of the flying instructions. Perhaps they just need crash helmets issued. I'm going to stripe that window with masking tape and hope it will help. May he—and all beings—be well . . . and mindful of their flying.

November 12, 2014

Sunshine, but with cold, heavy winds. The tree trunks move.

November 14, 2014

I'm reflecting today on how my father's sudden death from cardiac arrest in his early fifties influenced my life. I realized then that life includes death, and death is sure. It was a wake-up call at a young age to live life fully since tomorrow isn't promised. Impermanence is a continuous lesson, but not an easy one. We so want things to continue, want that stability, and so dislike change. Some of us cling to this more than others, but losing Dad made my grasping a little looser.

Last week Stephen Levine's book, *Who Dies?* moved me to write out some Death Directives for myself—especially since I travel so much, and could easily die far from home. I wrote out my wish to not be moved for 24 hours while I detach from the form I'm now in and my wish for cremation. I included the Phowa prayers that I hope someone will say for me, and the phone numbers and emails of my family. Included also are contacts for my closest Buddhist friends, who will chant for me, and one Episcopal priest, a cousin. They've all said they'll say prayers. It's now on one sheet of paper with the passport and medical information that I travel with. That old Girl Scout motto, "Be prepared," surfaces.

Then, the same day, I received a letter from home in the foodbox, news that a neighbor in New Hampshire whom I've known for twenty years died in a fiery Cessna crash in September. Some people might feel this could be distracting information, and that I should not have been told while on retreat, but I'm glad to be able to bring him to mind. For the next ten days I'll take time every evening to do a short ceremony, bringing him to mind along with a deity, visually washing and purifying his past karma and ill deeds, forgiving him, and letting him rise. The Phowa prayers ask for a good and peaceful death, and whether or not they help, they do no harm and could make a difference. They're also a way of saying goodbye. I too would welcome these prayers when I no longer walk this meditation path.

November 16, 2014

I wake to another lousy headache. Oh, me! I try some tea, a bit of breakfast, and moving slowly. Soon it will clear, but it's hard to wake up with a furrowed brow and an unhappy face to welcome this sunny Sunday morning. Ah, all is impermanent—even headaches.

Recently, I've been focusing on ways of looking at "waking up" or the path to enlightenment. One of our very senior Order members wrote an article delineating three models for this—Self Development, Self Surrender, and Self Discovery—that really speak to my experience.

Self Development, a path of regular steps, has been very much a part of my work and my life. Reflecting, I realize how truly intentional I am, wanting to accomplish as much as possible in this lifetime since I know that death will come. I've put a lot of effort into study, learning, and being of service and available to friends and family. Some would call me driven and intense. I practice as if my "hair is on fire" and with sincere intention.

Will this get me to enlightenment? Not sure. Certainly, it has resulted in a lifetime of meditation practice, a wide knowledge of Buddhist writings, a strong ethical life, and this year of solitary retreat. And perhaps a few insights with a small "i." Truth is, I'm thirsty for knowledge and I love study.

This self-development model speaks of effort, but it's only one of three models, and may relate more to where I've come from than where I'm going and what might be most helpful on this retreat. I realize how long I've labored under this model, reading, studying, and discussing. It's been most appealing to me, and I'll continue, though in a less concentrated way.

Self-surrender has always been a curiosity to me. This is something Thomas Merton speaks strongly of—surrender to awakening, surrender to God:

> The peace in one's own heart . . . resides in the awakening and attuning of the innermost heart to the voice of God - to the inexplicable quiet, definite inner certitude of one's call to obey Him, to hear Him, to worship Him here, now, today, in silence and alone. It is the realization that this is the whole reason for one's existence . . . Unfortunately, even in solitude though I try not to . . . I still depend too much emotionally on the idea of being accepted, approved of and having a place in society.[60]

So even though he speaks of surrender with such assurance, the mundane pulls him back. The Indian Buddhist monk Santideva speaks of surrender in *The Guide to the Bodhisattva Way of Life* as giving up a mundane personality to allow service, helping others, to work through us—essentially, a surrender to the good:

> "I gave my entire self wholly, to the good. Take possession of me, oh sublime beings. Out of devotion, I am your dove."[61]

Others surrender to a living guru or teacher, and some, I see, surrender to a husband or partner. Having seen surrender go very wrong—historically, emotionally, and psychologically—I'm somewhat wary of it as a model and am guru-resistant.

And yet I visualize Kuan Yin, the Bodhisattva of Compassion, "She Who Hears the Cries of the World," and wholly welcome her into my being, willing to give up this "self" to be of service to all beings. It was on another solitary retreat, at Brahma Vihara Arama Temple in Bali, that I wrote of my desire to take her on, to surrender, to wear her robe:

Putting On Her Robes

Slipping my arms through the robes of her garment,

Wrapping the cloth around me, raising the hood to my crown,
I dwell in her soft white raiment of love and compassion.

I open my eyes and see the world through her eyes,
Seeing the pain and suffering
With the graceful equanimity of the Bodhisattva
I wash it in compassion and reflective truth.

I smell the noxious fumes of anger and deceit
And transform it with the pervasive scent
of Lotus-born wisdom and truth.

I taste the labor and efforts of numerous caregivers
And hold the plum of generous effort
On my tongue—with gratitude.

I hear the tap of the elder's cane, the shriek of
Children's voices, the cooing of birds,
engines, and the swish of a felled tree,
And I am content—connected and in harmony
With the multiple beings that weave me
Into the net of interconnected humanity.

I stand, and step forward, in flowing robes
Moving through the vibrant air
As my Bodhisattva in body—in heart,
And with a quiet, focused mind—radiantly
... clear and sky-like
To experience the waking world as my yidam,
... to be awakened and transformed.

May my wisdom intentions bloom in this world
As relative Bodhicitta—aspiring to benefit all beings

And beyond this world, as the essence of great perfection
May I walk the Bodhisattva Path with the robes of the Buddha.
— Kiranada, 2/2011

Development, Surrender, Discovery—It's the Discovery model that appeals to me the most now, that beautiful image of the "cloud of unknowing" pulling away from the Bodhi moon is with me—the object of the spiritual search discovered, not developed—nothing to attain, nothing to surrender to. Subhuti speaks of self-discovery as the transcendence of duality in the here and now—waking up and shaking off the shallow dream that keeps us from enlightenment. He says it's like taking a blindfold off or removing a mask from your face.

These metaphors speak to me. I've been yearning to wake up for years, and aspire to in this lifetime. That yearning has brought me here, to be quiet for a year. To wake up to the truth of life, let go of the suffering, let go of attachment, of grasping; let go of the sadness and disappointments that grasping brings.

"Let Go!" is a poem by a Chinese poet that I copied down months ago and have just found, written on the back of this journal:

> You sentient beings who seek deliverance;
> Why do you not—let go?
> When sad—let go of the cause of sadness.
> When wrathful—let go of the occasion of wrath.
> When covetous or lustful, let go of the object of desire.
> From moment to moment, be free of self.
> Where no self is there can be no sorrow, no desire;
> The winds of circumstances blow across emptiness.
> Whom can they harm?
> Wrathful, Banish thoughts of selfhood;
> Sad, let fall the cause of woe;
> Lustful, shed lust's mental object;
> Win all by simply letting go.
> — Cheng-Li[62]

Will watching the wind move through the valley trees at sunset really teach me to wake up? Will learning the soft "whoop" call of the quail help me with that inner voice? Will bathing in moonlight every month at full moon lead me to banish the clouds of unknowing? I try them all—opening my mind, opening my heart.

At night in the quiet forest I hear the ruru, the morepork owl, hoot, and have such a feeling of peace and fulfillment. I feel myself in a lovely nest, warm and cozy, surrounded by all I need. Loved and cared for in my solitude. Such a strong feeling of wholeness and contentment. There is no other place I should be. The strength of this serenity is like no other in my past. I'm happy. I'm at home. I'm on the journey I was destined to travel.

November 17, 2014

It's a dull overcast morning—the forerunner of rain, I expect—and yes, here it is. I feel this is an unseasonably wet spring, but since I'm new to this land, have no weather reports and no one to confer with, I just observe and accept.

What a surprise to see a large, black brindle dog looking in at my porch door just now—the biggest thing I've seen up this way in months. I wonder if there will be a lost owner on his tail, but no one has materialized yet. I'm reminded of Thoreau's solitary retreat, when someone did arrive at his door looking for a missing dog. In the end, it seemed the visitor was more interested in discussing with Thoreau exactly what he did all day long than in locating the lost dog.

Wondering what my own personal answer would be to that man's question, I come up with a list that includes meditating, reading, cleaning, washing, cooking, and tearing up paper boxes for compost. Today I also dyed some silk thread and made scones. I watch the pine tree grow below the hut and the wind move in the trees on the far ridge. The pines have grown eight to twelve inches since July, a fascinating cycle. And although the wall of green on the far ridge looks dense and solid, I found last night that with careful concentration on a small area, I could actually see the wind move between the tree fern fronds and manuka saplings. I spent an hour with this as the sun set in the western sky.

Once, years ago, I heard my mother and sister chatting about me, and asking what on earth I did in that New Hampshire family cabin, alone and with no TV reception! Ah, in my mind I say, "I water the nasturtiums and feed the birds."

151

Everything stops now because of a sudden deluge. I move quickly to get buckets under strategic points outside to gather this rainwater. Although the water in my faucet comes from cisterns that store rainwater from the roof, I take great joy in gathering rainwater for the tub and clothes washing. What a joy to have this torrent pounding on my roof as I go back to preparing breakfast pancakes—beautiful golden discs in a black fry pan. I'm eager to share my perfected pancake skills with the kids when we have out yearly get-together next summer. Breakfast was never a big thing for me before. What was I in such a rush about?

I've moved back to a simple meditation practice that was core when I lived in Japan and started Soto Zen meditation thirty years ago—*Shikantaza,* or "Just Sitting." I've cleared my shrine for a while to have a patch of clean white wall to focus on and "just sit"—no focusing on breaths as in samatha, no visualizing Kuan Yin or sending loving-kindness, metta bhavana, except during my final evening meditation. I just sit, returning again and again to being present. It feels so right at the moment, with my exploration of the Discovery model and settling into a deep, deep space.

November 18, 2014

While reflecting in the night, I realized another page has turned, and my two months of life review have stopped almost completely. Just as some people speak of seeing their whole life flash before their eyes at the time of death, I've spent weeks and weeks watching my life flash through my mind. I've remembered conversations that took place fifty years ago, visited with people I haven't seen since childhood, looked down streets from my young motherhood days, and gone through memories of hundreds of acquaintances and relationships.

I found it curious that this came up now, but perhaps it's the first time I've *completely* stopped that very busy life and given myself over to quiet reflection. It's profitable. I feel clearer, more centered and at peace. My mind is quieter. I'm able to really be here in the moment now that so much of that old business is finished. I know some self-reflection will continue, but I feel a very big chunk of it has been accomplished in my first 100 days of solitude.

I'm here. I'm present, and I'm lighter, happier and more serene. Watching the mind is a true education.

November 19, 2014

Such a quiet, serene morning. The sun is out and the wind has stopped. I meditate, prepare breakfast, and slip out back to enjoy the intimacy of the bush with my oatmeal—away from the ever-changing grand panorama I live with on the front porch. There is such a different feeling to the space behind the hut under the karaka tree at this end of the meditation path. I've been pulled to this area more and more as I look at the Discovery myth.

Two young quail are working the earth for goodies, softly cooing to each other with their "whoop-whoop" voices. I realize what an honor it is to have all these beings share their space with me. I'm the big noisy, busy one—but if I'm very quiet, mindful and slow-moving, I'm welcomed to this land of theirs. They were here long before me, and they, and their coming generations, will follow when I'm long gone. It feels like a privilege this morning to be included in the family of quail, chaffinches and bees. I'm in training to be accepted in this treasure land. I have much to learn. So I'm quiet, watchful and patient for the lessons these little ones have to share.

Soon I must move my chair to stay in the warm sunshine and watch the floating white clouds. Present. Grateful. Nowhere to go. No one to be.

November 20, 2014

Ah. It's the morning after a food drop so I get a two-egg omelet with onions, red pepper, mushrooms and left-over parmesan polenta for breakfast. I'm eating only two meals a day but I still must watch my food costs since prices in New Zealand are often double, or even four times, the cost in the USA. I remember again and again that this is an island, and that what can't be grown here in season must be flown in, thus the higher costs. I come from a "land of good and plenty" with vast plains of grain and long growing seasons. Life is different here.

I watch the weather to see if today is a big-sheet-washday or not. Already at 9 AM there's a shower rolling in after early morning sun. But it quickly passes and the blue sky seems promising. Getting sheets and towels hand-washed and dried can be a challenge after years of an automatic washer and dryer, but I'm onto my fifth month hand-washing and wringing everything. This is actually one of the toughest parts of living remote for me. I've put out and taken in wash four times in one day. It's a lot of weather guesswork. But I'm back to my meditation cushion and thoughts of equanimity.

Recent reading and further reflection has brought up the subject of "stories," a topic I've visited numerous times in the past year. This retreat is a joy since it affords the time, space and quiet to explore areas that interest me but that I've had no time to really delve into. Pride, Fame, Fear, Self-Surrender, and now Stories: it's like shining a flashlight on areas with potential for insight.

Ajahn Brahm says that deep insight cannot fail to occur when one knows where to look. He speaks of the mind as a powerful flashlight that illumines all before it. But we need to know where to point it, where we might be likely to discover a hiding place of insight.[63] I resonate with that flashlight image, and hope that stories, myth and memory are not just sweet distractions; that looking deeply at the part they play in my life might reveal some insight.

I come from a family that told stories. We didn't so much live in the past, but rather we shared traditions and history with narratives. I was a receptive audience for my father's and grandmother's tales, a child who asked questions and learned much about my New England family's life a century ago, a base that I soon was passing on to my story-telling daughter.

From my grandmother, I learned of the first trolley on Rockaway Street hill in the Highlands of Lynn, early in the last century, and of the cow pastures and wild flowers that grew in fields where now there are only paved streets. I learned of the hoop skirt factory my grandmother worked in, and of the job she got at a nearby college so that she could sit in on the academic classes that she yearned for. I remember Dad speaking of "Black Jack" Bouvier in East Hampton, New York, where he grew up; of Jack's young daughter, Jacqueline, on her pony—the girl who later became a president's wife. I heard stories of Mom and Dad meeting in New York City at the hospital where they worked, dancing to Guy Lombardo's Big Band, and moving north to Mom's hometown outside of Boston when they wanted to start a family.

154

All these stories made up an oral history of my family before I was born. And I heard stories of me as an eighteen-month old, a two-year old, and a five-year old, of my friendliness, confidence, curiosity, and love of independence even then. These family stories supported the young woman I became.

We speak of stories as if they are fabrications or mere fantasy. But stories underpin memory. Bhante Sangharakshita says that memories of the past support ethics, love and friendship, and I believe this.[64]

Yet I remember a Buddhist teacher reprimanding me for going into story when staying present was requested. I was to focus on Direct Pointing—examining present moment awareness and experience—and not "the story." It was a good wake-up call for me. I also remember a Zen teacher in Japan who would speak of discursive thinking or stories that show up on the cushion as "going to the movies." And oh, how I loved to go to the movies; a habit that happens all too often for me. However, when he visited one of my art exhibitions in Japan, I admitted to him that some of the images he was admiring on the gallery walls had come to me while sitting on my meditation cushion. "Going to the movies?" I asked. "This is just fine," he said with a grin.

I've been thinking of our collective stories also, the ones most everyone in a shared culture believes. I was told when I returned from Japan to the USA that I'd need to find a good full-time job so that I could qualify for work health insurance (since the USA provided no care for those outside the job-supported insurance system). I asked why I needed health insurance, and was told it was for when I got sick or came down with cancer, so "they" didn't take my house to pay the bill. A story that has some basis in truth, I expect. But I didn't get a full-time job, nor did I find health insurance, nor did I come down with cancer—just yet. I couldn't let myself be led by fear of what might happen in the future. I had Dharma work to do. I put my money in vitamins, regular exercise and meditation —and so far, I'm doing well. I didn't believe their stories.

I also remember collective stories I heard in my childhood about those people I should be fearful of, people different from myself. I was shocked and confused by these tales, since I was raised in a culturally, religiously and racially diverse neighborhood. When I was told what to expect from "those" Catholics, Jews, Italians or Blacks, it didn't fit with my own experience. These minorities were my friends on the street. I found their families kind, benevolent and socially aware. That neighborhood strongly shaped my childhood and my approach to the world.

Some collective stories are responsible for horrific cruelty and injustice; those that led to the Holocaust, created the need for the Civil Rights Movement, supported the Indian caste system, and even the subtle caste systems in place now in Japan and England.

Some of these cultural stories are hard to see when we are immersed in them. I've found travel and living abroad deeply educational and revealing, helping me see with new eyes and question some of the assumptions of the West—the stories my community lived with.

Papanca—mental proliferation—is hard to stop, both on the cushion and off. Watching my mind helps me to understand my quick judgements of others, my story of what they did, why they were rude or unkind. If I stop, allow a gap, and step out of a reactionary story, I can step into their shoes, see the world from their viewpoint, and come up with a much more compassionate story of what might be needed.

Ah, will I ever be finished with looking at stories? For now, enough. I must clear my mind of the past and future and just be here, in this moment, present and aware. And that means the joy of clean, dry sheets tonight.

November 21, 2014

With all the lovely blossoms coming into fruition, I'm struggling with allergies and awake until 1 AM with a troubled head and a troubled mind. I was reminded of the verses on mind framing and worked at putting the troubles aside:

> As soon as disturbing emotions arise
> May I forcefully stop them at once
> Since they hurt both myself and others.

I'm moving slowly this morning, but so happy to see the lovely sun on this patch of bush.

Wild daisies are growing near my porch. I've watched them come up tentatively after the first tight bud got chopped off two weeks ago in a possum visit. With quiet on my roof for a week or more, three blossoms have opened their white petals and a fourth is just sprouting up. I'm pleased to have them. The young rata tree by the edge of the ridge is showing red globes, and the karaka behind the hut is covered with tight green tassels of buds, ready to burst. Spring is late, but here.

I hear a dog bark up on the hill behind me, a joyous, playful sound. I received a note in my food box, telling me I shouldn't be alarmed if Mojo comes through on "walkabout." One of the long-time residents has just returned, staying not so far from the stupa, and Mojo is his buddy, a happy, friendly dog, I'm told. This must have been that large furry visitor that appeared so suddenly at my door three days ago.

I read about the boatman in Buddhist literature who guides the vessel that crosses the river of suffering, and how he's willing to go back and forth again and again, across that river, helping to bring people over. This resonates with me on a cool, quiet morning, and I ask questions of myself. Am I creating a vessel for others with this solitary retreat? Am I some sort of facilitator for others' aspirations? Is this year in silence a container for others to pour in their hopes and intentions, and am I truly doing this as a surrogate for all those unable to be here? Am I a conduit for others' aspirations for enlightenment? I would be so happy to be the boatman and help to ease some suffering in this world. I pray every morning that all beings will be peaceful and happy, free from suffering, sorrow and delusions.

Maybe I'll have a few days off here to quiet my mind and my heart. It seems right just now.

November 24, 2014

Low clouds roll into the valley and a gentle rain begins—the first in four days. I've been taking my early morning tea out to the dense bush, finding a clear spot with a little sun, to sit, and connect with the day and the land. This morning I crawled down to the big pine and sat under those spreading arms with my tea for a half hour. It's been a silent wake-up to the day, a chance to welcome the bird life and all that grows in this overwhelming bush. And now the fog rolls in and whites out the valley. But the weather will change in twenty minutes, I'm sure.

I've had two days of no writing and one day of fasting—going inward more and more as I watch my needs change. Ten days ago, I took down the artwork on the wall, put away the small stitched pieces I was natural-dyeing, cleaned and simplified the shrine, and began meditating with a white wall. The quiet seems deeper, the contentment more real, and the direction of my retreat simpler—turning another page, stepping through another door. I'm pulled by the silence that the lack of wind supplies. When it's raging and beating the trees, my laundry and me, I hold on tight, enjoying that primal energy. But when it stops, I'm at home with contentment and the need to sit in meditation more.

November 25, 2014

A complete white-out upon waking: no valley, no far ridge, only white. The clouds have settled like a solid white sheet twenty feet beyond my door. The temperature stayed in the low 60s (17ºC) all through the night, and it seems as if the season has changed yet again.

I've stopped using my clock almost completely, relying on an inner timepiece to shape my days. With no monastery or Buddhist center bells to wake me or call me to meals, I wake with the light, eat when needed, and meditate between. It feels right. I noticed three days ago that it was 2:40 PM and I had yet to have lunch, but I wanted to sit, so I went and meditated, and ate one hour later. It's a curious existence, but a lovely experiment. There are many who set alarm clocks not just to get to work on time, but also to get in two hours of meditation or be on their cushion to welcome the dawn. It's been years since I've needed an alarm and I'm happier for it. When I need to be up for a 6 AM flight, I do set an alarm, and I usually wake intermittently through the night, turning off the alarm before it rings. Setting my mind at bedtime to wake up at a certain hour works for me.

Lovely oolong tea from Auckland and some grapefruit start the day. My porridge is waiting for me after my first meditation sit and yoga. It's a drop-dead quiet white morning. I'm sure the birds too are holding their breath in this eerie, dense fog, though I heard one hoot from a morepork owl testing the air. For a few minutes, a silvereye and a chaffinch come to feed, and then they too are gone. The wind stops, cloud movement stops. We pause, hold our breath—wait.

At 8:40 AM the clouds pull away from the lower trees and a magic show begins. I ride the clouds, get caught in the mist, become wet in the damp, swoop the downdraft like sledding on snow—I dissolve and re-form, taking lessons in impermanence, changeability and non-being from the weather. The sun breaks through for just a minute or two, and then it too is gone. A tree-lined crag is revealed, then disappears. All emotions—negative and positive—come into fruition and then dissolve. Riding the clouds of the Tararu Valley.

I should be meditating, brushing my teeth, preparing breakfast. But how wonderful to put aside the "shoulds" with weather as my teacher today and little feathered beings as my friends. I watch, open to experience.

I walk up to my drop-box to leave my food list, notes and weekly trash bag and see again evidence of pigs. Yesterday, at "tea time down with the pine tree," I saw the remains of digging and pig rooting. Last week they were very active on Slipglade Track, where whole areas were dug over and twelve-inch holes in the road furrowed out. I do wonder what could be so interesting and tasty about roots—but I guess they ferret out the much sought-after truffles in some locations. While I'd love to see these big Captain Cookers, as they're called here, they're nocturnal, as they are in Spain and Japan where I also encountered them. I wonder why they're so shy and why they became nocturnal foragers after being dropped here 250 years ago. I guess it's survival.

It's an interesting synchronicity that pigs, pork, and truffles have come up in my study of the Pali Canon this week and the Mahaparinibbana Sutta (16) of the Digha-Nikaya, the *Long Discourses of the Buddha.* Eating pork, or "pig's delight," may well be what precipitated the Buddha's death in 432 BCE, I learn.[65] it's said that at the age of eighty-three, after more than sixty years on the road, the Buddha died of food poisoning, though some contemporary doctors see symptoms of mesenteric infraction, a chronic intestinal blockage.[66]

That year, Buddha was feeling particularly frail and exhausted, and soon began telling his followers to ask their questions because he would be leaving this world in three months. He was working his way through northwest India, back to his place of birth, when he arrived in the village of Kushinagara (in present-day Uttar Pradesh). It was here that an unfortunate blacksmith named Cunda offered the Buddha and his devotees the meal that would be the Blessed One's final dinner. The spread included pork—or rather, "pigs' delight" (*sukara maddva/ sukara maddara*) —which has been translated in various ways, including "the soft, tender parts of pigs," or "what pigs enjoy," or "truffles." Buddha asked that the "hard and soft foods prepared in abundance" be served to his monks, and the "pigs' delight" be served *only* to him, with the leftovers buried in a pit. We are told that following the meal Buddha was attacked by severe stomach spasms, which seemed to bring him near death. He was clearly aware of what was happening, however.

And so the assumption is that Buddha died of food poisoning. It's possible. Others point to over-eating after an illness with chronic intestinal problems. However, the Buddha was very clear that his illness and death were not a result of Cunda's lack of mindfulness, and he should not be blamed.

Ahh, pigs' delight. Many Buddhists are vegetarians, following guidelines found in the Jivaka Sutta (55), in which the Buddha tells Jivaka that monks "must not eat the meat of any animal which they have seen, heard or suspect was killed especially for them." This follows the First Precept, not killing or causing harm to other beings.[67] However, living on daily alms as they did in rural India, the Buddha and his disciples would have deeply offended those who offered them food or starved if they had refused all meat.

I've seen non-vegetarian food offered to monks in Thailand and Indonesia at various monasteries and worked to hide my surprise. I might have encountered the assumption in Southeast Asia that shrimp, specifically, are neither meat nor fish, and thus acceptable. Temple devotees gain much merit by providing their local monasteries with the very best foods available, and I've watched huge feasts of shrimp presented to monks, while the parishioners sat nearby, glowing as the monks ate their offerings. The monks, in their kindness, consumed what was presented by the locals—the most expensive and special meal possible, as perhaps Cunda did in Buddha's time. Dear Cunda. I hope he had a good rebirth. I reflect on pigs in the night on Slipglade Track, and as a final meal for the Buddha.

November 26, 2014

Thinking about my earlier comments on not being bound by the clock or scheduling, I came across some writing by Anagarika Govinda, a close friend of my teacher Sangharakshita. His thoughts on solitary retreat in Tibet in the last century say:

> I have never felt a sense of greater freedom and independence. I realized more than ever how narrow and circumscribed our civilized life is, how we pay for the security of a sheltered life by freedom and lack of independence of thought and action ... when every detail of our life is planned and regulated and every fraction of time determined beforehand ... timelessness is suffocated ... when we accept its fullness, eternal life-giving rhythm we master it—make it our own. By accepting time, not resisting its flow, it loses its power over us and we are carried on the crest of a wave without losing sight of our essential timelessness.[68]

Lama Govinda, a wise man.

November 28, 2014

A deep rainy day. Many of my friends in the US are ending their Thanksgiving Day at this moment, full of their Tofuky—tofu turkey. I have oatmeal and chia seeds.

The day began for me with a deluge, the first rain in a week. I got my buckets out to collect as much water as I could. Happily, I work with chilly, cold fingers, delighted to be in this silent hermitage.

I enjoy watching the mist lift from the green-covered ridges and feeding the chaffinches. It's a delight to see them visibly fattening up with the spring, especially the small female who has become bold and chubby, almost the size of her brothers. I observe that when the wind ruffles their rust-colored chest and back feathers, there is BLUE underneath, the color of their caps. The swift-flying greenfinch has given up on the flax flowers, which have now gone into seed pods, and the daisies hold no nectar or attraction, it seems. I'll miss the lovely, black-masked, pea-green male and his duller, smaller female. He tried one last time for a nectar-producing blossom three days ago and found nothing. Watch-

161

ing, I saw him pull back, move upright in flight, and let out an annoyed "sqwack." He was off in a swoosh. I think that was my goodbye.

Bird watching is one of the quiet things I am now able to do. From a life full of activity, I now sit. Kamalashila speaks of our usual busy lives in his fine *Meditation* book, counseling that if you are now on retreat with little to do—when normally you are very active—the temptation is to fill your time with activity. Your energies will be looking for an outlet, so you will look for repair jobs, writing, study projects and elaborate meals.

I would agree on all these during my first three months here, and I'd add art projects to that list as well. He says that these may be all a cover-up, and perhaps unnecessary and a [poor use] of solitary time. As a very active person you may find you are attached to activity for its own sake. Doing nothing may be mildly threatening—to simply experience yourself. Activity may be "a substitute for experience, a way of covering up or hiding from a new depth of awareness."[69]

Kamalashila tells me to spend an hour each day doing nothing except experiencing myself! Can I break into this deeper level of mindfulness he speaks of?

I remember my childhood delight in "hiding out," or being up a tree, unobserved by the disapproving mother/father I created mentally as a child. I was always needing to prove my worth by accomplishment. It's still hard for me to relax that interior self-worth monitor and just be, spend an hour doing nothing.

Sona, a fellow solitary retreatant from my Order, sitting for three months in Wales, recently wrote:

Occasionally I felt lacking in enthusiasm, wanting something to do, to be more active, more productive. I tried to console myself with abandoning unskillful mental states thinking that that was enough. I wasn't always convinced. The results are not so tangible as a carpentry project or building a website—Lately I have been thinking how "identity" is tied up with what we do, with responsibility, status, etc. As I grow older, I feel I am reaching a kind of "use-by-date" [I found] the retreat a bit of a watershed—from being useful, responsible—to being grounded not outside but inside.

All these words resonate tremendously with where I am mentally on this rainy day.

November 29, 2014

Corn! Corn! How extraordinary. Word came through two weeks ago that corn had appeared in Auckland and there was a possibility it would be available here on the Coromandel Peninsula—possibly, possibly. Food can be such a big thing on solitary retreat. We work to avoid letting it be a distraction, but to keep our spirits up, a bit of variety is advisable. And corn—Wow!! I left New Hampshire as the corn was waist high and early varieties were already at the roadside stands. This is important summer produce for farmers there, and I hadn't really appreciated that the USA is such a big corn country until I moved away to Japan years ago and saw my country from afar. Corn wasn't seen at all in New Zealand, I was told, until recently—so what a thrill to get some wonderfully fresh ears in my food box this week. Bless the corn! And remembering others, all best wishes to my American friends and family as they celebrate their harvest holiday with cornbread, Indian pudding and pumpkin pie.

November 30, 2014

It's the last day of November—an overcast, cold day with raw showers that keep me putting out and taking in my jeans and sweatshirt, trying to get them dry. I gave up on trying to wear my summer cotton pants because of the cold yesterday and have pulled out warmer trousers until the weather is kinder.

Yesterday, I planted some new frilly-leafed lettuce and more silver beets. After three solid months of output, my original lettuce plants have finished. A small red leaf variety continues well, but the Romaine has put out all it was able. I moved the chive plant to a different location in the porch planter, hoping it would do better, and was surprised by the massive root system for so little show above ground. I would like to rely on it for my onions, but it has never been up to much picking. I've been happy to gather the majority of my greens here from my own porch garden. The only disappointments have been beets and the aru-

163

gula (gone to seed) and the small radishes, but it's all an experiment for me. Somehow, a celery plant appeared among the parsley, and is working to produce a sizable stalk. I've refrained from harvesting it to see how big it might get. The small shoots, I know, can be quite bitter. I'm reading my *Edible Wild Plants* book on Kindle and keep eyeing the dandelion greens along the walking path, but haven't tried any yet. Bless this Kindle for carrying thirty-six books and two dictionaries, yet weighing only a few ounces as opposed to twenty pounds.

I'm enjoying some leftover banana pancakes with tea as the sun goes down. What a good idea—to cook some extras and set them aside for a next-day snack. It's like having a good piece of banana cake full of sunflower seeds.

As I eat, I go back to re-reading May Sarton's struggles with solitude. It's true that I love reading journals. She gives me reinforcement for the writing I'm doing here, helping me to think that this writing truly might be worthwhile and of interest to others.

However, Sarton struggles with the idea that work on solitude may be the greatest gift she is giving *others*. I am also saddened to hear her struggle so with living alone and to hear her yearn so deeply for someone with whom to "share everything."

Who said: "We practice commitment to the way by helping and attending to others, and by doing the hard yards of coming to really know ourselves . . . " —the work of solitaries?

Clark Moustakas, quoted in Sarton's book, says:

I began to see that loneliness is neither good or bad, but a point of intense and timeless awareness of the self, a beginning which initiates totally new sensitivities and awareness, and which results in bringing a person deeply in touch with his own existence and in touch with others in a fundamental sense.[70]

Another of my fellow Order members, on solitary retreat for nine hard months, stepped into that retreat hearing that it would "make a better person of him." The account that I read following his return, after all his struggles with illness, both physical and emotional, over those

164

months, did seem to show change. He seems to be gentler, kinder, more patient and aware of others, even showing a true love of his fellowman that was not so evident before. Whether this will last beyond six months I do not know, but any "waking up" to self and others has some lasting effect, I believe.

Chetul hut in the sunshine after restoration.

Chapter 6 December

> How can we ever lose interest in life?
> Spring has come again
> And cherry trees bloom in the mountains.[71]

In the Coromandel it's not a dusting of pink cherry blossoms I see on the ridges, but scatterings of what looks like lavender among the fern trees and pines. It's the lovely manuka (tea tree) in bloom. The tiny white flowers on scraggly gray branches look like pale mauve sprinklings of powdered sugar all across the ridges. The wind rustles through them and all nod in answer.

My mountain peak too is ringed by bouquets of these white flowers, some growing low, but many 20' to 25' above the sloping ground— a banquet of flowers. It may be December, but here it's spring and the land is not unlike April in Japan when the wild cherries transform the mountains into pink clouds.

What a joy to have the moon return from the dark, renewed, refreshed, and pouring such brilliance into my hut. Moonlight is magical when it comes into a room to light up the dark night. Last evening I saw the sun set in the mist over the Firth of Thames and then turned to the other direction and spotted an early evening moon, already high in the sky. It was waxing into the three-quarter moon favored by Japanese artists, which they treasure more than the full moon renditions we see in the west. After a life in a fiery Zodiac, with my birth sign of Leo in five houses, I treasure this quieter, more serene moon in my later life and relish this silvery moonlight, now part of my name.

Ah, but what is it in the environment that has given me trouble four nights in a row? I'm still trying to discover the triggers for all this mucus reactivity so I can eliminate the full sinuses that bring me down. Soon, with summer, life might be drier and the pollen count lower. I'll be happy to trade this for a few mosquitoes. For now, I soak up the warm daytime sun, even when mornings are in the low 40s, and sleep almost vertically to get a good night's rest. I count my blessings, and they are numerous in this full land of flowering trees and friendly fantail birds.

And now, a startling Wedgewood blue sky with not one cloud, a quiet hush on the land, and a delicious morning of meditation and breakfast outside with little wind and only buzzing bees.

December 5, 2014

Although the past two days have been overcast, the moon does break through and is happily waxing into fullness with its apex expected in two days. It's such a comfort to see it in the dark night, like an old friend who has not forgotten me.

Today I've been watching my reaction to disappointments, and how patience and understanding are developing on this retreat. My one weekly contact with the world is the Wednesday food drop. This week, again there was a rotten grapefruit among the three I'd requested—two gooey soft spots that went to mold overnight—even after I'd asked for "soft spot" checks and praised "mindful shopping." I wish I could be there to squeeze the fruit myself. It's a real practice in patience and understanding to leave it to others. People who don't cook much are not so sensitive to produce about to go off. With delivery only once a week and no refrigerator, the freshness of arriving produce becomes a true issue. I'm already wiping mold off things and eating them, tossing bread that actually has spores growing on it, but often eating around them. I missed following through on that research I wanted to do on the advisability of eating rotten food, what I can get away with and what is ill-advised. I've done well so far, avoiding intestinal upsets.

As a friend said, everything is magnified on a solitary retreat. So, when food arrives already rotten, it can be a big thing. I considered whether I should say something or let it go and decided to write a note. Thanking the helpers for their hard work, I did list the grapefruit, kiwi, oranges, kumara (sweet potatoes), mushrooms and eggs that have not made it up the hill fresh enough to eat, and asked for a little more checking of the fruit and vegetables they kindly purchase on my behalf.

Wednesday is also the day when I receive any news or packages. There's the disappointment of no letter this week from a friend I wrote to a month ago, no book ordered six weeks ago, no Order newsletter I requested last week, no package from my daughter of things I asked for three months ago—and was there one more thing? The post is slow, over twelve days from the USA to New Zealand, while mail from the USA to Japan takes only six days. My patience is honed here, week after week. Ah, all part of my practice, I tell myself.

I'm looking at "The Four Reminders," found in the "Jewel Ornament of Liberation" discourses of Tsongkhapa and Gampopa. These are also known as "the Buddhist facts of life." They include the precious opportunity offered by human life; death and impermanence; karma and the realization that actions have consequences; and the disadvantages of samsara or "conditioned existence." One wise Order member writes:

> They aren't news and they aren't contentious, but, despite their importance, they easily slither out of awareness to be replaced by quite different assumptions. They are wake-up calls, jolts to our complacency, articulations of the troubling voice of reality as it speaks through immediate experience.[72]

I look at the first of these Four Reminders on this day of disappointment and impatience.

The first wake-up call deals with this precious human life. All the benefits of life come to mind; most importantly, the chance for enlightenment. I'm reminded how 'hard won' a human life actually is. The Pali Canon tells us of the blind turtle swimming in the deep sea who surfaces once every one hundred years for breath, and miraculously, slips his head into a yoke of seaweed—a remarkable chance likened to the rarity of a fortuitous human birth.[73] And I remember what an extraordinary opportunity I've been given.

I think about those verses of Tsongkhapa that are posted on the bulletin board over my computer at home:

> The human body at peace with itself
> Is more precious than the rarest gem.
> Cherish your body; it is yours this one time only.
> The human form is won with difficulty.
> It is easy to lose.
> All worldly things are brief,

Like lightning in the sky.
This life you must know
As the tiny splash of a raindrop.
A thing of beauty that disappears
Even as it comes into being.
Therefore, set your goal.
Make use of every day and night
To achieve it.

— Je Tsongkhapa (1357 - 1419 CE, Tibet)[74]

The first of the Four Reminders is a beautiful, poetic urging to use this precious lifetime to put our mind on enlightenment with strong intention. To practice with great dedication. This gift, this precious life in a land of plenty, this opportunity to meet the Dharma at a time in history when there are so many gifted teachers, in a country without war and famine, with supportive friends, leisure to study and apply myself. And now, a year without the usual distractions.

December 6, 2014

I saw my first eastern rosella parrot on the wing this morning as I enjoyed my morning tea with mist rising over the ridge. It's the rarest bird I've spotted so far, getting a number 3 on the 100 point chart of common sightings. It's a good-sized bird with a vivid red head and chest, a white throat, and a lovely yellow, black and green patterned wing going into blue. She has a long tail and was happy to perch in the blooming *hinau* sapling in front of my outdoor tub. Truly a spectacular, showy bird! I read that they're all descended from a southeast Australian bird, brought here caged about 1910, that later escaped—and that they're only seen near Rotorua, Northland, Coromandel, and a few in Wellington. Her shape reminded me of the rosy gray galahs that fill the skies every dusk in Brisbane, but the rosella is far brighter.

Last week I also saw a myna bird with its bright yellow eye patch and beak, alight in the same hinau tree. The hinau is similar to the mountain laurel back home, both in leaf and bloom, but this one is a taller, leaner version. Supposedly, the Maoris used its bark to make the black dye they used in flax weaving and tattooing.

Yesterday was a good day to look at the importance of this special life I've been given for a limited time. I consider using what I have to move a little further down the path to enlightenment every day, so that when I die I won't have remorse, to use Thoreau's language, "that I have not lived."

Knowledge of Impermanence and Death is the second of the Four Reminders, and it's good that I'm looking at it on this sunny, bright day clear of troubles. Blessed be. Ah, death. I know that one day I will die. I cannot avoid it. It comes to everyone and it will come to me. This is one of the things that is brought strongly to mind when I find the time to stop all the 'running along the shore' and really see.

As my fellow Order member, Devamitra, said, "Old age is no longer on the doorstep but has actually entered the house." And he's younger than I am by a few years. Old age links us to the reality of death, though of course many die before they're aged, through illness, disaster, accident, or violence. This past decade I've lost a number of family and friends, all younger than myself. It's been ten years of physical loss, but one of realization and accomplishment as well.

Mary Oliver's poem *When Death Comes* has always strongly resonated with me. I've turned to it again and again, taking courage and feeling the sheer exhilaration in life in the words. In that poem, she speaks eloquently of being a "bride married to amazement," and a "bridegroom taking the world into my arms." And, with the same, clear recognition as Thoreau and Tsongkhapa, she speaks of not wanting to reach the end of life, having just visited it.[75]

We typically act as if our lives are infinite. When one receives the shock of a terminal illness diagnosis, many step up with a new approach to the time left, aware only then of the preciousness of this life. The loss of a close loved one can spiral us into deep mourning and depression, but it can also inspire us to wake up to this life we have and appreciate deeply those who are still alive. This is what living with intention holds. I try to carry this in my life every day.

I decided to 'sit with death' this sunny morning as the flies and bees find their way into the clear silence of my hut, while I am feeling open and positive. When contemplating death I know it's important to set up the conditions with a session of Metta Bhavana meditation for myself first. I'm not going to mentally visit the charnel grounds or do the "Contemplation of the Decomposition of a Corpse" meditation. Someday, but not today. Instead, I set up some questions to reflect on.

1. Everyone dies. Do I think I'm exempt?
2. What would I do differently if I knew I had three years, or three months, or three days more to live?
3. Are my plans for the future provisional?
4. What do I need to face death?
5. What will matter when it comes?

Kamalashila speaks to me on impermanence in a contemporary way:

> And there is no way out—there is no escape from reality. Unless we can learn to sit more easily with the fact of impermanence, we are going to keep hurting ourselves and others. We need to realize that ending, renewal, death, birth, and change continue endlessly—and that it's actually a very good thing that they do . . . It is because of the very fact that life is so changeable that we can change our-selves.[76]

and continue to grow.

Here in this land of bountiful nature, where I'm so connected to the seasons, to the cycle of birth, fruition and death, it's all very real to me. The silver beets that have fed me for three months are now waning, the window sills every morning are littered with the bodies of gnats and flies that didn't make it outside the night before, the full moon now coming into its own will soon wane and go back to its dark time, to be reborn in fifteen days. My grapefruit will rot and become compost for the next cycle, or nourishment for insects going through their cycles. And I too will someday die and become nourishment for future genera-tions, physically, emotionally, spiritually. As it should be. A new month, dipping into a new year soon, and into a new decade of my life. As it should be . . . appreciating each day.

December 7, 2014

I was awake in the night with possums on the roof and on the deck, moving what sounded like rocks around and picking at the net covering my vegetables.

December 8, 2014

Another of the warm nights that seem to bring on the amazing, low cloud whiteouts. I awoke to an impenetrable wall of white twenty feet from the porch. Over the next two hours misty clouds lifted and some far ridges mysteriously appeared; then, as two weeks ago, the white curtain descended again. When it was clearer, I noticed that high up, the wind was moving from east to west, but in the valley and along the ridges it was coming in the opposite direction. I think the second belt of cloud cover came off the warming Firth of Thames, sliding back into the valley to bring more dense clouds.

Once the weather seemed to be resolving, I did my one-and-a-half-hour round trip tramp down the Dharma Road to the Community House library to see if I could pick up a Karma/Rebirth book I'd seen there earlier. There was still mist and the forest was quite wet but no showers materialized.

It was a lovely walk down, seeing the landscape change from winter to spring. Tall flowering manuka bushes were everywhere. Daisies lined the rough road, interspersed with beautiful stands of pink foxglove or purple loosestrife. It's grand to witness the seasons.

Now the sun is out brightly, the roof is cracking and popping with heat, and the roar of the Tararu Stream falls is louder than usual, speaking of rain up in the Pinnacle Mountains during the night.

Today I wanted to spend some time reflecting on the third of the Four Reminders—Karma. Recognizing this precious life, the evidence of impermanence, and the reality of death finishing us all off eventually, the reality of karma or "willed action and the influence or potential of an individual's previous conduct" is right there too.[77] I remember, reflect, and wake up to the truth that my actions have consequences. How I move through life, what I focus on, my attitudes and actions towards others all come back to me one way or another.

I'm reminded of a famous murder trial that consumed the American public for months in the 90s. It was televised daily with everyone speculating: did he or didn't he do it? I was teaching in Japan at the time and even there it was on everyone's mind. My students were convinced the man was guilty, yet he got off. They asked me how this could happen, in a country they admired. I myself felt that if he did do it, he wasn't free, that the result of his actions, karma, would come around soon enough. Nagapriya beautifully outlines this in his book *Karma and Rebirth* and says that with murder there's guilt, followed by fear of discov-discovery, which moves into insecurity, leading to alienation. I might add depression and ill health to his list.[78] It's sad to know that a murderer will indeed suffer in this life or the next, found guilty or not.

Thirteen years later, this man acquitted of murder is now in prison on another matter, broken and in ill health. He did not "get off" and is now perhaps paying for a violent act of passion so many years ago. Numerous adages speak to this, including "reaping what you sow;" "what goes around, comes around;"and "what you put out, you receive." Positivity and kindness also show up on your doorstep if your intention has been skillful and good.

When I was preparing for this retreat a year ago, and looking at the costs as well as a year with no income, a friend said, "But where will you get that money? How can you expect to find it?" These questions arose from her own financial insecurity. I felt that if it was important to my practice, and in some way of service to others, the money would be found. I moved forward with confidence, knowing that if all else failed, I could put the costs of airfare, a year's housing, and food on a credit card, and spend the next few years paying it off. Did episodes in my past give me the confidence that what was needed would arrive? Is it good karma that it all worked out and I'm here with the costs covered? Is our good luck or bad luck in this life a result of behavior in a former life—or can we see karma ripening even more quickly, within one lifetime? Vishvapani writes:

> I know that skilful actions have brought me happiness and fulfill-
> ment and have benefited others. When I have been kind or
> generous, I've seen others benefit and it has given me happiness.
> I know (also) that my unskilful actions have harmed others and
> harmed me too. When I have been unkind, I have seen the pain
> I have caused. Those actions have reinforced negative states of
> mind that make me unhappy and I've felt remorse and regret.[79]

In some religions and in ages past I was pushed to behave ethically and with kindness for fear of going to hell. In contemporary society, it's easy to see hell right here, played out every day. Behaving ethically, helping others, and moving through the world with awareness and compassion are the actions of my practice—I don't need threats of hell or bad karma showing up—the path is there. To be aware and awake.

December 9, 2014

On this cool, overcast day, I'm cocooned in this hut, meditating, and thinking of karma, regret and remorse, and remembering that the most direct result of karma is mental unease. I know that we suffer more through waking up to conscience as we develop spiritually. What we once thought was "not a big thing, since everyone does it" suddenly has us full of remorse and regret. And here is a confession. How I loved using that United States Postal Service plastic bin for other purposes, the one I received when I picked up three months of "held" mail. It was the perfect size for hauling my wash to and from the laundromat. I saw nothing wrong with this "repurposed use" until a postal worker, doing his laundry beside me, asked what I was doing using US Postal equipment for this purpose. What? A wake up.

And a second confession, again "taking the not given." I had quite a collection of airline teaspoons that I used daily, in Japan until I woke up to the fact that this was truly stealing. My developing Buddhist practice made me realize that collecting spoons from my flights to Scotland, Australia, Korea, Thailand and Japan was really not ethical. Remorse brought me to researching airline headquarters throughout the world, packing the spoons up with notes of regret, and returning them all. Again, I woke up and did my best to make amends.

And what is the karmic consequence of these ethical breaches? Retribution may still be coming, but there is also something called *ahosi* karma or "has-been" karma. Nagapriya writes that:

Since karmas require certain conditions in order to ripen, if those conditions do not appear it is possible that some karma will never fructify. One of the ways this works is through counteractive behavior. [My waking up?] For instance, we might do something quite unskilful, but before experiencing any negative results, we act very skilfully to purify ourselves and, in a way, 'cancel out' the negative

175

karma. Through a determined effort to develop the skilful, we can circumvent the negative vipakas [actions] that we would otherwise have experienced.[80]

What was developing in me during this time was something called *hrih*, which Kuan Yin actually carries in her heart. Hrih is the inner voice, the moral law, the voice of conscience. It has the power of illumination, of making things visible, and can include not just seeing ethical breaches, but making goodness, compassion and sympathy *visible* and illuminated.

With remorse, regret and shame for past actions, I work at letting them go, and not letting them define me in the future. This is not so easy in our western culture. The Dalai Lama tells us that remorse is different from low self-esteem. We can admit to remorse and grow from it. He wakes each morning thinking how he can use the day to bring happiness to others, rather than focusing on thoughts of self and remorse.[81]

Everywhere, things arise and pass away in dependence on conditions. Karma—cause and effect. I'm reminded of raising my first child so many years ago and trying to avoid locking horns with him by explaining the theory of natural sequences, a simple karma theory. If you don't wear your boots outside in the rain, your feet will get wet and perhaps that will be uncomfortable (or maybe not!). If you don't eat lunch or don't use the toilet before we start this road trip, you'll be hungry and have to pee later, when it's hard to stop. It was a different theory of raising children than my mother-in-law's views. She followed the "do so because I say so" school of discipline. Teaching natural consequences helps little ones see what happens—from this, there is that. My son had early exposure to the results of what we might call karma. He grew up with dry feet and a full belly and knows now to use the toilet before we depart.

December 10, 2014

It's another quiet, overcast day with a promise of sun, and I'm fasting. It seems the right thing to do before fresh food arrives later today.

Food. Without a refrigerator, I must plan my meals carefully and not expect to store things over a week. Tofu, which should be refrigerated and used within a few days, seems to last pretty well up to day six unopened, but once opened I must use it in the next two or three days. I've found a brand of multi-grain bread that will last even into the third week without mold—a great discovery. Of course, when food lasts so long, like the jar of peanut butter or my pot of miso, it makes me wonder how digestible it is and how many preservatives are in it to keep it from rotting.

The conscientious staff here have helped me rig up a "cold box" which sits outdoors on the ground out of the sun. It's an old metal filing cabinet with a towel over the top that must be kept wet. I pour water over the top two or three times a day and before going to bed, and the soy milk, vegetables, tofu, veggie hotdogs, bread and cheese I store in it do seem to last a few days longer.

December 11, 2014

5:30 AM. The valley is white with fog again and I'm awake early, wanting to end a dream that held threats of awkwardness and physical violence. I hope those guys in my dream sort it out while I'm awake and my daughter comes out okay.

I notice that my dreams are far less engaging than they were when I first arrived here five months ago. I seem to have filed through many years of life and have fewer conversations or incidents to go over than I did when I came with heavy buckets full. I feel more content and at peace than I did in July—a benefit of solitude.

I spent much of yesterday reflecting on merit, the rewards that come from good actions, and whether merit is transferable. This comes from a question Tenzin Palmo received in *Into the Heart of Life*, when someone asked if we can do anything to lessen a loved one's negative karma.[82] At the end of my meditation, pujas and Refuge Tree practice, I regularly recite a prayer of Transference of Merit that includes the phrase "May the merit gained in my acting thus go to the alleviation of suffering of all beings." Buddha was very clear that we are the owners of our own karma.[83] So can my actions change the karma of others?

Tenzin Palmo agrees that only the owner can lessen the impact of bad actions in their lives. However, she offers three ways of helping others with their heavy load, including purification rites, sending loving-kindness or merit, and example. Nagapriya reminds me of the

177

transformative impact we might have on others which can help them discard negative beliefs and habits and embrace a more creative outlook.'

In considering our own merit, he speaks of:

the influences we exert upon others . . . we do not live in discrete, insulated karmic bubbles . . . our moral behavior can significantly alter the course of people's lives for better or worse. . . learning to recognize the influence we have on others and using that influence . . . wisely and compassionately . . . is an essential part of spiritual growth.We can't directly change their karma, but "we can help them save themselves."[84]

This is something I feel too.

In my *Transference of Merit* prayer, I recite,

Just as the earth and other elements are serviceable in many ways to the infinite number of beings inhabiting limitless space, so may I become that which maintains all beings, situated throughout space, so long as all have not attained to peace.[85]

This I clearly support, yet when I first became a Buddhist, I had great worries about giving up all the benefits of my good actions—my merit—for others. I worried that this was like giving away all my money and not having enough left to pay the rent. Giving up my merit without regard to myself for the benefit of all beings—this deep, heartfelt generosity was new to me, coming from my self-sufficient, rocky coast New England Protestantism.

And yet it wasn't long before I was emotionally convinced and wanted to transfer whatever merit I incurred from my actions to others. Later, I read that when we give up our positive merit, it comes back to us ten-fold, but this has never been a motivating factor for me. I do remember once finishing a disrupted meditation and feeling that my miserable accumulation of merit from it couldn't possibly help anyone, but later I read that this wasn't true. Like the tiniest bit of water dropped into the ocean and dissolved, the ocean's vastness keeps that drop from ever drying up.[86] So I dedicate all the merit and positive actions so that all beings, including my enemies, may achieve enlightenment.

I learned that we gain merit in three ways: through generosity (dana), through ethical actions (sila), and through meditation (samadhi).[87] I'm only too happy to pass on any wholesome merit I might accumulate to others who are suffering or in pain. So, are we able to change someone else's karma? No. Can we help? Yes.

One part of me is eager to go on and look at that last of the Four Reminders—the Disadvantages of Samsara (cyclical existence)—but I put it aside and look at solitude more closely. What resonates at the moment is D.H. Lawrence's words about being alone:

> Be alone, and feel the trees silently growing.
> Be alone, and see the moonlight, white and busy and silent.
> Be quite alone, and feel the living cosmos softly rocking.[88]

Ah, off to my cushion to do some joyous meditation work. The valley is still white with fog and the birds are quiet. As light from the day wanes, I sit on top of the mountains and mist swirls around me again. I exist in a silvery white cocoon, embraced and supported.

December 12, 2014

So many words were running through my mind last night that I chose to read until late to quiet the narrative. It was after midnight before I put the book down and now I'm awake at 4 AM. But I can catch up on sleep later—the benefits of freedom from a set schedule.

At last, some fast-moving high clouds let that three-quarter waning moon blink out for me. When the dark clouds allow it to appear, the quality and intensity of that white glow is arresting—like a one-hundred watt light bulb in a dark forest. She feels like such a friend.

I realize it's the second moon month since our troubles on the hill ended, when my neighbor was taken away. Ten days ago, walking back from the stupa on the deep bush path, I passed his old hut. It's been transformed. With its new coat of paint, it glowed on that hill crest like this moon, or like a giant white bird—and I wrote:

Chetul Hut Watches

A snowy white heron resting on the high hill
Above the valley, radiating clear purity.
Made of wood and board, Chetul housed numerous
Meditators over these ten years.
Named for Chetul Sange Dorje, Bhante's Tara initiator,
It was a small jewel, deep in the bush—
Accessible only by a narrow, ridge-clinging path.

Chetul Hut, beloved refuge of a local practitioner
Who deeply connected with the land.
Buried nearby, his spirit
Could not becalm the troubled young hermit
Holding so much at bay, crouched in hiding.

Blackened with soot, covered in cobwebs,
Chetul heard the cries and howls of this
Demon-ridden young man—and wept.

The night they came for him, agitated screams
And shouted howls of "Get out! Get out!"
Echoed from the valley walls.
Before, the shouts and fighting were all gibberish,
Not understandable.
The language of demons and Mara.

Hard wars were fought in small Chetul Hut
Over the past two months,
Waking me from dreams of rescue.
Now gone.

Here Chetul glows in gowns of white
Painted inside and out.
Absorbing the kindness and healing
Sent by so many.
Reflecting the pure light of the Full Moon
Chetul watches from the ridge.

A snowy white heron perched lightly

On the hill, giving safe haven to all.
In the afternoon light, the clouds creep over
The far ridge, slow motion,
A hawk rides the valley up-drafts.
Chetul sits and watches.

— Kiranada

It's quiet now, but I'm reminded of that time when terror and anxiety wafted down the hill. I'm such a positive person that it's hard for me to look at that last of the Four Reminders—the Unsatisfactoriness of Samsaric Existence—but remembering October, it becomes more real. I can read Buddhist teachings again and again, but as Vishrapani says,

> . . . until we find emotional equivalents for them, they are only intellectual understandings. We simply forget them unless by emotions, we become convinced of them and take them on. The Four Reminders are meant to move our feelings, inspire and motivate, to wake us up to the truths. These reflections are a door that opens onto reality itself.[89]

It was a long time before I was convinced that I too was born into samsara—what Buddha called "this realm of ten thousand joys and ten thousand woes." To keep from drowning in a depressed, dysfunctional family, I would only focus on the joy life held. I couldn't contemplate the dark side of dukkha, or unsatisfactoriness, samsara, the endless round of the human predicament: birth, old age, death, ignorance. Not until later.

Even here on this quiet mountain, I see suffering that I can't avoid: from the physical trials of illness to the realization that old age is here, to the death which I know will come to me, and which is represented daily by those small beings on my morning window sill, and those I rescue from the outside tub after the rain. I see clinging, attachment and grasping even in my meals. Sometimes, fasting helps with that. Oatmeal this morning with THREE kinds of nuts on it as well as grated apple and fresh ginger. Really, Kira! Is this grasping or just greed?

Mental grasping is often there too. I remember the depression, fear and madness I witnessed this spring, and my own anxiety, stress and struggle—reacting rather than responding to the situation. How I wish for the grand equanimity of realizing all is in flux, knowing that I shouldn't cling and wish for constancy, solidity. Yes, agreed, it's futile to expect the world to make me happy—that expectation is a root of my suffering. It's best that I work to wake up as Buddha did, with heart and mind primed to respond out of wisdom, benevolence and kindness. To see this world as illusion and give up grasping—turn my back on samsara for a path that brings more permanent rewards. Remembering that I have this precious life to work through the suffering, realizing there is death at the end for all, that we are the owners of our own karmic actions, that samsara can be transcended, I can step off this wheel and do some good for others in this world.

December 13, 2014

I had a visit last night about 9 PM—one young possum checking out the front porch and getting a drink from a water bucket. Unlike in the past, this one chose to walk around the house rather than over the roof. When one is coming off the roof, I often hear the sound of long claws clattering over the metal and then a serious thump as it hits the porch wood. I know that others in rural New Zealand huts have had problems sleeping due to nocturnal possum activity; however, here there's been just an evening, or occasionally an early morning scramble followed by two or three nights of quiet. Perhaps their numbers are down this year with all the "pest control" efforts of the conservation folks.

As my visitor arrived, the sky in the west lit up like an orange-red fire scene. I've never seen such glorious, deeply colored sunsets any place else in the world. They're truly astounding.

During the night I had a wonderful visit with a colleague-turned-good-friend in a dream. It was a delight to recognize her bodhisattva qualities and appreciate the patience and kindness she manifests. Henri Nouwen, a Catholic priest who wrote on "Solitude and Community" (sounds like opposites, no?) in the 70s, says that "Solitude is essential to community life because in solitude we grow closer to each other." I've felt that happening numerous times during this retreat.

We take others with us into solitude and there the relationship grows and deepens. In solitude, we discover each other in a way which physical presence makes difficult, if not impossible. There (in solitude), we recognize a bond with each other that does not depend on words, gestures or actions and that is deeper and stronger than our own efforts can create . . . there we grow closer to each other because there we can encounter the source of unity.[90]

I need to reflect longer on that unity with this friend. Her goals in this world are very different from mine, but there's a clear sisterhood and respect for each other that transcends all. She traveled with me in Japan and Bali, and was the second person I phoned (for permission?) when the radical idea of a year's solitary retreat crossed my mind two years ago. The first person I called was my daughter. Both were so enthusiastic and encouraging that now I'm sitting on this ridge in the Southern Hemisphere listening to a roaring stream below.

Philip Koch writes further about relationships and solitude, saying:

social relationships have elements that can only be fully
experienced . . . and appreciated in solitude; just as the fullest
experience of self involves both un-reflective absorption
on one's projects and reflective distancing from those projects . . .
Accordingly, the fullest experience of other people, the awareness
of them which completes engagement and from which renewed
engagement ought to flow, demands solitude.[91]

Friends are with me here, and I expect I'm with them as they bring me to mind over this year away. A note that came with a package last month finished with this sentence: "You are missed and fully supported by all those who love you, you brave heart, you. Your fellow dharma-farer and admiring friend." Sometimes these friends feel very far away, and sometimes it feels that they're just right up the path, giggling in the bush. Who would expect that a solitary year would bring insight into friendship and a true deepening as a result?

December 14, 2014

A storm has moved in and it's been raining steadily for twelve hours now. The past three hours have been especially heavy, filling my two-gallon buckets with water cascading off the roof and giving me about fifteen gallons in the outdoor tub. Now the winds have picked up and the trees are barely holding on in these lashing gusts—truly an exciting weather morning on the hill. And in this blowing gale, a little chaffinch has worked his way up to the porch for some morning seed.

Philip Koch's book *Solitude: A Philosophical Encounter*, was sent to me here after my retreat started, when I realized that perhaps I really did need it. He's a great lover of solitude and writes,

> For just as one can feel a mystic identification with all nature in solitude, so can one feel an identification with all other people. I confess to feeling in solitudes of my own, an uncanny sense of presence of the great solitaries—as though we are all hauntingly together here in the windy countryside, just over the hills from each other. I feel, Merton might say, the mystical integration of my own church.[92]

With my love of research, I've done much reading on solitaries of the past and have blessed those folks who put pen to paper and shared their experiences. They've become quite real to me. Taking in Koch's quote above, I began to weave stories of these beings living "just over the hills from each other." The children's book on New Zealand-USA possum tales didn't get written three months ago, but I thought that with my vivid imagination, I'd try to report on all the (mythical) solitary retreats that are happening all around me. This could be the first issue of *The Solitary Gazette*, published in the waning days of 2014.

The news is that we are happy to have Hank Thoreau, the American naturalist, down at Pine Crossing in solitary retreat for a few years now. He came in and built his own small hut (10'x15') for only NZ $28 and has been observing the rising river flow, the storms, and the surrounding bush. Many of his neighbors continue to stop by to say hello when the water allows them to cross over the stream in their gumboots. He does tramp out for dinner with his mom once a week as he did in Concord, since here, town is just another mile further than his Walden Pond Retreat. Yes, he still refuses to pay taxes.

Up above him and much further out to the east we find both Tenzin Palmo in a high cave on the Pinnacles and Adm. Byrd doing his meteorological recording among the misty mountains over the next ridge. They are not in touch with each other but we hear that both are doing well, especially since Byrd has learned to set up the stove with fewer carbon monoxide fumes this time. And, of course, Tenzin has always been the most self-sufficient of the group with her annual food drops and serious Tibetan practices. Twelve hours a day of meditation does inspire.

Zen Master Bon Yeon Jane Dobisz is up at Chetul Hut. Though she is here for only three months, she is very serious about her practice, and like her Korean teacher, has set up a schedule of one-thousand full prostration bows a day and three hours of chanting. She's a true model of tenacity—but, of course, though it's been thirty years since her Maine woods retreat, she's still only twenty-five years old. A good solitary inspiration to us all. She brought more peanut butter this time.

As you may remember, many, many years ago, the Desert Fathers and Mothers arrived and found caves and small cells to occupy down near Thames. After twenty years, St. Anthony stepped out of his solitary cell to find that an entire community had grown up around him. It's now the modern town of Thames, and while no longer a working monastic settlement, it continues to share the Dharma with locals at Sangha Night on Tuesdays.

Not far from Thames, May Sarton settled in a lovely home that faces the sea. She is less troubled here by depression or by raccoons trying to come in the cat door for food in the night. As in New Hampshire, USA, she continues to write her poetry and that Journal of a Solitude. It's wonderful to have a journal writer over the next hill. It encourages.

And remembering writers, Bob Kull did get his PhD with his grand book on his year in solitude in Chilean Patagonia. He, too, is here in a very remote hut he built from scratch in the wilderness up along the Buddhaquest Track not far from the two big kauri trees. He likes it up there. Bob did remember to go to the dentist before "going remote" this time so perhaps there will be no teeth to pull on this solitary, but he now has the experience to share with others. Cat is not with him this time, but he's adopted a young possum who has moved in. She whines a lot less and has no epileptic seizures like poor Cat. He has good communication up there with solar equipment, like Dick Byrd in the Pinnacles. They both can be in touch with home base and email and chat on satellite phones regularly with their respective support teams.

It's an honor to have Thomas Merton down near the Community House in a small cabin (with a solar refrigerator!) He sees visitors regularly while on solitary retreat and there is always a pile of letters going in and out of that hut. Since he doesn't cook, the guys

185

at the Community House prepare a noon meal for him and he walks down to eat with them in silence. He manages with some soup or a sandwich in the evening and does a tremendous amount of writing on silence and solitude.

Kiranada at Abhaya Hut seems to be doing well, feeding the birds, painting lots of mani rocks that show up at various places on the retreat property, though we rarely see her. She worries occasionally about the gale force winds she calls hurricanes, but the staff have reassured her that they are just "big blows" in New Zealand lingo. The rat in the loo was solved early on and she has adjusted to the occasional rotten grapefruit in the weekly food drop. The outdoor tub is a hit at Abhaya and the camp stove oven her friend sent along feeds her love of baked goods. Her beloved Dhardo Rinpoche is there on the stupa hill. We hear she is writing—so maybe there will be yet another book on solitary retreat in the wind. She seems to need an extraordinary amount of both tea and books, but has the kind support of many friends in Auckland and Thames who supply her regularly and keep her happy.

We hear that Milarepa is living on gorse in the hills and we occasionally see some wisps of a smoke fire and hear some strange sounds—Tibetan song? If we pinpoint the area he is camped in, we'll see about doing a food drop of some brown rice and those Lorna Doone cookies that Zen Master Bon Zeon likes.

Phil Koch, Pete France, Vicki Mackenzie, and Tony Storr may show up here to interview some of these retreatants when they come out, as these writers have done in the past. Perhaps there will be some new books on hermits to add to what they have written. With all of those retreatants doing daily meditation and devotional practices, the land is infused with energy and kindness, and a peaceful aura prevails. May all be well among these hills of solitary beings.

What fun!

Remarkable weather is pouring in with a howling storm and small trees down. There's a roar in the valley I've never heard before. Is it the wind coming off the high ridges or a tremendous amount of water pouring down the river? I think both. I expect I'm cut off completely, and that the exit road is under four feet of water, as it was when I arrived. Very fine rain continues to blow east to west through the valley in vertical curtains. It's been twenty-two hours now of water from the sky, but breaks in the clouds show some late sun, and the promise of a half-moon tonight and a clearer day tomorrow.

I have a tremendous sense of just letting go, surrendering to this solitude, this time on the mountain. With nature blowing through me, I sing this song of a Zen priest from my Kyoto Nanzen-ji Temple;

> I sit at the moon-filled window
> Mind set free in the Dharma realm.
> Watching the mountain with my ears.
> Hearing the stream with open eyes.
> Each molecule preaches perfect law.
> Each moment chants a true sutra.
> The most fleeting thought is timeless.
> A single hair is enough to stir the sea.
> — Shutaku, Zen Poet (14th c)

December 16, 2014

I woke from a dream where I was in a bookstore, and was saddened that I hadn't been able to make some purchases before the dream ended. I worry that so often here, as in my other life, I'm lost in a book—either escaping to another land or striving to learn and understand concepts about this life that elude me—rather than living. Stepping onto the porch, I look at the vastness of this valley and realize how much I have to learn from simply being right here. As I write, a soft rainbow appears to confirm my realization, arching across my vista and riding on the curtains of vertical moisture that I've discovered only here. In thirty seconds the rainbow is gone. It reminds me of "taking darshan," sitting in the presence of a great spiritual being to absorb his/her essence.

I put aside all I'd planned to do to start the day . . . and stop, witness and participate in the magic unfolding at my steps. I again come back to gratitude for this grand opportunity to participate in this precious life. My cup overflows.

December 17, 2014

For the third day, skies are overcast, vertical curtains of fine moisture blow through this valley, and occasional gusts of wind send things flying into the hut. Little fern leaflets are airborne, sticking to every surface. And now, a profound, heavy rain cuts me off from all.

Yesterday, I put on all-weather garb and tramped up to have some time at the stupa, resting my head against its white, concrete hip, Dhardo Rinpoche's shoulder. No view of the sea, only blinding rain, but I did it. Coming home through the bush along slippery ledges, I wondered what might happen if, in a moment of unmindfulness, I slipped over the edge. How difficult would it be to struggle up again?

This morning I spent more time with my compassionate Kuan Yin, and listened carefully to the wind, trying to define the call.

> The wind has no voice
> Until it finds the valley
> The gorge, the trees—
> And then it howls
> And grumbles, whistles
> And groans. Roars!
>
> Wind against rock and crevice
> Between trees, limbs, and leaves.
> There is the voice!
>
> Silent until it encounters
> A surface, an obstacle
> And then, refining them
> As song;
> Using them to sing with
> Force, energy
> Power—of change.
>
> Oh, silent one—Oh roaring one. I send
> Praise for being that which
> Wakes me up, to source.
> — Kiranada

With rain pouring down, I wonder what life must be like for the birds. In light rain, I've seen chaffinches glide in to check out the food tray on my porch without too much concern. But when the rain gets heavy, they watch from the bush and time their arrival for a break in the downpour. Just now I watched a male and female quail, who often feed at the back of the house in early morning, appear out front, going through the grass looking for stray insects. As the rain got heavier and heavier, the female quickly headed downhill to protective cover but the male was either hungrier, better padded, or clueless. He was quite soaked when finally he followed suit, into the heavy bush. I imagine there will be a lot of feather fluffing under the ferns this afternoon.

December 18, 2014

I'm still socked in with wonderful land fog and rain off and on. Yesterday evening we had a break, and the sun appeared for an hour, setting in the west. The sunshine made all the trees and bushes twinkle in unexpected light, and it reminded me that the Northern Hemisphere is probably enjoying snow and the twinkling lights of Christmas. It's a beautiful time of year.

I'm doing some mantra visualization and chanting, and realize how much it's part of my life here—a current that runs just below the surface so that, if I step off to do walking meditation or tramp to the stupa, I'm chanting with each step. John Blofeld says that:

> The repetition of the sacred name (or phrase such as "Om Mani Padme Hum"—or "Lord Jesus, have mercy on me") is, properly speaking, another form or equivalent of contemplative meditation and is the easiest way of attaining one-pointedness of mind ... In time the sacred formula will continue to revolve in the mind even when asleep and dreaming. At a moment of imminent danger, the mind remains calm; no threat or fear to life or limb can cause a break in the chain of recitation.[93]

This reminds me of Mahatma Gandhi's assassination in the garden in New Delhi in 1948. His last words were "Ram, Ram"—one of the names of God in Hindu tradition, and something of a mantra for him. Stephen Levine, author of *Who Dies?*, tells me that some people, such as Gandhi, "are so connected to that essential part of themselves that even death cannot distract them."[94]

I'm not sure what was on my lips, other than "whoops," when I slipped off the slimy outside steps at six this morning. Ironically, the same right shoe flew off my foot as the last tumble two years ago, when

189

I suffered that horrendous concussion. That time too it was slimy steps and a light rain. However, this time there were only two steps, not four, and I was only carrying a plastic bucket. I did hit my head, though only lightly. My back and hips are aching mightily now, four hours later. This was a re-enactment of a decisive moment in my life that I did not need to replay again. I texted the guys to see if they might help me solve the slippery step problem and a bundle of outdoor carpeting appeared on my porch later.

I've been painting mani stones to place at the stupa with the mantra *Om Mani Padme Hum* as well as seed syllables for Amitabha (HRIH), Amoghasiddhi (AH), Akshobhya (HUM) Ratnasamabhava (TRAM) and Vairocana (OM)—the five Jinas, or archetypal Buddhas. I'm also doing Vajrasattva (HUM) and Tara's seed syllable (TAM). I came across some interesting information in Dilgo Khyentse Rinpoche's commentary on the *Thirty-Seven Verses on the Practice of Bodhisattva* concerning this seed syllable work:

> The syllables of Avalokiteshvara (and Kuan Yin as well) mantra "Om Mani Padme Hum" are a manifestation of himself. Whenever anyone, even ignorant wild animals, see these six syllables or hear the sound of the mantra, the seed of liberation is sown in his being and he is protected from rebirth in the lower realms of existence. The syllables of this mantra, even when written by an ordinary hand, are not ordinary syllables but have been consecrated by the wisdom mind. The syllables are made of his blessings; they have the power to liberate.[95]

I'm happy that the possums, rats and birds, as well as visitors to the stupa here, are benefitting from my work these past three months. It's a joy.

December 19, 201

Finally the weather god decided to shine on the Coromandel Peninsula and we have glorious warm sunshine. It's up to 24ºC (75ºF) at 1 PM, the laundry is quickly drying, and the pansies are flapping their petal faces gleefully. What a long haul of rainy weather! As for the grass and foliage, it seems that the bush flourishes even in the rain though I know my vegetables need sun. I sat outside for my pancake breakfast this morning and ate mindfully, later noticing all the bees gathering nectar.

Spring is moving into summer at last, and the solstice will be here in just three days, at the dark of the moon.

My tumble down the steps yesterday has me achy and stiff, but two soaks in an Epsom Salt bath yesterday have helped immensely. The knot on the back of my head is uncomfortable, but since I haven't had any dizziness or nausea, only a night-time headache, I assume it's minor, with no concussion. Hallelujah! I've nailed a piece of that outdoor carpeting to the slimy steps to ensure this does not happen again.

I've been reflecting more on mantras and how the singing of a repeated phrase is so conducive to one-pointed meditation, focus and internal grounding. More than twenty years ago, I was part of a group that focused on devotional chanting. Every day at the ashram there were hours of continuous chanting. Some of my deepest meditations came following those chanting sessions but I've fallen away from that extended chanting practice.

Here, I'm reluctant to speak at all. I watch myself saying the mantra to myself in a whisper rather than vocalizing it as I would with a group. It's a curiosity. What chanting I do each day is done very softly. It seems that I love this great silence and don't want to break into it in any way. Speaking and singing, bringing that voice up, takes such energy and effort; something we don't really notice until we take a vow not to speak. So many people told me that they'd find being silent a most difficult part of a solitary retreat, that they would surely be talking out loud to themselves. I remember my son saying to others, "Can you imagine Mom not talking?" and yet here I am—with no words, and delightfully happy in it. Silence. How delicious! So, I write my mantra on stones and whisper it softly 108 times each morning on my cushion to start the day.

December 22, 201

A quiet morning with wonderful sun creeping over the ridges. Yesterday I awoke again to rain, had all my buckets filled with three hours of constant downpour. I was happy for the sound and the bounty. Rain is a comforting old friend now, despite the small hardships when it's continuous. But today I have the sweet, cool smell of a clear morning.

Yesterday was summer solstice here and I planned to get up to the stupa early to do a Refuge Tree practice as I've done on other solstices and equinoxes. The rain delayed me, so it was 11 AM before I tramped up the wet road. I heard joyous voices chattering above me, and just before I hit the junction of Slipglade with the Dharma Road, I heard the rumble of an approaching ORV ferrying white-bearded Steve and two little four-year olds singing at the top of their lungs en route to the stupa as well. I stopped and turned back, realizing there must be a retreat going on and that it was Sunday, a busy day for visitors in the bush.

We've stepped into the school summer holidays, and the next six weeks will be the busiest time here. Just when I was so enjoying the sweet silence and quiet! But as retreat life is arranged at Sudarshanaloka, even the school holidays should not interfere with my quiet very much.

Later in the day, I trekked along Slipglade with my boots and shovel, doing roadwork after the big rains, draining the water that collects in the muddy tire ruts four to six inches deep. The digging of the pigs over the past month has helped me create culverts for run-off, and it was lovely to arrive on the track and hear the tinkling of a small running stream draining the water that comes off Chetul Hill.

I worked along the road to the end, and so wanted to see the stupa on this day that I just left my shovel and gloves, and climbed up the road in my gumboots. Of course, in the next half hour I encountered more people than I've seen in months. As I passed them on the path, they looked into my eyes with such expectancy, with such warm, friendly, kind smiles, hoping, I think, that I might speak—but I cannot. Putting my hands together in a *gassho* greeting is the best I can do. I slipped past and was gone. I wanted only to return to my hut to watch the clouds and moving trees. I've been alone and silent so long I can't manage even a hello. A part of my old self pulls me to greet them, to ask about their story, how they're doing, to chat as I would have so much enjoyed before. But now, the best I can be is alone.

Through the early evening and night, my back began to ache tremendously. Whether it is emotional or physical, I don't know. It seems that the pain has a physical base, yet I've spent more than a day in deep self-reflection, picking apart behavior and past history and going quite deep, so it could be emotional pain as well as the fall. I'm just with it, feeling it, moving very slowly, learning acceptance, not being too disap-

192

pointed that it may interfere with my meditation today. This, too, is a teaching I must realize and remember. I keep learning.

But I decided today that it was back to the tub for some more soaking if I could lift those full buckets to fill it with this bad back since the faucet has again stopped working from the hillside spring. I did much better than I expected. There's still the pain, but I can sit. Contentment. A fine day—the longest day of the year in the Southern Hemisphere.

December 23, 2014

As the fiery sun dipped over the horizon at nine last night, taking us into darkness, the possum paid a noisy visit. These days she just makes a ten-minute call to be sure all is in place and I'm keeping up the neighborhood, and then is off to more interesting pursuits. It's nice to have someone keeping a regular eye on me, even if she must drag that noisy bush tail behind her.

Last night the sky carried brilliant stars, though no moon. This is the dark time, but that bright, starry night was a joy. With all the overcast skies, I've not seen stars clearly for more than three weeks. It's wonderful to be alive and awake to nature. I reflect about why I'm not open to it more at home, too busy with house and car. It certainly beats the internet and Facebook for nourishment and quiet stimulation.

Life was quiet at six this morning with only the light growl of water over rocks down below in the ravine—the constant and enduring heartbeat of the valley. I was on the porch. listening—watching the day begin. I felt part of it at last, integrated and entwined. I saw the sun break on the ridges at 6:10 (5:10 standard time) and remembered back six months ago, when that happened at 8 AM. The days are long now and dawn comes early.

The sweet little silvereyes were out first, so shy, and with no bird cry, just busy about their work. They cover each of their favorite branches and fern fronds, rolling up and over, hanging upside down looking for insects. When a new spider or caterpillar tent attracts their interest, they're off after it. Their olive-green bodies and white bellies now sport soft russet side feathers that I haven't seen before. Meanwhile, the russet chests of the chaffinches have paled, now that breeding time has finished. My chaffinch couple make a showing but pass on, far less demanding than before, now they know that seed is out, and they can come by later. Well-trained, I am. A few male chirps will bring fresh birdseed to the porch.

The daisies are in full bloom—a profusion of twenty or thirty in three different parts of the front and back garden even as the flax blossoms have gone to deep green, dangling seedpods. The paths through the bush are scattered with small flowers from the manuka as their season ends and another begins. I can still see many dusty white trees across the valley where this invasive tree has filled in along with tree ferns on land burnt off fifty to seventy-five years ago for farmland.

I am here. I'm part of the silence. My heart is open, my ears are watching, and my eyes are hearing.

December 24, 2014

Solitude tames my energies to investigate, to answer, to complete. In recent years, our technology and communication have grown to the point that we move quickly, expecting to find answers fast, complete tasks and go on to the next thing. Here, I must sit with what I don't know and hope for answers. Expectation and disappointment loom very large. In my other life, disappointment was a small thing. They say that in solitude all things are intensified and emotions magnified. I'm learning to sit with disappointment, with not getting answers, with not receiving parcels, learning to master my patience skills. I look and see how little it all matters and laugh at what seemed so utterly important the day before. I've lived a life of accomplishment, of finishing tasks and going on to the next one. This inaction and inability is new to me. It feels like a breaking down, like a step backwards, or towards death.

But it also feels like yet another page has turned, another decade has begun—one of deeper reflection and inner wisdom. How surprising that this new decade should come with an unmarked birthday during this year away, alone. With age in the room, not at the doorstep any longer, I have less of the energy that's fired my life and gotten me around the world five times alone. Less energy, maybe, but time to look more finely and reflect more deeply.

This writing keeps me from artwork and I'm not sure it's as satisfying as moving color and pattern across a page. Paintings have sat half-finished here for a month, and now the trees have changed color and the impetus is gone. Some of it is the weather. With a constant blowing mist, it's too wet to paint outside. Some of it is this writing, which distracts me from focusing on art. Each day, with meditation, cooking, cleaning and study, there are just a few extra hours available. My energies have gone into putting down these words rather than putting color on paper or threads on silk. But it's another creative expression, an exploration that maybe needs digging into.

May Sarton speaks of this in her *Journal of Solitude*: "I have written every poem, every novel, for the same purpose—to find out what I think, to know where I stand . . . to become what I see."[96]

I've been reflecting on why I'm writing this journal, what the purpose might be. Is it a gift for others and a way of carrying them with me, sharing what I see in a year alone? Is that too much to expect? Many who have undertaken long retreats have *not* written because they felt it the distraction that it is. I can see my mind wrapped around painting and color, or around finding words to write. It could be dwelling in open spaciousness or the transcendence of a deep meditation. It can't be all places.

But on this quiet, overcast day with the wind just picking up, I'm happy to look at why I do write. Is it truly for others? Annie Dillard says with force: "The impulse to keep to yourself what you have learned is not only shameful, it is destructive. Anytime you do not give freely and abundantly becomes lost to you. You open your safe and find ashes."[97]

Yet Bob Kull questions journaling on solitary on his retreat and says that ". . . writing tended to pull me out of the present moment and mute the intensity of the experience." He found himself distracted by mentally composing what he would write. Yet like Sarton, I've found that writing has actually helped clarify what I'm seeing if I do it slowly, mindfully, and with reflection. Kull goes on to say that when he wrote, ". . . I wasn't really in solitude but in an imaginary future when someone else would be reading my descriptions. During those times I remained embedded in language and my social identity rather than free to experience my inner identity as part of the universe." Later, he does agree that putting experience into words has benefits and that it did encourage him to look more closely and reflect more deeply. And "the journal now allows and invites me back into the days and months of solitude."[98]

I'm curious about this 'social identity' that Kull speaks of, and wonder if I carry this too in my writing. I've been keeping a daily journal for almost 20 years now: musing, recording events, examining, fingering wrongs, working out feelings and noting small insights and thoughts. It's been a personal journal, never meant to be shared. So I have a history of daily journaling that has little to do with social identity. I write to record experience and insights. This journaling I'm doing here is somehow a substitute for a chat with a friend, as well as a working out of thoughts and observations. Little self there, I feel.

Philip Koch has some wonderful words for the wise from his experience of writing in solitude and speaks of a desire to tell the "secret truths," those things that solitude has revealed to him. He speaks of how "truth wants to be told" but how it needs to be received by those who can understand, respect and even revere these insights. If those conditions cannot be met, there is reason to keep the "solitary visions secret".

He continues with:

> observations are recorded in a journal with a sense of the importance of the recording... Thoreau's journals, Anne Frank's diary ... What is that importance? Is it not the feeling that truth, as truth should be recognized, recognized by all knowers? ... the cognitive side of reflective perspective in solitude, reflects outward towards other people. When that reflection is caught in another eye, a kind of completion of this gift of solitude occurs.[99]

What a beautiful, generous way of explaining how this Bodhisattva Path of caring for all beings manifests in a solitary retreat, alone and silent except for a pen—his gift of solitude shared with others.

I write with the hope of sharing this meager effort further. The deep gratitude I feel for those writers that made an effort to share their solitary experience spurs me on. Yes, as Annie Dillard says, to NOT do this could speak of selfishness. For someone to hold this precious thing close to their chest and not share could be due to a fear of defiling the experience, I expect. But again and again, I bless those who've written of solitude and helped to open the door for me.

And with my fellow solitaries, Kull and Koch, I have come to realize that this journal is a record, a teaching tool for my future life, a way of remembering and connecting once more. As Kull says, "Like Hansel and Gretel, I'm leaving a trail of crumbs to lead me home again."[100]

And so we come to Christmas Eve.

December 27, 201

I'm coming out of some hard days of back pain that had me crawling along, feeling slow, waking up to a body that I usually depend on without a second thought. Every difficulty, even a noisy fly during meditation yesterday, was ground for anger, irritation and annoyance. But I also look at this with positive eyes and see it as a chance to practice, to be more aware and awake. Hot water bottles, three soaks in an Epsom hot bath, and a tennis ball placed under pressure points have all helped to release some of that pain. Ahh, dealing with the idiosyncrasies of the body.

I did have a wonderful Aunt Betty's Chocolate Pudding, a Christmas cake that arrived in my Wednesday food drop. It's a great holiday indulgence. I've been rationing my sugar and chocolate intake since my concussion, knowing they can contribute to those nasty headaches but here I am. Back better—head not.

I remember Stephen Batchelor, a former Zen monk, encountered problems when he did his three months in, three months out retreat for three years. He speaks of confronting personal demons and says that being alone was of enormous value with this. Coming up against ourselves, we have to respond to our reality using the tools we've been given.[101] This is one of the reasons I'm here, and yes, it has been enormously helpful.

This morning I have great remorse for my behavior as a teenager, and my lack of care for one relationship in particular. I wonder if my friend perceived it as I see it now, if I truly discounted and withdrew from daily contact with her to be with other, more interesting friends, if I lacked concern for her feelings? Looking back so many years, she's one of those for whom I still carry great love and compassion, and now she's gone. Is this a demon from the past? Disrespectful behavior concerning a friend?

Yesterday I was looking again at the achievement demon that has driven me for so many years. He's quieter now, but something in May Sarton's *Journal of a Solitude* brought him up once more. To be so driven, so achievement and accomplishment-oriented, overwhelms . . . but there's a good side too. Society does recognize the self-motivated, the self-starter, and even the self-actualized. These characteristics often spell success in this world. I seem to have been born with motivation, though I received little encouragement or modeling to succeed. A kind but bewildered family was there behind me, wondering who this strange duckling was.

May Sarton speaks of how important achievement was to her—and of her neurosis about work, inherited from an academic father.[102] The expectation to produce something, to account for her time, was always there, the feeling that a day was wasted if she did not get to poetry. I've been reflecting more on how and why I've felt so pushed to produce— whether there was any external pressure, or if it was entirely an internal drummer that's had me marching so hard these many years.

It has taken me years to come to this realization of myself, as this solitary shows me. And it takes time alone, unobserved, without the feeling that I'm being evaluated in some way, to know this. So much benefit comes with relaxing into "being" and not always "doing." Time alone, unstructured, gives me some precious breathing space to investigate such lifetime habits—whether they be demons or not.

I relish a banana pancake breakfast on the porch, a break from all this internal work. As I meditated just an hour ago, I heard the chime-like tones of the dawn-dusk bell bird, but the give-away chirps at the end identified it as a tui, that great mimicker of birdcalls. Tui are almost four times the size of the bell bird (120 grams versus 28) and are far more in evidence here. Both songbirds have a whirring flight due to a notch in their outer wing, but I've yet to see a bell bird. I only know her from her call and that wing sound.

I saw two tui going through an extraordinary raucous courting dance, followed by some small chaffinches chasing along behind each other with some serious stuff on their minds other than food. I'm delighted the finches have had less interest in my wild bird seed these past two weeks and expect it's the proliferation of flies, gnats, mosquitoes, spiders and ants now that warmer weather has arrived. I've also been pleasantly surprised by a very busy, fast-moving bird couple who swoop under my porch roof about 5 PM each day, diving back and forth. Twice, one has hesitated in mid-flight to look into my hut, but I wasn't quick enough to see what they were. They do have forked tails like swallows and move like them, flitting quickly like a bat, but they seem bigger. I didn't glimpse a russet face or a blue cap either. I hope one will scoop into the hut in the next week or so and I can get a better look.

Even though the bird population has become more varied in the past six months, I'm still surprised by the lack of numbers compared to the northeast USA. Is this a decimated bird population because of egg-eating predators or possum control? I'm reminded of the artificial piped-in birdcalls along Shijo-dori Street in downtown Kyoto, meant to give shoppers a sense of well-being now that the bird population is gone.

Besides the farmers' harmful use of pesticides in this modern, high-production world, New Zealand is one of the few countries that still using a controversial aerial drop "1080 poison" to control the possum population. While Prudence the Possum and her buddies do enormous damage to flora and fauna, stunting trees by munching on new shoots, eating native birds' eggs and killing baby chicks (which, thank goodness, I haven't seen), the poison kills not only possums, but native birds as well. I've been told this is going on just over Ridge Road in the National Conservation Wilderness in the hope that the native bird population will come back in greater numbers once the possum numbers are down. Here we have life in the modern bush, with external rather than internal demons.

December 29, 2014

Today brings clouds but also patches of sun. The temperature has gone up to the mid 20sºC (mid 70ºF) every day for three days. Hooray!

I'm waking up to things I've become innately aware of. The hoots of the ruru owl and the descending tones of the bell bird have finished for the morning, and now, at 9 AM, we have a quiet lull—the space between dawn and mid-morning when other songbirds take over. It's a strangely quiet time in the bush. Even the bees and flies wait for the sun to warm up the air before starting their buzz-work.

Openings, awakening, insights. A number of them rushed in this morning and I hope they're strong enough for me to retain and grow from them. I came across an interesting quote in my Order newsletter two days ago: "With dependence on our practice, insights will arise again and again. On a good day, one can have three insights before breakfast!" Some of my insights have to do with mind and consciousness, their workings, and what I'm experiencing. And some are just—mundane.

I've had a clear sense of "happenings" in my life over the past five years, but the mundane wants to be mentioned first: something has been evolving on this land since the summer solstice arrived in rainy gales. It reminds me of a scene from *Mary Poppins* when the weathervane twirls on the top of the London house, and they say that a new wind is coming in and life will be different.

I felt it when I climbed to the stupa a week ago. The breeze was kinder and softer, and the energy on the land is one of expectancy and harmony. Perhaps it was those happy four-year olds in the back of the ORV, riding up the steep Dharma Road with Steve, singing their hearts out. Or another time when alone on the stupa hill, grass recently mowed and raked, the sun bright but not blinding, I felt that cool, gentle breeze, and a palpable difference. It seemed that the land had come into its own. The struggles and fear had gone out of the bush and sweet Dhardo Rinpoche's compassion and love had settled back down on a harmonious ridge. Even this morning, stepping out onto the deck, the air welcomed and enfolded me. Something has truly changed here, and I celebrate it.

And another realization. Today I woke up feeling some things about myself, and noticing that there are some things I do well, many things I have just average intelligence about, and some things that I just miss on,

200

ending up with apologies and remorse. And here I must apologize to the trees.

Between my after-breakfast meditation and my before-lunch one, I took my cup of tea out to the bush to sit and watch. I chose a large grove below the Slipglade Track where the rain run-off disappears in dense growth. There are nine forty-foot nikau palms—almost a grove, some noble young kauri, and three long-limbed puriri trees spreading their arms thirty to forty feet on each side of their massive trunks and supporting lots of vegetation. I sat, watched, and listened, and came to the insight that it was completely inappropriate to climb trees as an adult. Perhaps young children with little realization might do this, but these noble mothers have been here, in some cases, longer than my years, and are due the awareness and respect of matriarchs with quiet wisdom. Some notes left in the Hut Notebook to help retreatants with acclimation, allude to this, saying "The more mature trees respond to darshan (just looking) or to touch if you are patient and sensitive. They can be a great source of joy and inspiration." I'm not sure who prepared these *Notes for Newcomers to the NZ Bush*, but it was someone local, someone more awake than I. If I find a tree mother who'd welcome me, I'd love to rest in her loving arms. But if not, I'm firmly on the ground, respecting their grandeur.

This insight shows me the strides in sensitivity I've made since stepping off an international flight six months ago. I'm truly waking up, becoming more aware of the preciousness of my surroundings, and seeing all I have to learn from this bush. It's humbling.

I remembered another solitary person who was brought to his knees with the shame and humility I'm experiencing today. Admiral Byrd, after hiding much and revealing it only in the written word, admitted the mistake he'd made in going off alone to the Advance Base for an Antarctic winter alone. Even when ill health hit and he was close to death, he wouldn't admit his (arrogant?) mistake to Base Camp in their twice-weekly calls. Only their perception that something was radically wrong saved his life. It seems he'd rather die than say he needed help. Byrd writes:

the self-preservation instinct of leadership and a sense of shame over my flimsiness drove me to wall-off the immediate past [even when rescued]. I wanted no one to be able to look over the wall . . . something deep inside me demanded that I close my mind to the notion that I had been rescued.[103]

He calls it Pride, in the next paragraph.

One of the tremendous benefits of a long solitary retreat is the chance to pull out these failings or humiliations slowly—even the ones we've forgotten about—and look at them when grounding and safety allows. Without that solidness, confidence, and integration, the response is limited.

As Bob Kull found on his year alone, you either "embrace it, avoid it or—go mad."[104] I've seen all these alternatives here, even in my short six months.

And now, strawberries have arrived and some books I've been hoping for. Those weeks of waiting, being patient, and trying not to manifest disappointment, start to resolve. Word came through the grapevine that one long-awaited book ordered in October and mailed November 6th has been lost. A trace is on it in Thames, and I might see it this week. There's also a letter explaining the troubles of a close friend, and why I've had no response to my October letter to her. When folks don't share travails with me, thinking they're shielding me, they don't realize that I'm picking up on their troubles anyway. The ether is thin, my connections strong, and I sense when something isn't right. It's been good practice to learn to set these emotions and premonitions aside, and focus on what is in front of me. But there's also a sense of release in learning what's behind the feeling and being able to follow through with action, if appropriate. I send loving-kindness. I send thoughts of healing.

There are drawbacks to having strong intuition and just knowing, without obvious evidence. This has been with me from childhood, a source of survival in some cases. It's been encouraged and developed further in thirty years of meditation—an aptitude.

December 30, 2014

I wake in the night to a silvery half-moon behind clouds at midnight. After twenty minutes, it floats free in all its shiny glory. Perhaps, this summer season will bring clearer skies.

Today gunshots went on for twenty minutes or more while I was doing an early evening sit. In such a quiet land, they were disturbing and seemed out of place.

As I come into a new year—always a time of reflection for me—I've been looking at the five years since I was ordained. While I loved being in the mountains of Spain for my ordination with seventeen women from five countries, sleeping outside for eleven of the twelve weeks, some disturbing things came up at that time that are only now moving to resolution. While some experiences were high and transformational, I also had some ego-shattering experiences, and often felt quite alone, thrown back on my own resources. Along with deep sadness and personal reassessment, I had the great joy of meeting my lovely yidam, Kuan Yin, who slipped into my tent window one morning at 3 AM in the form of moonlight. I remember it well. She's been with me since, guiding me on this Bodhisattva path, modeling compassion and care for others, a true teacher and protector.

In my practice over the next few years, I yearned to work with dhyana absorptions, and in 2011 was able to do a retreat with Leigh Brassington that was most helpful and encouraging. Then, before I could get very far, I had that tumble down the back stairs with the ladder in hand—I've been working my way back to normalcy since. Now I see that it has been a transformational five years. I've grown and learned so much and continue learning.

"Oh, the sweetness of being able to realize I am my experience. I am this breathing. I am this moment and it is changing continually, continually arising in the fountain of life."[105]

December 31, 2014

It's 23ºC (72ºF) at 10:30 in the morning, another warm summer day at last. I'm so glad for this change in the weather. I'd grown tired of wearing the same long-sleeved layers for five months. At last, some new blue things to put on.

The wind has picked up today. Since I have no weather report to rely on, I try to be sensitive to weather patterns and wonder if this means rain will figure in the next few days. Yesterday, I watched layers of clouds—the high, stationary ones, and the ones closer to me that skimmed across the sky. Both were the cumulus type I remember studying as a ten-year-old Girl Scout.

Today is the last day of the year. It's been a significant year of healing and openings for me. I began it in San Miguel de Allende, Mexico, with the fine Meditation Center folks, doing Paramita study with a Dharma friend, giving talks and workshops, supporting the new Center in nearby Queretaro, and connecting with new Dharma friends. Between late March and early June, I did three art workshops in Georgia, Michigan and Montreal, Canada; a very condensed teaching schedule for me, but I needed the money. I took the month of June to organize, clean, pay bills and make arrangements for being gone for the coming year. In early July, I was off for the other side of the world. 2014 started as a year of travel, a year of dealing with concussion headaches and nausea, a year of connecting with treasured old friends and meeting new ones, a year of doors opening and deepening practice.

And now, in sunny Tararu Valley, I take my mid-morning cup of tea out to a glade in the bush to sit and reflect on all of this among my tall, leafy mothers. Communing with nature. Why do I have to go 10,000 miles to another hemisphere to receive all that the woods have to offer? Setting aside the time; making it a high priority. It certainly lifts my spirits, even if rain comes.

I sit with "heavy duties" today: watching red wasps circling, observing a very large spider amble over leaf litter, listening to the flutter of those tui wings I know so well, watching the sun and shadow patterns on the tree trunks and letting go of me—entering and participating in forest life. I think of other times when I take myself out, follow an ink line, feel the emotion of color—and that's when I'm doing art. We can call it "blissing out," and put it down, or "dropping self" and elevating it, but it's real. It's what feeds artists. It's why we pursue our work even when it's not economically intelligent to do so. We do it because it's a "calling," because we **have** to, because we've found the sweet, dhyanic, absorption-like bliss that losing self produces. It's similar to losing self out in the woods or in meditation for the serious, receptive practitioner.

Five years ago, on retreat, I responded to the question of why I disappeared into the scrub vegetation and up the buttes to draw. What did I get from this? Others suggest that it is pursuing fame, glory, being special, unusual, someone with talent. No, no! I thought. No 'me'.

> They ask—why do you draw?
> Why do you paint?
> My answer: to lose myself.
>
> To slide into the land
> And lose my busy mind
> To drop my sadness, my suffering—
>
> To fly and soar with the wind——
> Climb tall pines
> Follow a line up ledges.
> Cling to precipices I cannot climb
> Except with this freedom.
>
> To live on the high peaks
> Swoop with the vultures
> Open my beak and caw,
> At the beauty
> Of sunlight on rock, on pine.
>
> To lose myself;
> To turn empty, boundless;
> So that wind blows through
> The space where I once sat.
>
> — Kiranada, 2009

Reading this again five years later, on the cusp of a new year, I'm reminded of Li Po, a poet who does it even better:

> The birds have vanished into the sky
> And now, the last cloud drains away.
> We sit together, the mountain and me
> Until only the mountain remains.

"Twelve Moons," indigo-dyed silk hanging depicting the twelve months at Abhaya hut including the full and new moons; stenciled, quilted and embroidered.

206

Chapter 7   January

"May all beings be well." This is what I said on my rainy porch at midnight as I listened to the haunting call of the ruru owl far down the valley. In the distance, I could hear the rumble of fireworks explosions, but I just sat on my cushion of rain.

I had hoped to walk up to the stupa before midnight to welcome the New Year under a bright, waxing moon and to be meditating as the clock hit twelve. Most years I'm on my cushion some place in the world. Two years ago, I was at a hotel near Kansai Airport in Japan for the night, en route to Indonesia; three years ago, I was on a porch in Maui. This year though, I woke close to midnight and realized that a walk to the stupa in blowing rain with no moonlight was ill-advised. I'll try a night walk before I leave, but I need moonlight as well as my head torch to safely navigate the aptly named Slipglade Track. Once the rain cleared, I did walk to the stupa and spent two hours there meditating and doing a Bodhicitta Puja for the welfare of all beings. I am always moved by this puja and especially by these verses:

> For the whole procession of humanity,
> Traveling the roads of existence,
> In search of Happiness,
> This will give them joy…
> I invite the world to be my guest,
> At a great feast of delight
> For those in poverty,
> May I be wealth.
> For those in pain,
> May I be balm,
> May I be a light, for those who are lost.
> May I be a harbor,
> For those who need shelter.[106]

My years in Japan have honed me to note all the New Year "firsts:" the first dream, first thought, first words, first sound, first view, first letter, and first poem. I was happy to find my first thought was wishing all beings well, safe from hunger, suffering and ignorance; and my first sound was that of the lovely owl. I wrote no first poem this morning, but recorded a short haiku I wrote last September.

> My cup of gratitude
> Is so full
> It spills.
> — Kiranada 9/2014

And then I wrote out a favorite Li Bai poem that sounds very close to my present experience:

Sitting Alone on Jingting Mountain

> Flocks of birds
> Fly up and vanish.
> Single clouds
> Roll on, at leisure, but alone.
> While two of us here
> We will never be bored—
> Myself and the mountain.
> — Li Bo (701-762)

Alone, happy, content, I'm moving into the seventh month of this retreat with delight.

January 2, 2015

Ah, what a wonderfully bright moonlit night we had last night, the one I'd hoped for on the 31st. So, I learn again and again that with hopes we have disappointment and then suffering. If we are just present, we can dwell in quiet serenity. As soon as moon shadows appeared on the ground, a possum slid down my roof in a great racket, landing square in my water bucket. That did it. He was gone in a flash, soaking wet.

Small insights continue to bubble up. Yesterday I began reflecting on speech ethics, coarse language and why we use it. A sentence in Kull's book, which I'm enjoying re-reading, says something like: "... at last, I saw the ducks f**king." Why not mating, I asked myself. Was this written for shock value? In Buddhism, we have speech precepts that train us to relinquish such language. The precepts are a working ground, not commandments though. We start with training in truthful speech, and later, if we choose ordination, we follow additional speech precepts, working to make our speech kind, helpful and harmonious, and also to know the appropriate and kind time and place to share truthful speech. We train to abstain from harsh, useless and slanderous speech as well as false speech. Nothing there about profanity, yet it is not usually part of the Buddhist life.

One forty-year old told me recently that using the f-word was tribal, connecting a generation. Yet I know it brings on negative emotions. In all the instances I could think of, the use of profanity, even as an adjective, for example, "f**king possums" or "bloody weather," seems to show misdirected anger, suffering and frustration. Sometimes I look at the speakers and see a lot of unresolved hostility coming out in language, as if they're carrying big sticks. I wonder if they are building up self-esteem by using coarse language. I feel that it does do harm on very subtle levels, both to the hearer and the speaker. So, I ask myself, is coarse language a marker of anger with the world, used to abuse self and others? Perhaps. In many cases we grow out of this, but not in all instances. How would our language be different if we dealt with where our anger comes from and addressed some of those negative mental states that tie us to such suffering, rather than letting them spew out all over the dinner table in coarse language?

Many young parents make a conscious decision to clean up their language when the children arrive. My father did, and I know my husband and I did. I remember an amusing incident when my son was just over a year old. As with many children learning to talk, he had pronunciation issues for a few years—especially with "s." Sesame Street became Tetame Tweet, and since his name was Sean, shhhh, our dog Sasha became Shasha. This dog was in obedience training, and I was using hand and verbal signals to teach her to sit, stay and lie down. The toddler watched and listened. I remember so well my beautiful fourteen-month old son standing up in his high chair, and with appropriate hand signals telling Sasha to 'sit,' "sit," "sit." However, his "s" came out as "sh." My visiting mother-in-law was shocked to her core. She looked at me with eyebrows raised, questioning whether I had truly cleaned up my language, since Sean had picked this up someplace. I calmly turned to him and said: "That's right, Sean," "sit, sit,'" with good, clear pronunciation. His anger and coarse language did not appear for many more years and his pronunciation cleared up by the time he started school.

Whoops! Going back to the source of the duck quotation, I see what was actually written: "I saw the butter-bellies [ducks] screw today" (p. 192 Kull)—not f**k as I surmised. How could I have misread that? It still sounds rough to my ears. However, I'm told that the author took out most of the profanities that were in his original manuscript. He would agree that yes, words have power. Further clean-up possible.

I'm also looking at insights connected with self-cherishing. I'm brought back repeatedly to the underlying reason for doing this retreat: to prepare and train myself so that I can be of more benefit to others. It's the ultimate aim of this life in samsara, to wake up and be able to genuinely help others. When someone thanks me for doing this retreat for them (as one friend whispered in my ear before I boarded my flight) or sends a note that says "Thanks for meditating for all of us," or a text message to say "Your bravery and determination are my inspiration," it's a strong reminder. All those hours of walking and sitting meditation, all that time scanning clouds and moving trees for answers, all that work delving into my negative emotions and shortcomings are to help others—not to cherish myself or be self-referential. That wonderful net of interconnectivity that does away with duality and selfishness and creates the open spacious mind is so needed in this work and in this world.

January 4, 2014

It's intriguing to see the changes in perception as this retreat goes on. The ridges that face the hut on the far side of the valley looked to be a wall of green trees—only green—when I arrived. A month later I began to see different shades of green, and now they appear full of color shadings. What I know now as distant manuka-tea trees have lost the lavender hue they carried for a month or more as they blossomed, and now, with petals dropped, new growth makes them appear a dusty rose. The mamaku and ponga tree ferns are a startling chartreuse or yellow green and the native rimu pines have a reddish-green cast that browns out. Some startling red blossoms have appeared high on the crowns of the tall rata trees—bright spiky balls close up, but across the valley they look like a crown of red poinsettia. It's a joy to be able to "'see" more

clearly as I've slowed down, become more mindful, and more perceptive to my surroundings.

I've picked out new sounds as well in the past two months as summer has influenced the birdlife. Some calls may well be newly arrived
birds, but some are refinements—new vocalizations from birds I now
know well. The "cheep-cheep" that always told me a male chaffinch was
on the porch looking for food was transformed this morning into a thir-
teen-syllable call by a young one, high in a nearby tree. With his head
thrown back and an open beak heading for the sky, he repeated a full-
throated "chip, chip, chip, tell, tell, tell, cherry-erry-erry—tissi cheweoo"
for more than five minutes. What a surprise!

I'm spending some time in the sun most days, cutting grass, and enjoying the warmth; the temperature goes up to 26-28ºC, and once to
30ºC/86ºF. I'm still using the three-inch scissors and cutting about a
square meter of grass a day. It's tranquil and rewarding. Where I've
done no clipping at all in past months, the grass is now twelve to fourteen inches tall. The scissors make slow work, and I know that I could
complete all of this in less than ten minutes with my noisy electric
weed-whacker from home, but the quiet communing with the earth and
slow clipping of three or four blades at a time is contemplative. I'm reminded of the monks at the Zen temples in Japan sweeping the gravel
with their long brooms every day, every day.

These observations bring to mind Alexandra David-Neel and her
time in Tibet early in the last century, for we both connect deeply to nature and seasons:

> Then it was spring time in the cloudy Himalayas. Nine hundred feet
> below my cave, rhododendrons blossomed. I climbed barren moun-
> tain tops. Long tramps led me to desolate valleys studded with
> translucent lakes—solitude, solitude! —Mind and senses develop
> their sensibility in this contemplative life made up of continual ob-
> servations and reflections. Does one become a visionary, or rather,
> is it not that one has been blinded until then?[107]

January 5, 2015

Two wonderful moonlit nights. It's the Hay Moon, and aptly named
as the grass grows high during this month. In December, when we were

still in the rains, it was a Strawberry Moon, telling of the coming strawberry crop. I've enjoyed two baskets so far.

Last night, as the fiery red sun set in the west between 8:30 PM and
9 PM, I turned to the east and saw the grand full moon rising—peeking
out between slow-moving clouds. Finally, with the dark, it sat high in
the sky, and later flooded my hermitage with glowing light. Through the
night, I awoke again and again to check if my friend was still there.
There's something enormously comforting for me in the moon's presence. Having it show up month after month is reassuring on retreat.
Even when it's stormy and the sky is filled with clouds, I remember it's
always there.

From my musings yesterday on doing this retreat for others—for
all sentient beings—I concluded that I should indeed polish and clean
this jewel of practice as I would a gift. My mind's eye envisioned a wonderful orb—my "actions". held in my hand, cleaned, buffed and polished
to a glow. It came to me that I could do this by carrying clear, clean intention to every prayer, every recitation, every mantra that I do—as
though I was preparing to hand them to someone as a present. I quietly
watched my recitation of the Refuges and Ten Precepts, and rather than
just singing them out by rote and memory, I stopped after each one, letting the intention and the sound echo in my being. I visualized the one
hundred-eight mantras as an exquisite string of beads, preparing each
mantra as a jewel for others. I polished the loving-kindness prayer,
heard the words, watched my articulate enunciation, and made it as
purposeful and beautiful as it truly is. This whole life here and all that
I'm learning is a jewel to be given away to others, but the start is the
"waking up"—polishing that orb, letting it shine and gleam in my hands
as I offer it up.

Today I'm fasting. It seemed the right thing to do during the first
week of the New Year. I'm reading of Buddha's life (in *Gautama Buddha*
by Vishvapani) and of the homeless, renunciant monks who went into
town every day and, with eyes downcast, received in their begging bowl
whatever was given.

I reflected on my situation, and felt so very greedy and demanding,
to have presented a specific food list each week for six months now. I'd
prefer to just receive what someone might give me and rely on that with

non-attachment, knowing I'd have enough and would make do. And so, this week, I drew an image of a begging bowl on the first page of the Abhaya Shopping Notebook and asked the guys to fill my begging bowl with whatever they were moved to place there. Perhaps this will become a regular practice. But I feel it may put more stress on the staff, and they would perhaps prefer a list to follow without the concern of choosing for me. We shall see. New doorways to step through.

January 6, 2015

A quiet, sunny morning. It's been in the high 20s (75-85ºF) each of these first days of January, and twice the temperature has gone up to 30ºC (86ºF). Summer has finally arrived! Though I had grave doubts about what summer in New Zealand might be like when I still was wearing a hat and gloves for meditation, two weeks ago. While the days get quite warm, once the sun starts its descent, the evenings cool off quickly and the nights are quite cool and pleasant. There seems to be very low humidity right now—unlike the muggy Japanese summer and that in the New Hampshire woods. It really is a fine climate with mild seasons on this North Island.

As my solitude continues, I go deeper into self, seeing my failings and habits. I again remember the comment that the most important experience a solitary retreat provides is an undiluted experience of self. This "facing self" is not easy work. It takes strength, bravery, sincerity and perseverance to really look within at the negatives. Coming from the Islamic tradition, Bayezid Bistami, a 9th c Sufi, says poetically:

> For twelve years at a stretch I was the smith of my own
> being. I laid it on the hearth of asceticism, heated it red-hot
> in the fire of ordeals, set it on the anvil of fear, and pounded it
> with the hammer of admonition. Thus I made it into a mirror
> by acts of piety and devotion.[108]

This image really resonates with me. I can see that. Solitary retreats are one big reflection of all that we need to work on. While hatred (ill-will) and delusion (ignorance) can manifest and trip us up almost daily, it's greed or grasping that catches me most often. I get upset and irritated when things don't go the way I expect them to. I can be grasping and greedy for food and find myself snacking non-stop. Only a day of mindful fasting can put me back on track.

The things I've done that I'm most ashamed of seem to come from grasping and greed, and the antidote is so simple—just letting go into contentment. We can combat greed by focusing on generosity, of course. It's so easy to see the faults of others while our own messes are more opaque, and even at times seem just fine. It takes the mirror of self-reflection and self knowledge—one with the rust removed—held up during the quiet of solitude, to see clearly where work is needed. Facing ourselves, getting an undiluted dose of what needs looking at, and seeing our failings, these are among the benefits of solitary retreat. It's not the ecstatic, joyful part of retreat, or what we want to write home about, but it's real.

January 7, 2015

What a sweet summer day: the temperature up to 30ºC (86ºF) at 3 PM, but comfortable out of the bright sun with that cool breeze. I love it. Though I do keep listening for rain. It's become an intimate friend over these six months and will surely be missed if this summer weather continues.

My experiment of asking the staff to fill my begging bowl from my food allowance was such a joy. To see what they chose for me, including in-season fruits and vegetables—what fun! Along with some wonderful blueberries and strawberries, a dear Order member sent along some much appreciated kukicha tea, and there was a bag full of fresh spinach from the Community House garden. What a treat! My jar of miso has lasted well without refrigeration for more than six months now despite the note saying refrigerate after opening, so I looked up the recipe for "Spinach Bundles with Creamy Miso Sauce" from Mollie Katzen's book *Vegetable Dishes I Can't Live Without* on my Kindle, a dish inspired by Japanese *Ohitashi.* It turned out delicious.

Spinach Bundles with Creamy Miso Sauce

1 pound spinach (fresh)
¼ c. miso
½ c. cider vinegar
2 T. honey
¼ t. minced or crushed garlic
2 T. roasted peanut oil (or almond or sesame)

½ c. mayonnaise
Red pepper flakes, to taste
A few toasted sesame seeds
Dried bonito flakes (optional)

1. Place the spinach in a colander and rinse well. Shake to remove most, but not all, of the water. Place the miso in a medium size bowl. Whisk in the vinegar, honey, garlic, oil and mayonnaise and beat until smooth. Add the red pepper flakes to taste. Set aside.

2. With the water still clinging to the leaves, cook the fresh spinach in any pot over a medium-high heat for about 1 minute or until wilted. Watch carefully. Turn with tongs.

3. Remove from heat and transfer spinach to a colander in a sink. Let cool until comfortable to handle, pressing out any excess liquid with the back of a spoon as it cools.

4. Divide the spinach into 4 sections. Use your hands to squeeze out as much liquid as possible and discard, then press each section into a tight little bundle of any shape.

5. Spoon the sauce onto 4 or 5 small plates, and place a spinach bundle on top or next to each puddle of sauce. Top the spinach with a light sprinkling of sesame seeds. Serve cold or at room temperature.[109]

While practicing letting go of food attachments, I came across a quotation by Sangharakshita that encouraged me to reflect more on grasping and attachment. Besides having contentment as a traditional antidote for grasping, I think patience or *kshanti* (Sanskrit) is key to working with this.

It is difficult to translate *kshanti* by one English word because it means a number of things. It means patience: patience with people, patience when things don't go your way. It means tolerance: allowing others to have their own thoughts, their own ideas, their own beliefs, and even their own prejudices. It means love and kindness. And it also means openness, willingness to take things in—and, especially—it means receptivity to higher spiritual truths.[110]

To wait, to watch, to receive.

January 8, 2015

I had real trouble getting to sleep last night (too much salt yesterday, I bet). The unusual occurrence of planes flying over at 10:45 PM and 12:15 AM also had my mind elsewhere rather than with sleep. When I did drop off, the possums decided to pay their weekly visit and seemed to be reconstructing something on my metal roof. I thought that with this bright moonlight I might be able to get some good photos of them to share, especially when they slipped down onto the deck, but I couldn't get myself out of bed. So it was a late morning start today. But I'm being kind to myself and taking each meditation slowly.

I'm feeling down today, which is somewhat unusual for me. With multiple sneezes and three tissues full this morning in ten minutes, I wonder if it's a cold starting or more allergies kicking in. My eyes feel like I've been crying all night, though I haven't.

The other possible reason for the dumps I'm in today could be a reaction to looking at my faults and failures in the past few days and taking them in deeply. I know that they should be looked at without judgment and without beating myself up too much or losing all self-esteem. I re-read a chapter on "Practicing the Good Heart" in Tenzin Palmo's *Into the Heart of Life* that highlighted some important things to remember when doing this hard work. She speaks about happiness and unhappiness depending on the mind.

Consider that one companion whom we stay with, continually, day and night, is our mind. Would you really want to travel with someone who endlessly complains and tells you how useless and hopeless you are; someone who reminds you of all the awful things you have done? And yet for many of us, this is how we live ... with a tireless critic—that is our mind. It entirely overlooks our good points and is a very dreary companion. No wonder aggression is so prevalent in the West. We have to befriend and encourage ourselves, remind ourselves of our goodness as well as consider what may need improvement.

This may be my hard work today. I need to send some good metta—loving-kindness—to myself and get back on track.

I have sweet potatoes boiling now, and have a mushroom spinach sauce to put on them. All this comes with clear planning and forethought. The spinach and mushrooms will 'go off' soon and I do my best to never throw out food. Planning. Ah—life in the wilds. I should just eat lentils and dried vegetables every day, cooked in a pressure cooker, like Tenzin Palmo at thirteen thousand feet, but here too is an attachment—to fresh food and variety. I come across a note from last week's food box drop that I saved: "Mince pies from Akampiya and the season's first strawberries from Lisa and me. Enjoy!" ... and I remember the kindness of strangers, and all who are supporting what I am trying to do on this solitary ridge in the bush.

Rain showers are blowing through. Sweet rain. Sweet friends.

January 9, 2015

A misty, quiet morning with clouds clinging to the peaks. I practice "dissolving" by being with each thin cloud as it rises, loses moisture, moves, and dissolves into emptiness. As each cloud vanishes, what is behind it is revealed in more clarity. It reminds me of the last piece of art I was working on before departing for this retreat. It was called "The Clouds of Unknowing." I use my art to explore concepts, reflections, and Dharma, the Buddha's teachings. These sources inform and inspire my work.

This morning I did a forgiveness meditation, something I usually do in late December with my close Buddhist friends. We ask forgiveness for harm we may have done towards others as well as ourselves, and forgive harm we've encountered at the hands of others. It seemed fitting to do it today during this first moon of the year, especially as I try to accept and transform those failings I've been focusing on recently, and the hurt and grievances I came up with in the fall/spring. This meditation speaks of how we all long to be safe, and the importance of treating others and ourselves with respect. Sometimes we carry layers of fear, cynicism, pain, and old wounds deep within to try to protect ourselves from injury. To dig them out, look at them, and let them go is an important practice. Many religions have a forgiveness practice at the year's end. It can be deeply transformational and purifying, the start of letting go of old wounds, guilt and anger that keep us from growing—letting go of those "Clouds of Unknowing."

January 12, 2015

A dull, overcast day with a lovely light wind, 22ºC (71ºF), but I'm chilly in short sleeves. I just received messages from home that the package of things I asked for in August was mailed late last week. News also arrives telling me that the paper work I have prepared for a visa extension will be filed for me by an Order friend in Auckland. Without it, immigration could pull me out of here in early April. I have my fingers crossed that I've completed all the necessary papers saying what I'm doing here, that I have the funds to support my last three months, that I haven't been working in this country and have an exit ticket. I've had experience with visas from years of living in Japan and know how to read the fine print and give the immigration folks what they need. However, I still feel insecure knowing that all might be canceled, and I could be given two weeks to leave the country,

I'm so aware and appreciative of the web of kind friends and family that have taken on parts of this organization for me. I usually handle these issues myself, so it's a stretch and good learning practice to ask for and receive the help of so many, both in New Zealand and the USA. I received one very kind email almost two years ago from that Order member in Auckland who is helping me now. She'd heard that I was hoping to come to New Zealand for a solitary retreat. The note said she was prepared to help me in any way. Such extraordinary kindness from a stranger. This web of Indra that weaves all sentient beings together across the universe is very real and comforting.

I've had some dealings with the local critters and crawlies the past few days. The possums have taken an interest in the hanging basket of pansies, which has been so showy and bright over the past six months. Pru possum and her guys have been trying to stand on the top of the planter netting and paw with their long claws at the basket that holds the pansies. If it came down, it would make quite a crash.

And then there's the recent infestation of ants—on the toilet seat and in the kitchen—floor and counters. I spent a good hour sweeping up hundreds of little running beasties and ushering them outdoors two nights ago. I've sprinkled salt along my baseboards and cupboard/sink edging, and for the moment, interest in invading Abhaya kitchen has waned. I didn't resort to bug spray since it's poisonous for them and me. I'd prefer to relocate them if possible. I've gotten quite good at catching

218

flies and bees in a small jar and helping them outside when I want a quiet, non-buzzy meditation. At other times, I just leave doors and windows open and let things fly through the hut, enjoying this lovely change of season both inside and out.

While I was preparing lunch, I thought to share two other ways to use miso—one of which was part of today's lunch, *nasu dengaku* (braised eggplant with miso). I've found that eggplant will last more than a week without refrigeration. My one big Greek-style eggplant gives me three servings—added to spaghetti sauce, in eggplant curry with sweet potatoes, apples and raisins, and then as *nasu dengaku*.

I had no idea I'd be sharing recipes when I started this journal, but I do like to cook and eat. I wish Vicki Mackenzie had shared Tenzin Palmo's sourdough bread recipe, cooked on a woodstove at thirteen thousand feet, when she wrote *Cave in the Snow*, so that desire encourages me to include some of my favorite solitary recipes here. I'm living under somewhat extreme conditions, and I'm vegetarian, so perhaps some of the food trouble-shooting I've done here might be of use for others on retreat (or at home).

It only takes a cup or more of boiling water and a heaping teaspoon of miso paste pushed through a tea strainer submerged in the hot water pot to make soup. Sliced green onions (spring onions in Kiwi lingo), some cubes of tofu, and a few slices of shiitake mushrooms make a great Japanese soup. Today, I also made braised eggplant with miso.

Nasu Dengaku

1. Slice a large eggplant diagonally to get four 1½ inch thick slices.
2. Brown the slices in a little oil in a fry pan, placing a bowl on top of the slices to press them down.
3. Turn them after about a minute.
4. Thin 2 T. of miso with a ½ t. of water and a ½ t. of vinegar. Spread this
on top of the braised eggplant, as if you were lightly buttering toast.

Traditionally, in Japan the sliced eggplant is placed under a broiler, turned once for browning, then a healthy layer of miso is spread on top and it's returned to the broiler to braise. My fry pan method is "outback" simple.

January 14, 2015

What a very surprising morning this was. At 11 AM the moon was still up, a lovely waning half to quarter moon very clear in the blue sky. Who says the moon is only for night time? I'm hoping to see it set over the western hills if the fluffy white clouds hold off. How extraordinary to watch it slowly dissolve into emptiness, disappear into the soft blue of day. Moon sitting!

January 16, 2015

I found half a quail egg with a feather inside it on my tramp up to the stupa today. At first I thought someone had raided a nest as hedgehogs are notorious for eating quail eggs, but after looking over the shell I decided it was from a recent hatching. I read that quails lay up to 22 eggs at a time on the ground, so they're easy marks for hedgehogs. Hopefully, this little one is off with his mama in the undergrowth.

I'm doing contemplative stitching between meditation sits and enjoying the focus very much.

January 17, 2015

A small sliver of a witch's moon at dawn.

The tree cutting that my valley neighbors have been doing off and on for the past week is finished. The visitors who had Woof and Yipper yapping for the first time in a month have departed and the cattle are quiet, the chickens at rest. This is the morning time when even the birds are busy with things other than vocalization—a quiet, expectant time, full of anticipation and good for meditation. I'm feeling more alone this month than in the previous six. It's okay—but today I would enjoy a chat and a friendly face. Instead I get birds, spiders, and itchy bites in the night.

It has been a week of looking more and more at Bodhicitta (enlightened mind) and the altruistic dimension of my practice. Bodhicitta practice means:

> to bring our awareness to the ground of being that we share
> with all living beings;
> to experience more deeply the suffering that we
> share with all beings;
> to bring heartfelt energy to a deep wish for all being to be free
> from suffering

Two hundred and fifty years ago, Ryōkan, the Zen poet of Japan, wrote of this very thing in poetry that I was reading this morning:

> O, that my priest's robe was wide enough
> To gather up all suffering people
> In this floating world.[111]

And another short Ryōkan poem:

> When I think about the sadness of the
> People in this world,
> Their sadness becomes mine.[112]

Taking on the sadness and suffering of others is the focus of tonglen, a Tibetan Buddhist practice, and is something that drew me long before I found a name for it in Buddhism.

Today others are with me, and I feel their unbearable longing to be free from suffering: the Nepalese hill tribes I'm reading of, the sick in local hospitals, the men down at the Community House on retreat this week, and even the cow bellowing in the valley.

To take on this longing to be free, to see our interconnectedness, to reflect and notice its origin, to wash it in moonlight for myself and other sentient beings, to dissolve the imperfections, hindrances and unskillfulness that produces each suffering and transform it into bliss, clarity and purity—this is the practice of Bodhicitta—the way of the Bodhisattva.

Earlier in the week, I was doing this meditation practice and looking at the troubles and suffering prevalent in the lives of so many, my own life included. I kept coming up with the emotion of fear, which seems to lie just below the surface, running through so much of our lives. I looked at fear last September /October but wanted to consider it more deeply. So, the past few days I've carried a notepad with me, writing out all the things we fear, how it controls our lives, dictates our interaction with others, and even infiltrates the politics of our countries. Buddhist teachers say that fear of death—of dying—is at the root of all of it, but my list includes the more immediate fear of the unknown, fear of loss, fear of pain, of danger or being harmed, of our loved ones being harmed, of losing power over our own lives, and of confrontation. The three poisons in Buddhism—greed, hatred and ignorance—all have fear at their base. It shows its face in anger, anxiety, timidity, doubt, jealousy, craving, envy and pride. And that fear for our own safety and that of our loved ones can contort and warp our relationships, our behavior, and our ability to reach out with compassion for others.

Women, especially, live with this fear for safety. The reality of rape and assault is borne out by statistics. In Canada, one in four women are assaulted before they're seventeen years old while 53% of women born with disabilities and 80% of aboriginal women are assaulted or abused.[113] I'm sure it's worse in many other countries. And yet, women are in this world with much to do, with travels to take, with the need to show compassion, care for others, and see all as ourselves with an open heart. Fear is countered by awareness, trust, confidence and *shraddha* (faith). We should be safe and free from fear.

Fear keeps so many people from becoming all that they could be. Some have come from severely abusive childhoods that keep them from developing roots of trust, and they limp through adulthood learning what they can. Some go into the depths of depression and delusion with drugs, alcohol and dependent relationships. All this moves through my mind when I think of fear.

I've been extremely lucky in my life, and attracted some good karma, it seems. I've also developed good "street smarts" and avoided many difficult situations in my travels alone, thanks to the heightened awareness that fear can bring. I remember one incident when I used that helpful awareness.

In the mid-nineties, while visiting New York City from Japan, I found myself in central Manhattan, crossing a wooded area of Central Park en route to my hotel. This "shortcut" would take me over a small knoll and through some light forest. Suddenly, I noticed in my peripheral vision three young lads, each walking towards this same knoll from different directions not sixty feet from me, and each nervously watching me and each other. The closer I got to the point of disappearing over that knoll and out of sight of others in the park, the more aware I became that this could be a set-up, that I might easily be a target for confrontation and theft. Using the "street smarts" that come from being a single female with some urban experience, I stopped, threw my hands in the air, and with a shout of "Whoops!" as if I'd forgotten something, I turned around and walked swiftly back to the more populated street nearby. All three lads also stopped, looked at each other, and seemed to be confused. I've shared that incident with others, especially the young women in my life, my daughter, and nieces. I tell them it's okay to "act the fool," turn around and go the other way, or step back on a foot behind you on a crowded subway if there appears to a threat to your safety or intrusion of your person. You don't have to be positive something is wrong. Fear hasn't kept me from being out in the world, but it has taught me to be awake, to couple compassion for others with the realization that things happen. I'm not weighed down by the unskillful actions of others, but I look to divert them. Life is full of suffering, and side-stepping some of it requires being awake and present to the moment.

January 18, 2015

Rain through the night, the first since New Year's Eve. I imagine this will bring the mosquitoes everyone has spoken of. I'm already battling the increasing number of ants that want desperately to move in. I should be looking upon them as lovely little visitors with whom to share my small hut. My only real worry is if they get into my foodstuffs.

There are two significant birthdays today and tomorrow in Japan. One is that of my beloved, and the other, a poet turning ninety-eight years old. Her photo is on my shrine this week and my thoughts go to her. For this dear friend, struggling with the sufferings of old age, I mentally send one of my favorite poems of Ryōkan:

The rain has stopped, the clouds have drifted away,
And the weather is clear again.

If your heart is pure, all things in your world are pure.
Abandon this fleeting world, abandon yourself,
Then the moon and flowers will guide you along the Way.[114]

January 20, 2015

I've been waking at 4:30-5:30 the past few days and on my medita-tion cushion for dawn. I've had more energy this week and have been up to the stupa three days for meditation. On that walk this morning I encountered three coveys of quail dashing across the road and piping in the bush, probably trying to distract me from nests of hatchlings. Soon, I expect I'll see some little ones. I've also been down to Pine Crossing for a dip in the river. What a joy to have my head under a small waterfall and be cool all over! Tomorrow I'll hike down to the Community House library—the first trip in six weeks—before the afternoon heat hits.

January 21, 2015

What an extraordinary sky, from a brilliant orange pink and gold sunset—deep, deep colors—to a dense, starlit night. It's the dark of the moon so the stars look like full strength light bulbs on a blue-black background.

The season is advancing and pink foxgloves are blooming on their showy stocks next to the road. Through binoculars I spy something yel-low and profuse happening across the valley, too far away to identify.

I've spent time the past three days gathering fallen leaves from the karaka tree in my back garden. The tiny balls of fruit have grown to the size of plump olives now, and with this fruit comes a cascade of yellow, rubbery leaves. It's been like a New England autumn to wade through the leaf clutter, much like home when the maples and oaks drop their leaves in October/November, but here it's summer. After two requests to borrow a rake and no response, I went to improvisation-mode and made a Maori broom from downed manuka scrub bound together with recycled cord. It makes sweeping the leaves into piles possible.

Food is low—there's a delivery later today. I will admit that I spend much of my time hungry with my simple diet of two meals a day and little to snack on. It's hard to produce a list of all the nibbles I usually eat at home, plus it adds to the weekly costs I'm trying to keep down. Food is expensive here so being frugal is good practice. And I'm mindful of cravings. Since my life on retreat is somewhat sedentary and I'm on the cushion so many waking hours, it's good to reduce my calorie intake. I've lost a bit of weight but not a great deal. I'll be happy for some Indian, Chinese and Thai food when I get out, and a big bag of peanuts to snack on. Meanwhile, I become friends with my cravings and know that it's okay to eat simply.

My 4 PM meditation walk along Slipglade Track revealed a small family with a recently hatched baby quail. She was the size of a two-day-old chick, but with a longer neck and fluffy brown markings rather than the fuzzy yellow of baby chickens I know. With all the clicking and tek, tek, teking going on from both sides of the track, I suspected the adults were calling to other babies as well. I hope so. It would be sad to have just one chick survive from a possible twenty-two eggs laid. What fun to cross paths! And then I found a short brown quail feather further down the path to go with the black and iridescent green tui feather I found three days ago. It enlarges my heart to be part of nature and the life of these feathered beings.

A few days ago, I wrote that I was feeling more alone this month than the previous six or seven. Then I came upon four guys washing the stupa for the coming summer retreats. They were part of the Australian/New Zealand Men's Training for Ordination group, I expect. While there was no interaction— I just climbed the hill above the stupa and quietly meditated—it filled my heart to see them working with each other. Some were horsing around, splashing water, and two-stepping to the Vajrasattva mantra. Just to see some human beings filled me with pleasure—no interaction, just seeing. My life is full, but I do notice what is missing and this becomes a treasure.

January 22, 2015

Breakfast outside in the bush after yoga and meditation. It's a chilly 17ºC (63ºF) but I appreciate the weather change and love the fresh air with my cup of kukicha. Gusty winds and fast-moving morning clouds. When I went out to the deck to feed the birds this morning, I found a possum calling card from their visit last night. They don't hang around long, but have decided that the front porch is a good place to take a dump. It's not messy, just provides a morning giggle. Life in the bush.

Most mornings between sits I've been working on recording stitches in the Twelve Moons indigo-dyed hanging that I have been working on since the early part of the month. It has two panels and six rows of lines in blocks of four. When I analyzed what I had done abstractly in wax and dye, I realized that it could easily represent a year calendar for me. I stenciled full moons in white where they might have appeared each month and dark moons fifteen days later. Now I'm quilting and adding color threads to it. I got in lots of angst-ridden red embroidery stitches around the September and October moons, and now I'm adding some white windy storm stitches for November and early December and yellow flower stitches for the turn of the New Year. I sit, stitch and chant for hours, reflecting on my months here.

It's true that I'm setting up all the conditions I've been told will help me to wake up, to become more aware. And then there are Suzuki Roshi's succinct words: "Gaining enlightenment is an accident. Spiritual practice simply makes us accident-prone." Love it! The Soto Zen practice is one of living, working and sitting regularly—without a goal—knowing that wonderful *satori* awakening just comes (like possums in the night) and rattles our cage of consciousness. Aware and awake.

January 23, 2015

Another great day, though with a few mosquitoes biting at breakfast time. I walked up to the stupa to do my second sit as the clouds moved off and was delighted to see my second quail family with babies in two days. This one seems to have six or seven chicks, five days to a week old. They're big enough now that if frightened (which happens easily at this age), they flap and flutter into the undergrowth.

I pulled out my wildflower reference book after my walk down to the Community House library yesterday, and was quite amazed when I made a list of what's blooming at the moment. The ox-eye daisies have been going strong for a month now, but this week scotch thistle, a lovely orange montbretia and Queen Anne's lace (wild carrot) have popped out. In the low grass are purples, oranges and yellows—including purple forget-me-nots, pink centaury blossoms, scarlet pimpernel, white clover, and what is listed as "lotus," which in New Zealand is a small multi-petalled yellow flower on a vine. Some are climbing up my tub frame. The tall yellow flowers I saw across the valley with binoculars could be ragwort, but more likely a heavier tall flower such as evening primrose not yet blooming on this side of the valley. There seem to be a lot more wildflowers than I see in the New England woods.

Since the guys here on retreat bought out all the veggie hotdogs before my helper got into the store on Wednesday, I'm without one of my protein sources this week. Unfortunately, I hadn't added tofu to the list, expecting that the hot dogs would do for three days. I don't care to rely heavily on eggs and cheese for protein (and I can eat just so many nuts), so I reluctantly opened the can of beans left by a retreatant seven months ago. Truth be told, I'm not a bean eater and have never been—even as a child when beans and franks were standard Saturday night fare for my Boston family. I do try to have no preferences since I know they only cause suffering, but beans don't seem to agree with my digestion. I eat them only when necessary and feel as if I'm "taking medicine" for my health. However, I was encouraged to see that one can of beans carried thirty-two grams of protein, so today I made the effort. The one bean recipe I enjoy and seem to tolerate is a Brazilian Black Bean soup with mandarin oranges and a nice curry flavor. Here it is, thanks to Mollie Katzen, delicious with a bit of sour cream to top it off.

Brazilian Black Bean Soup (5 - 6 servings)
1 hour to prepare (not including bean cooking time).

Begin soaking beans at least 4 hours before assembling:

2 c. dry black beans
3 ½ c. water or stock
2 t. salt

A	B
1 c. chopped onion	2 oranges, peeled, sectioned, seeded
3 cloves crushed garlic	½ c. orange juice
1 large chopped carrot	1 T. dry sherry
1 stalk chopped celery	¼ t. black pepper
1 t. ground coriander	½ t. fresh lemon juice
1 ½ t. ground cumin	¼ .t red pepper
(2 T. oil, approximately)	
(optional: 1 c. chopped green pepper)	

1. Rinse the beans. Cover them with water and let them soak several hours. Pour off excess water. Place in sauce pan with 3½ c. water or stock and salt. Bring to boil, cover, simmer 1½ hours over very low heat.
2. Sauté group A, beginning with the onions and garlic. If necessary, add a little water to the vegetables to steam them along. When everything seems as it should be, add sauté to the beans. Let the soup continue to simmer over lowest possible heat.
3. Add group B to the soup. Give it a stir, cover, and sit down for ten minutes. Now, return to the soup refreshed. Look at it and ask yourself if this soup suits you. Is it too thick? Add water. Do you want it thicker? You can puree some or all of it in the blender. You can make it hotter with more red pepper.

Serve topped with sour cream or yogurt.[115]

I'm re-reading (for the third time) Vicki Mackenzie's book on Tenzin Palmo, *Cave in the Snow*, and thinking about her commitment to Buddhism at twenty-one. Her retreat period in the Himalayas came when she was thirty-three to forty-five years old. We're actually just a year and three weeks different in age. When I've heard young ones boast about how they're so glad they found Buddhism at a young age, I've replied, perhaps too quickly, that I had three lifetimes to complete before I got there. In some ways that's very true. And yet I wonder if those multiple lives I lived—years learning art in Japan, raising children, four relationships, being part of the Civil Rights Movement, Women's and Gay Movements—were necessary or a distraction. They certainly added to my education, and my understanding of and empathy for others. Tenzin Palmo just skipped all this and went into a cave. She has been out twenty-five years now, working to establish a nunnery for others and committed to her "vow to attain enlightenment in the female form—no matter how many lifetimes it may take."[116] And I'm right behind her with that commitment, taking notes and picking up her dropped breadcrumbs with deep respect.

Reflections on lives lived . . . and then miraculously, a package of frozen Quorn Mince protein appeared on my porch this evening when one of the helpers realized I'd missed the veggie hotdogs this week. Such thoughtfulness. Bless them.

January 24, 2015

I'm again amazed at the quiet of the mornings here before the birds, bees and flies start and the rest of the ridge wakes up. Woof and Yipper greeted some strangers passing by at the bottom of the ravine about 8 AM today, but other than that, you could hear a pin drop. I'd expected that these school summer holidays (January-mid February) would bring more boisterous visitors, but so far it's been delightfully quiet. The men's retreat ends today and I'll no longer hear their voices on the road in the evening, coming up to the stupa. I'll miss hearing them—they've been joyous.

The possums had a meeting on the grass out front two nights ago that resulted in a pile of cast off fur tufts. At first I thought the remains were from a scuffle though I heard no shrieks or outbursts in the night; after closer examination, I realized the scattered fur was mostly undercoat with no roots pulled out. Somebody with a big itch must have done a lot of scratching. It's the softest down I've ever touched, gray with some brown tips, so very, very soft. These are amazing beasts of the night.

229

It's been interesting to watch my emotions stabilize in the past month or two and serenity grow. Now, I take each day as it comes without a strong variance of emotion. What bothered me so intensely months ago is no longer important. Peeing in a bucket every night, not having piped hot water, washing sheets and clothes by hand, dealing with a limited diet and no refrigerator—a few months ago they were irritants to be surmounted, but all of that is just okay now.

I've also settled into a schedule that varies very little from day to day. While Tenzin Palmo in Lahoul, India, and Zen Master Bon Yeon in the American woods were up in the dark of the night to meditate and do prostration bows for three hours, I feel I don't need that. Perhaps I'm lazier, older, or less intent, but this schedule has worked for me over the past six months and is loose enough not to feel harsh or restrictive:

5:30–7:30 I wake, heat water for tea, start breakfast preparation, wash a bit, have tea and do some yoga.

7:30–9:00 My pre-breakfast sit has grown into a double sit with a ten-minute walking meditation in between.

9:00–10:00 Breakfast outside, then cleanup—sometimes putting in laundry to soak.

10:00–11:00 Third morning sit.

11:00–12:30 Tea in the bush, reflection, mani rock painting, stitching art work, studying notes, writing. Some lunch preparation, finishing laundry, sweeping house, cleaning rugs.

12:30–1:30 Fourth morning sit.

1:30–2:30 Lunch preparation, lunch usually outside, then cleanup.

2:30–3:00 Rest. Sometimes a nap, sometimes just a lie down to rest my back.

3:00–4:00 Afternoon meditation followed by tea.

4:30–5:30 Walking meditation and purification mantras (Vajrasattva).

5:30–7:00 Cloud-watching, reflection, grass clipping with scissors, leaf gathering, baking scones.

7:00 Puja, Refuge Tree and Prostration Practice.

8:00–10:00 Reading. Occasionally, writing and study.

10:00 Bed.

230

This gives me five to six hours of meditation each day, which is less than I've done in the past but seems to fit this long retreat. It feels as if I'm never far from my cushion.

January 25, 2015

A lovely thin moon in the Western sky last night as the sun was setting. I'm still trying to understand its movements. The phases are easy, but the times that it's evident in this southern sky vary tremendously. It still surprises me why sometimes it rises at 9 PM, and at other times at 2 AM. I hope the promised mail from my daughter will carry the 2015 moon chart a friend sends as an annual year-end gift.

I woke this morning from a very angry dream that should not have surprised me, but did. All of this practice may bring changes in my actions, and hopefully temper my speech, but thoughts, and with them, the dream world, will be the last frontier to change. I'll be so pleased when my compassion, caring and serenity show up regularly in dreamland and transform my quick reactions there too. Last night, my long dead uncle was laughing at me angrily stomping my foot about something. And a few nights ago I woke from a deep dream of loss, worrying about the welfare of my daughter, now quite grown and capable. I was happy to be able to sit with last night's dream, contemplate a clearer, kinder reaction to the anger, and transform it into what the Buddha would say: it truly is samsara, full of suffering but only an illusion, a true dream.

January 26, 2015

It's nice to be cool in the mornings when the afternoon temperatures go up to 31ºC (almost 90ºF). I sleep with the windows open, with wonderful fresh air pouring in, even when sometimes I need to pull on a "watch cap" during the night to keep my head warm and avert headaches.

Even while I'm dealing with unpleasant physical things, (no, I haven't mentioned the bugs yet, but I will!) my mind goes to what I've learned from the Dharma. Often, I review the antidotes to the five hindrances (doubt, sloth, restlessness, anger and greed) and they help me to see what I'm dealing with—my habitual reactions—in a clear light.

While I still have some knee-jerk reactions, I'm more receptive to considering a different way of looking. I take the presentation of the antidote or "opposite" as a challenge, an intriguing and creative new way to look at things.

I come to creativity easily and enjoy the opportunity to get out of my own shoes (my stuck position, my frame of reference, my view) and try on another person's shoes. The challenge is like two creativity exercises we did in art school. They really did have us crawl under a desk, or stand on top of one, to push us to change our view physically and see things differently, develop more flexibility and give us a way to grow. Now I use the same concept to start seeing things as they really are.

When I come up with anger, the antidote is "love" or metta—not always an easy reaction when I'm fuming. Along with love and patience, forgiveness and peacefulness are additional antidotes to anger. I also look at just letting go, asking if what I'm angry about is really so important. Pride fits right in there too, and is another of the poisons. It's good for me to come out of that space of self-cherishing and apply antidotes of "other-regarding" and "cherishing others." To forget about self and self-importance, I look to others and our commonality, and wish to help others as much as is appropriate.

Greed and grasping have bases in cravings and attachment. I love it when I find patience as an antidote to grasping. It seems to work to stop "wanting, wanting"—to just step back and be patient. That's a prime one for me, one I need to look at again and again since I'm such a fast mover. Patience, ahhh! And of course, contentment is the opposite, and a good antidote for greed. To be content and happy with this, right here.

Buddha says greed and craving are the primary cause of all human suffering. A big one. Craving is ignorant, self-centered desire. It leads to addiction in many forms. Enlightenment is sometimes called the freedom from craving. Not having what we want, "being parted from what one likes, being unable to keep what one has, being unable to get what one wants,"[117] all are a basis for clinging and craving. Clinging to whatever gives us a feeling of security (money, food, loved ones, status) denies the reality of impermanence, and in the end, results in deep suffering. So to really look at my craving is of paramount importance. Milarepa, the great yogi of mountains and caves who worked so incred-

232

ibly hard to gain enlightenment in one lifetime, spoke eloquently about craving and impermanence:

> The lovely flowers of turquoise blue
> Are destroyed in time by frost—
> This shows the illusory nature of all beings,
> This proves the transient nature of all things.
> Think, then, you will practice Dharma.
> The precious jewel that you cherish,
> Soon will belong to others—
> This shows the illusory nature of all being,
> This proves the transient nature of all things.
> Think, then, you will practice Dharma.
> A precious son is born.
> Soon he is lost and gone—
> This shows the illusory nature of all being,
> This proves the transient nature of all things.
> Think, then, you will practice Dharma.[118]

And then there's the deep samsaric suffering of dealing with bugs in places I feel they should not be. Birds too suffer from lice and mites, and solve this problem in a number of ways: with chimney smoke, sand dustings, and individual ants rubbed into their feathers as a natural insecticide. I wasn't interested in trying any of these solutions though they sounded interesting. So, my response last night was to start boiling underwear and sheets. They're hanging out this morning drying in the sun.

While trekking in Nepal, Charlie Pye-Smith resorted to soaking clothes in thermal hot springs to deal with lice in his shirt seams. I'm comforted to know I'm not the only one handling these pin-sized irritants. I do wish there was a better way than boiling water. On the other hand, lice transmit typhus and other diseases.

January 28, 2015

I wake from a dream of being on pilgrimage in Japan, staying at monasteries, and open my eyes with precepts on my lips. I'm singing them in the Indian style, or rather, chanting them in my head, for I've lost my voice a bit, not speaking for so long.

At 2:30 AM a rainstorm came through and refreshed the air and the land. Today, my two hundred and first day in the wonderful quiet of the New Zealand bush, I have peace. A lovely, soft rain begins at 11 AM. How I've missed it! I noticed that some parts of Slipglade Track had dry weather cracks yesterday, so I expect the earth is enjoying this wet day too.

Today is food drop day. Good, since I have no fruit, vegetables, tofu, cheese, or bread, only one egg, no cookies, no scones, only a can of tomatoes, a can of corn, and one package of crackers. Yesterday afternoon I was so disturbed by the lice infestation that I ate ten peanut M&Ms when I usually have three a day for my treat. Since there's rain today, the food drop may be late but I've had breakfast and some soup for lunch, so I'm really fine until tomorrow. I remember years ago, when I was newly married and still in college with a law school student husband, some days there was no food. One day we had only potatoes, and another day only noodles. This austerity lasted just one year and was not so very bad, but it made me empathize with those who truly are hungry and struggling.

January 29, 2015

Brother Sun—Sister Moon. Is she a woman? She shines in my window as I prepare to turn out the light for bed. Clouds move around her like a dance, covering and dissolving her and then framing her brilliant luminosity— the waxing moon of late January. If I arrange my pillow just right, I can fall asleep in that moonlight. I feel so extraordinarily happy, so extraordinarily peaceful. This is so very far from where I was three or four months ago, when I was struggling to hold positive thoughts and a neighbor was yelling at demons on this hill. I'm so very glad that this retreat is long enough to have lived through all that, and come out in the moonlight of peace and serenity.

I finally got Jane Dobisz's *One Hundred Days of Solitude* in my box. Re-reading it, I came to the section where she, too, sings the praises of long retreats. It sounds so familiar:

> I am so at peace. There's nothing more to need or want. No-
> where I'd rather be. The humming of my mind is at rest, like
> sediment that has settled to a bottom of a glass of water. It's still,

perfect. There's a warm, deep, calm feeling permeating every-where. How could I have missed this pleasure for so many years?[119]

I would wish this experience for all beings—if they only knew and could persevere to this point. Ecstasy in quiet moonlight.

Alone, happy, content, I'm moving into the seventh month of this retreat with delight.

*Kererū, New Zealand wood pigeon, high
in the fruit-laden karaka tree.*

Chapter 8 February

Nine in the morning and a quiet rain begins while I eat my oatmeal on the porch. The rumble I hear far up the valley seems to be someone's generator, but soon it will be drowned out with the sound of rushing creek water if the rain persists.

I had a text message that there is much snow at home and "it's beautiful." I remember one year when my usual early January departure meant I missed seeing the stark outline of dark tree limbs against the glow of white as the landscape is transformed with a clean blanket of monotone color. To those who live in New England it would be inconceivable that one could yearn for snow, after three months of heavy shoveling, plowing and cancelled events. With one heavy storm after another, it becomes tedious, and we yearn for spring to arrive.

Here, the clouds are descending on the ridges and a mysterious white shroud appears on the high bush. I do love weather, and here I've learned to appreciate all its variances. To resist its changing forms is only to suffer.

The past three days I've dealt with sun, showers, and washing and boiling water day after day to deal with the lice-infestation. Where they came from I do not know. It could have been from that possum fur I picked up, or that wonderful collection of bird feathers I gathered. They are the size and color of minute body lice and have the usual six legs, but do not bite, only crawl everywhere. Do you need to know that they were in my bedding, in my underwear, in my hair and elsewhere? They were multiplying in the outhouse on the toilet ring, and every time I sat down, I was picking up more. So, I wiped that seat off before sitting and left the lid up to discourage a moist environment and proliferation. Yes, I got a package of lice treatment in my food box, and followed the directions in addition to washing everything in boiling water. (This continued for the next few weeks.)

Despite the shock of all these bugs, I've found that every time I submerse an infested article of clothing into hot water and bring it to a full boil, my thoughts go to boiling live lobsters, and to a scene from the novel *Shogun.*

Am I taking life? Yes. Before I was awake to the non-harm precept, like all good New Englanders I ate boiled lobster and relished it. Yes, we boiled them LIVE. Yuk. Then I read that chapter called "The Night of Screams" in *Shogun,* Clavell's novel of 16th century Japan, when the western barbarians arrived at the port for a confrontation of cultures. It wasn't lobsters the Japanese were boiling live that night, but a human. Thinking of these incidents, my heart cries out. Lice and bugs are not crustaceans or human beings, but I'd rather not be doing this. It's hard stuff I'm learning here. I wonder what the next test will be. Meanwhile, I take joy from the descending clouds, those magical ridges, and this grand valley view I've been given this morning.

It's true, I've come up against serious aversion, perhaps for the first time. What I learned is that "this too will pass," and if all you have energy for is meditation and washing, then that's what you do.

Yesterday afternoon I was feeling quite low, so gathering my mala beads and my Vajrasattva purification mantra, I walked Slipglade Track out to the Dharma Road where it branches up to the stupa. There's a bench in the bush on the side of this road as the two tracks meet, and there I sat as the day ended, chanting my mantra a hundred times, looking out to the Firth of Thames and the distant sea.

February 2, 2015

Fast clouds skim across the sky from the north today, and white fingers glide down between the far ridges. Now, night has come and I sit at the window, waiting for the dark sky to give up my moon. Patience.

February 4, 2015

A morning in the upper 50s (14ºC) when lately we've had nights in the 60s (19-20ºC). It's almost 10 AM and only now am I sitting for breakfast. I could see myself as disorganized, lazy, and not staying on schedule, but there are no appointments or classes to rush off to. And those of us who are lucky get insights before breakfast. For me, today, there were three. I'll get to them soon.

First, I want to sing the praises of quail in New Zealand. Are quail insights? I've been walking up to the stupa more often (three times in six days) to get veggies from the great garden that an Order member put in to help us long-term retreatants. But often, I'm up there to just sit, meditate, take in that very different atmosphere, and enjoy the growing covey of quail that live nearby.

Yesterday a regal male perched on a rock overlooking four grown birds and a gaggle of six babies. The quail's markings fill an artist's heart with joy. Such deep black markings, a topknot trimmed with white, and such a beautifully patterned body is a gift to any viewer. The male squawked when I got too close, and was off into the grass, signaling the others, who cooed and clicked as they hustled away. Twice, en route to the stupa, I've squatted on the side of the road for five minutes to let them cross over, and to watch the babies show off their black-striped heads, which will grow into those remarkable headdresses. As Andrew Crowe's bird book says, if you sit quietly in the bush for five minutes, the birds will come.[120] They teach us patience.

I'm not sure why, but after coming home from the quail families, I was remembering two human Bodhisattvas who stepped into my life, demonstrating all their loving-kindness for this very busy, intentional, and driven young one. My wonderful childhood neighbor, who radiated kindness and concern for me as she raised five children under difficult conditions, was always there with adult wisdom, listening, and encouraging me. And my equally wonderful best friend from college years, who was in my life for forty-three years, a friend through so many different lives, always modeling kindness and grace. Neither were perfect beings, but both were deeply loved and noted as remarkable people. And both passed away too young, as Bodhisattvas seem to do.

This morning I had some clear awakenings concerning illusions, emotions and the equanimity that I yearn for and admire in others, especially those two Bodhisattva friends. Again and again it comes through to me that I can choose to suffer, to be led around by my emotions, my views of right and wrong, "should be" or "should not be"—or I can let these things go like the illusionary bubble that all this grumbling hurt really is.

Buddha says that many emotions lead to suffering and all phenomena are illusionary and empty. I keep learning and learning—taking in all these things I've heard hundreds of times, but only now—with this quiet life of meditation and silence—am finally being able to hear, as if for the first time. Young Dzongsar Khyentse Rinpoche reinforces this, saying "All it takes is one situation when the conditions are precisely right and one piece of timely information is provided, and your point of view can change."[121] He tells me that I can see through some of this mess as the illusion it is, and not get stirred up or sad, or angry, but have confidence to leave the drama behind, and the clear understanding to walk away because "it is just a movie." By understanding emptiness, you can maintain an appreciation for all that appears to exist, but without clinging to the illusions as if they were real, and without the disappointment of a child chasing rainbows. However, many of us stay in the dark, without the courage to break out of the network we're plugged into.

This was demonstrated twice to me only this morning (and before breakfast!) Doing some simple yoga asanas every morning has relieved my incapacitating back issues. I knew I had to do something on this retreat since I'm on my own with scoliosis, stenosis, moderate bone degeneration and arthritis, and have no acupuncturist or chiropractor to rescue me. Having the courage to break out of my usual patterns, having no excuses for not getting down onto the mat each morning, and unable to rely on my preferred exercise (swimming), has been an eye opener. Daily yoga works, as it worked for Tenzin Palmo in her cave for twelve years.

The second eye opener this morning is a big one for me, an emotional issue that has reared its head three or four times in the past six years when I'd hoped it was done with. I saw that my attachment to right and wrong, to being "justified" in my heart, and suffering at the hands of another, was really an old pattern of grasping and clinging to ego—and that harmful words and perceived criticisms are really illusions. In this instance, I'm reminded that others heard this harsh criticism and were saddened, but not incapacitated like me—rather, they heard and let go, into equanimity. This is a difficult one for me. Even receiving a long letter of apology, which acknowledged unskillfulness, didn't completely defuse my hurt, despite my desire to be done with it. I carried these accusations around for almost six years like a heavy load of rocks on my shoulders or a wound that opened periodically when I was low and began oozing again. Now, it's gone. All illusion. I realize at last that there is no self to be hurt or defended, criticized, or beaten up—unless I choose to cling to and grasp this defensible ego. What woke me up this time was Buddha's Wisdom of the Four Seals:

1. Nothing compounded can permanently exist
2. Emotions can bring pain and suffering and are never sources of permanent bliss
3. There is no truly existing self—phenomena are illusion and empty
4. Enlightenment is beyond concepts—beyond time and space

I'm seeing things as illusions at last, and making the choice not to suffer over this anymore. What a breathrough!

Re-reading *What Makes You Not a Buddhist* helped me with this. A book which mentions going off to a cabin in Kennebunkport (Maine) and a hut in Costa Rica by page twelve, and was mostly written in a cafe in Ubud, Bali, was sure to catch my attention. I've been to all three places and loved each for different reasons. Dzongsar Khyentse may be a Buddhist born in Bhutan, but he is of this world, and as the flyleaf says, ". . . is one of the most creative and innovative Tibetan Buddhist lamas teaching today." Thank you, Lama Dzongsar, for this morning.

Thinking of criticism, I'm reminded of two of the eight verses of mind training I say each day. One has to do with first giving victory to the other and accepting defeat, and the other is particularly applicable to my present situation:

If someone insults or blames us and it is justified, then this criticism is actually helping us by pointing out faults of which we may not be conscious. We should feel grateful. If the criticism isn't true, it's just words. And just an illusion. We should just see through it.

February 6, 2015

Being here on this precipice with nothing to watch but the weather and my mind, I'm learning. I heard, somewhere that the changing moon patterns strongly influence the weather. Really? Maybe sailors and farmers know this, but we urban dwellers just go to the internet or newspapers for weather reports, and whatever shows up, we deal with it. But with no wise companion with which to discuss concepts, and no electricity for an internet connection to do research, I'm thrown back on myself, with only observation and no confirmation.

What I have here is the full-moon phase and a sudden drop in temperature from the high 80s to low 60s F, much higher winds, and lots of precipitation. It feels like summer finished in three weeks, and we're back to October winds and storms. I'm sad for those local folks who have rented a beach house for a week or two of sun.

I watch the weather. I have little else. And I'm learning. Two nights ago, when I was expecting a glorious full moon, the valley turned white—not with glowing moonlight, but with that dense fog of last winter/spring. Twenty feet from my porch, it was solid white, so very eerie and mysterious. This continued from midnight until 6 AM, when it became wispy showers, and then downpours for the next two days. Yesterday it cleared a bit, but the winds were extremely high, wrenching the door to the hut out of my hand and banging it against the wall, then swinging it back and hitting me in the shoulder. It's the most violence I've felt in months. I managed to have a chilly bath between showers and blessed the burners under the metal tub that brought the water temperature up to "warm." The whipping wind somewhat dried the towels and underwear, and the rest of the wet wash is inside the hut for the night.

I've also recently noticed that I am reluctant to go to sleep. I've always enjoyed my sleep time, but despite being exhausted and ready for bed, there's some apprehension now. It's not a fear of bad dreams, but rather the reality that I wake up many mornings with a headache. I've learned that if I get up, do my yoga, and have a cup of tea, it usually wanes. But that pain is still there, morning after morning, and it's often two hours before I feel well. A curiosity. I have no opportunity to check out the reason for this.

However, what has changed are the lingering side effects of that concussion of two years ago. In truth, these morning headaches are the last of the last. The cognitive symptoms, excruciating pain, dizziness and nausea are completely gone. So I try to accept what's left and be happy for my relative good health.

In a world where an email or a text goes off and is often answered in minutes, I'm learning the quiet, peaceful, patient life of thirty years ago. The importance of patience is high on the list of things I've learned here. I wrote to a friend in October, she received the letter in November, but then broke her ankle and misplaced my address. I've heard she answered the letter in December and mailed it in January, but it's February and I've yet to receive it. Patience. It's like the *One Hundred Days of Solitude* book that took a hundred days to arrive at my hut after a friend ordered it for me. It was lost in the mail, reordered, and then took another month in delivery. These delays are good for me.

I've noticed when I carry my prompt American efficiency off to Spain, Mexico or Indonesia for winter retreat or studio time, I have to re-learn that slowing down. There, I need to walk and speak more slowly, and carry fewer expectations. Those three winter months each year are a saving grace, my acupuncturist friend says. Can you imagine what I was like thirty years ago before I started daily meditation? I accomplished a lot with my high expectations of myself, but over these years away from my efficient environment, I've learned that being kinder and more mindful is truly beneficial.

February 7, 2015

The winds have stopped, rain clouds departed, and there was a waxing moon in today's powder blue dawn sky. Before sitting down for my pre-breakfast meditation, I opened the porch door to check on that moon and flushed two large quail in my front garden. I'm happy to see them back, and have hopes that these two may be raising a brood of chicks in my garden, like the stupa gang are doing. As I came out of one contemplation and moved into another the day was quiet enough that I heard light tapping on the porch. I expect some small chaffinch found the seed I left out. I'm serving it on a green plastic tray now, which produces a noticeable "ping" sound when pecked.

It was a raucous night. Had I not been so very tired, I would have gotten up with my flashlight to take stock of all the guys visiting. I thought the possums were rearranging furniture on the metal roof when I heard a long slide and crash. It seems one of my metal frame porch chairs was involved because this morning it was upside down next to the tub. It must have been an interesting transaction, coming off the roof, tumbling into the chair and flipping four feet off the deck. I'm

243

sorry I missed it, but I just could not pull myself out of bed. The best I could do was to note the time: 3:10 AM. The roof/porch activities went on for almost thirty minutes, and as usual, the possums left a bit of scat as a calling card in case I didn't know who was visiting. Such fun.

I've been enjoying dipping into some paint the past few days. The idea of doing a watercolor painting each month for twelve months hasn't come to fruition though I've been careful to watch what seems appropriate to paint. My first few months here were very full of not-ing—a slowing down, nature observations, adjustments to hut living and many life reviews. I'm now going into my eighth month feeling free and light enough to look around and work with the stupa in a visual way. It has such a reassuring presence. Each time I visit it, after my bows and my three circumambulations, I put my head against its shoul-der and talk to Dhardo. He was such a kind, compassionate and wise Rinpoche. It's important to me to have this connection here.

Painting the stupa is a visual challenge since it asks for lots of mindfulness and observation. Each shape and swell above and below the center bell-form is different, but all are graceful and refined. Then there's that very challenging six-sided base—times three, which the bell-shaped stupa sits on, with four additional box altars, signifying four of the archetypal Buddhas—facing north, south, east and west. All this is topped with a small cube-shape, a twelve-ring spire and a cornice. It all has deep significance. The base cube represents the earth element, the round bell the water element, topped by a cone-shaped fire element, a disc-shaped air element, then space and consciousness in the cornice jewel drop portion. Until last week it was just too overwhelming for me to step into visually despite knowing the elements it represents. But at last I'm here at the foot of the stupa, as if I'm with an old friend that I want to become more intimate with, pencil and paintbrush in hand, ready to open my eyes and heart. It's quite amazing to see this "self," Kiranada, transform, change and grow over these months. Again and again, I find myself deeply grateful for a full twelve months.

At 4 PM on this quiet Saturday afternoon, the valley echoes with gunshots for thirty minutes. I wonder why. Practice shooting? Hunting? Protecting crops? Killing animals for sport or food? KILLING? Who? Why?

I think of my young quail in the garden this morning, and a sentence I read in a Venetian mystery novel by Donna Leon last evening: "Two tiny quail lay between a pile of fresh peas and an even larger pile of tiny roasted new potatoes, the whole dish redolent of the cognac in which the quail had been baked."[122] Sounds yummy. It's Guido Brunetti's dinner. But it also makes me sad that someone would relish eating these noble little birds who click and coo so lovingly to their summer chicks on my front grass. Once you know who they are, it would be hard to kill and eat them, I imagine when bought at the supermarket, wrapped in plastic, their deaths have been sanitized and they're only something good for dinner. I try to be sympathetic to the views of others, not be judgmental. But perhaps beings are dying in the bush today from gunfire. And my own stomach is upset after eating a chicken egg for lunch and contemplating Guido's quail dinner in Venice. Is it time to fast again?

February 9, 2015

I see clearly now that my mood and emotions can often be a reflection of the weather, and that there's something about a dull, overcast day that brings out the morose. Morose, sullen, ill-tempered—those are not quite the correct words. Gloomy and down are closer.

But, something always cheers me. This morning it was seeing the white horse far up the valley on the Sanctuary Ridge actually walk. WALK! I had to get my binoculars because I couldn't believe that this white statue, which seemed to stand still over three or four months, was actually moving. It looks as if he's neither tethered nor fenced, but has been placid enough to just stand for days. He's out at 7:45 AM and in these summer months is still there at 8:30 PM, but today he walked off and disappeared behind greenery. Escape? Off down the road? I was so thrilled. "Go for it," I said out loud.

And on this quiet, dull day when I'm searching for something else to be enthusiastic about, some huge, noisy New Zealand kererū pigeons arrive. These birds are the size of ducks. They flap noisily over the hut, flop around among the karaka tree limbs, and thrash about to eat the recently ripe, olive-sized fruit that's now turning orange. They're the latest excitement at Abhaya Hut. These karaka kernels are highly poisonous, causing violent convulsions and permanent paralysis in humans, my resources say, but the pigeons obviously relish the bitter fruit. They're awkward and ungainly, which makes their eight to ten-pound weight seem even heavier—more like a duck up in a tree than a pigeon. They do have elegant black-green necks that stretch out, and glamorous snow-white bibs and underwings that make them one of the world's most beautiful pigeons. What excitement to watch them!

I sat this morning and listed the things that enliven my life here or make me happy. That's when the joy of the white horse's escape and the pigeons came in. On my list also is the time to delve into topics, consider and reflect on them, and write in my journal. Without this venue to share my thoughts and observations, I could become morose—and even ill-tempered. God forbid!

I regularly have topics to reflect on and the latest is the practice of rejoicing in the merits of others and singing their praises. Is this unique to Buddhists as a "given" practice? It comes from the Mahayanists, I expect, and is found in the *Bodhicaryavatara* (*A Guide to the Bodhisattva's Way of Life*) written by Santideva in the eighth century, translated by Adrienne Bennett, and used by Sangharakshita when he prepared a version of the Sevenfold Puja in the 1960s.

I happily rejoice in the virtue of all sentient beings which relieves the suffering of the miserable states of existence.

I rejoice with delight in the good done by all beings through which they obtain rest with the end of suffering.[123]

To delight in the virtue or merit of another is to practice mudita—sympathetic joy. We can derive strength and inspiration from noticing and sharing the skillful, generous and kind actions of others. In sharing this merit, we counteract any unskillful mental states of our own, such as jealousy, envy, pride and egotism. We should never end up feeling inferior or "looked down upon" by using this practice. It's a practice about others, not about ourselves, for sure. Bhante Sangharakshita reminds me that there's an important psychological aspect in this rejoicing in the merits of others: we cannot be happy for others if we are not happy ourselves first. If we're out of touch with our own spiritual practice, it's hard to appreciate what others are doing without resentment or criticism.

I've watched this practice in both the USA and in Britain, and have found some subtle differences that may have cultural roots. Sharing good news—a publisher is finally found for a book, a scholarship has come through, a media interview is in the works—in the US bring comments of "Terrific!" and sincere enthusiasm. Yet, it seems sharing these same things in the UK carries shades of boasting or "being full of yourself." In the UK, it seems this sharing brings out subtle comparisons on the hearer's part. Is there truly a difference between a brash, enthusiastic egalitarian country where anyone can rise to the "perceived" top and the old hierarchy of ranking in another country? I just keep watching this to see if it's really true.

I continue on with thoughts of mudita—sympathetic joy for those who receive good news—and rejoice in the merits of those who are doing fine work in the world. I learn so much from them. Truly, as Nagapriya says in *Exploring Karma and Rebirth,* ". . . learning to recognize the influence we have on others and using that influence wisely and compassionately is an essential aspect of spiritual growth." He also says, "Our skillful actions can have a transformative, even revolutionary effect on the lives of other people, which may enable them to discard limiting beliefs and habits and embrace a more creative outlook."[124] If Tenzin Palmo, Henry David Thoreau, Bob Kull and Zen Master Bon Yeon hadn't gone off on their solitary retreats and later written of them, I might not have realized such a thing was possible, nor have received the encouragement to follow their example.

So when the day is dull, there are things to explore that can lift me right out of those doldrums—with gratitude. In the end it was a sweet, happy, centered day. Amazing.

February 12, 2015

Listening, watching, experiencing the quiet of the bush, I continue to learn from it. Raindrops splash into buckets and I watch contemplatively. When a small chaffinch comes to feed, I stop any movement that might distract or frighten her. Yesterday, my 6 PM walking meditation flushed one of the huge kererū pigeons from the karaka tree. This is their chosen hour for feeding on the ripening fruit, so I quietly moved my walking to the deck in front. Ten steps in the limited Zen-style duck-walk (right heel next to the left instep, lift, small step, left heel at right instep) down the new wood walk, then four steps to turn and another ten small steps in the soft ending of the day.

It's a food delivery day, and I'm happy to have two notes. One comes from Australia, where a fellow Order member is doing a nine-month solitary and has me in mind, and another from a mitra (a friend of the Order) in the USA with news of her family, her practice, and the small meditation group I support in my local village. It's good to bring them all to mind, acknowledge that external world, then sink back into my quiet inner world.

The fellow hermit in Australia writes: "Loneliness is painful; solitude is bliss; the only difference is the heart opening."

Mindfulness—mindfulness of body. I've been considering bowing as a moving meditation practice. I look at the motivation, and the thought behind it, and find that bowing may be a sign of respect, devotion, or even protest. At the height of the Vietnam era in the USA, two American Chan bhikshus did a ten-month Pilgrimage for Peace, taking "three-steps, one bow" from California, along the Oregon coast, and into Washington state above Seattle. They logged over one thousand seven hundred bows per mile over 1150 miles, with aspirations for peace with every step.[125] Zen Master Bon Yeon (Jane Dobisz) did one thousand bows per day during her one hundred day solitary retreat in the woods of Maine, finishing three hundred prostrations before 4 AM with her Zen practice of bowing to her "true self."

Yet I know that the practice does not come easily to Westerners. In the US, we're raised thinking of equality, and to bow before another person, or a statue, brings up visions of servitude, subservience and "bending the knee" to some graven image. Yet bowing can be transformational. Suzuki Roshi says that to bow is to give up ourselves, give up dualistic ideas, drop all distinctions and merge. To bow we must give up our self-centered ideas and be willing to lay ourselves low, to turn over our attitudes of pride, conceit, arrogance and delusions to equanimity.

I read that Suzuki Roshi's teacher had a callous on his forehead from bowing. He knew that "he was an obstinate fellow and so he bowed and bowed and bowed,"[126] always hearing the voice of his own teacher in his ear scolding him for coming to the monastery so late in life. The Zen roshis tell me that I should be prepared to bow even in my last moment, at death. It's a serious practice. So I'm ready, if my knees hold up.

I started bowing when I first arrived in Kyoto thirty years ago. In Japan, we bow instead of shaking hands. We bow to acknowledge the other person (or even an object), out of respect. At tea ceremony class, I bowed to the tea room space, to the teacher, to the tea towel and to the matcha powdered tea in the bowl. At the temple, I bowed before entering the zendo, bowed to my meditation cushion, and as acknowledgement to the practice, I bowed before and after the bell. But it was not until I returned to Kyoto three years ago that I could find the courage to bow to the Roshi carrying the long kyosaku training stick, receive a swat on my shoulder, and bow to thank him—receiving a bow from him in return. It was an accomplishment for me to overcome that fear and take on that humility, and it was totally refreshing.

To bow, to pay respect, to be humble, to relinquish self, to become low, to give up ego, to lay pride, envy and negative emotions down there with the candles and incense. I move up down, up down—the physicality crawling into my bones and muscles, into my being. The joy I find in bowing even here in a small hut in the bush is immense.

February 13, 2015

Breakfast and, later, tea in the back garden. Can I call it a garden when it's just a clearing in the bush where the ORV turns around, next to the two water cisterns at the back of the hut? It's always pleasant, whatever I call it, and is presided over by a friendly fifteen-meter-plus karaka tree. She has to be an old one since there are a number of rotted splits near the base. Her deep green, glossy, rubbery leaves are like those from a rubber plant. They say these leaves help to heal wounds and draw out pus. And the kernels have karakin in them, known to kill grass grub larvae.[127] It's here, under this tree, that I hear the noisy swoosh and flap of whistling wings as the kererū pigeons arrive for breakfast. I'm continually amazed at the noise and the size of these beauties, three times as big as any pigeon I know and close to the bulk of a duck—airborne.

It's only in the mid 60s (18-19ºC) but I'm happy to be outside under the clouds with the promise of afternoon sun. Even at this temperature, some insects are humming—cicadas or what we call "sem-is" in Japan? In other locales, they'd be an indicator that summer is upon us and the temperature has just broken 80ºF (26.7ºC), but not in New Zealand. Here, these insects just show up with their occasional zinging sound. The temperature, it seems, is irrelevant.

A generator kicked over far down in the valley about 9:30 AM but has stopped now. All of the farms and homes along this river depend on solar electricity, so these overcast days put a strain on reserves and the noisy generator is needed. As they say, sound travels well in the bush, so I'm sure they're a long way away—but in my silent life I hear every-thing and take note.

This evening I saw a kererū pigeon asleep in the high limbs of the karaka tree, just napping, soon to wake and begin eating again. He was accompanied by two sizable ladies. They really do take these large, olive sized kernels whole, one after another. My belly aches to think of how all those great pits (2.5-4 cm—that's over one inch long) must feel as they go through the digestive system of these big girls, but I guess they're built for this. They spread the seeds, propagating these trees, and eat over seventy other plant species. Other small birds seem to keep their distance from these white-bibbed giants. I would if I were little.

Sitting under this tree, I notice that among the many yellow leaves and whole kernels that come down in the night are many partially eaten ones. Either the possums are interested in them, or perhaps it's our res-ident rats. Whichever it is, they make quick work eating this downed fruit through the hours before dawn. It leaves an interesting mess for my morning raking, but I love observing and learning from all of it.

February 16, 2015

I was awake much of the night—up and down, reading, having a plum, thinking of putting on tea—returning again to thoughts and wor-ries about the visa renewal. I ask myself if I am here for only another six weeks and in need of winding up, or will I be here for another four months? With five feet of snow at home, the mailing of the application papers to my New Zealand supporter is slow to arrive, so the wait con-tinues. At 1 AM I write a note to myself, "Nothing can be done, so let it go."

I consider papañca, the conceptual proliferation of thought that complicates and entangles. I go to the question Who is worrying? and let it sit with me in the night. If there is no self to worry, then it's just activity—to be noted and dropped without more thinking, without more judgment. I watch the stillness of my mind and try to catch the moment when thought rolls in. And then watch it dissolve, without added input. It's interesting to watch it slide back into stillness/silence. One teacher suggests we notice how the walls of the mind dissolve when conceptualization is absent.

I sit outside in the warmth of the morning sun, eating my oatmeal and listening to the kererū pigeons enjoying their morning meal. Life is very sweet and gentle. I pull out something I wrote earlier this month:

On Solitary:

Things that bring comfort:
The glow of the shrine candle;
The full moon in the night window;
A dried plum at 6 AM;
Clean sheets, warm bath water;
A chaffinch welcome at dawn.
Time to appreciate all things.
But,
Reliance on the ephemeral, the impermanent
Brings disappointment, brings sorrow.
The candle dies, the moon changes phases,
The sheets need changing and water cools.
The small chaffinch finds other realms,
And no longer comes.

To take my mind up that ridge
To the very edge;
To let go of all thought;
Make my mind like non-stick teflon,
Where thought finds no root.
To let go into emptiness
And quiet;
There is the bliss. There is stability and joy;
Returning again and again,

To the other
Just becomes a temporary joy,
On solitary.

— Kiranada, February 2015

February 17, 2015

A soft, quiet morning. A tui calls, and the suddenly prolific white cabbage butterflies flutter.

I've been working with papañca and the bubbling-up of thoughts, and reflecting on their nature. To see the very edge of a thought, to watch it bloom, is fascinating. A mind with no thoughts is a blissful mind, serene and quiet, but the usual state is one thought, one story, one plan after another. I can have meals arranged; exhibitions organized, completed and hung; trips planned; tickets bought and bags packed in my mind in a matter of minutes. Other times I watch my mind flutter, like the moving pages of a thumbed dictionary . . . or become dense like the deep morass of the bush vegetation with nothing in focus.

When a thought shows up and I shine a spotlight on it, I watch it scuttle off, hanging its head or with eyes focused at the ceiling, saying "Me? Who, me? Proliferate? No way! Just sitting here twiddling thumbs." Thoughts and mind really don't like the glare of the spotlight—but unobserved they multiply like rabbits and take off. Is it really true that caffeine and coffee encourage papañca proliferations, as one Order member has written? Does caffeine encourage the firing of brain neutrons, which encourages runaway thoughts? It's something to consider.

So why spend time watching and investigating thoughts and the workings of the mind? The *Dhammapada* says "... the world delights in conceptual proliferation, Buddha delights in the ending of that. There are no footprints in the sky. You won't find the sage out there."[128] The development of suffering is closely connected to this perception.

> Mind is the forerunner of all actions
> All deeds are led by mind, created by mind.
> If one speaks or acts with a corrupt mind, suffering follows,
> As the wheel follows the hoof of an ox pulling a cart.

All deeds are led by mind, created by mind. If one speaks or acts with a serene mind, happiness follows, as surely as one's shadow.[129]

— Dhammapada

When there is papañca, there is desire, and with that come likes and dislikes, which move on to greed and even envy, and the unhappiness of it all. To be able to control thought, to be familiar with it and see it proliferating at a distance, gives me some choice about whether to follow and chase it or whether to pull back and sit in serenity, equanimity. It's a life work for sure.

I have a noisy belly right now. Today is a fasting day and I had some immediate kickback from a sour stomach when the vitamins hit it an hour go. I'm not really hungry, just noisy. If I keep my stomach full of liquids—that means water or tea here since I have no juice nor means to make juice—I usually get through the day quite happily and even without hunger. On another day, I can be hungry all the time— something like that proliferation of thought. Once it starts, it just runs on.

I'm off to meditate at the stupa and later do some painting up that way. A happy day, with a noisy belly.

February 18, 2015

Morning sounds: Watching . . . Listening . . .

5:56: the click of a light switch as I find my way around my one room hut before dawn . . . 6:15: the swish of the yoga mat rolling out into the center of the room and the sounds of legs raised, back twisting, breath in, breath out . . . 6:30: the sound of a soft shawl wrapping around my legs and waist as I settle onto my meditation cushion, the snap of a lighter as the candle flares and incense catches the flame . . . 7:05: the growl of an early fly who slipped in my open window, alighting on my wrist and forehead, and the purr of an airplane heading north, up the peninsula in early dawn light . . . 7:15: the crunch—oh so quiet—of a slow-moving car creeping up the valley road to one of the farms upstream . . . 7:25: the sound of precepts, mantra and prayers as I transfer any merit from my first sit to all beings, to relieve suffering . . . 7:50: the sizzle of frying potatoes and green tomatoes, the bubble of poached egg and the slosh of tea water poured into a pot, and later into a green cup . . . 8:00: the noisy flapping of kererū pigeons arriving at the backyard tree, the gasp of discovering an eight inch pigeon wing feather on the lawn, stuck in like a regal dagger . . . 8:15: the peep and flutter of three busy fantail piwakawakas as they dance and cavort between tree limb, bush, fern tree . . . 8:20: the quiet tap of metal fork on solid plate as I eat breakfast outside and the sun breaks through the rough, low clouds . . . 8:25: the melodious tones of a bellbird or tui trying out an imitation in tentative notes. The amazing hush, when all activity and sound stops and the forest takes a breath or two, anticipating the day, practicing the same silence that infuses and transcends this hut. Waiting, contemplating, reflecting on what silence really is—the space between breaths. If only I could wrap and package this and offer it, with head bowed, to all of you with my deep respect.

Anyone reading along could have anticipated that breaking a fast, even a one day fast, with fried potatoes and green tomatoes is inviting disaster. How foolish! I paid for this with a lousy stomach and the runs most of the morning and now a queasy headache. Just plain foolishness. My usual warm oatmeal would have been kinder.

February 19, 2015

I slipped down to the Community House library to drop some books before two retreats begin, bringing twenty to thirty people to the center, and started back up the Dharma Road while it was still somewhat cool. Later, the temperature will climb to 28°C. As I passed a clearing on the side of the Dharma Road that I've seen before, I decided to investigate this shady glade. From there, I followed a path through the bush, and after a three or four-minute walk, descended to the river edge and a miraculous space. Perhaps this was the swimming hole I'd heard of? What an enchanted miracle!

Guarded by a massive thirty-foot boulder that wedged in the ravine hundreds of years ago, a delightful waterfall cascaded into a sandy pool with dappled sunlight and mossy rocks edging the area. It was so inviting that I stripped off my clothes and slipped into the chilly water for a dip under the waterfall. Afterwards, I sat and meditated there to the sound of bubbling, moving water. And later, I explored both down river and up, finding a fine table rock and three more bathing pools. What a truly enchanted area, so beautiful and serene! I could have been up on my ridge in silence the whole year and have left without hearing about it. It was only serendipity that led me to investigate. I look forward to returning.

February 21, 2015

I'm feeling low and tense today. One of these days I may be ready for a good cry, but it hasn't happened yet. It would be good to know what I might be crying about, rather than just free-floating angst. I know that at present I'm fingering worry about the visa, whether I should be preparing for an exit from this abode or not. I'm hoping they'll accept my extension under a special category which allows longer stays than the usual nine-month maximum for those from the USA. I don't know how often this happens, but I've been told of at least one refusal at this center.

I've gotten word that all the paperwork is with authorities, as of yesterday, and this next week a decision will be made. There's nothing more I can do except burn some candles and incense, so I took my low spirits and nervousness off to the bush with my eleven o'clock cup of tea.

Not knowing exactly what area would fit my mood best, I found myself hiking down Mill Track and making a turn up the steep Rata Trail, which I've never explored. I didn't have my good tramping shoes on, or my pack with map, water, whistle and Epi-pen, so I couldn't go too far. And I was still carrying that tea cup with me, no less. Three or four minutes up the track, I came on a wonderful tall grove with five or six really fine sixty to seventy-five foot rata trees. I was able to put down my mat and the tea, and just listen and watch. I spent time doing darshan, taking in that forest energy. Rata are capped by great red puffs of flowers in late spring, but these are finished now. Their limbs are quite unusual as they grow out horizontally from the tall trunks, some-times twisting and turning so they look like knotted biceps traveling through the upper forest canopy. Later, I put my head against the larg-est tree and absorbed the vital natural energy that had it reaching so high into the sky.

Sitting in nature is healing and nourishing. I found myself returning home to my little hermitage, lighting a candle and feeling real ac-ceptance for whatever will come. Whether I'm to remain here to finish a full year, or go onward to Indonesia for the last three months—in either case the outcome will be correct and will offer the best possible conditions for me to learn what I have to learn on my Path.

February 22, 2015

Gifts from the Rata Grove

From the environs: deep peace and serenity.
From the majestic rata tree: groundedness, vital energy,
upward flow.
From the tui bird who left an iridescent green/black feather:
the promise of flight.

I have a deepening connection to both Kuan Yin and Dhardo Rinpoche; I feel their profound kindness and concern for all beings and their work in the world as they hear the cries of suffering. With Dhardo's stupa so close by, I know I'm part of that presence. Wherever I meditate, I often envision Kuan Yin on a lotus, high up on a white cloud. Here, I see her on the far ridge. In Spain, at Akashavana, she was on the bluffs with the vultures, and in New Hampshire she's up my tallest pine tree, resting on a giant nest instead of a lotus. Today, following my mala bead mantra chants, I felt a flow of red light cascading down from her onto me: blessings of strength, wisdom and fearlessness. My connection with her has grown in this peaceful land. I feel blessed to have had this quiet extended time to develop and deepen that link.

February 26, 2015

I'm surrounded at last by bugs. I wondered where they were when I arrived in July, but of course, that was winter. Now they're flying into my tea, into pots of soup on the stove, and up my nose. I had one jump in my open mouth last week too. So I learn to keep my mouth shut and keep lids on my pots and tea.

There were some lovely days of rain early in the week that refreshed all of us. I had a bath and got some sheets and towels washed. Sometimes taking time off from daily journaling allows me to finish some art—this time it was two watercolors and the Twelve Moons/Twelve Buddhas fiber piece, which now has a row of hazy Buddha images in the third week of each of the twelve months. At last, the piece has pulled together.

Yesterday morning I found the usual possum "calling card" placed in the exact center of the top step of the porch as if to say "I was here." No need to tell me. I knew it by the scampering and rumble on the roof in the night. It still sounds as if they're skipping rope or assembling new furniture up there—and then the slide and thump as they come down the beams to the porch with a thud, dragging their clattering jump rope tails and tap dance claws with them. They're quite interested in the karaka tree fruit just now. Everyone is but me.

This seems to be the month for mating possums. Their eerie Boooo-raaaah, Boooo-raaaah mating calls echo in the night. These are BIG growling calls, not soft and gentle, and appear to be coming from a much larger set of lungs than those of the cat-sized possums I've seen. They're indeed spooky, like nothing I've ever heard, reverberating like a low cello string. Fascinating bush sounds. I love these discoveries.

The half-moon was bright last night at midnight. I slept with all my curtains open to enjoy it. Fast moving clouds skittered across the heavens, but they didn't dilute the brilliance of that persistent moonlight. Glorious! I occasionally wonder how I might carry this back to that other life I lead in the forest of New Hampshire. I just need awareness and intention.

I am still working on mind and watching my thoughts, trying to "container" them when on my cushion. I'm sitting with this for a few days to really know it, doing it again and again.

Bhante reminds us that we are strongly conscious of the body as our own personal body. In dropping duality and merging, we recognize our deep connection with others and unite. We begin to feel that their bodies too are ours; our attentiveness to those who are ill, who need help, should be as strong as our attentiveness to the needs of our own body. And we should expect or yearn for nothing in return—do it selflessly.[130]

Late afternoon, after a sit, I thought I'd go walkabout and see what was happening on the horizon, down at the Firth of Thames. I looked up the word "firth" since I only knew it from the Firth of Forth in Scotland, and found that it's a Scots word for a fjord or narrow inlet of the sea. In this case an inlet between the landmass that includes Auckland and the finger that protrudes, the Coromandel Peninsula.

I walked down to the end of Slipglade where it joins the Dharma Road and I have a wider view of the sea than the little bit I can occasionally view from the hut. Moving leisurely and quietly, I came upon a convention of quail right in the middle of the road, all having an afternoon dust bath. I'd wondered where the quail families had gone, as it's been ten days or more since I saw them up at the stupa, and here they all were. The perceptive adults heard my approach and popped up, five or six males and females shaking out clouds of yellow dust. Then a little one hopped up as I approached closer. I counted fourteen babies. Quite a gaggle. As I sat on the roadside bench and enjoyed watching them waddle down the road, five more teenagers hopped out of the bush to join them, just seven feet from my feet. The young ones are already forming their distinctive top knots, which will later be larger on the males. My bird book says that in autumn up to fifty birds join up to make large social groups.

The view of the Firth was lovely. Afternoon showers showed as sheets of gray coming down out of clouds, with rough water below. The showers seemed to be coming this way, though I was sitting in beautiful sun.

I'm a great lover of "no-self" poetry, as I call it, and that poem from Li Po, the Chinese sage who does it so well, came to mind:

> The birds have vanished into the sky,
> And now, the last cloud drains away.
> We sit together, the mountain and me
> Until only the mountain remains.[131]

It feels as though he's here, living my solitary life.

258

Squash from the upper retreat house garden.

Chapter 9 March

I've been sleeping in the glow of the waxing moon the past few nights. It's at my window at 9 PM, heading for the western ridge about midnight, then ducking down, and gone by 2 AM. The wonderful silver light turns my front porch into eerie daylight, casting long moon shadows behind the planters of vegetables. How extraordinary to be part of this! To be present.

Today began at 14ºC (58ºF) in the early morning and went up to my record high of 32ºC (91ºF) in late afternoon. It's great to have cool mornings and nights when the daytime temperature is that high. Life in Indonesia and the Arizona desert, as well as the sultry summers of Japan and New England, have me somewhat acclimated to this hot weather. I just accept it—and put my head under the cold water tap before sitting down for the next meditation.

I'm learning to live with the flies. They've become more prevalent indoors with the warm weather, though smaller and without the noisy buzz of their larger brothers. They're fast-moving, and like sitting on the floor, especially in the kitchen area. I've become quite adept at capturing and releasing their larger brothers, which gather on the window pane or glass door, but these are far more skittish. I've made a vow to just live with them and shoo them out as best I can, since angrily swatting at them disturbs my open heart and meditations. It's summer in the bush, and they are more a part of it than I am. All mind states are illusions. Seeing flies not as dirty, irritating pests, but as entertaining friends, turns them into illusions.

With the flies comes the problem of keeping food fresh without a refrigerator. I make small portions to eliminate left-overs, but sometimes I miss. Yesterday I had to throw out some soup with coconut milk, as well as one third of a moldy loaf of bread, some slimy green onions, and a head of broccoli that I missed steaming up before it turned yellow. This morning a cup or more of soy milk had to go down the drain. It turned sour after three days in an open carton in this heat. The cool-box does well, but only keeps food at 14-18ºC (high 50s-low 60s ºF) and not the 4ºC that most products need. This is one of the challenges I live with.

March 2, 2015

It often surprises me when my current reading slips right in behind an ethical decision and reinforces it. Reading Nagapriya's *Karma and Rebirth* again, I came across descriptions of both hrih (*hiri* in Pali, translating as personal conscience) and *ottappa*, known as social conscience. I knew swatting flies was not a good idea, but knowing that they were both in my outhouse toilet and also lighting on the rim of my teacup minutes later, I was concerned about health and another way to deal with them. However, my experience of hrih intensified my ethical sensitivity, expanded my awareness, and helped me see my moral failings more fully.

If we're ethically sensitive, we actually suffer more, empathizing with the suffering of others. No fly wants to be squished with the whack of a rolled newspaper, and I certainly do not enjoy carrying dead flies outside to the bush. Not good for them or for me.

This increased sensitivity gives the possibility of self-transformation, which is one of my reasons for being on this retreat. I'm learning to cover my teacup when it's not in use, wipe down the cutting board, put lids on pots and wash my hands more often, letting the little winged insects bring me some joy and fun with their antics. And then I notice that fewer are coming inside, and how much quieter they are without having the crazed newspaper-whacking being come after them. This morning, two even allowed me to capture them and assist them outside along with a lovely large spider. I'm learning to live and let live, learning that a personal conscience and a social conscience can be beneficial to all living things, myself included. Today, I don't even need to meditate with a sarong over my head to keep them from crawling across my nose. All seems quiet and in harmony at last.

March 3, 2015

Yesterday was again a very hot day. By 3:30 PM I decided to hike down to the river at Pine Crossing, where I could have a cool dip and do my late afternoon meditation next to moving water. I found a striped bird feather (from an akaka, or native parrot) and a surprising redpetalled pinecone on the way. The water level was the lowest I've seen it yet, but still refreshingly cold.

Lots of sweet little black and white tomtits are around lately. They're sparrow-sized birds with an oversized head and a curious manner. One followed me, branch to branch, down Slipglade, obviously interested in who I was. Who am I? I don't know myself, right now. For the second time in four months I passed another woman arriving at the ford just as I was departing.

I returned home to find two disturbing text messages on the cellphone. The visa processing has been postponed because the credit card number on the application I completed last June was incorrect and was refused. The immigration office is willing to try again with a corrected number, thinking I had misrecorded it. They wrote that I still have time for this, but my fear is that the credit card is being refused because the bank thinks it's a fraudulent charge coming from New Zealand. Though they've been notified that I'm out of the country, this has happened before, even when I've informed them of my travel plans.

Tenzin Palmo speaks of the fruits of retreat not being realized until the final three months, three weeks and three days, and that's beginning right now. She was forced out of her three-year retreat in the last few months by a "Quit India" notice from an immigration officer who appeared abruptly at her cave door and wanted her out of the country in ten days. That's not the way to finish a retreat. I too may be forced out in the next week or so I realize. But I have the support and help of a dear one in Thames who has agreed, by text messaging, to see this through for me. I'll work to put it out of my mind— or at least, not dwell on it when I can do little to help.

I have a message that someone else has just entered a one-year solitary retreat at the Zang-ri Hut across the valley, and it buoys me up to know there are two of us sending prayers and watching cloud movements on these auspicious ridges.

March 4, 2015

My sweet daughter's birthday. Standing on my tip toes and holding the phone over my head, I tried to send a birthday cake symbol to her on my cell phone, but it didn't go through. Even the very occasional texting I do can "pull me out," involving me in the world I'm retreating from. But today it was important to send a birthday wish to my daughter. I finally did it when a cell connection opened up.

Starting my ninth month on retreat, I've had two support meetings with Senior Order members in the past week, one visiting from the UK and one from here. I was told before coming into retreat that any visitor or meeting would mean a one week disruption in my practice. I can see that now. Balancing the plusses and minuses, I chose to have a support meeting every four months, knowing the consequences. With my emotions already on edge because of the ambiguity of the visa situation, the disruption seemed to make less difference.

Both visitors asked what I was missing now, and what I was looking forward to in the next four months. My response was, "I miss going out for a good Japanese meal, going to see a great film, and having a chat with friends." They reminded me that these things will be there waiting when I come out of retreat. But what will not be there is this lovely, supportive silence, this grand expanse of time to practice and reflect, this spacious valley and color-filled sky. This is here and now, and soon will be but an illusion, a short blip of memory, one year in my long life.

Am I looking forward to more months of silence, my visitors asked. When I focus on the difficulties and the tedium of the same meals, the same schedule, the same view, I can lose enthusiasm and wish for the diversity of life "outside" and away from biting insects, flies up my nose, and bread that goes moldy in two days. But life "there" involves suffering too, just a different kind—too much activity, too many demands, too much anxiety. What I have is this here, this now, and I love it—my arms wide and full of bounty and appreciation. Looking forward? Yes, to some completion, to some fruition.

I've found an activity that centers and grounds me between my meditation sits . . . and that is stitching. This week I've spent two to three hours each day doing additional quilting on that Twelve Moon piece that I thought I'd finished, stitching with greater calm and serenity. It seems to fit what I need right now.

March 7, 2015

When I was preparing to come here, again and again I was asked, "But what will you *do* there, alone for a year?" I'd reply, "Anything I want to that seems appropriate." And all too flippantly, I would add, "Heck, I could throw a disco party if I wanted to." I've learned to eat my words too many times in this short life because that's exactly what is happening in this peaceful, quiet bush at present—a disco party! Or as the note in the box says, a music festival in the valley.

I didn't hear many cars crunching along the lower road this past week, but I had noticed (through my binoculars) that the beehive boxes had disappeared from a grassy knoll in front of the farmhouse way down in the valley. My binoculars are inexpensive and the focus at that distance is somewhat fuzzy, so I didn't quite know what was going on. Little did I realize that this farmhouse was preparing to host a festival on the full moon weekend.

Music festival, hmmm. Would this be like Woodstock—lots of loud live music and amplification? So far there has been a solid hour and a half of screaming and shrill announcements, followed by a percussion of drum rhythm, followed by a night of amplified disco beat that only stopped during a 6 AM rainstorm. It's quiet now at 10 AM as everyone dries out and prepares for another all-nighter. It hasn't really been disturbing, and I'm somewhat glad that the valley is filled with lively people. I hope they travel home safely and that the event is successful for the promoters. And that the beehives return to the grassy knoll next to the sweet manuka trees in place of the colorful tents and gaggle of cars and motorcycles.

I sit on the cushion with the Heart Sutra, going through the five skandhas—of body, feeling, volition, perception and consciousness, saying "This is not me, this is not mine, form is only emptiness, emptiness only form," to the sound of cars crunching down gravel roads ... to enlightenment.

March 9, 2015

Out on this wooded point hanging over the valley, facing the welcoming distant wall of trees, the sky and the clouds, I have a feeling of deep safety and security, of being held. Every night my door is open, never locked. My curtains are pulled aside so I can see moonlight flood into this hut as it works its way up from the east to the zenith, then down to the west. The reassuring, repetitive call of the ruru owl sounds all through the night, every night—out in the valley, calling to its mate. Even the rumble of the possums reassures me. In all the places I have lived on four continents, here I feel safest. This is extraordinary after such a tenuous start. But now I'm secure, happy, content. I'm here with my Heart Sutra commentary, my sketching, lunch prep and leaf raking, and hour after hour of sitting in front of a small shrine with a white porcelain Buddha *rupa* raising his hand in the abhaya mudra of fearlessness. So many things that disturbed me at first—the size of the tea kettle, the height of the shrine, the small Buddha Amoghasiddhi, (rather than Shakyamuni or Amitabha), are now so familiar—comforting and perfectly fine. I wonder at that first reaction, and why I felt so rigid and judgmental. Now, this is home. Even the two flies that have taken up permanent residence inside the hut are just fine. There is endless quality to life now. No place to go, nothing pressing to do. Just being, experiencing, watching with awareness. Here is deep, deep silence. Quiet like I have never heard before. Only the ruru owls marking time for me.

March 11, 2015

When dawn lit up the sky at 7:10 AM, the waxing moon was still high in the sky. The seasons are changing, and daylight comes more slowly and departs sooner. A half-moon in two days.

An old friend visited in my dreams, someone who came to say goodbye to me at the airport just nine months ago. When we each packed up books, dishes and art in Kyoto in 2000 and moved back to New England, did we know it was the end of one era and the beginning of a new one? There are so many lives to live while we keep learning.

Soon this chilly summer morning (14ºC-58ºF) grows into an exceedingly warm autumn day. I light a candle for my visa approval.

March 12, 2015

There has been a turning point this week; an opening of my heart, a deep settling, an embracing and welcoming. It may be a little strange since I'm still in bureaucratic limbo, not knowing if the government will allow me to stay or not. But despite the uncertainty, the retreat seems to move on its own energy, proceeding through a new gate to a different level.

Ten days ago, when I was asked if I was looking forward to another three or four months of retreat, I couldn't say I was truly "looking forward," just willing to do it. Now I feel much more eager, more joyful, anticipating and open. Something has turned—and though I still don't know if I must leave in three weeks, I completely accept this, confident that things will unfold as they should, and that I will be lovingly carried along.

I opened my Kindle to find a quotation, and was faced with the words "As though given new wings." This is how it feels—the sunlight after the shower, the promise of a rainbow in the east. "When the meditation drops from the head to the heart and is felt, then transformation begins to take place."[132] That quiet inner joy is there now, resistance weakened and open-handed acceptance accomplished.

Two nights ago, after a Refuge Tree Prostration Practice, the hut seemed nestled in a giant open lotus, and Buddha Amitabha came down to settle on the roof—or was he hovering? The space was infused, perfumed, saturated with love and compassion, with the air of a lotus-filled spring. So very present. No place in the world I'd rather be.

Now, a field of flitting white butterflies echoes the white of the nearby stupa. Dhardo Rinpoche is near, with all his kindness and generosity. This afternoon, I finished reading, for the third time, *The Wheel and the Diamond*, the story of Dhardo's life. As always, I'm brought to tears by the story of this Lama, the thirteenth in his lineage. Seven years ago, I was fortunate to visit the Tibetan school and orphanage where he lived until his death in 1990. He started the orphanage in 1953, responding to the growing number of children arriving from Tibet, and it continued on as the Indo-Tibetan Cultural Institute. Before I flew to New Zealand, I met his young tulku, or reincarnation, a graciously soft-spoken young man, as kind and present as his incarnate predecessor. What an amazing being the 13th Dhardo Rinpoche was! I'm in awe that such a being lived. And what a time to have lived, through the fall of Tibet to the Chinese, the establishing of monasteries in India, and the continuation of the precious culture that he held so close.

We're fortunate that our teacher, Sangharakshita, was a young Theravadin monk early in the 1950s in Kalimpong, India, and befriended this high lama or Rinpoche, taking instruction and initiations with him, and making this intangible link that continues today. The young 14th Dhardo Rinpoche Tulku is even now in New Hampshire, at my home center, dedicating a stupa containing some of his predecessor's ashes. And I'm here with another glorious Dhardo stupa, feeling his venerable presence in my daily life.

March 13, 2015

Jane Dobisz (Zen Master Bon Yeon) writes that one of her reasons for going off to the Maine woods to sit a solitary retreat for one hundred days was to get her mind and body in the same place at the same time. I too feel this strongly. I'm much more present with this moment than I was in the past. My life before I set my bags down in this hut feels fuzzy and barely remembered after eight months here.

I feel the ginger in my fruit cup fire some heat in my mouth and slide down my throat to get some good heat going in my stomach for digestion. I hear the whine of a neighbor's generator far down the valley, in between the melody of the bell bird's pristine tones. I watch my scraggy little female chaffinch work her way up the morning grass, seeking insects and contemplating the safety of a hop onto the porch for some waiting seed. I watch my laundry drying in the sun after a day of lovely showers and a night on the line inside. My experience is narrowed by this retreat, and is also as wide and boundless as space. I have the grace of time to be present, to watch and notice, to truly feel and take in so much that passes by quickly in that other life. I feel blessed and appreciative to have this time for presence. I notice that too: the gift.

March 14, 2015

I wonder if subconsciously I feel time is running out. Or if the fruition of all those hours on the cushion, all those stitches pieced with mantras, all those hours of opening this heart to other people and to birds, bees, flies and possums, is leading me to some answers. This week I'm beginning the three month, three week, three day time when the fruits of a long retreat are to be realized.

A senior Order member with a long history of retreats said he could not write a journal on his solitary retreat because, for him, it would be "selfing" too much. A new word for me: selfing. Caught up in self or self-image. If there is no self, how can there be selfing?

I look at this idea and realize that some retreatants may not want to give reality to their failures, their blunders and their unskillful thoughts by writing them down and sharing them later. They choose to learn from them internally, and grow into better beings in order to do the work more effectively. Others use a retreat like this to add to their credentials, or to make them feel good, even though it is incredibly hard. Some hold the solitary retreat tight to their chests, knowing it involves 10,000 bows, or crossing an ocean solo, or surviving sub-zero temperatures, or not speaking one word or seeing a human soul for months. Others welcome the macho challenge, and look at it as an Everest to conquer, either resulting in failure if not completed according to their rigid rules, or success with laurels bestowed for being a tough Marine and coming through it.

Do I need to prove myself? Is this a competition? Is it all smoke and mirrors, this "self" stuff?

It all tumbles out now as I watch this mind, watch motivation, feel the deeply held wish to be of help and service in this suffering world. Seeing how, in my limited time left, I may serve and listen, and be present for others. No self—no one home to receive praise, to be criticized, to gain or lose anything. No one home.

Do you know this, if I don't write it down? I will tell you that on March 14, the moon was an exquisite half-moon at 4 AM as it rose in the east. At 10:30 PM it was still high in the sky over a quiet small hut in New Zealand. I see this, experience this, and receive the grace. If I don't write this down, how can you see it too? And is it at all important that every day the sun rises and moves across the continents to bring light and warmth to you? That the sky has not one cloud in it after intermittent rain showers? That there is suffering in this world and that there is an end of suffering? It all tumbles out now. Reading again, as I do most mornings as I begin my meditation sit, I share;

> "Where water, earth, fire and wind have no footing;
> There the stars do not shine and sun sheds no light;
> The moon does not appear and darkness is not found;

"...When a sage or Brahmin through wisdom,
has known this for herself (himself),
Then he is freed from form and formless, from bliss
and pain."[133]

— The Buddha

I learn from this, yearn to rest in it, and not hold it tightly since there is no me or mine, only openness that flows into the world.

For me, this "selfing," awareness of self, comes when I have doubts—when I wonder if this hard work of retreat has value, when I wonder if this is worth sharing with you. Back I go to my cushion to find the treasure, to crack the nut, to open to the place where stars do not shine and no darkness is found.

March 15, 2015

An extraordinary morning of high winds and lashing gusts beating on this little hermitage. The wind howls and groans and whistles. My usual quiet meditation echoes the action outside. Some find coffee, stress, anxiety, or a high number of demands the most likely disturbances, but here in the bush it seems it's howling wind that pulls at my emotions and creates papañca, the proliferation of thoughts, on my cushion.

I try some walking meditation and then fifty bows, increasing that callus on my forehead, and this seems to help with my second sit. Once my heart rate descends, I feel myself moving in to core. My arms become more leaden and my breathing and thought activity quiet. Earlier, I could move from thoughts of my ordination in Spain six years ago to cleaning closets in New Hampshire to redesigning art work—all in five minutes, and each ridden with angst about the inclement weather. That active mind. But finally I settle into quiet space, happy that this schedule gives me a framework to drop into. I remind myself that it should be not so tight (like violin strings) that I snap and spring, but not so loose that I don't get out of bed. Something in the middle that deals with howling wind and quiet "no self."

March 17, 2015

How refreshing it is, the day after rain! The air is cool and clean. Every being is taking a breath. It began raining two days ago, and went on heavily for twenty-four hours. There was no going out for walking meditation. Solid, hard rain. I'd had word this severe weather was coming. I wondered how the quail families were doing, battened down in their nests, hopefully in a dry part of the forest. A male and female chaffinch did appear on my porch after eighteen hours of rain, looking for food. The male flew under the covered porch and shook all over, like a dog coming out of a lake. How do you fly with a feather coat when it is so exceedingly wet? This male is a round, plump guy that I named Mr. Chubbs six months ago. He was so very greedy and put on so much weight with my birdseed that he would squat in the middle of the seed tray like a sitting hen, and just reach over to peck and keep feeding. Now he's lost a bit of weight, and his spring breeding color has dulled, but he's still double the size of the shy female. I'm glad they both got their food and that the weather broke at noon for everyone to dry out.

Today was wash day, the heavy wash, so sheets and towels are out in the sunshine along with shirts and underwear. Yesterday's rain was so strong that I was able to fill every bucket to overflowing and even have almost a full tub of fresh water for a bath this afternoon. Tony came by last week to repair the tub's gas burners, which had both quit, so I should be able to take the chill off the water for an outdoor soak this afternoon. Life in the bush.

. I'm enjoying an in-depth study of the Satipatthana Sutta and looking at "ardent, clearly knowing mindfulness" and all that means, seeing how mindfulness can be a balancing factor, a guardian at the sense doors, and a help in training the mind. I'm much more settled now, and the increase in meditation sits, bowing practice and "guarding the doors of the senses" is paying off.

I hear some very serious roadwork being done below in the valley. Some heavy equipment, maybe a road grader, is moving slowly up the ravine, perhaps repairing washouts on that metalized road that services the distant farms up the Pinnacle Range. In September, we had a landslide outside the Community House that entailed bringing in earthmoving equipment to give accessibility. Perhaps this is what I'm hearing. In solitary, I don't really know. I'm just here: sitting, watching, experiencing the bush, experiencing the mind.

March 18, 2015

I wake to a cold morning with the autumnal equinox just two days away during the dark of the moon. I'd decided that I would hear of my visa renewal by yesterday, and when nothing came through, I was most dismayed. I decided that today needed to be a day of purification, of less grasping and attachment. So, I woke with the one-hundred syllable Vajrasattva mantra on my lips and went on to thirty more recitations of the full mantra through the first hour. It will be with me all through the day, with my mala counting beads not far away. I also decided to let go of more grasping and make today a fasting day— in fact, I've decided to fast until the visa notice comes through, however many days that takes. With this decision, I feel positive instead of being full of regret.

With this resolve came a look at confession and purification of ill-thought. With so little interaction with others, my unskillful actions, words and thoughts are minimized, but they don't disappear completely. Two instances of aversion came to mind during a morning sit. Both happened at the sacred stupa, where I'm more likely to see or have contact with others.

I always try to avoid being there on the weekend since that's a time when visitors and sightseers are likely to be wandering about. But there I was on the hillside, about thirty meters above the stupa, working on a painting on a Sunday—ten days ago. Two women appeared in shorts, tank tops and hiking shoes, carrying water bottles and striding up the hill. I often note whether visitors move to the left or right of the white dome to circumambulate. This gives me a clue as to whether they're sightseers there for the view or are coming to the stupa as a sacred site. One woman strode swiftly to the right (sightseer) and started to come up the hill to where I sat with my brush in hand. She kicked a tarp left on the grass from a past ceremony, and then was surprised to notice me sitting above and, looking guilty, shouted a "hello." I didn't speak, didn't nod, didn't make eye contact, but rather looked down at my painting as both women, moving fast, passed behind me up the track that leads to the mountain trail.

I noted unskillful emotions arising fairly quickly—aversion and some definite unfriendliness that I regretted in a matter of minutes. My lack of acknowledgement came from fear of an unwanted conversation—being in silence—but also, I realized, from aversion to and judgment of their actions. I felt bad enough about my reaction that I considered writing an "I'm sorry for my unfriendliness" note and leaving it in the middle of the trail for their return.

There was an earlier interaction with a more mindful couple who appeared in the same place two weeks earlier. They were quiet and, noticing me, made a point of sitting on the far side of the stupa out of my view, protecting their privacy and mine. And yet, some aversion and judgment arose in me when I noticed they'd left the engine of their car running during what turned out to be a thirty-to-forty-minute visit to the stupa. At first I was confused by this since New Zealand seems to be an aware and awake country, worried about pollution, carbon footprints and global warming. New Zealanders buy organically raised food, support farms working towards this, and are strongly against GMO products. But it seemed these folks were running their air conditioning to keep the vehicle cool for their trip down the mountain on this 75°F day. Or else they had ignition problems, feared they'd be unable to start their engine, and so left it idling in the clean mountain air. Again, aversion on my part as my critical self arose. It seems that some things have lessened after being out of contact with society for nine months, but old habits of approval and disapproval linger.

The Eight Verse Mind Training prayer that I say each morning reminds me how negative emotions hurt both myself and others, and should be forcefully stopped as soon as they're noticed. Today I send good wishes to these visitors, saying "May all beings be peaceful and happy, free from suffering, sorrow and conflict," and to myself, "that I might be free from ignorance, craving and aversion." I'm working on this as I sit, out in a spot of sunshine on this chilly morning and get into my day of fasting with gratitude. A tui bird chortles, clucks, whistles and buzzes in a cacophony of calls, and a small tomtit comes for the feast of insects I've uncovered as I passed along the track. Friends in the bush.

March 20, 2015

Another cool, overcast day that flows into sunshine later in the afternoon. The quiet here is interrupted only occasionally by the buzzing

273

of bees that have appeared suddenly. I welcome them and find them friendlier than the anxious flies, which have lessened with the rain and wind.

Fasting slows me down. I could see my lack of energy when I walked down to the Community House to drop some books off yesterday. The walk back is all uphill, and fairly steep in many places. I usually stop once or twice to catch my breath during the homeward trek, but yesterday it seemed like I stopped every fifty or one hundred feet, and had a good sit down at four different places. I kept daydreaming of someone coming along and giving me a lift up, though that never happens in this quiet land. But before too long the climb was over, and I strolled into my grove and put my head under the outside faucet.

It's hard to believe that the Immigration Office has had my visa extension application for a month now and no reply. Luckily, Kate in Thames is monitoring my application and will text me with news when there is any. It was difficult to turn in my food order this week, not knowing if I should be finishing off what I have on hand or continuing to stock up. Do I need two rolls of toilet paper or the bargain twelve pack? Such decisions. So I ordered none.

What I did conclude, late one sleepless night, was that if the renewal doesn't come through, perhaps I could just fly out of New Zealand for twenty-four hours and return on a three-month visa on arrival permit, granted automatically to US citizens. It would mean a disruption in my retreat, yes, but perhaps it would be possible. The hoops that bureaucracy presents for us to leap through! I know that it's all part of practice—but this one has truly set me back. A distraction from the Heart Sutra study.

March 21, 2015

It's the beginning of a new season, a re-dedication and a reflection on my reasons for being here. Dead quiet. Not a pin drop. Not a birdcall, dog bark, neighbor's generator, wind howl. Just deep, expectant quiet. Silence to contemplate the moment.

March 22, 2015

At 11ºC (50ºF) in the morning, I'm cold. More to come, I'm sure. I have yet to fire up the stove and will wait until it's really, really necessary. I'm meditating with hat, muffler, gloves, sweatshirt, outdoor vest and a blanket—*again*. Coming full circle. If my alarm clock worked, I'd be up earlier, but for some reason I can't get a ring out of it, so I wake up naturally. There are folks who pride themselves on how early they're up and on the cushion each morning, and I admire them. Then I watch them during meditation sessions all day long, echoing the nodding head of my night-working mother, who was always sleep-deprived. So I sleep when I'm tired at night and wake when I'm finished. We're still on Southern Hemisphere Daylight Savings Time, so dawn doesn't come until after 7 AM, with sunlight on the ridges by 7:40. I remember it was after 8 AM last July.

I enjoy and appreciate this morning time to think, watch, and observe a self that I sometimes drag groaning with me all day— the one that worries and then gets angry and dissatisfied. The one that is graspy and moves to clinging. Not my true self. Not the one I'm growing into more and more. It's great to have the time to watch this happen. To be the observer, the knower.

This long, long wait for a visa reply has been an excellent time to watch this self and all its habitual actions and reactions. Growing up in a chaotic household, I became super-organized—someone who acted on things that needed doing and made careful future plans, preparing even months in advance. All this to avoid that last minute, disorganized, angry, fearful chaos of my youth. It was a way of controlling my life, of putting some grace and ease into it, and making it more peaceful. Then the New Zealand Immigration Agency took control and I was told— wait. Local friends write, "just put it out of your mind for now."

So I'm learning to put it out of my mind. I'm left with more meditation, more bush-watching, more stitching, more reflections on Dharma, and more compulsive tearing of cardboard box pellets. I'm learning to see those habits and compulsions that ruled my life for fifty years more clearly. I'll still be the active "go-getter" and not the quiet sister with the blissful smile, but I'll see what I'm doing more clearly and not just react to conditions, but make choices. Without the bindings of reaction and angst, I'll have more time to sit and reflect than before, and be able to just be quietly in the moment. Perhaps I'll irritate others a bit less too. That's the positive side of all this.

I find a small patch of sunshine outside to sit in and eat my breakfast porridge. I go through my mala beads and my one hundred mantras, and feel the resistance of a special bead near the end that I mentally call my "confession bead"—a time to stop, review the previous day, and see if I have an unethical action, thought or word to bring up, confess and make a resolve about. I do this each day, as Dhardo Rinpoche did, and as the current Dalai Lama does.

Today, I remembered the counsel of a very senior Order member who advised that I could just ignore the rules and overstay my visa if necessary. I discarded the idea even then. I've spent too many years living abroad to ignore my host country's rules. I realized that ethically, this would be breaking my second precept—the taking of the "not given," i.e. stealing. I need to sit peacefully on this cushion, in harmony with all, sliding the next bead along, chanting "Homage to the Jewel in the Lotus"—honoring those precepts nestled in the center of my heart that I have chosen to give me guidance in this life.

I had a delight during a late afternoon meditation at the sunset bench on Dharma Road a few days ago. I was in a deep, peaceful space when some clicking and cooing encouraged me to open my eyes to see fourteen quail hoofing it up the road to sit opposite me and join the meditation. The babies are all doubled in size, almost full grown—with little respect for their elders, whom they pester by snuggling up for a late afternoon sit or snooze. It's been a special joy to watch these little ones grow to young adulthood over the two months since I found that quail eggshell on the track.

I remembered, too, the six lovely quail that bobbled into my front yard yesterday. Following some insect hunting, they all settled down and nestled together on my pile of dead grass for a community snooze. They remained that way for almost thirty minutes; then distant gunshots shocked them awake and they scampered into the bush. These sweet beings were on their own, without an adult bird, and were somewhat smaller than the Dharma Road covey with the two black-faced males and four females. Elegant birds. I was so happy to see quail again so close to my hut. I remember their moms and dads from last December.

March 24, 2015

Yesterday I walked to the stupa to water that large vegetable garden. I gathered some ripe tomatoes, chard, beans and small onions, and made a small bundle to drop at the Chetul Hut food box with a note for another retreatant. The fresh produce is a delight. I came home with a lovely pumpkin squash after a fourth morning meditation in front of the stupa with Dhardo Rinpoche joining me. It's the anniversary of his passing this March—twenty-five years ago—and he's still remembered with love, deep respect and appreciation.

When the far Zang-ri Hut came into view on my walk down the stupa road, I stopped, waved my hat, and bowed to that far hill, and Pemasati there in her first month of a one-year solitary retreat. Numerous times throughout the day, I mentally reach across that valley to join hands with her, and then reach up north over the sea to Nagarakshita in Australia in the last months of her retreat, taking them in with a group hug, and giving support and understanding. I include all others on retreat, wherever they are, working through their loneliness, demons and joys.

At home I prepared scalloped potatoes and ginger tofu with great fresh greens on top and a grand sliced tomato. Instead of an afternoon lie-down, I got a bath going and cut my hair to half an inch all over before my last two late afternoon sits. I finished some Satipatthana Sutta study on the porch with the sunset watching, then did an evening puja and some nighttime reading before lights out—praying that my dreams would be helpful, heart-opening and of benefit to others as I grow and awaken on this mountain.

I'm never far from my meditation cushion, never far from mindfully watching the arising and falling away of phenomena. Never far from the grounding that has kept me happy and content to be here, watching it all unfolding, watching the bush and pastures go brown with the fall.

This morning I awoke from dreams of friends, lovers and family in time for first light. Finding my slippers and a flannel shirt to offset the morning chill, I lit the stove and drew water for tea. I dumped the pee pot outside and rinsed it out as I took in the new day and the falling rain. Back inside, I hopped out of my nightclothes and into my day clothes and had a bit of a wash-up with warm water, and made tea.

The blue yoga mat got rolled out. I had a sip or two of oolong tea and got down on all fours for my daily practice. I start with some shoulder rolls and the cow, cat, cow, cat, cow, cat, downward dog routine that has my backbones cracking, then on to some kneeling triangle and thread the needle poses followed by the plank and hold pose. I continued on with knee-crossed backward twists, then onto my back for bent knee window-washers and five backward lunges, then up for the moon salutation repetitions and some standing poses, finishing with Warrior One and Two. Although I've been taking yoga classes for forty years, this is the first time I've had a daily practice. It has stood me in good stead. A few more sips of delicious tea and I was on to my cushion, bundled up in hat, gloves, muffler and shawl for Refuge and Precept chanting and the longer Tiratanavandana salutation. I slipped into a lovely quiet place with my shoulders settled, breathing slowed, and mind calm.

Soon I was up again, bowed, and quietly, gently, slipped out the door for ten minutes of walking meditation before my second sit. I paused at the door to see if the one fly in my hut this morning would like to exit with me, but the answer was "no." He had more inside housework to do. I walked the track behind the hut, lifting, swinging, placing each foot mindfully, noting the arising and passing away of body sensation, feeling each step in my toes, ankles, knees and hips, and looking for the result in my chest and shoulders. The tall fern fronds swished across my head when I didn't remember to duck as I proceeded down the track and turned.

There, at waist height, was the leaf I noticed and loved nine months ago, with a few more insect holes than before. I'm pleased I didn't pick it six months ago to place on my shrine. It's there, in place each day, to greet me and remind me of the love that bubbled up in me when I first saw it so long ago.

Moving so very quietly, the walking was part of my cushion time— an extension of the meditation that I went back to with my second sit before breakfast. Kuan Yin came down with the recitation of my mantra and I slipped into her robes for the day. I recited the "Eight Verses of Mind Training" and finished with transferring any merit gained from this sit to all beings everywhere: my family, friends, strangers, and those I have difficult times with.

I gave up that vow to fast until the visa came as just too willful, so this morning I oiled the frying pan and mixed flour, ginger, pumpkin seeds, dates and bananas together for my pancakes since the last banana was ready to go off. Eating breakfast, I watched the rising and falling away of my taste response, mindfully chewing each bite thirty times (following the advice of Thich Nhat Hanh) and occasionally looking up to the ridge outside my door. A little chaffinch arrived for his breakfast of birdseed too. Clean up, a small sweep, and bed making, and I was back to my cushion for another sit. Then, with bells, bows, and more transferring of merit, I was up for some free time of stitchery, reading and writing, listening to and watching the birds, and getting the wash out to dry.

I've just received a text message that my visa extension came through this morning!!! I guess we provided all the right things (sixteen pages of forms plus three more from the bank, the airline and a center trustee). What a learning experience for me, and an opportunity to watch my habitual reactions. Wow! I wouldn't ask for this one again.

March 25, 2015

The cool weather has blossomed into one more summer day with the temperature up to 28ºC/82ºF, but the brown pastures and dead fern fronds tell me that fall is upon us. Soon we'll be sending this lovely warm sun up north to my other friends for their spring and glorious summer. The seasons arise and pass away, and I'm awake more and more to this change around me.

Arising and passing away. While I can feel calm, centered and at peace, my body knows I'm handling some stress. When it hits a certain level, canker sores manifest on my upper lip. This visa extension was a "two canker sore event" that arose and is passing away.

Once, I came up with five sores at one time. That was ten years ago, when I returned from Japan to help my younger sister, hospitalized by the graft vs. host disease (GvHD) that finally killed her. Driving the one-and-a-half-hour trip to the hospital in Boston every day and helping her young family brought on enough internal stress that I came down with multiple canker sores and was banned from her isolation room for almost three weeks. So, even when I think I'm doing well and taking things inside, my body says waiting five weeks for a visa renewal is stressful.

Relationships, physical body, thoughts and perceptions are all arising and passing away. The practice of mindfully noting them keeps me minute by minute in touch with the work I have come here to do.

March 26, 2015

Some people have told me that after nine months alone on a ridge, they would start talking to themselves. I've not found that, yet I greet the moon, especially after five or six days with only stars. She's like an old, dear friend. Last night, I was surprised to see a lovely moon low in the northwest sky as early as 6:30 PM. Before 10 PM, she'd set behind the mountains for the night. I'm learning her pattern after all these months, and know now that the waxing moon will be in the early night, and then she'll show up later and later each night afterwards . . . or maybe not. It's all very mysterious, this sky route.

The moon is the most endearing friend of this retreat, often present, always glorious, always guiding and encouraging. The little chaffinches run a close second. And the chirpy piwakawaka fantails that are always so happy to see me, and fly from branch to branch around my head during walking meditation, are running a near third.

On my cushion this morning I had such a sense of being in a lovely nest of caring and compassion, surrounded by so many beings. I receive notes from friends who say they think of me daily as they sit in meditation, or even when their oatmeal bubbles. They're all here, there is no separation. I am part of them and they are part of me. Indra's Jeweled Web brings us into this interconnected mesh of life. To be able to sit on retreat with them is a treat; to have all beings part of this practice, an honor. To hear them murmuring in the cool breeze, in the dancing raindrops, in the chortle of the quail, feeds me. They're part of the white mist that yesterday morning filled the valley again and again and again, three times in one hour. All are here with me, sharing this experience; all present, part of life on this wet ridge. To say "I'm doing this solitary retreat for you" is erroneous. You are here. We're doing this together. To walk through the long, quiet nights and live out the endless repetitive days is to do it with you, with all beings. And it is a joy.

March 29, 2015

Last night, the half-moon ate through clouds and flooded my pillow with silver light, purifying, illuminating and holding me. She was in the early evening sky, and disappeared in the west by 11 PM.

Now I'm engulfed in another kind of cocooning white. A delightful rainstorm has moved into the valley, bringing misty clouds and a deluge of rain. I have a front row seat for all the changes of weather, here on this exposed precipice.

March 31, 2015

Like sediment settling to the bottom of a glass of water, I'm here, cocooned and enclosed. It's the last day of a most difficult month with the angst and uncertainty of whether I was to move to another country or, by the grace of the immigration office, continue here. I've watched my emotions rise and fall, watched equanimity slide in and out, watched ethics challenged and distraction tramping through.

In a matter of days I was settled and deep into the Heart Sutra. It was coming anyway since emotionally I had come to a resolution a week or two ago. Now I'm settled, and happy to just be, letting go, at last.

Who is this "self" that needed a visa? She left with that last full moon.

Knotted supplejack vine, like those vines that tangle the floor of the New Zealand bush.

Chapter 10 April

What a special day today has been! I had a rough night sleeping, and was awake to see the three-quarter moon set just before 4 AM. I decided today might be a good "day off," to read, have breakfast (dry rice cereal, as well as a poached egg) and just do what meditation came naturally. Without a schedule, I slid into a double sit without noticing it, eager to be on the cushion. Who would guess?

The food delivery arrived on a corner of my porch at 12:30 and I continued a day of food splurging with a toasted sesame bagel, veggie bacon, a grilled tomato and silver beet greens for lunch.

The day flowed with such grace and loving joy, topped off by the arrival of the quail family, who took over the steep front grass area. They love to hunt insects in that grassy clearing, so different from the dense bush all around. With so many fern fronds underfoot, the dark bush may be great for sleeping and protection, but for food sourcing, I guess it's challenging.

I fired up the double burners on the tub and had just slipped into the steamy warmth when a number of little silvereyes flew over and perched in nearby shrubs, curious about what was going on. Suddenly, a young male quail appeared on the edge of my tub, not six inches from my toes, checking me out. I watched and enjoyed, but soon became concerned he might tumble into the hot water, so I did a few squeaks, which he echoed. He then hopped down to join his covey of five, who had just returned for another food search. A pretty, self-confident, bold bird. It seems the sounds of splashing and swishing water around are not as frightening as large body movements, and this group of six quail are becoming increasingly familiar with me being here. When I meditate, they doze. When they're foraging, I try to stay motionless so I don't spook them and send them scampering.

The birds have trained me well. I've learned to freeze as I exit the hut, sit in an outside chair, or recline in the tub—waiting out their visits and trying not to disturb them. The patience I've honed in all those hours of meditation has made these waits an easy joy—a chance to observe and be part of their lives. It's with great respect that I become motionless for them. They're born to this land, bear their young here, and probably die on this ridge after five to ten years. I'm just a temporary interloper. I've learned respect and know that this place is theirs, not mine. Such very beautiful birds! And such a gift to have them nearby almost daily now.

The sun goes down. I sit inside in my one chair, pulling stitches on a shibori piece, and loving this life.

April 3, 2015

The sun is setting again after a good day of meditation, study, food preparation and a trip up to the stupa for a meditation sit. The sun is less harsh now, so I was able to sit very close to the bare stupa, where the words "Radiate Love" shine back at me.

I've taken on the weekly care of the lovely vegetable garden that Dharmamudra put in this past season before departing for five months in the U.K. His kind intention and great gardening skills have been a boon for me. The cucumbers and silver beets are waning, but we're heavily into beans and tomatoes now. I try to keep an eye on the tomatoes and carry some almost ripe ones back to the hut before they drop and tangle with the ground bugs. My windowsill has seven beautiful red balls in different shades ripening as I write. I give them a squeeze each day to see which one needs eating before it gets too soft. Two of them went into spaghetti sauce last week, and I've learned the joys of cooking green tomatoes as well. Eight corn stalks are still filling out, and some small pepper plants, and three more squash plants are almost ready.

In New Hampshire, squirrels did in my squash every season, eating the blossoms early, but here all seemed well until last week, when something tampered with one squash that has now rotted. Others have sizable gnaw marks, but they have tough skins, so will probably survive.

The possums seem to have accepted D.M.'s four-foot metal fence at the upper retreat center and the protective netting on my porch boxes as part of the neighborhood, and are no longer climbing on top or nibbling through the end of the net openings.

I carried the biggest squash down to my hut earlier in the week and have had two meals from it so far. It lasts well without refrigeration, and I should get two more meals from it. Today was squash soup and left-over scalloped potatoes with cucumber and tomatoes.

I try to judge the weather, and if there has been a day or two without rain, I'm up there watering with a hose using rainwater collected from a cistern that D.M. set up. I discovered a bag of manure nearby, which I expect is part of the reason for D.M.'s great success with this prolific garden. I brought a little back for my porch planters. The planters did so very well last fall, but they stopped growing as December and January's warmer weather came on, so manure may be a good boost. The silver beet here has already taken notice, putting out new leaves and getting a growth spurt.

The sky darkens; a golden glow begins on the edges of dark clouds. No red tonight, but a magic dance begins as the sky softens to celadon. Pink and red mix with gold for a minute or two and then are gone.

April 4, 2015

It's Saturday, early evening, and gunfire rings out across the valley for a full hour. Every ten or fifteen minutes, five or six volleys seem to come from the deep forest where the Argosy stream comes down from the higher ridge. Zang-ri Hut, where Pemasati is doing her second month of retreat, is right above there, and I wonder how upsetting this must be for her. Of course, sound travels easily here, so the shots could even be coming from over the ridge, deeper in the Coromandel Range. It's normally so very peaceful and quiet here that this occasional gunfire is surprising. It's usually at a weekend. After it stops, the quiet seems especially heavy, permeating the tree tops, the swaying ferns, and the deep ridges. A comforting blanket is pulled up over the valley and the sky lights up red.

April 6, 2015

Morning comes slowly today with an overcast sky. Clouds are clinging to the upper peaks, and I just manage to finish a before-breakfast sit and walking meditation before a hard rain descends. The valley is socked in, with curtains of rain and mist until after 9 AM. As the white shroud starts pulling away, a small male chaffinch arrives for his morning meal. Arriving, passing away.

Observing how these tiny, twenty-one gram birds with no hands or fingers can pick up a seed, shell it, drop the casing, and swallow it in a matter of seconds while I need fingers, lips, teeth and tongue to do the same, has me fascinated. Of course, I'm speedy at cracking open pistachio nuts with my lower front teeth when I'm after that nut myself.

I'm reminded of my house in Japan, where I heard a persistent ringing sound, like someone tapping a gong or a pipe, in the summer. Upon inspection, I found that the neighborhood crows had discovered the dried kibble I put out for the feral cat, Kuro-chan. They would pick up one kernel in their beaks, fly up to the metal patio roof-frame, and bang that kibble on it until it broke into bite-sized pieces. Such ingenuity. It's now quiet and misty again with clouds lying low on the valley. The nasturtiums I've planted from wild seeds are just breaking ground and will welcome this rain. A full moon always seems to bring weather changes. Last night, a glorious large moon sat in a sea of dark clouds from 10 PM to 5 AM. This April moon is called the Grass Moon where I come from, but since we're in the Southern Hemisphere, this could well be the Harvest Moon of fall just after the equinox.

April 7, 2015

The neighbors down below on the other side of the river who care for the cows and Woof and Yipper are doing some construction this morning. The whine of an electric saw echoes through the bush. Rather than disturbing me, it's welcome evidence that there are others in the world, while I see only my own shadow for weeks on end.

Sitting out in a spot of sun, in a different part of the bush, I have a new view of the valley. Closer in, I watch the glints of shining webs that crisscross between the leaves. Seems that it's spider web season as well as mushroom season. Aware and attuned.

Now, on all the tracks I walk through the inner bush, I carry a twig or fern in front of me to keep from walking into these webs, which always seem to be at face height. Some are so dense I have to stop and step backwards to actually disentangle myself. But this morning I'm thinking of what they represent—all the miraculous effort these little spiders extend to weave these beautiful nets of silver glints. I remember raising silkworms, and the strength of of the silk protein in the webs that they put out—silk coupled with serum glue to make a minute thread stronger than steel fiber.

When I take time to watch minute life, insects and birds become a deep fascination. I'm not anthropomorphizing the spiders, not thinking they feel the same dismay I might manifest if someone walked into my six-hour construction and destroyed it, but I certainly see fear, greed, friendliness, curiosity and tenderness displayed, at least among the birds that surround me.

Bob Kull delved into these same reflections I'm having here:

"I'm not claiming I actually know what animals, or the wind, think or feel, but in solitude the visceral experience can be intense and magical—at times terrifying. And if I can't logically claim to know the thoughts and feelings of animals (birds/insects), neither can I dismiss such intuitive identification. Perhaps in solitude I become more sensitive to connections usually invisible to our city-dulled senses. I simply don't know. In any case, personalizing animals and elemental forces seem to happen naturally in solitude."[134]

This perceptiveness, receptiveness, and opening of the heart when we need not be "on guard" or toughened up, is a very real part of solitude. I expect it's there, too, in those who are more spiritually evolved, or have been raised without the fear that modern life instills.

I'm thinking of a remarkable teacher at my art college, who was easily moved to tears by snowfall; of the present Dalai Lama, who cries and laughs so very easily as he opens his heart to each of us; and of a story about Gyalse Thogme Rinpoche (1295-1365), who wrote the *Thirty-Seven Verses on the Practice of a Bodhisattva* that I refer to often. From a very young age, this Rinpoche displayed a degree of compassion and understanding that is the hallmark of the Bodhisattva. Watching a leaf twirl into the wind while in his mother's lap, he wept and said "another being is carried away to the sky." As a young child, he once came inside naked because, he found: "Someone outside was feeling cold." His mother went out to find his clothing wrapped around a frost-covered bush, held in place by stones at the corners to keep it from flying away. He grew up to become a generous, kind man who regularly gave up his own food and clothing to those in need, a great teacher to all through these centuries.[135]

All this was on my mind on this sunny morning in the bush. When I stepped back out onto the track, a small piwakawaka hopped onto a branch next to my shoulder. He chirped a hello, and followed me back to my hut. It's hard not to think of this as friendliness, and to feel the joy of contact, especially on a remote, forested precipice.

April 9, 2015

Tomatoes are bubbling on the stove with some green onions and garlic chopped for this week's spaghetti sauce and I'm about to sit for my third meditation. It's one of those overcast, quiet days with no wind, no birdcalls, and no sound. A feeling of reflection pervades the valley.

I've been looking at this word "reflection," and how it might differ from "thinking about." It seems that when I reflect, I hold the topic more lightly in my hands, finger it, turn it over, examine it, and let conclusions or images come more softly than when I pick through ideas and think deeply. Reflection feels more intuitive and less goal-oriented.

The quality of this retreat has again changed as I move into this last quarter. I'm so very pleased I didn't have to stop after nine months. These last three months feel like a wide, quiet meadow with much still to explore that I would not want to miss. It's a more inward time. I sent off three postcards and a short letter last week, and may now be done with any further communication from here. I'll look at the phone for a text message just once a week. If there's a real emergency, I expect someone will come up here and find me. For now, I'm going more deeply within and am so happy to be doing that. I feel that I'm in a welcome container, a warm and cozy meditation nest, and have all the help and support I need.

A point of reflection this morning had to do with loneliness—what it is. Loneliness has a very different feel from solitude. Loneliness is an emotion: solitude is not. Tenzin Palmo and Henry Thoreau both said they were never lonely, yet others have struggled hard with this.

Loneliness is defined as an unpleasant longing for human interaction, a sadness, an unsatisfied desire. It's something I've felt rarely here, but I do remember it from being out in society. Perhaps I've learned more clearly that it stems from a feeling of duality, of separation, maybe with flavors of grasping, attachment and not getting what I think I need. When I recognize this, the suffering I'm causing myself stops. I'm not separate from others; I'm not really alone if I recognize the web of interconnectedness that exists. It's tangible. Being alone is a treasure, a gift, a chance for deep inward explorations, and for building the confidence and assurance that come from this. Paul Tillich says loneliness is the pain of being alone, while solitude is the glory of being alone. Solitude: physical isolation, social disengagement and reflectiveness—all three need to be there. And at last, with the visa solved, lice under control and my physical environment secure, I'm able to disengage, detach and step into that well of solitude I came here for in a much deeper way. I keep watching, keep listening for all I have to learn; watching with my ears and listening with my eyes.

April 12, 2015

Cold nose, cold ears. Half moon rising after 2 AM in the dark night. Yes, another day alone and just fine. As Lawrence says:

> Be alone, and feel the trees silently growing.
> Be alone, and see the moonlight, white and busy and silent,
> Be quite alone and feel the living cosmos softly rocking.[136]

April 13, 2015

Rain in the night and no moon. A cool morning once again. Though it's 16ºC at 9 AM, it was down to 11ºC/58ºF in the night. This would be balmy weather in mid-winter, but my fingers and nose are cold as I adjust to this weather change. Just last week we had some days in the upper 70/low 80sºF/26-28ºC.

I'm enjoying the multitude of birds arriving outside the hut. In the past it seemed I saw one bird at a time, but now, like those coveys of quail, I see three to four chaffinches and silvereyes flitting from one bush to another, seeming to play with each other, enjoying company while they hunt for insects. I guess this is typical of late summer/early fall bird behavior when, according to my bird book, great groups of birds join together for harvest holidays.

I have a vivid dream life here, often "going to the movies." In last night's dream, despite a visit by noisy possums rearranging furniture, there was quite a rumble and the front two corners of the hut seemed to drop, as if we were having an earthquake. Having lived through daily rumbles in Japan, and even one in the UK when I was speaking in a lecture theatre, I'm not shocked by mild earthquakes. I just ride them out. In my dream, I did get up and found both planters gone. One was on its side in the grass and the other had completely disappeared. For some reason, I decided that possums had sped off with my 100 lb box of growing silver beets. I looked around and found nothing, but was prepared to do a thorough search of this precipice later. Soon, my dream melded into maple sugaring, with my friends and family tapping the maple trees and boiling the sap down to make syrup. This will actually be happening back home in New Hampshire now if the right weather conditions prevail. With this sugaring dream feeling so very real, it was a surprise to wake up to blowing winds and misty New Zealand mountains.

I realize that dreaming is important for mental health. Some people believe it's an information-processing function, putting new experiences into the right slot in permanent memory. Though I wish for dreams of great insight and realization, this does not seem to be part of my life right now. However, I've noticed that my concern for ethics and loving-kindness for others does carry through to my current dream life. When feelings of envy, greed and competition with others show up, I'm shocked enough to wake up with concern.

Dreaming, prayer, meditation and even the creative process are all linked with the need for solitary time to process and produce a harmonious state of mind.

On this retreat, the deep quiet I've felt has provided daily experiences of what I call "life review," which has been most beneficial. The first six months were busy with remembrances and ordering my life experiences. That has lessened now, but is still occasionally present. It's food for thought, helping me to know myself better, and to transcend the life I've been given—learning from the past, forgiving myself for past regressions, and creating aspirations for growth and new knowledge.

April 14, 2015

A third night of lashing wind and rains that abated at 5 AM—the quiet after the storm— and then started again until 9 AM, when the sky cleared, the sun came out, and all that heavy weather was forgotten. The temperature still holds at 7ºC/44ºF. I gave in, started up the heater for the first time in months, and brought the indoor temperature up a few degrees, but not much. This seems to be the start of that weather I had lived through the first three to six months here, and I'm remembering where all the blankets and warm clothes are located. After my first sit, I did walking meditation in my full length Gortex raincoat and boots, and came in to do thirty bows to Buddha, Dharma, and Sangha for devotion and to get more blood flowing. After some spinal twists and shoulder crunches, I was back on my cushion for a second sit, warm and toasty, before my hot porridge breakfast. Just after 9, sirens went off way down in Thames—the first time. With my usual prayers, I sent metta that all are free from danger.

It's a new day in the bush and the chaffinch has come twice for food. I have much cleaning up to do outside, a wash to hang out, and some roadwork to do on Slipglade Track to trench the water flow and avoid having standing water for two weeks. It's comfortable, satisfying work. I don't stop to question it, just do it with love and an open heart.

At noon, I went up to the stupa for a sit and finished roadwork en route. I gathered up some corn there and some ripening tomatoes after this big storm. I'd like to start up the tub, now full of rainwater, but the quail family have arrived and are feeding below it, and I don't want to disturb them.

April 15, 2015

Patience is much on my mind this chilly morning as I blow my nose six times, sneezing between each blow, and deal with the post-nasal drip that has been present throughout my stay.

Ah, patience. It's something I've had a great opportunity to work on during this retreat. Being a self-starter, a quick mover, used to taking care of my own needs in a timely manner, it's a trial to slow down and rely on others. If all went smoothly, if the visa whizzed through in days, if people responded to texts and notes quickly, if my food requests were understood and products were always available, I would have no chance to work on patience.

With this wretched post-nasal drip flooding my sinuses every night, and washing over me whenever I lie down to do yoga, dripping into my already upset stomach, I asked for some decongestants to be posted to me more than three weeks ago. If I were at home, I could slip out the door, hop in the car, swing by the pharmacy, make a purchase, and ingest a wonderful decongestant in under thirty minutes. Here, it takes weeks. Yet in some situations I do well with patience, as my mother and others have mentioned the great patience I show with students and little ones in my teaching.

Patience means accepting or tolerating situations without annoyance or anxiety. I worked so hard to have patience with that visa situation, to not be anxious, but despite rising above the angst and worry again and again with all those hours of meditation and the many candles burnt for the Immigration Service, I ended up not only with stress-related cold sores, but also now two weeks of belly trouble. My pre-ulcerative condition, on hold for thirty years, has shown its painful face. So this morning, with all my complaints of drippy noses and pain in my gut, I'm still working on patience.

I'm lucky to have the support and inspiration of fellow solitary retreatants. I've gone back and re-read how Kull survived a year on an island off Chile (no food delivery) and Tenzin Palmo managed three years at 13,000' in Lahoul, Himalaya. When a pre-arranged six-month delivery of grains, flour and apples didn't arrive, Tenzin Palmo rationed what she had, lost a tremendous amount of weight and came close to starving. Their harrowing experiences give me confidence and reassurance that what I'm doing, they have done, and hardship is valuable. Delayed medication deliveries are so insignificant by comparison that they give me a chance to see myself clearly and work on these faults.

As my morning confession goes, "I acknowledge my flaws and my unskillful habits that keep me from enlightenment. I acknowledge the actions that have built up my faults."

April 17, 2015

With that need for patience comes letting go. Letting go of expectations, attachments to preferences, desires. I've gone from winter into summer, and now am heading back into a second winter. Psychologically, I felt this would be difficult. My preference would have been to have a summer to look forward to, not another harsh winter in an uninsulated hut with high winds and rain. But here I am, accepting it, and finding after nine months of meditation that it's just fine. All that resistance to cold weather, those desires and attachments, have softened and loosened. I'm letting go. Nothing is permanent, even that lovely warm weather. I'm a little sad not to have patches of warm sun to sit in outside for morning breakfast, but maybe there will be some warm days. I pull out that hot water bottle, long forgotten, and bless its invention again and ask, "Why do Americans never think of this?" I locate those few pieces of fleece and the one flannel shirt and one sweatshirt that I'll wear every day now for weeks and months, and am grateful for their warmth. I slip into the routine of lighting a fire each morning for a short time to take the chill off. I snuggle into my meditation nest of shawls, caps and wool blankets as if it were an old home I'm happily returning to. And this too will be impermanent. It's the practice of letting go.

I'm still studying the Heart Sutra and learning about mundane, metaphysical and transcendent wisdom—to be free of "view," to be empty of self-existence. To know that form, sensation, perception, memory and even consciousness are OK. Without attachment to them, seeing them as empty, there's no place for suffering to rest. Taking it in, daily, hourly, moment by moment—and letting go.

April 18, 2015

What a day! Tonight it's the dark of the moon, and with the coming new moon, I'm hoping for some purification and cleansing. It's raining, and just as the landscape weeps, I found myself on my cushion this morning in tears. Stuff coming up again. Am I really not done with this? Truthfully, I realize that this is all illusion and am happiest to just drop into no-self and let it all wash away in the rain. Or have I come to some clearer understanding that needs integrating? Integration—the work of solitaries.

I'm looking at personality traits, whether certain styles of moving through this world are culturally based, and whether this may have put me in conflict on a long retreat in Europe, some years back. I come from a young country full of self-starters, a country that appreciates individuality and over-achieving. America was built on this, and our current president, Barack Obama, is a clear example. We don't get out of the ghetto or the lower middle class without over-achieving—and that's me also, to a lesser degree.

I carry confidence and self-esteem and some level of dignity (as is typical of all of us Leos!) How surprised I was to come across a reference to a "tall poppy" in my New Zealand guidebook's glossary: a tall poppy—someone who excels . . . and discover that cutting down tall poppies to bring over-achievers back to earth is every Kiwi's perceived duty.

Wow! Is this what I run into when I visit the UK? I do know that Japan encourages sameness, and anyone sticking their head above others is liable to get it lopped off. Yet I found that as a foreigner, I was expected to be different. I was useful to that society. But in a three-month retreat in Europe with a predominance of Brits, I ran into some very painful incidences that felt like head-lopping. I ended up with some of the lowest amounts of self-esteem and confidence of my life, and am still healing from this.

Question: Does culturally acceptable behavior differ that greatly between English-speaking countries? It's true that I'm the one who steps off the curb and crosses the street with confidence when nothing is coming. I don't stand questioning at the edge of the curb.

What I learned during those painful three months was to duck and hide. I became the last one, not the first, to speak or move. It was most stressful since I was not able to be myself, authentic or present. And was I also criticized for hiding? The land was extraordinary, the spiritual dimensions superb—yet the experience left a bad taste in my mouth, for which I am sad.

With this pouring rain and these flashes of lightning, I'm here on this precipice to heal—to integrate, to grow, and to fall deeply in love with the world. And to forgive myself and others. Only illusion.

Wow! Wow! What exciting weather! Weather can be the best channel in town. The rain is so heavy this afternoon that I have to turn on the overhead light in order to write. The rainwater cisterns and my tub are almost overflowing. I wonder if there will be flooding from all this. I'm happy to be on such high ground, and have no worries with that, but what of the others? I hope everyone is hanging on and safe.

Maybe I needed this heavy rain and this purging to loosen my attachment to what might have been during that previous retreat. It was what it was, and I continue to learn from it. And are these kind, thoughtful Kiwis really interested in lopping off the heads of over-achieving Americans, or is Obama safe to come here?

April 21, 2015

Has the rain stopped for a few days? I hope so, since it has been a very wet week. Yesterday was another day of continuous showers, and the hut is full of clothes still drying from a wash done days ago.

I have six little quail on the tub boardwalk just below my steps—also drying out. They look as if the wet weather has been rough on them, and are really enjoying the bit of sun we have this morning—spreading their feathers, preening, and settling into groups for a warm snooze. The two young males hop up on the logs bordering the grass. Are they standing guard on the four sleeping females, or is that just some male bonding?

As I did my walking meditation an hour ago, feeling a bit glum, I was comforted by three fantails that sought to lift my spirits. They came so close that they twittered about my face, landed on twigs, cocked their heads, and almost perched on my shoulder—and then they spread their glorious white and black tail feathers like miniature peacocks in a lovely morning welcome. They're such curious, friendly beings. It's hard not to smile in acknowledgement of this outpouring of kindness. Bless the birds.

I'm now putting out two dishes of seed for the chaffinches to try to reduce the bullying. It hurts my heart to see one piggy female pushing off the others, and frightening the more timid. Maybe I should be sending a little metta to them as well as an additional feeding dish, and asking what this greed issue is all about. Perhaps that bullying female has a nest of squabbling hatchlings to contend with back in the bush? They all certainly give me great entertainment, and a morning of small insights.

After many days and weeks of stitching pattern into Ahimsa cloth during that long visa-wait, I've soaked the pieces, pulled up threads, and knotted the silk into resist work. I'm on to dyeing them now. They're a series of explorations of the Heart Sutra—taking my experiential and intuitive response, and translating this ephemeral quality into images on cloth. Not an easy challenge. "Form is emptiness." "No feeling, thought or choice." "Holding to nothing, whatever." "Beyond, beyond, way beyond." How do you translate that into image? It's a challenge, yes, but a good conundrum to play with between meditation sits. I'm grateful to have this work, and try to do it with an open heart, with no "self" involved, with little judgment or criticism of the outcome. Assessment can come later. For now, it's just joy in colors and pattern.

I'm just back from a walk along Slipglade Track. It's my first time off this point in a week. I went out to clear fallen fern fronds off the track since it's Tuesday and Tony will be coming along in the ORV to pick up my weekly food order from the dropbox and my little trash bag. I was surprised to see much fresh digging and foraging along the side of the path, far more than ever before. Obviously, the wild pigs were hungry, and quite busy last night. Walking along, I flushed the Dharma Road quail covey (now up to fourteen) that I've often seen gathering in the road.

At the upper retreat house garden there were still a few tomatoes and silver beets for picking. I'm on the last small ear of corn and a few green onions, but the beans seem completely finished. There were two squash blossoms and two cucumber flowers, so there's hope for a bit more in the future if the temperature doesn't drop too far too quickly.

It's been great to eat off the garden since my own porch planters are putting out so very little these past few months. I see lots of mushrooms, three different types all along the stupa path and here in the sunshine at my hut. I wish I knew more about them since I'd be happy to eat from this wild bounty, but I'm clueless. I read last week of a Thich Nhat Hanh group in Japan in the 90s that had sixty hospitalized and one losing his sight and temporarily the use of his legs from eating poisonous wild mushrooms, so I'm very cautious—but interested.

I was so very sorry to hear the news that Thich Nhat Hanh was hospitalized for a severe brain hemorrhage six months ago. I'm glad to know he came out of the coma, and I'm joining in with the prayers from around the world in hope that he'll recover. He is eighty-eight though, and has lived a long, extraordinarily significant life for the benefit of so many people. He's been a spiritual father to so many, and a model of deep compassion for me.

I find these words of his so moving at this moment:

This body is not me; I am not caught in this body. I am life without boundaries.
I have never been born and I have never died. Over there, the wide ocean and the sky with many galaxies all manifest from the basis of consciousness. Since beginningless time, I have always been free. Birth and death are only a door through which we go in and out . . . playing a game of hide and seek.[137]

He shows us the way.

What a delight to spy the tiniest fingernail slice of a waxing moon low in the northwestern sky as the sun sets. I gather a blanket and blue watch cap to sit outside and honor its descent to the ridge until the odd mosquito sends me inside with three bites. It's good to see that old friend. The new moon is always a bit hard for me when it's so very, very dark here.

April 22, 2015

How sweet to wake up chanting mantras.

Can I write this? Can I get it down? While I'm meditating on my cushion in front of my shrine, it's as if I'm transformed into a busy train station. As I follow my breath in and out, a thought may arrive like a train pulling into that station. At that moment, I have a choice. I can board that train and depart with the thought as it travels through multiple stations, and end up, thirty minutes later, far from my intended concentration focus, or I can continue sitting. I noticed this morning that

297

there really could be a gap, a conscious decision to board that train or let it pass through, to put energy and content into that thought or not.

That image reminds me of the great benefit I've received from suffering that concussion. For the first time in my life, I could actually sense my brain and carefully watch the slow, slogging process of forming thoughts, which used to come with lightning speed. When I was in the deep throes of it, information that would have been "on the tip of my tongue" before became less accessible. That was embarrassing, but I accepted it and hoped cognition would return. The injury gave me access to watching a thought actually form. I saw myself put tremendous effort into scanning for the answer to a question. That experience now helps me watch thoughts form and develop when I don't want to take that train.

This morning I heard the stationmaster singing out the departing trains; "Lunch—What to Have," "Generosity—How to Volunteer," "Japan Pilgrimage—Planning" . . . "All Aboard!" Without me putting energy into the topic, those trains departed on their own and left me sitting quietly on the cushion, in the back of the station, watching my breath move in and out, inhale, exhale, long breath here, short breath there. Just aware. I saw the train station for what it was, and chose not to ride any of the outgoing thoughts, not even the fast moving through-station express.

I saw that there was no "I" sitting; no thought coming, no subject, no object, just the doing, the sitting and the being. No "me," no "my," no "mine." Just sitting, a blissful, relaxing, out of body space. Nobody. No sensations, no thoughts or perceptions, no history, memory, or choice. Not even consciousness connected to a "me." Empty and full. Wind blowing through. Nobody home. No "one" to be home. No doer of the deed, knower of the known. Vast. Limitless. No train station.

April 24, 2015

A vivid rainbow greets me as I fill the tub for a morning bath. All is impermanent: rainbows, sleeplessness, me.

April 25, 2015

The almost half-moon is low in the sky, about to set behind the ridge at 9:30 PM. It will be another cold night after some wonderfully warm days. I'm acclimating to fall and the coming winter after an all too brief summer.

I've had a lovely day of intermittent showers. I worked on a new, longer sadhana visualization of Kuan Yin, the Bodhisattva of Compassion. It's been developing for months, and this morning it all seemed to come together. I spent an hour or more between meditations writing it out longhand before doing some polishing and typing it into the computer before the battery got down to 8%. I use the computer very rarely, perhaps once a month or less, to listen to a Satipatthana lecture or hear the words and pronunciation of the Dhammapalam Gatha that I'm trying to memorize. There's no internet connection up here, so I have no pull to email or search the web. Just the birds and me.

April 27, 2015

Yesterday was a lovely day of full sun and buoyant feelings. I was up early and went through the daylight hours with deep happiness. I enjoyed having Kuan Yin so present with this new, vivid sadhana visualization I've prepared which speaks to me and calls her into my life more clearly. Then this morning broke with cold, dark rain that went on all day and my spirits fell. I watch my reaction with acknowledgement and awareness.

For the second time in two weeks we've had a day of rain that rivals Noah's deluge. Rain buckets are filled to overflowing and I have a tub outside with water two inches from the top. The rain stopped finally about 3 PM. The half-moon is now out and the valley is roaring in the dark with gallons and gallons of water running down that river and out to sea. The growling roar reminds me of that first big storm when I arrived; as soon as it stopped, I had to march down Mill Track and see where all that noise came from. Now, I know. I also know that by tomorrow morning all will be quiet and the deluge over.

I'm getting so very tired of being bitten through the night, and can't quite put my finger on why or who. I'm still boiling my sheets and clothing as a final rinse, but wonder if washing that dries on an open line may be picking up creepy-crawlies I don't know about. I'm particularly sensitive to bug bites and my warm metabolism seems to attract every mosquito, flea and spider within miles. While I love this life in the semi-wild, bites in the night I will not miss.

I remember a night at a guesthouse on the Li River in China thirty years ago, where there were more mosquitoes inside than outside the mosquito net. I knew I was being bitten, but decided to be a good Zen student and let the insects have their meal, and then they would be done. My travelling mate heard me whimpering in my sleep. We counted sixty bites on one arm alone, and over two hundred bites on my legs, arms, back and face. As I said, insects love me—I make a great meal.

Complaints, yes. But truly, I do love it here. I'm relishing the quiet, the roar of the river, the gusting of the wind, and the chirping demands of hungry finches and cooing quail. I'll deeply miss this in two months.

April 29, 2015

I awoke to the voice of my little sister asking if she could go out and play—her child's voice clear as day. She's been gone for twelve years.

The sun was out at last, so I put some clothes in to soak and sat for meditation, missing that sister. It started to rain. The arising and passing away of phenomena. I keep learning to keep letting it go.

Later, I was out in the wet world for walking meditation in my raincoat and purple boots—lift, swing, place; lift, swing, place my feet on wet grass. A shaft of sunlight broke through the forest and brought the bush to life. I turned, and a shining jewel caught my eye and stopped me in my tracks: an exquisite drop of rainwater glowing on the edge of a leaf. A diamond on an emerald curve. I stood still and took it in as two tomtits flew through to see what was happening. I remembered Dogen's Zen poem of a drop of water on a heron's beak and was pulled into deeper reverence. "What speaks of our fragile life as the moonlight shining in a teardrop of water trembling on the tip of a heron's beak?"

Back inside to begin my second morning sit, I took a sip of hot tea and saw my breath vaporize in the chilly room. Wrapped in a shawl and blanket, I was absorbed in emptiness, the void, the vastness of sunyata, as the rain began again.

This is the solitary life, the ups and downs, ins and outs of a mind struggling for enlightenment in this lifetime. Such a grand aspiration, but an aspiration worthy of effort, of focus.

April 30, 2015

Warm sunlight poured through the window, touching my crown, filling me with love for the world and compassion for all those suffering. I felt happy and joyous, filled with this red light blessing from Kuan Yin. It connects to the sadhana I do, but is especially inspiring when the rays of the sun or moon cascade down and become blessings and purifications in themselves.

The surface of the land here on the Coromandel peninsula is always moving. Because I'm surrounded by tree ferns, not stout pines, or oaks with solid trunks and strong limbs, the fronds bounce. In spring I counted as many as twelve to fifteen brown, furry fiddleheads as big as my hand developing together deep within the trees. These grew and unfolded over two months to become full fronds, many of them six feet long. With the gusting autumn winds, they're always in motion. Many of last year's fronds have dried and withered, and I was pulled to do some tidying up and cut these off, but soon realized that they give the small birds a good roosting perch, and so they stayed.

I come to the last day of the month, a joyous month of grounding and developing. I feel more and more that this is my home. I feel established in my practice and free from former worries. I could easily stay on and make this a LIFE of solitude, as Milarepa did. Soon, it will be time to come out and be in the world again. But not quite yet.

More rain and blustery weather—typical fall weather, it seems. It keeps me close to home and that meditation cushion.

Brilliant red mushroom along the Slipglade Track.

Chapter 11 May

During the night, I awoke to a bright moon shining into my room and spotlighting my meditation cushion and mat. It always inspires me when this happens. To have that cool, silver light shining right on that spot where I sit hour after hour asking for nirvana is a small miracle. Tonight is the "becoming" moon, with the three quarter waxing into a full moon in just a few more days. This moon of poignant promise, the moon becoming.

I sing praises to the weather gods for coming up with this gloriously sunny day after so much rain and wind. I thought that we were marching on to winter but then this . . . this.

Today, the glowing sun crept over the eastern hills and sent a shaft of light onto the northwestern ridges on the far side of the valley at 7:20 AM. Not one cloud in that porcelain blue sky. It was cold, 7ºC or 44ºF, and the temperature stayed there for another hour or so. I was up for two meditation sits, with ten minutes of walking meditation in between and then breakfast. All this swift, organized activity was so that I could get the fleece pants and navy sweatshirt off my body after ten days and into a wash. I hoped there would be sunshine to dry them before I needed to wear them again. And, yes, it worked. I got sheets, underwear, nightshirts and turtlenecks into the wash as well. All of them were out on the line before a meditation sit in the sunshine and a walk to the stupa and vegetable garden by 11 AM.

Everything is happily drying, and still not one cloud to be seen. We're up to 16ºC/62ºF. What a day!

Today is the day I should have prepared a tub bath—not yesterday, when it was still so chilly and a cold rain started as I slipped into the water. After all that time heating the water up, it was still only tepid when I hopped in. It was a sorrowfully short bath.

303

May 3, 2015

It's hard for me to consider the first of May as fall, but here, it certainly is. The winter solstice is next month and the second of the three autumn moons is coming into fruition. I think of those in Japan, the USA and Europe who often sit full moons with me in mind on a cushion above a roaring valley.

Zen Master Ryōkan wrote lovingly of the autumn moon—a special time for moon-viewing in Japan.

> The moon appears in every season, it's true,
> But surely, it is best in fall.
> In autumn, the mountains loom and water runs clear.
> A brilliant disc floats across the infinite sky,
> And there is no sense of light or darkness,
> For everything is permeated with its presence.
> The boundless sky above, the autumn chill on my face.
> I take my precious staff and wander among the hills.
> Not a speck of the world's dust anywhere,
> Just the brilliant beams of moonlight.
> I hope others too are gazing on this moon tonight,
> And it's illuminating all kinds of people.
>
> Autumn after autumn the moon comes and goes;
> Human beings will gaze upon it for eternity.
> The sermons of Buddha, the preaching of Eno
> Surely occurred under the same kind of moon.
>
> I contemplate the moon through the night,
> As the stream settles and white dew descends.
> Which wayfarer will bask in the moonlight longest?
> Whose home will drink up the most moon beams?[138]

May 4, 2015

I extended my hands across two oceans and the Tasmanian Sea to celebrate this full moon, shining so patiently in the cold night sky. It's Wesak, the celebration of Buddha's enlightenment under that Bodhi tree 2550 years ago. Such a miracle, and such an inspiration to us all to know that we mortals can wake up from all our dreams of suffering and pain and see them as illusion. My mate in solitude over in Australia is finishing her nine-month retreat with this full moon and coming out today. A short note from her in January said "It's been a great comfort to know that you too are on this amazing journey just across the water."

The land was cold and frosty this morning after that full moon. I no longer hear the possum's mating call of "Boooo-Rah" hissing in the night like an ethereal ghost, only the persistent ruru owl. The flowers have mostly gone. All that remain are a stray daisy or two and the lovely Himalayan honeysuckle with trailing red flower tassels dangling from deep green leaves. But the mushrooms are prolific, popping out of the damp forest along every path. I delighted in some brilliantly red ones as big as my hand that appeared this week in two places. What a chance to notice all the joys of the forest floor. It takes seclusion and quiet to wake up to all the beauty that lives right next to my feet.

I was so excited to spy six gray bunnies feeding on the grass near the outside tub, but then a black-masked face with a great topknot popped up, and I realized it was the quail family, not rabbits! They've grown into beautiful rotund adults in the past month or two, filled out to the size of soccer balls. After twenty minutes of foraging, they nestled down into two groups for a snooze, and ten minutes later were back to insect hunting before the evening chill descended. No bunnies in this bushland so far.

Today is the 300th day of my retreat. I'm surprised. I came across a note I wrote to myself in September, which starts with: "All of life does not need to be exciting" and goes on to remind me to "honor the ups and downs of this retreat. Be humble, eat your words. All will change. Don't be lazy, but learn to put less pressure on yourself. Watch what's going on internally and externally." All still important.

Three hundred days! My inclination is to take a morning and evaluate, though I will try to put that aside a little longer. It's more important for me to continue to be aware, be here this day. To be present until I'm not. I've done well, and am so very content and settled here that it will be a pull to get me out. To have this very wonderful opportunity to stop all that activity, that compulsive response to demands—email, phone calls, schedule—to stop and be. This morning, I realized I have nothing that needs doing. I can sit longer, chant longer, and stay with a thought as long as it takes because no one is waiting for me. It will be hard to pick up that pressured life I've built for myself again. This contemplative seclusion suits me quite well. I have concerns that I'll not be finished exploring *sunyata*, emptiness, and the void when my days are up. Perhaps I never will be finished.

May 5, 2015

At 6:32 AM I see the "hazy moon of enlightenment." Where does that quote come from? Eihei Dogen again?

May 6, 2015

A lovely, mild day with sun, temperatures up to 20ºC/68ºF, and not much wind. Quiet. But then I heard the sweet cooing start of the quail call. I couldn't see them in the grass out front, but soon, six of them slipped out from under my front porch to eat and forage just four feet away. They're such beautiful birds.

I set off to the stupa to share my happy day with Dhardo Rinpoche and photograph a group of brilliantly red mushrooms that I discovered on Slipglade Track as I walked out yesterday to the Community House library. I wanted to leave a big note of WOW! next to them to share this joy with another human, perhaps with Tony as he brought my groceries, but I'm sure he saw them. Such a startling contrast—this brilliant red in a land of green and brown.

I came home from the stupa trek to find some very juicy scat on the edge of the outdoor tub. I bet it was the quail calling card—though this is a first.

This journal has so many reference to the little beings that I live among. Reading other solitary reports, I find similar references. We even assign them personalities, noting who is the shy one and who's an aggressor. This is a retreat of possums and birds, yet thinking back to my other solitary retreats, I realize that I made friends with the sheep in Wales and the friendly dogs in Mexico, observed the aggressive roosters and their hen wives in Bali, and the hierarchy of temple dogs in Thailand. The New Zealand birds are much more agreeable, and with my quiet and respectful ways, we get along well. I have learned from them.

May 8, 2015

Every so often, I come across a sentence that grabs me with its poignancy and has me re-reading it again and again. Gretel Erhlick has one in her evocative book on sheepherding in Wyoming, *The Solace of Open Spaces.* "Last week a bank of clouds lowered itself down summer's green ladder and let loose with a storm."[139]

It sounds like what happened last night when the rain started, then echoed all through the night. It's still pelting down now after breakfast. Fluffy white clouds are coming down the yonder ridges, and my valley neighbor's electricity-producing waterfall is running strong. The valley roars with moving water.

Despite the rain, I see birds flit in and out of the scrub, and two entertaining silvereyes are hanging upside down on the red tassels of the Himalayan honeysuckle, getting what nectar remains.

Indoors, the ants have not given up. I observe them on the kitchen counters as well as on the bedside nightstand, foraging for crumbs from last night's scone snack.

May 10, 2015

After thirty-six hours of intense rain, the deluge stopped. I was happy to see a fine, white-throated tui in the trees above my path as well as a hefty woodpigeon as I stepped outside for walking meditation early this morning. Once these woodpigeons were hunted for food, killed almost to extinction. I was pleased that this one was comfortable enough with me that he could sit above on a tree limb as I did my quiet walk below. I got another view of him as I turned and continued my slow walk back. I've spotted nineteen different bird species in the ten months I've been here, from mynas and eastern roseda parrots to yellowhammers and greenfinches.

Today, I continue to observe the ant population. They seem to be busier in my kitchen in fall than they ever were in summer. I now have to set my honey and maple syrup bottles into water jars to keep the little ones from taking them over. Banana pancakes are not so delicious with baby ants cascading over them as they come off that yummy syrup bottle. What would appall me elsewhere, I just deal with here . . . with equanimity and some smiles. Life is simple here.

Likewise, the last of the tomatoes have many spots and mushy parts as I'm coming to the end of this crop—but they're food, and I persist in cutting off bad parts. I stew them up with celery, onion and garlic and they're delicious.

It's hard to go out and sit in the bush for reflection when we have no sun, but here I go—down to visit the big pine—even as gunfire rings through the valley again. I squat in the forest, put my shoulder and head against the trunk, and breath in her protection.

May 11, 2015

I sleep, bathed in the soft light of a half-moon, and woke two hours later, now bathed in sunlight. Amazing.

Today, I'm reflecting again on solitude and loneliness. My reading brings me to the story of that great man, Nelson Mandela, who spent twenty-eight years incarcerated, winning freedom, dignity and equality for his fellow South Africans. This deeply forgiving, brilliant and compassionate man writes that the hardest time was his last year, when he was placed in a three-bedroom prison home (with swimming pool!!), away from fellow prisoners. He said it was the loneliest time of his long imprisonment and the most intolerable. Loneliness is an emotion.

Isolation and loneliness are not the same thing. I wonder if Mandela's loneliness at the age of seventy was perhaps connected to the remorse and regret he talks about experiencing—his feeling that he had caused his loved ones great harm and suffering. His political activities and ensuing incarceration meant he was not present to help and protect them. In truth, he took on the suffering of many, rather than the suffering of the few, as a Bodhisattva might do.

When I re-read the story of Tenzin Palmo, I found that her time of loneliness was not during those twelve years in that cave, where she was most happy in her practice, but rather, when she was surrounded by many people at a monastery. As the sole woman in a sea of monastic men, she was excluded by tradition from hearing the communal teachings and practicing devotional ceremonies with them. She suffered immeasurably, and writes of deep loneliness until she realized that this was all emotion. She identified it as attachment and grasping, and saw clearly that it was causing her suffering. With that knowledge, the loneliness dropped away.

Am I lonely in my small hut in the bush? No, not really. I have so much: the company of birds and insects; the beauty of the bush, with every path and leaf and stone to explore; the liveliness of unpredictable weather; the chance to research, explore and reflect on what I see and what is within; the blessings of a healthy mind, full of creativity and imagination; and a practice that gives inspiration and encouragement. I'm here with the support of so many and they're with me in spirit. Loneliness is not possible with so many beings sharing my life in this interconnected web.

May 12, 2015

As I was meditating, the floor trembled, the windows howled a mournful tune, and the new mushroom in the front grass was toppled by gusting wind. A storm had broiled into the valley from the southeast. I'm so used to stormy weather coming from the north in New England; it continues to surprise me that here it's the southern gales we fear most. But Antarctica is down there, swiftly moving into the dark, polar winter.

I know the temperature (minus 60ºF) on this day, May 12, eighty-one years ago in that dark Antarctic wilderness because of Adm. Richard Byrd's journal. A fellow solitary retreatant, Byrd writes that the "aurora flamed brilliantly ... and danced its frenetic excitement . . . for hours." I have no aurora australis here, but I do know that brilliance from my time in Iceland, forty years ago. Byrd was doing well this week in 1934, having arrived six weeks earlier. Like him, I'm cold and wet, but his conditions were so much more severe than my blowing gale. He writes of being utterly at peace in that present moment with the aurora australis, and I share that peace with him, deeply.

When I put on my raincoat and my wellies and trudged up to Slipglade Track to leave my food list for the week at the drop-box, I found a true joy inside that box . . . another book on silence that an Auckland friend mentioned, dropped off by an intermediary. A book! It's not tulips or daffodils, but so welcome.

And then, alas, the dark side showed its face. I'm still not sure what precipitated it today, but in my mind I was back in last September and October when my neighbor, a five-minute walk away, was going mad. I again relived the sounds. The screaming and fighting were disturbing enough, but the shouting in tongues in the dark added to my confusion and unease. I realize now that much of the angst of that time was being in the deep bush, not knowing what was happening up in that hut, and not feeling reassured that my concerns were heard down below in the community.

I wanted to be tough and to be okay. My heart opened and I worked daily to send metta—loving-kindness—to my neighbor in his troubles, and metta to myself. All that helped keep me here. But to be told that although he was threatening the retreat environment, he had been promised the legal one month's notice to vacate, and would not be leaving for another thirty-five days!

So here I am, eight months later, feeling nauseous and weepy when I thought all this had passed. Obviously I've not yet recovered. Knowing that disturbing emotions only harm myself and others, I got up from my meditation cushion, put on my boots and raincoat, started chanting the Vajrasattva purification mantra, and marched through the rain to the stupa. Now, one hour later, I'm better, and the orange-date scones are in the camp oven on the stove. I think of a course I could teach: "How to Deal with Trauma, Alone on Solitary Retreat: 101-102." This is an experience for the tough, and only for those with sincere intention. The wimps left months ago.

May 13, 2015

I awoke at 5:55 AM with moonglow coming in my window. The headache from yesterday's angst was almost gone. Did the headache precipitate the emotional pain or did the emotions bring on the headache? Chicken and egg. But a new day was here. With distance, I was able to unplug that fiery emotional element, examine it again, and reflect.

I sat in the moonlight and let that beam nourish and heal me. It was a delicate waning quarter moon with a hazy oblong glow around it, not yet at the zenith. I watched the horizon turn from Wedgewood blue to powder blue, and then to white on this moon path. Finally, one hour later, the moon slipped behind low clouds as the eastern horizon turned a golden orange glow, preceding the sunrise.   My emotions too moved into the clarity of a new day. I realize now how much anger I still carry connected to the happenings of last September. Not knowing what was going on, or what the retreat staff were striving to do, or could do in this delicate situation, I saw only that they weren't helping him with his demons or me with my fears as much as I felt they should.

While I have trouble owning anger, it does erupt from that intense, fiery core I carry. It's usually fired by seeing others harmed by seeming incompetence, irresponsibility, or lack of mindfulness. Yet the anger that pops out of me harms others, I see. And it harms me as well. People make decisions based on what they know, and the lack of action last September came, I expect, from good intentions: wanting to provide a haven for someone who was agitated and needed a quiet retreat, wanting to honor a promise of one-month's (legal) notice, wanting to provide a safe place for all retreatants—which, in this case, was not possible. Physical safety, emotional safety and psychological safety have different faces. Somehow, through this episode, I lost a bit of trust in the powers that be, and felt very much on my own, without needed support.

I know that every solitary retreat brings up some crisis to learn from. From health issues to mechanical breakdowns to psychological crises, they all show up. Hopefully, the crisis doesn't become life-threatening. Those who act as "guardians at the door" of a retreat need to be trained to respond to all of these issues, and have a support team in place to help. The tenacious retreatants survive, though some of us hold on only with our fingertips. I'm surprised that, eight months later, I'm still walking through this morass, trying to understand what happened, learning to accept and forgive others and myself.

Yet, meditating outside in the warmth, I feel deep peace pervade the valley. Finding my breath, no thoughts cling. Only breath. Breathing in, breathing out the blue. Breathing the sky, that vast, infinite, deepest, most transparent blue. The void, the emptiness. I too am made of this, my mind blue, full of the clarity of the nature of ultimate voidness, vastness.

May 15, 2015

I've come here partly to study silence. This week, Sara Maitland's *Book of Silence* has helped me put my finger on a number of its qualities She's been studying silence for fifteen to twenty years, focusing on a secular rather than religious context. Maitland uses the experiences of long-distance sailors, arctic explorers, wilderness adventurers, mountaineers and those marooned to back up the observations of religious retreatants. She's found a number of common qualities that I too have observed, and in some cases shared: an intensification of physical and emotional sensations; a feeling of interconnectedness; a lessening of inhibitions; some kinds of auditory confusion such as "hearing voices"; boundary confusion that perhaps results in risk-taking; a sense of bliss or joy; and experiences that can't be put into words. But also, a significantly lowered energy level, or even lethargy. This was something the monastics fought against, seeing it as sheer laziness.

Lazy is something I've never been called. Since childhood, I've always been known for my energy and activity. These have brought recognition, accomplishments and praise. While it is perhaps an innate part of my personal physiology, being busy became a habit early in my life. I couldn't feel good about myself unless I checked off everything on my "to do" list for the day. Internal drive as well as external rewards have defined my life ever since.

And so, this year away has been an experiment for me. I was intrigued to see how much I might accomplish when I was no longer observed, free from any judgments or criticism. That habit of being busy continued for a number of months, but eventually I settled into a deliciously quiet, still space. I sang that refrain easily, "Nothing to do, nowhere to go".

Maitland discusses this lack of activity on solitary, how there comes a feeling of drowning in silence where it becomes harder and harder to move. Some retreatants feel slightly drunk or elated, but others have reported being somewhat uncoordinated, dreamy, entranced or uncaring. Gontran de Procius, the French Arctic explorer, wrote of the stillness that began to weigh on him—the flame of life within him withdrawing further and faster into a secret hiding place, and his heartbeat slowing. He spoke of feeling almost paralyzed, and of a sinking feeling, as if he was in a well from which he couldn't pull himself out without inconceivable difficulty.[140]

Is this a mental, emotional or physical reaction to silence? Or a response to cold, lack of activity, lack of a proper diet? I read in Maitland that deep silence can carry an element of bliss that's truly mourned when closure comes, a bliss that can also be an aspect of a classic mystical experience. With a twist, this reaction to silence can also move into depression if one is predisposed.

Or this response to silence can be seen as *acidie*—mental or spiritual apathy—as the Desert Fathers argued. It can be viewed as sloth, a lack of enthusiasm or interest, listlessness, a lethargy that can become a pathological need for sleep. Anthony Grey, who was placed in solitary confinement by the Chinese Red Guards, said his life was becalmed on a flat sea, empty. The early Christians just called it sin and pushed the threefold discipline of study, physical work and prayer.

What I learned from former solitary retreats is the need for a plan or a flexible schedule that one keeps to. This comes naturally and easily for me. I'm never far from my meditation cushion. Secular solitaries, especially those incarcerated, have practiced a variety of activities that kept them sane: Edith Bone, in solitary for seven years in Hungary, recited poetry and translated it into the six languages she knew; an incarcerated musician went methodically through the four parts of each Beethoven quartet; Anthony Grey created crossword puzzles and learned Chinese on his own; the Birdman of Alcatraz studied ornitholgy and wrote three books during forty-three years of solitary confinement. They echo religious retreatants like Tenzin Palmo, who followed a heavy schedule of twelve hours of meditation practice a day.

All this makes that silence, that solitariness, tolerable and even productive. But my usual energy is definitely down. Has that energy I've been known for in the past been fueled ego-assertions? Or am I just feeling my age, perhaps? I seem to feel exhausted easily, but I'm happy to be in a deeper place, tuning into myself. I monitor my food, activity, thoughts, rest and reading—realizing that higher states of consciousness and awareness will come from this time, and hopefully also integration. I'm changing. I'm different from when I came in.

May 16, 2015

Today, the temperature didn't rise above 8°C/46°F until 10 AM. Continued belly pain had me getting up from my third sit and texting home to ask my daughter to call my doctor for a consultation. I've been having problems for six weeks now, though I've been mindful of how much fried food I was consuming since it has caused problems in the past. The acid reflux pills I've taken don't seem to make a difference. Am I manifesting an ulcer? Should I just sit with this for another two and a half months? Will that risk damaging my stomach lining?

What a delight to have that small emergency cell phone come alive with a return message in under a minute from the other side of the world, saying "I'm so sorry to hear you have belly pain." Across sixteen hours of time difference, two oceans and a landmass, I'm cared for. It made my heart fill and a real smile appeared on my face.

Meditating outside with eyes closed, I heard the familiar click, click, coo, coo of quail coming in. They join me regularly, wending their way through dense bush. The repeating soft "macwerta, macwerta" of the male call confirmed their arrival. When I opened my eyes, I found them foraging for insects three or four feet away. Soon, they settled down for their ten-minute snooze. When I finished meditating, I opened my eyes and they were gone.

Ahh, the joys of meditating with quail. I resolve to continue to wake up to the joy that is right there in my daily life, even when not on retreat.

The Desert Hermits of the 4th c tell the story of three young monks. One was assigned to reconciling enemies, one to visiting the sick, and one went off to the desert. The first two were quite unsettled, overwhelmed by responsibilities, and discouraged by their progress. When they asked the third how he was getting on, he demonstrated his realizations by pouring water into a jar. It was murky since it was desert water. However, a little while later, the water had settled and cleared. "The former water is like the man who lives among others," he told them, "Because of their turbulence, he cannot see his unskillfulness. Yet, when he lives alone, especially in the desert, he can see his failings."[141] In silence, all settles and life becomes clearer. How very true. After this time of quiet, reflection, and some life changes, I can go back and be of more help to others.

May 17, 2015

I've been awake since 4:30 AM. Hilarious! Two young possums visited during this chilly night, sliding down the porch posts from the roof. They forgot to bring their wirecutters, so the silver beets were safe for another night beneath the netting. The best the possums could do was sniff and smell the greens, and leave some poop on the porch. When I got up, I used my bramble brush to sweep away the remains and managed to flip it eight feet into the air and into the full bathtub. Yuk! Luckily, possum poop floats, and I was able to scoop it out in minutes. Life!

May 18, 2015

A white sky and temperatures in the 40s (6-8ºC). I woke from a dream of seeing my days as mala beads on a string—round, smooth, the same again and again, snuggling next to each other, supporting each other. The days on that string rarely had a shining jewel among them, but they were beautiful and precious in their own way. A dream that echoes my life here on the hill.

Leaving my warm bed, I drew some water for tea, snapped on the heater, and placed the pee bucket out one door to be dealt with later. The bird seed tray went out the other door. A flutter of shadows on the fogged-up glass told me the birds had come. I prayed Grayhead wouldn't boss and harass the others, but would let them have a bit of seed on this cold morning. All the delusions—the greed, anger and ignorance of human life that brings so much suffering— are played out each day on my porch as I watch these feathered beings. It's a gift to see some show kindness and joy, but Grayhead, especially, has serious problems that need looking into. I send metta to her.

In silence. No one to share insights with. A quiet year.

I look down at these hands, which are often grasping a ceramic tea cup for warmth when I'm not in a meditation pose, and am surprised once more. These brown hands framed in dark blue fleece are not my hands, or the hands of a New Englander. These brown hands arrived last October or November after a few months of intermittent sun. They belong to New Zealand, and probably won't be seen again: rich nut brown with a glow of yellow—nothing I have seen on me at any other time in my life. They remind me of the hands of Vikasini, who arrived in Spain from Auckland to support my Ordination retreat five years ago. They belong to a New Zealander. I'm continually surprised to see this anomaly at the end of my own blue cuffs.

May 20, 2015

A quiet, cold morning. It was 9ºC (48ºF) when I woke at 6:30 AM and now at 9:20 it's moving up to 12ºC (54ºF). I believe it got to 20ºC (68ºF) yesterday as I was slipping into a warm bath outdoors among the tree ferns. It felt so good to be clean.

Some small insights that have been cooking on the back burner for a week or more came rolling in today. They make this whole year of quiet worthwhile. One of those insights is my need (habit) to be "other regarding." This echoes the insight of that third desert monk, alone so that his internal water could settle and he could see more clearly.

I was raised and trained to always think of others, and perhaps be defined by others. That focus has changed somewhat in the past twenty years as I've been drawn to meditation and more inner reflection. I woke this morning with friends on my mind and how I might be of help to them. Noble thoughts. But I'm here on retreat. I should be focusing on self-awareness, my internal workings and my busy mind, with the aim of becoming a better person. If I do this work now, then I'll be more able to serve others later. I realized how this tug and pull between inner and outer has been going on for the last 320 days with no resolution, but something happened today that gave me a little insight.

It's my nature to be drawn to, aware of, and concerned for others— often with too little awareness of myself. I do take care of my health and safety, but I've often been puzzled by those who are deeply conscious of themselves and worried about what others might think—focusing on themselves, examining themselves, even hiding for fear of being seen. It's been my tendency to be out there, busy doing, helping and befriend-ing, but with little awareness of the "me" I was presenting to others. You could call that confidence but it's also a lack of awareness, a lack of real inner focus.

316

Being less than aware means not noticing the impact my words or actions might have on others; not seeing that my own emotions, when they bubble up, could actually cause harm not only to me but to others. This whole year has been one of looking within more and more. It's been painful at times, but illuminating and, I hope, helpful for the future. I expect and hope I'll carry more humility, respect and awareness of others, and do more listening and watching before "helping." I'll still cross the street to assist a stranger struggling out their door with a wheelchair, to help them down the stairs, as I did forty years ago to my companion's amazement. But I hope that I will wait and watch more.

Some of this insight has come from looking closely at my yidam and her posture as she sits on her lotus throne. It was just yesterday that I opened my eyes and saw that the Bodhisattva of Compassion, Kuan Yin, clearly demonstrates this inner and outer quality that I aspire to. Her left leg is tucked under in the posture of seated meditation. She holds a blue lotus in her left hand, a symbol of purity growing from muddy waters into illuminated enlightenment. Both seem to be symbols of "looking within." But her right foot is down, as if to step forward to respond to the cries of the world. Her right hand is raised, with her fingers in a mudra of exposition, perhaps teaching, perhaps sending forgiveness and blessings to all. Left and right—inward and outward—balanced.

Kuan Yin is teaching me "the middle way"— a path not weighted towards the silent ascetic in the cave for a lifetime, but also not weighted in the direction of the world. She's not always out there helping, at times over-extending and burning out from responding to the constant needs and suffering of others. That balance speaks to me. All of this I knew, but didn't really "get" until the time was ripe for this wake-up call. It tells me how to be on that Bodhisattva Path, to be of benefit to others, but with a more mature, awakened mind. I'm grateful for these lessons.

7:30 PM. How great to see a young possum passing through in the night, two days after the new moon. He went across the porch, past the loo, out to the front, and on to the boardwalk by the tub—investigating every place I'd dug when I transplanted grass sprigs to bare spots today. He seems to use my buckets for a watering spot as well. His tail is almost longer than his body, and thick, though not fluffy. He rose up onto his hind legs to get a taller view, posing with his small forepaws tucked under his wrists, and stared with shiny eyes into my flashlight. A little pink pointed nose, big eyes and small curled ears—adorable, yes. He reached up to the tub, investigating, but careful not to disturb anything. This is not a "stupid" animal, as I've read, but a mindful, instinctual one. Off he went, down towards the pine tree path, disappearing in the dark.

May 24, 2015

It's been a few days since I've written. Yesterday was a dark day, emotionally and physically. I experienced all of the flatness, listlessness and sadness of the solitary prisoner, the cave dweller, the long-distance sailor, the anchorite with door sealed to the outside world. It was good for me. It gives me appreciation and empathy for what my fellow solitaries go through.

There was rain from when I woke at 3 AM until after 9 PM, when my day ended. I was trapped in my small hut as a prisoner might be, going out only twice to empty full water buckets into the tub and gather more water for the future. Bird activity was the only relief. I wondered what life would be like if I was truly enclosed, unable to see out, and with no other moving thing but my shadow.

Human beings thirst for communion with each other or other animate beings. Occasionally, I hear a vehicle crunch on the dirt road that runs through the valley far below, and I instinctively rise on tiptoes to see if I can catch a glimpse of this moving object that speaks of human life. I follow every plane and helicopter that travels overhead until it disappears at the horizon. I smile at every bark I hear from Woof and Yipper though I can't see them three-hundred meters down below me in the valley. Without these interludes, life is quiet, continuous, less than stimulating, becalmed. It would be too easy to slip into depression if I didn't have a clear reason for being here, a curiosity about the process and experience, and a spiritual practice that supports and guides me.

And then, this morning, I awoke to light and sun. Blessed impermanence! Between sits, I walked outside and saw such a glow of bright sunlight down one path that I was pulled to follow it and stand in the light. The forest was still wet, with dark tree trunks and dripping leaves, but the glow was magical after so much rain. The vertical greens were spun with silver spider threads, glinting and shining, crisscrossing the view, and moving slightly. My ever-present tui bird toned what seemed to be a welcome in descending notes. I'm so happy that he's accepted my presence in his wood and my strange human habits. It's a quiet, peaceful day, pulled out of the dark of yesterday.

There were one or two showers through the day, but I've learned this is typical winter weather. The solstice is one month away and my delightful friend, the moon, may be back tonight at half phase, after a week or more of dark. It's cold enough to see my breath inside. I've been struggling to dry my one warm sweatshirt after washing it two days ago. I finally put it on, even with slightly damp hem and cuffs. It's the only thing I have that I'm truly warm in and I wear it every day. Some day I'll have other clothes to wear. Will I appreciate them?

I'm reminded of Pemasati, who shares this ridge with me. For two months I bowed and waved to that far hut across the valley where I thought she was living. It was only earlier this month that a message told me she has moved to a different hut, down below me. I thought perhaps this was the woman I'd seen once or twice coming down the road from the stupa. Four days ago, I saw her again, along the stupa path and thought to speak. With a bow, I pulled up my voice and asked if she was Pemasati. Yes, she was. She told me she was so grateful I'd spoken, and that knowing I was nearby gave her great support.

Every day, my thoughts fly to her as well as all of those on this land, down the valley, in Thames and Auckland, back home, and around the world— and I send out blessings that they may be peaceful, happy and free from suffering. It's very precious to have this time to be so focused and this opportunity to learn so much.

The rain buckets on the porch send patterns of refracted light dancing on my inside walls and ceiling. It's an unexpected by-product when the day turns sunny and hits the water surface, constantly changing, better than any film or light show.

Sara Maitland writes of those who "live" silence and how they become writers of "observed" nature, weather and birds. She often quotes my fellow New Englander, Henry Thoreau, in his observations of life alone in nature:

319

In the streets and in society I am almost invariably cheap and dissipated, my life unspeakably mean . . .But alone in the distant woods or fields, in unpretending sprout-lands or pastures tracked by rabbits, even in a bleak and, to most, cheerless day like this, when a villager would be thinking of his inn, I come to myself, I once more feel myself grandly related, and that cold and solitude are friends of mine. I come home to my solitary woodland walk as the homesick go home. I thus dispose of the superfluous and see things as they are.[142]

May 25, 2015

A rain shower, sun, and then the temperature dropped *at noon* to 8ºC (45ºF) and the skies opened. Luckily, I had a sense that rain was coming and got up from my meditation to pull in my Kindle, which was charging on the steps in the waning sunlight. I slipped back to my cushion, and ten minutes later the sky opened with a racket of hail, ice balls flying down from the heavens. And then sun again, and another bout of hail to follow. Now, dead quiet. Weather! Love it!

At 6 PM I watch a glorious pink sunset through one window, and then turn to another window and see the silvery half-moon I've missed so much.

May 26, 2015

How wonderful to find nine quail in my front grass, foraging around, looking for their bug breakfast while I eat my oatmeal. It seems three cousins have joined the tribe. Soon they all topple over a log like sheep over a fence and hustle down the dense path to the tall pine below. Earlier, Woof was disturbed by something and kept up a steady bark for an hour, then Yipper took over the braying. Now, quiet. Rain showers but no hail today.

Henry Thoreau speaks of the forest as though he's using my voice—or rather, do I speak with his? He says in Walden: "every little pine needle expanded and swelled with sympathy and befriended me." Absurd language to many people, but intimate to those who've been on retreat for many months, sensitized to all of nature that surrounds and supports us.

He goes on with some of the joys of rain that I too have felt:

Some of my pleasantest hours were during the long rain-storms with the spring or fall which confined me to the house for the afternoon and the forenoon, soothed by their ceaseless roar and pelting; when an early twilight ushered in a long evening in which many thoughts had time to take root and unfold themselves. In those driving northeast rains . . . sat behind my door in my little house, which was all entry, and thoroughly enjoyed its protection. [143]

May 27, 2015

This morning I went for a brisk walk to clear my mind from some troubling thoughts. It turned into an extraordinary day. I went up above, along the ridge, taking a trail that's new for me, through a deep, ancient forest. Huge trees, dense undergrowth, and not a whisper: no wind or tree branches rustling, not an insect, wasp or fly buzz; not a bird peep, not a rattle. Just deep, penetrating, pervasive silence. Way, way off, I thought I heard the soft rumble of water over rock, but it seemed to be in another land. I struggled over huge downed tawa trees, balancing on top and sliding over to the other side. The trail was sign-posted, but rugged and unkempt. I came across a huge standing tawa tree (twenty plus meters) with well over twenty-three (count them!) kahakaha or perching lily plants among the high branches. Some of these large baskets of fan-fingered leaves are quite heavy, I've been told. The bushmen's memorable nickname for them is "widow-makers." It seems these beauties have killed all too many woodcutters when trees were felled and that unexpected basket toppled off a high branch and landed on a head. Knowing this, I always move carefully under tawa trees. What an amazing forest!

Now, I'm home for a meditation sit, lunch, and a soak in the tub in the wonderful May sun. After time out in the bush, I can't possibly wrap my mind around those troubling thoughts that were present three hours ago. The forest does that. Clean slate.

May 29, 2015

A quiet, dark night. There was a crystal-clear three-quarter moon at 8 PM. At 10 PM the light poured through my window and I slept in its glow. After moonset, I woke at 3 AM to read more of Ryōkan's praises of the autumn moon.

> True, all the seasons have moonlit nights.
> But here's the best night to see the moon.
> The moon and earth are one, and myself one
> with them.[144]

Wrapped and bundled against the cold, I'm with Ryōkan, in praise of the autumn moon once more.

At 5:30 tonight I sang to the sunset, then turned and sang to the moon, one in the west, the other in the east. It seems impossible, but such is the May autumn moon in New Zealand when seen from a precipice hanging over a deep valley with a wraparound view. This would not be possible back home in my New Hampshire hollow, surrounded by tall pine, hemlock and oak. So I sing praises to this time, to this month, to this moon, to this experience.

May 30, 2015

I hear tramping around and scampering almost every night as I'm drifting to sleep. It doesn't go on for long and isn't loud enough to keep me awake. Droppings tell me these are regular visits by my neighborhood possum. Every two or three nights, there are droppings from Morrie the Rat as well. Morrie confines his explorations to the outhouse, and I'm sure spends many nights peering into that hole, eyeing the fruit and vegetable scraps, and wondering how to get at them without being trapped as he was last July. He hasn't tried a fishing pole yet, but I'm sure that's next. The lid is up for his viewing to cut down on the build-up of moisture on the seat and development of bugs on the toilet rim since my events of last January. Seems to work.

I did some research to see if possums might be a predator for rats and mice. It seems not. Possums are more interested in seeds, eggs, birds and their chicks, and plant life, than in eating rats. My books tell me that possums eat 21,000 tons of vegetation PER NIGHT across the two large islands of New Zealand. Is that possible?

All these predator thoughts came up as I watched the "war of the feathers" this morning. Young Grayhead chaffinch continues harassing and taking out Red every time he tries to feed. She really has it in for him. Many mornings he flies in on a circular run, lands, she dive-bombs him, he takes flight again and circles, and they come in again for another round. Three, four, five times it can go on. I cheered when I saw him arrive early one morning and get a feed in before her appearance. A visitor to my hut saw this and said it was most unusual chaffinch behavior. I think it may be adolescent love, but this harassment makes for a really nervous guy.

With thoughts of predators, I'm also thinking a lot about equanimity, something that could benefit me as well as Grayhead and Red. It's a quality that has drawn me since I was first introduced to the concept in Buddhism many years ago. I came across a definition by Tsongkhapa (1357 – 1419 CE), who calls equanimity the freedom from powerful reactions (positive or negative) to another person or an event—the ability to be even-minded toward everyone, no matter how they behave.

My gentle, steady friend, Tracy, someone who has often defined equanimity for me, was in last night's dream. We met in college on the first day and became buddies for life. While I was fiery, passionate and out there, she was the gentle, quiet soul, yes, perhaps a bodhisattva. She loved me dearly. My closest friend for forty-three years, and now gone.

I'm often attracted to equanimous people since I so admire their qualities—stable, settled, without grasping, seemingly wise, seamless, unchanging, and even empty. I look at equanimity as a very settled foundation for life. Helping my dad mix concrete and pour footings for our summer house in the New Hampshire forest when I was nine years old gave me an early understanding of the need for solid foundations. Tsongkhapa writes that one must flatten hilly ground to create a stable base for building. It's equanimity that evens out the mind's attachment to some people and disdain towards others, and allows love, compassion and joy to develop. I wonder if Grayhead chaffinch is listening to these morning reflections?

Letting go of strong, passionate reactions, and banishing desire, jealousy and hatred, leaves us free for wisdom to develop. Perhaps some of this equanimity comes with age, when we've learned to settle more and let go, when our grasping and needing seem less, when we can just sit.

323

To listen to the silence. To compare the morning silence, so thin and expectant, to the nighttime silence, so thick and rich, dense as a good chocolate cake. To listen, to learn equanimity. This is something to which I aspire.

May 31, 2015

Nowhere to go. Nothing to do. No phone calls, no emails, nothing to reply to, no one to respond to. Alone for a year. People say, "How wonderful! I want this." Do they understand what they long for? Here are the harsh negatives of a life set aside: alone, yes, and without the intimacy of a friend's smiling face, without another human to share this path with. And the glorious positives that make it all so very worthwhile: the opportunity, without distractions, to look within. The chance to experience the past again, to approach it differently, consider changes, truly experience the present, map out a possible plan for the months and years that may be left to me. Aspiration.

The opportunity to just sit in the forest, to be with all this verdant nature, to watch it grow and transform daily. That leaf I fell in love with ten months ago at the turning spot for my walking meditations is still there. The insect holes have enlarged and joined together. They flute the top edge. The once glossy, deep green surface has dulled and grayish yellow spots have appeared in three places. It's no longer the dazzling fresh growth it once was—it looks like me after a year—but it speaks of endurance and holds a strength, a presence. Soon it will lose its tenacity, its lifeblood, and will drop and become leaf litter, returning to the earth from which it grew, as I will. I watch it. I learn and appreciate.

Again and again I'm reminded of how I'm just a small blip on the huge screen of life on the ridges of the Coromandel Peninsula. All these trees, shrubs, plants, paths, streams and mudholes existed long before I showed up. I've been given the pristine opportunity to share time with them—to watch clouds and rain form; to see fiddleheads be born and develop, see them untwirl and become fern fronds; to watch quail families mature; to learn that no matter how many trenches I dig, how much work I put in, the Slipglade Track will always flood and will become deep, squishy, quicksand mud every winter.

324

I'm just a temporary visitor, humbled by this forest—a novice, an apprentice here to learn the lessons of impermanence.

The sky lightens, Woof gives a morning bark far below, the soft gray clouds move and form, and the eastern ridges pale with misty showers as rain moves into the valley. Do I love this place? Yes. Yes! A new day of nothing to do, nowhere to go.

Kiranada in front of a giant 800-year-old Kauri tree.

Chapter 12 June

I welcome this last full month of retreat.

I was expecting a glorious full moon tonight, but instead, I got lashing rain beating the house. Thunder bubbled up in the north, rolled and rumbled across the valley and over the top of the hut, and burped and pounded out in the south. Ten minutes later—dead silence: no rain, no thunder, no wind. Quiet on this dark, wet precipice. Wow!

I'm wondering when the understanding will come; when the clear seeing, the realization of what I've done here, what I've gone through, seen, heard and experienced, will come. Will it come to the top like good cream, and need to be shared? Perhaps, in the next few weeks. But not yet, it seems.

Woof and Yipper were disturbed last night. Barking went on for ten minutes or more after 9 PM. I expect it was some animal coming around their farm, something that didn't belong: possums, wild pigs, feral goats, or a weasel. The same night I had possums on my porch, passing through as usual, getting a drink from my buckets.

I've enjoyed dabbling with paint during the past three days of intermittent rain, watching the clouds from my covered porch. It feels good to see color on absorbent paper. I realized yesterday that these watercolors are my observations of the external—the clouds in the valley, the light on trees, the majestic stupa. But over these eleven months I've done other artwork on fiber that explores the internal side of my retreat. I've used both watercolor and stitching to investigate the silence that has permeated these months so deeply. I've realized that my attempts to illustrate the Heart Sutra in stitch and cloth were misguided. It was actually silence I was searching for with thread and color.

Making silence visible with my needle and non-harm silk is not easy, but it's something close to my heart. I reflected on this yesterday morning, considering the capacity of cloth to absorb, mute and hold sound between the tines of thread: silence woven in and held. Looking at my work, I see ruffles and ridges of silence embedded in the weave; layers of silence, quiet and pristine, articulated and reflected in the process of making and remaking—woven, stitched, pulled, and marked with plant essence, with plant residue, washed, steamed, stretched and re-stitched. Marking the surface, listening to the rhythm, the repeat of thread on thread. Here are repetitive stitches, meditative spacing, plucked and metered—recording silence. This is some of the internal world I've been working with these eleven months, in my hands, in my fingers; listening, hearing with my eyes; watching with my ears.

June 7, 2015

Yesterday was a second clear day, and while the morning was still cool, I decided on the spur of the moment to climb up to the Ridge Road and walk over to see the giant kauri trees at last. I woke a bit late, so I ate breakfast, packed up the equipment I might need, and was off. A twinge in my ankle, the one that I've broken three times, sent me back to the hut quickly for an Ace bandage and my ankle support, but it turned out I didn't need them. Carrying art materials, water, half an apple and my mat for the wet forest floor, I was just fine.

Climbing up behind Chetul Hut and past the Tawa Trail, I reached the Ridge Road Trail and began a half hour trek upwards along an old forest road strewn with fallen tree growth and other debris. I soon left the tree ferns and regenerated manuka forest and climbed into an area of old growth tall pines and rimu. What a delight to be in old forest! Up, up I went, through ankle-height ferns. It was that very quiet time of morning, and I heard no birdcalls, and saw no birds until I descended three hours later.

The Kauri Tree Trail is rarely used, so I was stepping over downed branches, scampering over huge fallen trees, and watching every footfall for tangled, tripping supplejack vines. The ground is well trenched by wild pig furrows and foot-deep holes cross the path, with lots of loose dirt left over. The trail and its edges seem to be prime hunting grounds for tasty roots. I delighted in seeing brilliant red mushrooms on green moss, clusters of brown and black puff balls, a gaggle of thirty mushroom caps running up the side of a dead log, and then a spectacular fourteen-inch Turkey Tail mushroom with overlapping bands of black and white. They had me stopping for photos.

Deep, deep in the woods, after sliding down a hillside supported by guide ropes, over roots and windfall, and crawling on my hands and knees under downed tree branches, I arrived before a giant. I looked up, up into the high canopy, to the first branches sixty feet above my head. The small leaves were so high up it was hard to see them.

Hanging on the side of the steep hill, I tried to take in the huge trunk. It would take more than ten people with arms outstretched to encircle it. This great kauri is a remnant of the thousands that once covered much of New Zealand, but are now found only in the north. Like the giant sequoias of California, the kauri are among the largest trees in existence and can live up to two thousand years. This one only survived because of its inaccessibility. All of its sisters and brothers were harvested before the end of the nineteenth century, I read, brought down by teams that cut through their ten-foot diameter trunks and slid them down this hillside to the river, where they floated out to the Firth of Thames.

Standing beneath this six hundred to a thousand year-old beauty, I was awed by its size and by its smooth light gray trunk in a forest of dark trees. With reverence, my fingers slid over the bole and circular flakes of pale gray green bark peeled off with each touch. Underneath, the wood felt hard and tightly-knit, extremely dense.

After a few hours of meditation and darshan, I climbed back up to a path fork and slipped along a dense, muddy trail leading down toward the Tararu River to find the Twin Kauri Sisters, younger but just as stately and awe-inspiring. They stand not more than seven feet apart, reaching up into the high forest canopy and disappearing from view, as graceful as two old Victorian sisters garbed in gray. It's hard to believe that such gods of the forest were harvested for commercial use, almost to extinction. Two-foot slices were sent off to museums around the world for display while other trees became humble church pews or post office and shop counters. I learn that young kauri were the perfect spars for sailing ships. Many were used as ship and home building materials and made into furniture as well as traditional Maori canoe hulls.

As I was leaving for this retreat, I received a poem by a fellow Order member who stood on this same ground twelve years ago, and honored these giants. She wrote, in part:

a vast citadel of gray bark
smooth and rising sheer, with leaves so far
and ferns and orchids sprawling
in a wide spread of branches
higher than my eye could reach
wider than my arms, older than my life
I stood still before it
Then sat at its feet.

— Satyalila "Big Kauri," October 2002

Writing now, the day following my trek to these giants, I am still feeling the benefits of this auspicious meeting. As I sit on my cushion to meditate, I can feel the effort I made to get up there in my legs and arms and back. It was good to break my usual schedule and extend myself for this trek—one that I so much wanted to do before I left, but doubted I could accomplish. These giants could have been saplings when the first Maori canoes arrived 800 years ago and the first humans walked this land. Emotionally and spiritually, I feel as if I've met the guardians of this land.

There's a sense of peace and completion in me now. As with so many things lately, I feel I've entered a month and a decade of endings and completions. In exactly thirty days I'll be boarding an airplane to leave this land. Perhaps that will be the last time I'll see this part of the world. I'm preparing for that. I'm walking through this with eyes wide open, with deep awareness, carrying peace and contentment, with gratefulness and appreciation. In some ways, I'm sorry to not have a leaf or circle of bark from those queens of the forest to place on my morning shrine here—but instead I have memories, photos, a small painting, and a deep sense of awareness. Such strength, such nobility, such awe-inspiring presence. May all beings—flora, fauna and trees—be happy.

June 10, 2015

Between meditation sits, I enjoy tidying up in the hermitage. Not wanting to leave everything to the last few days, I'm tackling one drawer or cupboard each day. It feels good to put things in order for the next retreatant. With that in mind, I've also copied out lists of birds sighted and some recipes I've enjoyed, to add to the book that stays with the hut. Perhaps this will help others as they adjust to this noble hill.

I'm in the last twenty days before I break silence and begin the slow walk back into the world, but I feel so at home here that I'm not eager to leave. This chance to more clearly see myself and my life has been immensely helpful.

I realize what I've gained and also what I've missed, being in seclusion for one year. I'm eager to have the answers to two silly questions. I remember well the cultural updates we were given at the end of our three months of seclusion during our Ordination retreat: we were told who won the Wimbledon tennis match (important to the Brits, I guess) and of Michael Jackson's untimely death. I only wanted to know if Barack Obama was still alive and healthy. There had been so much press in the spring of 2009 that he would never survive six months in the presidency, but he did, with grace. After a year in seclusion here, my two big political and cultural questions are *What happened in the Scottish Referendum last October?* and *What is the sex of Kate and Will's second child?* Really earth-shattering questions.

On a more significant note, I'm very sad to be missing the Sakyadhita (Daughters of Buddha) Convention, which begins in Indonesia next week. I'd hoped to be at the India gathering two years ago but my concussion put a stop to that. This time I'm nearby, but on retreat. I'll once again miss putting my palms together to bow to Tenzin Palmo, who always attends, and to thank her deeply for the inspiration she has given me. They say there's always a next time, but I'm so aware of impermanence that I have few expectations about the future. I've lived a life of "do it now", but I've mellowed recently. I'm letting go of many things.

I was pleased to hear that Tenzin Palmo knows of our small Triratna Order and our work with the Dalits of India (the former untouchable caste), some of whom have converted to Buddhism following the example of the social reformer, Dr. B. R. Ambedkar. Triratna involvement began as early as 1978, when the Order started setting up hostels, medical treatment and education facilities in Dalit communities as well as teaching the Dharma to this under-served population. The programs have brought results, but the need is endless. I was heart warmed to know that Tenzin Palmo, who works hard to train Buddhist nuns in the Tibetan tradition, had noticed.

Looking toward the end of my retreat, I'm dipping into the writings of Alexandra David-Neel as she completed three-years in a cave/hut under the supervision of the Gamchen of Lachen. She came to the end of her stay knowing that the servants who supported her needed to get back to their families, and realizing that despite all she'd learned, the contemplative life would only be an episode in her life as a traveler and Buddhist researcher, "at best, preparation for further liberation." When she looked at the threadlike path below her that led out into the valley, and knew the day would come when it would lead back to the world, deep sorrow, beyond description, took hold of her.[145]

And Lama Govinda (1898-1985) comments on retreat, saying that:

"Far from closing his eyes and being dead to the world, [the con-templative hermit] . . . opens them and becomes wide awake; far from blunting his sense he develops a high awareness and a deeper insight into the real nature of the world and his own mind. And this shows him that it's as foolish to run away from the world as to run after the world; both extremes having roots in illusion that the world is something separate from ourselves."[146]

It is this lesson that Govinda taught his disciples.

Alexandra David-Neel and Lama Govinda, so many years ago, are both commenting on the way contemplatives step back into the world, just as is unfolding here, right now at Abhaya Hut.

June 13, 2015

It's close to the winter solstice and I open my eyes to look at the clock in the dusky room, and am surprised that it's almost 7 AM. I've been pleased in the past to rely on light to wake me, but no longer. With the reversion to Standard Time almost two months ago and the coming of winter, I must reset my internal clock.

By the time I put out some birdseed for my early callers, put the pee pot out the other door, get on some water for tea, have a quick cold-water wash, put on cold clothes, and roll out the yoga mat, the sky is lightening and a new day has started. I have the heater on for a short time, and warm some oatmeal on its top surface. Using the heater means a few windows must be cracked open for ventilation, which seems quite counterproductive, but it's the only way to keep the air fresh and eliminate headaches. The heater goes off as I settle in for meditation with a shawl, a blanket, a hat and gloves.

A real morning treat is stepping outside between morning sits for ten minutes of walking meditation, and enjoying that sweet, sweet fresh air. I do love being outside in the morning, and will even put on a raincoat and boots to do that walking time. Today there are just gusty winds roaring from the south, promising colder air and rain perhaps. I haven't seen much sun in three days, but this is the New Zealand winter I know.

When I've had trouble sleeping the past few nights, I open the curtains drawn against the night-time chill and allow the brilliant half-moon to spill its silver across my pillow. I'm asleep in five minutes with a smile on my face. It happens every time.

June 16, 2015

I'm learning so many different things. Some are internal insights, and some are merely things that I've slowed up long enough to see, having missed before, being too preoccupied with the internet or the *Boston Globe* Sunday edition to notice.

This morning it's the realization that the coldest temperature comes just before dawn, not in the middle of the night. Watching the temperature dip from 7ºC to 3ºC (that's from 44 to 38ºF for Fahrenheit friends) between 5:30 and 8 AM surprises me. I've also noticed that as winter begins, it takes the day longer and longer to warm up, with that night time chill holding until 10 or even 11 AM. These are insights, but not from the meditation cushion. Now the sky is changing to a light powder blue on the eastern horizon and the day is starting. Off to my yoga mat and meditation cushion for me.

June 17, 2015

I was moving quickly, putting things in order—cleaning up after lunch, dumping the compost, returning things to the cold box and moving to the front porch to cover the tub and bring in the wash—and then I was stopped in my tracks. All of that went to the back burner because the quail had arrived and were foraging in the grass.

I sat quietly to watch, not wanting to disturb the best show in town today. It's been almost two weeks since I've seen them and the ones who were once babies have become gray butterballs—all filled out. Their distinctive black headcombs bobbed and quivered, their black masks were pristine, and all the faces looked so distinct that I had trouble picking out any female markings among the showy male masks. They reminded me again of what's important in life—not accomplishing tasks, but appreciating what I've been given: being present for each moment in this glorious bush country with all it offers. Covering the tub could come later. I sat on my cushion, eyes closed, enjoying the comforting sound of cooing and cajoling just outside.

June 20, 2015

It's winter solstice, but through the night the wind picked up, a warm front arrived with winds from the east, and the temperature climbed to 15-16ºC (60ºF, no less). I got up numerous times to take off my hat, gloves, and the silk underwear beneath my nightshirt. I even opened a window!

And then the heavy winds and rain showed up. New Zealand 'big blows' always feel like hurricane warnings to this New Englander, but locals take them in stride. Soon it was blowing hard enough that the windows were banging and whistling a tune, I almost lost my watch cap off my head outside, the front door flew out of my hand, the rod-iron porch furniture slid across the landing. The birdseed tray did a flip and landed in the brambles ten feet away. Wow! It's winter in the bush. Wind!

I've been inside meditating, transcribing a lovely puja, and doing some cooking. It's a noisy howling day outside but I'm quiet and serene. Nine days before I start my walk out of silence.

My shrine has a lovely bouquet of purple verbena daisies with a sprig of sage and thyme intermixed—a gift in my food-box from our new staff member, who's buying groceries for me now. It's nice to have her. I'm sensitive enough now that I can tell who's driving the ORV once a week by the depth of the tire tracks in the mud. After being in silence for so many months, the ground, the air, the bush all speak to me, bringing news of passages.

Tonight will be the longest night of the year with sunset close to 5 PM and no sunrise until well after 7 AM. Though I tend to sleep more during winter, the past two nights I've been awake from 2 AM to 4 AM, counting the stars, listening to the wind, chanting and meditating. Soon my life will change drastically as I move into community again. I'll go slowly, carefully watching, and trying to carry some of this serenity with me to my sweet home and to others.

June 23, 2015

It was a joy to spy the lopsided grin of the quarter moon two nights ago, moving to set over the north ridges at 8 PM. The temperature dropped rapidly and held at 3ºC (37ºF) all through the night, which put frost on the pastures across the valley. I've come full circle. I carved the letters FROZEN into the deck with my fingernail once again.

Today, the quiet is deep and pervasive. I'll miss this deep presence, this tangible woven hush when I step off this precipice in just six days. I plan to join the Thames village evening meditation program as I break silence. Someone from the community will come in the thick twilight, find me on the road, and take me down. A stepping out in the darkness.

The full moon will guide me out of New Zealand in ten days and the next full moon I see will be over a lake in southern New Hampshire. It's hard to wrap my mind around this. It feels as if I'll just live out my days here on this ridge, doing my daily meditations and regular chores, feeding the birds, filling the outside tub, and contemplating what arises and what passes away. After a life of traveling and learning, always feeding that internal need for stimulation, I've come to a place where life has been defined by four walls, almost a cave, for a full year. Watching, experiencing and learning through each cold moment, I've been appreciative and grateful that I can do this, at last.

For my first morning meditation today I was wrapped up and still in bed. My cheeks were so chilled that I meditated through a haze of woolen shawl. I've noticed that I haven't wanted to break the silence in these last weeks, even with prayers, chants or mantras. I do all three regularly, hourly, but only in my mind or in whispers. In the past few days I've looked at the effort it would take to find my voice, and haven't been able to work up that energy. Curious. How much effort does speaking take? An infant vocalizes even at birth, but the silence seems too precious to break. Even the birds seem to respect this in the morning. Tomtits, fantails and tui flit around and join me on my meditation walk but none speak until later. Silence.

To renounce speaking. I know of someone who lived in society and did not speak for six months as an experiment. Renunciation interests me, but not the renunciation of speech, at least not once I'm off this retreat. Contemplatives renounce as a means of non-attachment, a way to drop grasping, to loosen the hold that so much of samsara suffering has on us.

What will I renounce after this solitary retreat? On every other retreat I've spent time mentally going through my closets at home and later, divesting myself of many material possessions. Ah, material goods. After my ordination retreat, the hair went, jewelry (including a large collection of artisan earrings) went, and the colorful, exotically patterned batik clothing went. Slowly, I became the short-haired woman in the simple blue I was ordained in. It seemed right and freeing.

Last week I watched the navy-blue gloves and hat come off, the navy-blue fleece vest, sweatshirt and pants set aside—all in a pile of blueness. I watched the navy nightshirt pop over my head along with the blue silk undershirt and noticed the simplicity of this. Sometimes I yearn for other colors, especially since, as a fiber artist, I relish the use of multiple dyes and shading in my art, but I find this blueness liberating. Renouncing all that grasping has been good. And now I'm contemplating a further big renunciation, that of taking on Anagarika Vows, renouncing relationship, family, career and materialism. That may take a year of consideration before accomplishment. We shall see. I will sit on it. (This was completed in August 2016 when I became Anagarika Kiranada.)

Kobun Chino Roshi counsels me again, as he did when I stepped off that ORV last July: "When you realize how rare and how precious your life is, and how completely you are responsible for how you live it, how you manifest it, it's such a big responsibility that naturally such a person sits down for a while."

June 25, 2015

It's the third morning of temperatures below zero and the land is noticing. The water buckets on the deck are frozen. A crust of frost covers the porch and makes the steps slippery. The grass has a white dust of ice across it all. I was awake for part of the night, chilled with the cold, even with four wool blankets and a feather duvet. Cold, yes, but I manage.

Over in the pastures on the other side of the valley where five cattle have grazed and Woof and Yipper once frolicked, the land is deep white, as if snow has fallen, though I think it's only frost. The sky is a clear safflower blue. Not a cloud. As the sun rises, slowly the roof starts dripping from melting frost.

I've learned to manage this chill in an uninsulated hut. The cold is outside and I dwell in the interior, inside my body. I see so clearly that this long, long period of aloneness brings benefits I wouldn't see or feel in another environment. I'm here to face myself, to see my true connection with all that is outside, with the world. As Marchaj Roshi says, ". . . you sit by yourself with a level of honesty and openness." He tells me that we enter this sitting practice by finding our kind-heartedness and considering how to offer it to others. All the teachings support us and tell us we can do this. We can see the pain, and we can release it.

The daily rhythm, the tasks to do, the meditation sits, the times for reflection, have developed into a tangible whole. I'm at peace, deeply held, serene, and filled with a calm equanimity I've long sought in the outside world. How much of this can I carry with me out of here? How much can be transferred to a busy life? Do I want a busy life any longer?

I feel as though I've changed, as if a new person sits here with eyes opened to what surrounds her, with ears and senses attuned to what slipped by before. If so, I may step into life off this hill with new perceptions, awareness and sensitivity. In these last few days I'll look at what I've learned from 360+ days alone.

There have been no grand awakenings, no major enlightenments. Yet the small insights have built an encouraging stream of confidence and support. Just to receive a note or text message saying "I have thought of you often and of what you are doing" lets me know that the effort has multiplied, the hours of sitting quietly in meditation have in some way touched others, and there must be benefits beyond this room.

The ice melts, the frost softens, and the land and I are gentled by the sun and transformed. What arises, falls away. I'm warmed and nourished by this knowledge on a cold morning.

June 27, 2015

I stepped outside in the evening chill to get some cheese from the cool-box, and was caught by a silvery three-quarter moon with rings of hazy pink and blue. I hesitated to watch the fast-moving clouds. In the short seconds it took to then open the bin, locate the cheese and close it up, the sky changed—no more pink aura. Changes come so very quickly here.

What has interested most people about this year of mine is the solitariness, the being alone for twelve months. This has come most easily to me. What has interested me, and continues to, is the observation of silence. To be a witness of deep silence, to watch and listen; to pick up the difference between the silence of night and the silence of a quiet mid-morning. To listen to the weather moving, changing; to hear the silence between the storms. The depth of silence in this remote bush is something I will remember, and I know I'll pine for it. It has been most precious. It has woken me up.

Silence. I remember talking with an audiologist about my mother's deafness in her later years and her resistance to wearing a hearing aid. I felt she was missing so much of family life. The doctor said to me, "But you have to realize the deliciousness of silence for the profoundly deaf." I thought I would miss music, the sound of laughter, children's voices, a call from my daughter, but truthfully all this quiet has been worth it. A new door has opened for me.

In two days I'll step out of this silence and travel to an evening service at the Thames Sangha—breaking silence after a year. They've asked if I'll do a reading. I'm apprehensive, shy, wanting to just sit in the back and watch, but then I feel perhaps this would be a good start. I hope I can find my voice, that it isn't completely misplaced. Starting slowly, little by little, watching and listening.

June 28, 2015

A dark morning. I'm awake early after a dream of Japan, a dream of "not fitting in." Maybe this is a prediction about the coming weeks as I try to re-integrate into western society. One part of me looks forward to feeling the warmth of friends again and hearing of all that's gone on in my absence, but a larger part of me wants to head for the woods, hang out here longer, continue this sweet, quiet life of solitude that is now so familiar. I can easily understand those hermits that hide out when someone visits, ducking any human contact. I feel it. Someone commented on a photo of Augustine Courtauld, who had been six months in a tent in the arctic winter, saying that he looked like a man "stripped of his persona, his public self stolen, leaving only his true self naked"[147] before the world. I feel like that right now. I'd like to hide rather than step out of this. It's as if, "silence unskinned me."

And yet the fearlessness that brought me here, that allowed me to sign up for a year with only the experience of six two-week solitary retreats and one of twenty-eight days, will be the fearlessness that takes me into the world, the confidence that helps me put one foot in front of another and walk out of this.

I've thought about tackling the chaos and busyness of the world I left. I've been told it can be harsh, disorienting and painful. Thinking this through, I've considered wearing my robes on my flights home. Would that give me some protection, some excuse for walking more slowly, speaking less? Putting on the robes does set me apart. It may signify that I'm coming from another place, that I'll not be as quick to understand what is expected. It sometimes feels that robes encourage others to be more gentle and kind, though not always.

After living in the bush for a year, my eyes are wide open like a baby deer in headlights. I'm confused about what is expected; I'll be a novice learning the way of moving through this world that I once knew so well. Yet I feel it's okay to be like this.

Having lived abroad and returned numerous times to a culture that I should be very familiar with, but wasn't, I realize that 'returners' need time. They also carry a special insight: the ability to see their own society with fresh eyes. In 2000, after eighteen years abroad, I allowed those new eyes to question many cultural assumptions and this led me to choose a lifestyle that diverged in some ways from the norm. I expect this, too, will be a significant re-entry. It's frightening, but welcome, and completely part of the solitary year—the in and the out.

July 2, 2015

Full moon light pouring through a window and descending to my meditation cushion: one of the most poignant and enduring images that I will carry away from this solitary retreat. I open the curtain near my bed and the moonlight comes in to lull me into sleep after an exhausting day.

I've had two days with people, catching up, running errands, and using my voice after a year. Yesterday my voice gave out after lunch and I was down to a croaky whisper. I hope today will be quieter, but I have meetings with three people planned. My last two days on this ridge will be quieter, with plans for cleaning, packing and retreat-closing. It's been an extraordinary year and feels like only three or four months. I'm exceedingly happy.

I walked through a supermarket yesterday, picking up some last-minute food needs, and was truly dazzled by all that was available, the variety and color. I could easily have been overwhelmed, but I was just joyous and appreciative of the bounty. And now I have the rising sun, the light in the eastern sky and a new day to appreciate.

I was so pleased to have a chance to visit the Wass farm down below and see my dear barking friends yesterday. I found that Woof and Yipper are actually Oscar and Lela to others. They seemed to know me, and I them, by whatever name. I saw some chooks that I've occasionally heard up here on the ridge and said hello to a few of the grand, white-faced beef cattle that come to the upper pastures. All these friends I've only heard or viewed through binoculars over the past twelve months, and am now meeting. The Wasses, Peter and Ann, were in town having a lunch break and I was pleased to be introduced to them and let them know how much I appreciated being across the valley from their homestead for a year.

So the circle closes. The July full moon sends me off as it welcomed me so many months ago, setting at dawn over the southwest hill. Like others out in the world, I too wonder what will come from all these months of silence. I watch and listen.

July 4, 2015

My last day here.

To let go, be purged, purified, washed by the night rain, seen-through by the full moon; to be liberated, freed, let loose from all the samsaric bonds of suffering. To step out anew, cleansed. To see with fresh eyes. To listen to others, but not be entangled. To be aware of the deep silence that supports us. To return to source, drink there, be renewed and step out again. To let that compassionate heart flow and spill over. To listen. All these things I have learned over twelve months.

Ready for departure after 360 days.

Epilogue

Dawn in Bali—23ºC (74ºF). There's no space between the bird and reptile sounds to sink into the silence I found at Abhaya Hut, but I'm held in soft, green, loving arms. The roosters began their encouraging calls between 4:30 and 5 AM. It wasn't long before the frogs took up the song, and soon I was aware of three or four different voices coming from different parts of the rice field, welcoming the light in the east above Mount Agung.

Soon a farmer in a white shirt and dark sarong steps out to walk his rice paddies, hands clasped behind his back. He pulls up his sarong, knots it, and steps into the mud with a machete in his hand to weed between the rows of vibrant green seedlings. I listen, I watch. A motorbike growls in the distance—not unlike the growl of generators up the Tararu Valley. As the sky lightens, I pick up dots of color between the palms and shrubs: red hibiscus, white poinsettia, yellow allamanda flowers, all reflected in the moving water that surrounds the bungalows and walkways. I'm home here. This is my eleventh or twelfth visit to this land, a stopover, a week or two to acclimate to life outside. I chose this place for the softness of the land and the kind, respectful awareness of these lovely people.

Five days of visits at the retreat center, a day or two in Auckland, and a rough and difficult trip out of New Zealand through Sydney to Denpasar have left me with a need for rest, silence and simplicity. I always say that traveling is for the tough. At the Auckland airport check-in, what could go wrong did go wrong. Amplified announcements, roaring jets, exuberant children, inebriated travelers, alarm bells and confusion, all welcomed me. Again and again, I repeated that I couldn't hear or couldn't understand directions given me. Mostly, the airport personnel were not annoyed to repeat, but the stress was tangible.

And here I am back in nature, watching roosters in beehive baskets being carried out for airing and sun, cooking fires starting, smoke rising and life beginning in a land away from concrete and traffic. I listen. I watch.

July 23, 2015

After two weeks of being somewhat in the world, I find myself wonderfully engaged with others but very much exhausted with social encounters. The stress has been enough to attract a respiratory infection. Being away from other human beings for so long, away from germs that I normally would have developed resistance to, has me struggling with a summer cold. Is this a metaphor for that active, engaged society with its expectations and built in protection/resistance —compared to the open-hearted, aware, sensitive and somewhat fragile life of the contemplative? Something for reflection.

"my relationship with myself has deepened,"[148] Bob Kull writes after his year alone. It's so true. But I also acknowledge a deep, deep love of others, a true joy in being with them and watching them. "Sympathy with nature blended with the boundless heart toward all beings".[149] So very real—all cultivated through love, kindness, meditation and reflection.

I'd love to take these genuine heart-filled emotions out into the world, but I realize that I must go slowly and cautiously. The world, the chaos, the stress—these are exhausting and this soul/being is still fragile, perhaps not quite as ready to engage as others would wish. Slowly, quietly, reflectively, I need to move in this thick green water of life.

As I flew through the night skies, en route home, I sent this poem through cyberspace to my friends, family and supporters:

After Solitary—Handle with Care

Sitting without my armor
Able to manage in the bush
With harsh conditions
But without the protection
For life in the streets, in the marketplace.

Doe-eyed, unknowing, fragile,
Open-hearted, without a buffer,
I am prey to the long sword of anger
The short knife of envy;
Without emotional armor
That was checked at the door
Twelve months ago.

I rise above it
Close my eyes to insidious comments,
See all, for what it is—
Illusion, not real.

To let go of self, to not respond,
To walk with kindness
With awareness
And to remember
How interconnected we truly are.
Life after silence, after solitary

June 30, 2015

And it has not been easy.

I arrived in Bali en route to the USA and stayed for two weeks to get my water-wings. I remained quiet, separated, peaceful but then, as I prepared to board the plane for a thirty-three-hour return flight from Denpasar to Doha, Qatar, to Philadelphia to Manchester, New Hampshire, the airport was shut down for twenty-two hours because of volcanic ash from an eruption in east Java. I looked at those long lines of unhappy people, crying babies, angry parents, disappointed honeymooners—and my heart blew wide open. I truly loved them all. I began talking, helping and laughing at it all, making myself at home with them

345

on the floor, doing what I could and loving it. People offered me an iPhone and urged me to call my daughter about the delay, found vegetarian food trays for the four hour stand in line, insisted I step in front of them and go first. I just glowed and loved them. Humanity, all that I had not seen or heard, for a year.

I came home always remembering that woman who whispered in my ear, as I boarded the plane a year ago, who said, "Thank you for doing this for me." And so I share and comfort and encourage others, even if it means just standing by and witnessing.

I slipped into New Hampshire with the words of the Zen Poet Shutaku on my lips:

> Mind set free in the Buddha realm
> I sit at the moon-filled window
> Watching the mountain with my ears,
> Hearing the stream with open eyes.
>
> Each molecule preaches perfect law.
> Each moment chants a true sutra.
> The most fleeting thought is timeless.
> A single hair is enough to stir the sea.

Endnotes

Chapter 1

[1] Kornfield, *Teachings of the Buddha*, 84-5.

[2] Kull, *Solitude*, 143-44.

[3] Mingyur Rinpoche, "Why Do We Take Refuge," 16.

Chapter 2

[4] Catherine, *Focused*, 77.

[5] Storr, *Solitude*, 62.

[6] Santideva, *Guide to Bodhisattva*, 34-5.

[7] Tsangnyön, *Milarepa*, 59-60.

[8] Ibid., 156.

[9] Thoreau, *Walden*, 66.

[10] Kull, *Solitude*, 255.

[11] Mitchell, *Enlightened Heart*, 47.

[12] McAra, *Land*, 56.

[13] Beck, L. Adams, *Splendor of Asia*, 127.

[14] Maitripala, Unpublished puja.

[15] Kamalashila, *Meditation*, 151.

[16] Ibid., 224.

[17] Sarton, Journal, 99.

[18] Brahm, Bliss, 77.

[19] Storr, *Solitude*, 28.

Chapter 3

[20] Philips, "Take a Hard Look," 83.

[21] Quoted in *Cave,* 171.

[22] Ibid., 195.

[23] Ibid.

[24] Ibid.

[25] Ibid.

[26] Twichell, *The Snow Watcher,* 17.

[27] Drake, http://news.nationalgeographic.com/news/2014/04/140412-moon-faces-brain-culture-space-neurology/

[28] Kamalashila, *Meditation,* 93.

[29] Kull, *Solitude,* 211.

[30] Nouwen, *Way of the Heart,* 27.

[31] Dilgo Khyentse, *Thirty-seven Verses.* Appendix 5. 227-28.

[32] Harper et al, *Rough Guide to New Zealand,* 1021.

[33] Ryōkan, *One Robe,* 59.

[34] David-Neel, *Magic,* 162.

[35] Govinda, *White Clouds,* 22.

[36] Crowe, *Native Plants.*

[37] Brahm, *Bliss,* 175.

[38] Ibid., 258.

[39] Tenzin Palmo, *Heart,* 135.

[40] Ibid., 61.

[41] Storr. *Hermits,* 39.

[42] Dilgo Khyentse, *Heart,* 66-67.

Chapter 4

[43] Hahn, Thich Nhat, *Sun My Heart,* 63.

[44] Goddard, *Buddhist Bible,* 46.

[45] Sonam Rinchen, *Eight Verses.*

[46] Tenzin Palmo, *Heart,* 140.

[47] Kull, *Solitude,* 131.

[48] Merton, *Silent Life,* 150.

[49] France, *Hermits,* 27

[50] Sonam, *Eight Verses.*

[51] Katzan, *Vegetable Dishes,* 67.

[52] France, *Solitary,* 170.

Chapter 5

[53] Thoreau, *Walden,* 96.

[54] Simpson, *Touching the Void,* 21.

[55] Gunaratana, *Beyond Mindfulness,* 66.

[56] Koch, *Solitude,* 118.

[57] Ibid., 126.

[58] Koch, *Solitude,* 125.

[59] Cheng, *Life and Death,* 130-31.

[60] Merton, *Vow,* 188-189.

[61] Santideva, *Bodhisattva,* Chapter II, Vs. 8.

[62] Cheng-Li.

[63] Brahm, *Bliss,* 183-184.

[64] Sangharakshita, *Living With Awareness.* 10-11.

[65] Walshe, *DN.* 127-141.

[66] Mettanando,
http://www.lankalibrary.com/Bud/buddha_death.htm)

[67] Bhikkhu Bodhi, *Middle Length Discourse,* Sutta 47.

[68] Govinda,*White Cloud,* 60-61.

[69] Kamalashila, *Meditation,* 119.

[70] Sarton, *Journals,* 158

Chapter 6

[71] Ryōkan, *One Robe,* 61.

[72] Vishvapani, "Four Reminders," 2.

[73] SN 47.7, MN 11.169, SN 3:25.

[74] Tsongkhapa, *Readings From the Refuge Tree,*78.

[75] Oliver, *New and,* 10.

[76] Kamalashila, *Meditation,* 82.

[77] Nagapriya, *Karma,* 1.

[78] Ibid., 59.

[79] Vishvapani, "Four Reminders," 5.

[80] Nagapriya, *Karma.* 77-79.

[81] Tenzin Palmo, *Heart,* 133.

[82] Ibid., 27.

[83] Bhikkhu Bodhi, *Discourses of the Buddha's Wisdom,* 75.

[84] Nagapriya, *Karma,* 77.

[85] Santideva, *Guide,* 35.

[86] Tenzin Palmo, *Heart.* 102.

[87] AN 8:36.

[88] Lawrence, *Complete Poems,* 538.

[89] Vishvapani, *"Four Reminders,"* 2- 3.

[90] Nouwen," Community," 18

[91] Koch, *Solitude,* 245.

[92] Ibid., 352.

[93] Blofeld, *Compassion,* 131.

[94] Levine, *Who Dies?* 27.

[95] Dilgo Khyentse, *Thirty-Seven Verses,* 50.

[96] Sarton, *Journal,* 12.

[97] Quoted in Koch, *Solitude,* 79.

[98] Kull, *Solitude,* 43-44.

[99] Koch, *Solitude,* 144-145.

[100] Kull, *Solitude,* 263.

[101] Quoted in *Cave,* 195.

[102] Sarton, *Journal,* 89.

[103] Byrd, *Alone,* 220.

[104] Kull, *Solitude,* 130-131.

[105] Macy, *World As,* 190.

Chapter 7

[106] Unpublished Puja, based on Santideva Verses, Ch. 3.

[107] David-Neel, *Magic,* 64.

[108] Buber, *Ecstatic Confessions,* 30.

[109] Katzen, *Vegetable Dishes,* 108.

[110] Sangharakshita, *Drama of Cosmic,* 13-14.

[111] Ryōkan, *One Robe,* 75.

[112] Ibid., 76.

[113] Koch, *Solitude,* 273.

[114] Ryōkan, *One Robe*, 23.

[115] Katzen, *Moosewood*, 26.

[116] Mackenzie, *Cave*, 4.

[117] Sangharakshita, *What is the Dharma*, 59-60.

[118] Milarepa, *Hundred Thousand*, 244.

[119] Dobisz, *One Hundred Days*, 111.

Chapter 8

[120] Crowe, *Which NZ Bird*.

[121] Dzongsar, *What Makes You*, 81.

[122] Leon, *By Its Cover*, 113.

[123] Sangharakshita, *Ritual*, 33, 39.

[124] Nagapriya, *Exploring Karma*, 27.

[125] Heng Ju, *Three Steps*.

[126] Suzuki, *Zen Mind*, 45.

[127] Crowe, *What Tree*, 51.

[128] Sangharakshita, *Dhammapada*, 259.

[129] Ibid., 1-2.

[130] Sangharakshita, *Living With*, 44,

[131] Li-Po, http://poetrychina.net/wp/poets/li_po

Chapter 9

[132] Mackenzie, *Cave*, 12.

[133] Udana Sutta 1:10 -37.

Chapter 10

[134]Kull, *Solitude,* 132.

[135] Dilgo Khyentse, *Heart,* 9.

[136] Lawrence, *Complete Poems,* 538.

[137] Quoted in Badiner, *"On the Path with Thay,"* 45.

Chapter 11

[138] Ryōkan, *Dew Drop,* 30.

[139] Erhlick, *Solace of Open Spaces,* 26.

[140] Maitland, *Book of Silence,* 71.

[141] France, *Hermits,* 26 – 27.

[142] Quoted in *Book of Silence,* 155-56.

[143] Thoreau, *Walden,* 99.

[144] Ryōkan, *Zen Poems,* 56.

Chapter 12

[145] David-Neel, *Magic,* 65.

[146] Govinda, *White Cloud,* 101.

[147] Maitland, *Book of Silence,* 57.

Epilogue

[148] Kull, *Solitude,* 164.

[149] Blomfield, *Gautama Buddha,* 186.

Glossary

abhaya   (Sk) literally "fearlessness"; a symbolic hand gesture, palm facing forward, fingers pointing up; a symbol of protection that dispels fear. (See mudra.)

ahimsa   the principle of non-violence; harmless in relation to life; non-injury; a tenet of Mahatma Gandhi's campaign for Indian freedom. Ahimsa silk refers to silk produced without killing the pupae or moth to reel off the silk thread, allowing the worm to mature, pierce the cocoon and emerge.

Akshobya   the blue Buddha of the East, representing Mirror-like Wisdom; called the "Immutable One". (See jina.)

anagarika   literally a "homeless one"; a person who has given up most or all worldly possessions and responsibilities to commit full-time to Buddhist practice; one who renounces relationships, family, career and materialism.

Avalokiteshvara   an enlightened being, said to be the manifestation of Buddha's compassion; called the Boddhisatva of Infinite Compassion.

Amitabha   the red Buddha of the West, representing Discriminating Wisdom; associated with the Pure Realm; Buddha of Boundless light and Compassion. (See jina.)

Amoghasiddhi   the Buddha of Fearlessness; green Buddha of the North; representing All-Encompassing Wisdom. His name means infallible (amogha) success (siddhi). (See jina.)

Bhante   (Pali) literally means "Venerable Sir"; teacher; in the Triratna Buddhist Order Bhante refers to Sangharakshita, the founder.

bhikshu   (Sk) also *bhikkhu* (Pali) an ordained monastic monk, one who lives by gathering alms.

Bodhicitta   (Sk) altruistic intuition; the mind dedicated to attainment of enlightenment in order to benefit all sentient beings most effectively.

Bodhisattva   (Sk) in Mahayana Buddhism, one who has attained enlightenment and is on the way to Buddhahood but postpones reaching the goal with a vow to help all beings attain salvation.

body scan   a form of meditation; to mentally be aware of each region of your body in sequence; a way to be in touch with the body, to let go of feelings, to release pent-up emotions and to train attention.

Buddha Shakyamuni   literally, "the Awakened One, the Shakyan Sage"; usually refers to Siddhartha Gautama who lived in India 563-483 BCE; the Indian price who became an All-Enlightened Being; the historical founder of Buddhism.

Chan   (C) from the (Sk) *dhyana* meaning "meditation"; a Chinese school of Mahayana Buddhism; called Zen in Japan.

Dharmachari/Dharmacharini   literally "dharma-farer," the word used as a title for Triratna Buddhist Order members.

darshan   (Sk) a silent transmission of spiritual experience.

Dharma   (Sk) also *dhamma* (in Pali) the Buddha's teachings; also dharma: the way, the law; the truth, righteousness, and reality.

dhyana   (Sk) also *jhana* (in Pali) sublime states of mental absorption; a state of strong concentration focused on a single sensation or mental notion; dynamic meditation or contemplation. (The words *ch'an* and *zen* are Chinese and Japanese derivatives of *dhyana*.)

dukkha   (Pali), also *duhkha* (Sk) Buddhist word meaning suffering, pain or "unsatisfactoriness".

enlightenment   total knowledge; a state of perfect wisdom and unlimited compassion; the only permanently satisfying solution to human predicament; the achievement of a buddha.

gassho   (J) a gesture of honor and greeting, with palms of the hands placed together; it signifies interconnectedness, union of opposites.

Going for Refuge   the central act of Buddhism; to seek refuge in the Three Jewels: the Buddha, the Dharma and the Sangha; to make Buddhism an integral part of one's life; a necessary step for ordination into the Triratna Buddhist Order.

gorse   a yellow-flowered shrub of the pea family; its leaves form prickly spines; native to western Europe, it was imported to New Zealand and has become a "nuisance shrub" taking over the native bush plants.

hrih, hrī, hiri   (Sk) a "seed syllable" meaning personal conscience, mature self-awareness; also defined as shame, to blush.

jina   literally "conqueror"; the five jinas are archetypal Buddhas representing an inter-related mandala communicating Buddhist truths; each of the five jinas embodies a wisdom aspect of enlightened vision: Akshobya (wisdom of the great mirror), Ratnasambava (wisdom of equality), Amogasiddhi (wisdom of discriminating awareness), Amitabha (wisdom of all-accomplishing work) and Vairocana (wisdom of the dharma realm).

karma   (Sk) literally "action"; actions or thoughts whose results are felt in this or future lives; the law of "cause and effect".

kauri   (Maori) among the world's mightiest trees; the largest species of tree in NZ, standing up to 50 meters tall and with trunk girths of up to 16 meters; kauris covered much of the North Island when the first people arrived, 800 - 1000 years ago.

kesa   (Jp) also as *kasaya* (Pali) a collar of fabric worn by Triratna Order members bearing the three jewels embroidered on each end. Anagarikas wear a yellow kesa in reference to the saffron robe of the Theravadan monastics, while Dharmacari/nis wear a white kesa.

kleshas   (Sk) mental states that cloud the mind; emotional obscurations poisons or defilements such as ignorance, hatred, desire, pride and envy.

koan   an enigmatic question; the contemplation of koans is a central meditation practice of Rinzai Zen School, intended to by-pass the habitual rational mind that often overly relies on intellect and reason and thereby to trigger insight and awakening.

Kuan Yin, Guanyin (C) or Kannon (J) the Boddhisatva of Compassion and Mercy; a great being who aspires to help all sentient beings; venerated especially by Mahayana Buddhists, known as she "who hears the cries of the world".

kyosaku (Soto Zen) or *keisaku* (Rinzai Zen) a flat wooden stick used during periods of Zen meditation to remedy lapses in concentration.

Mahayana the "great vehicle"; a broad school or movement of northern Indian Buddhism found in Japan, Tibet, Mongolian, China and Korea; characterized by its focus on the bodhisattva vow.

mala a string of Buddhist prayer beads used for spiritual practice; 108 or 111 beads used to count repetitions of mantras.

mani literally "jewel"; mani rocks are stones painted or carved with the sacred Buddhist mantras; carving mani stones is considered a form of meditation.

manuka (Maori) New Zealand tea-tree, or broom tea-tree; a flowering plant in the myrtle family native to Australia and New Zealand that often grows to 20 – 30 feet tall in scrub areas.

mantra (Sk) literally "mind protection;" a Sanskrit or Tibetan phrase or string of sound-syllables recited to concentrate and protect the mind; phrases that embody the energy of an enlightened being.

metta (Pali) or *maitri* (SK) meaning loving kindness, friendliness, amicability, benevolence, affectionate kindness, good-will, amity and sympathy.

metta bhavana meditation practice to cultivate feelings of loving kindness

Milarepa, Jetsum (1040 – 1123) Tibetan yogi, poet and teacher, whose biography and poetry are among the best-loved works of Tibetan Buddhism; an archetypal disciple, meditation practitioner, hermit and teacher.

Mitra (Sk) "friend"; in Triratna Order, those who have made a simple going-for-refuge ritual.

morepork New Zealand owl; ruru (Maori)

mudita (Pali and Sanskrit) sympathetic or vicarious joy; also the pleasure that comes from the success of others.

mudra a mystic or symbolic gesture of hands and fingers; the mudra *abhaya* is done with the palm facing forward and fingers pointing up symbolizing "fearlessness".

Om Mani Padme Hum a Tibetan mantra translated as "jewel in the lotus"; recitation of this mantra along with counted prayer beads is a popular religious practice in Tibetan Buddhism; it is believed that such continuous recitation can lead to liberation and eventual Buddhahood.

ottappa (Sk) social conscience.

Pali the language of the Theravada Buddhist canon said to be the language used by Buddha.

papañca (Pali) the proliferation of thought.

phowa (Tibetan) the transference of consciousness at the time of death.

piti (Pali) also *priti* (Sk) rapture; a mental factor of concentrative absorption (see dhyana); joy associated with deep tranquility; the arising may have physical manifestations such as goose flesh and shaking.

Prajnaparamita literally "perfection of wisdom"; direct intuitive insight into the true nature of things; a term for the enlightened being.

precepts the way of ethical training recommended by the Buddha and other Buddhist teachers; directions given as a rule of practice or conduct.

ponga a silver tree fern that grows up to 12 meters tall and 160–450 millimeters in diameter with fronds 4 meters long and a distinctive silver-white coloration on the underside; a symbol commonly associated at home and abroad with the country of New Zealand.

puja a ceremony showing reverence through invocation, prayers, chanting, devotional attention; ceremonial worship.

puriri evergreen tree of New Zealand.

rata a tree of the myrtle family with hard wood and red flowers in early summer.

Ratnasambhava the archetypal Buddha of Generosity; the yellow Buddha of the South; his name means "Jewel-born One." (See jina.)

refuge to be sheltered, to rely on; a place to put your trust; Buddhists "take refuge" in the Buddha, Dharma and Sangha.

Rimpoche (Tibetan) literally, a "precious one"; an honorific title given to a Tibetan Buddhist master, especially one who is believed to be the rebirth or emanation of a previous highly developed Buddhist.

rimu New Zealand red pine.

rupa a form, shape or figure; a Buddhist statue.

sādhanā a personal meditation practice in which one identifies their own form, attributes and mind with those of a deity (see yidam) for the purpose of transformation.

samsara the present world we live in; the cyclic realm of birth and death.

sangha the spiritual community of the Buddha's followers.

Sangharakshita (Dennis Lingwood) 1925 - ; Buddhist teacher and writer; founder of the Triratna Buddhist Order (known as FWBO until 2009.). Ordained as a Theravadin Bhikkshu in the period following World War II, he spent over twenty years in India where he had a number of Tibetan, Chan and Indian Buddhist teachers. He was active in the conversion movement of Dalits (Untouchables) in India and has authored more than sixty books. Sangharakshita devised a non-monastic ordination system, and allows the taking of "anagari-ka" precepts of renunciation.

seed syllable   bija; is a Sanskrit letter regarded as the concentrated essence of an enlightened being. The seed syllable for Kuan Yin is "hrih."

shibori   (J) bound and stitch-resist dye technique for patterning fabric.

shraddha   (Sk) faith.

skandhas   (Sk) literally "heaps," aggregates, or groupings; the five factors that constitute sentient beings' mental and physical existence: body, feelings, volition, perception and consciousness.

stupa   a circular mound or monument often containing relics, used as a focus for meditation; originally a mound or structure built to commemorate a Buddha or other highly developed persons. It has become a symbol for the mind of Buddha.

sunyata   emptiness in the sense that all things are empty of intrinsic, unchanging existence and nature.

sutta   (Pali) also *sutra* (Sk)   literally "a thread on which a jewel is hung"; a discourse attributed to the Buddha or a disciple.

tantra   the esoteric practices of the Vajrayana; yogic practices of visualization, mantra, mudra and mandalas, as well as symbolic ritual to work with subtle energies.

Theravada   the "School of the Elders"; a branch of Buddhism now found in Sri Lanka and South East Asia that preserves the Pali Canon as its doctrinal core.

Three Jewels   Buddha, Dharma, Sangha.

tonglen   (Tibetan) a meditation visualization practice for exchanging self with others.

Tiratnavandana   a chanted salutation to the Three Jewels of Buddha, Dharma and Sangha.

Triratna Buddhist Order   (formerly Friends of the Western Buddhist Order, FWBO) an international ecumenical Buddhist Order founded in 1967 in the UK by Sangharakshita.   Its six defining aspects include its base as an ecumenical movement; Going for Refuge to the Buddha, Dharma and Sangha as core; a unified Order, not propagated by monastic lineage; with emphasis on spiritual friendship; team-based right livelihood; and the importance of the arts in spiritual development and devotion.

tui   (Maori) a native New Zealand songbird.

tulku   one who inherits a specific lineage of teachings in Tibetan Buddhism; a tulku is given empowerments and trained from a young age by students of his predecessor; he is believed to be a reincarnation of the predecessor.

Vajrasattva   a bodhisattva associated with purification.

Vajrayana   the "Thunderbolt" or "Diamond Vehicle" tradition of esoteric Buddhism, commonly called "tantra".

visualize   to envision; to conjure up an image; the building up of a clear and stable image in your mind's eye.

visualization   a common form of Buddhist meditation involving the use of imagination to create vivid symbolic forms.

yidam a type of deity associated with tantric or Vajrayana Buddhism said to be a manifestation of Buddhahood or enlightened mind. In meditation, practitioners identify their own form, attributes and mind with those of a yidam for the purpose of transformation.

References

Badiner, Allan. "On the Path with Thay", Tricycle, Spring 2015 vol. 24 no. 3

Beck, L. Adams. *Splendor of Asia: The Story and Teachings of Buddha*. NY: Dodd, Mead & Co. 1926.

Bianco, Frank. *Voices of Silence: Lives of the Trappists Today*. NY: Anchor Books, 1992.

Blofeld, John. *Bodhisattva of Compassion: The Mystical Tradition of Kuan Yin*. Boston: Shambhala Publications,1977.

Bloomfield, Vishvapani. *Gautama Buddha*. London: Quercus, 2011.

Bhikkhu Bodhi, Trans. *In the Buddha's Words: An Anthology of Discourses from the Pali Canon*. Boston: Wisdom Publications, 2005.

———. *The Connected Discourses of the Buddha: A Translation of the Samyutta Nikaya*. Boston: Wisdom Publications, 2000.

Blofeld, John. *Bodhisattva of Compassion: The Mystical Tradition of Kuan Yin*. Boston: Shambhala Publications, 1977.

Bodhi, Bhikkhu and Bhikkhu Nanamoli (trans.). *The Middle Length Discourses of the Buddha: A New Translation of the Majjhima-nikaya*. Boston: Wisdom Publishers, 1995.

Bodhicitta Blessing. Adapted and edited by Karunadevi. Unpublished doc.

Brahm, Ajahn. *Mindfulness, Bliss and Beyond*. Somerville MA: Wisdom Publishers, 2006.

Buber, Martin. Ecstatic Confessions. San Francisco: Harper and Row Publishers, 1985.

Byrd, Richard. *Alone*. New York: Putnam and Sons Books, 1938.

Catherine, Shaila. *Focused and Fearless: A Meditator's Guide to Sates of Deep Joy, Calm, and Clarity*. Somerville MA: Wisdom Publications, 2008.

Cheng, Nien. *Life and Death in Shanghai*. NY: Grove Press, 1987.

Crowe, Andrew. *Which Native Forest Plant?* Auckland: Penguin Books, 2009

———. *Which Native Tree?* Auckland: Penguin Books, 2009

———. *Which New Zealand Bird?* Auckland: Penguin Books, 2001.

Cooper, David A. *Silence, Simplicity and Solitude*. Woodstock VT: Skylight Paths Publishing, 1999.

David-Neel, Alexandra. *Magic and Mystery in Tibet*. New Delhi: Harper Collins Publishing, 1993.

Dilgo Khyentse Rinpoche. *The Heart of Compassion: The Thirty-Seven Verses on the Practice of a Bodhisattva*/Commentary on Root Text by Gyalse Ngulchu Thogme. Boston: Shambhala, 2007.

Dillard, Annie. *The Writing Life*. New York: Harper Collins Books, 1990.

Dobisz, Jane. *One Hundred Days of Solitude Losing Myself and Finding Grace on a Zen Retreat*. Somerville MA: Wisdom Publications, 2008.

Drake, Nadia. "Why People See Faces in the Moon." http://news.nationalgeographic.com/news/2014/04/140412-moon-faces-brain-culture-space-neurology/

Dzongsar, Jamyang Khyentse. *What Makes You Not a Buddhist*. Boston: Shambhala Publications, 2007.

Ehrlich, Gretel. *The Silence of Open Spaces*. NY: Penguin Books, 1985.

Evans-Wentz, W.Y (ed). *The Tibetan Book of Great Liberation*. London: Oxford University Press, 1962

Fermor, Patrick Leigh. *A Time to Keep Silence*. NY: The NY Review of Books, 1957.

France, Peter. *Hermits: The Insights of Solitude*. New York: St. Martin's Griffin, 1996.

Goddard, Dwight (ed.). *The Buddhist Bible*. Boston: Beacon Press, 1970

Govinda, Lama Anagarika. *The Way of the White Clouds*. London: Riders and Co., 1966.

Gunaratana, Bhante Henepola. *Beyond Mindfulness in Plain English*. Boston: Wisdom Publications, 2009.

Hahn, Thich Nhat. *The Sun My Heart*. Berkeley CA: Parallax Press, 1992.

Harper, Laura, et al. *The Rough Guide to New Zealand*. NY: Rough Guide Publishing, 2006.

Heng Ju, Bhikshu, Bhikshu Heng Yo. *Three Steps, One Bow: American Buddhist Monks' 1000 Mile Journey for World Peace*. Burlingame CA: Buddhist Text Translation Society, 2014.

Jamgon Kontrul's Retreat Manual. Trans. by Ngawang Zanpo. Ithaca NY: Snow Lion Publishers, 1994.

Kamalashila. *Meditation: The Buddhist Way of Tranquility and Insight*. Birmingham UK: Windhorse Publishing, 1992.

———. *Buddhist Meditation: Tranquility, Imagination and Insight*. Cambridge: Windhorse, 2012.

Katzen, Mollie. *The Vegetable Dishes I Can't Live Without*. NY: Hyperion Press, 2007.

———. *Moosewood Cookbook*. Berkeley CA: Ten Speed Press. 1977.

Keller, David G.R. *Oasis of Wisdom: The Worlds of the Desert Fathers and Mothers*. Collegeville MN: Liturgical Press, 2005.

Koch, Philip. *Solitude: A Philosophical Encounter*. Peru IL: Open Court Publishing Co., 1994.

Kornfield, Jack. A Path with a Heart. NY: Bantam Press, 1993.

——— (ed.). *Teachings of the Buddha*. Boston: Shambhala Publishers, 1993.

Kull, Robert. *Solitude: Seeking Wisdom in Extremes*. Novato CA: New World Library, 2008.

Lawrence, D.H. "Be Alone". https://notes-in-nature.org/tag/ponderosa-pine/

Leon, Donna. *By Its Cover.* NY: Grove Atlantic.2014

Levine, Stephen and Ondrea. *Who Dies? An Investigation of Conscious Living and Dying.* NY: Doubleday, 1982.

Li Po. "Zazen on Ching t'ing Mountain". *Crossing the Yellow River: Three Hundred Poems from the Chinese.* Translator Sam Hamill. Rochester NY: BOA Edition, 2000.

Macy, Joanna. *World As Lover, World As Self.* Berkeley: Parallax, 1991.

Mackenzie, Vicki. *Cave in the Snow: A Western Woman's Quest for Enlightenment.* NY: Bloomsbury, 1999.

Maitland, Sara. *A Book of Silence.* NY: Counterpoint, 2008.

Maitripala. *Kuan Yin Puja.* Unpublished doc. Adapted from *Santideva's Guide to the Bodhisattva Path.*

McAra, Sally. *Land of Beautiful Vision: Making a Buddhist Sacred Place in New Zealand.* Honolulu: University of Hawai'i Press, 2007.

Merton, Thomas. *The Silent Life.* NY: Farrar, Straus and Cudahy, 1957

———. *Thoughts in Solitude.* NY: Noonday/ Farrar, Straus, and Giroux, 1956.

———. *A Vow of Conversation: Journals 1964- 1965.* NY: Farrar, Straus and Giroux, 1988.

Mettanando, Ve. Dr. Bhikkhu, "Did Buddha Die of Mesenteric Infraction?" http://www.lankalibrary.com/Bud/buddha_death.htm.

Milarepa, *The Hundred Thousand Songs of Milarepa.* Translated by Garma C.C. Chang, Boston: Shambhala Publications, 1999.

Mitchell, Stephen (ed.). *The Enlightened Heart: An Anthology of Sacred Poetry.* NY: Harper Collins Publishers, 1993.

Mingyur Rinpoche. "Why Do We Take Refuge." *Buddhadharma.* Summer 2014, 48.

Nagapriya. *Exploring Karma and Rebirth.* Birmingham, UK: Windhorse Publishing, 2004.

Nouwen, Henri. *The Way of the Heart: Desert Spirituality and Contemporary Ministry.* NY: Harper Collins, 1981.

———. "Solitude and Community," *Worship* 52. 1978.

Oliver, Mary. *New and Selected Poem,* Boston: Beacon Press,1992.

Philips, Douglas. "Take a Hard Look," *Buddhadharma.* Summer Issue 2014

Politzer, Anita. *A Woman in Paper.* NY: Simon and Schuster, 1988

Ryōkan. *Dew Drops on a Lotus Leaf: Zen Poems of Ryōkan.* Translated and edited by John Stevens, Boston: Shambhala Publications, 1991.

———. *One Robe, One Bowl: The Zen Poetry of Ryōkan.* Translated by John Stevens, Boston: Weatherhill Publishers, 1997.

――――. *The Zen Poems of Ryōkan.* Translated by Nobuyuki Yuasa. Princeton University Press, 1981.

Sangharakshita, Urgyen. *Dhammapada: The Way of Truth.* Birmingham UK: Windhorse Publishers, 2001

――――. *Drama of Cosmic Enlightenment: Parables, Myths and Symbolism of the White Lotus Sutra.* Cambridge UK: Windhorse Publishers, 1993.

――――. *Living with Awareness.: A Guide to the Satipattana Sutta.* Cambridge UK: Windhorse, Publishers, 2003.

――――. *What is the Dharma?: The Essential Teachings of the Buddha.* Birmingham UK: Windhorse, Publishers,1998.

――――. *The Religion of Art.* Glasgow: Windhorse Publishing, 1988.

――――. *Ritual and Devotion in Buddhism.* Birmingham UK: Windhorse Publishers, 1995.

Santideva. *A Guide to the Bodhisattva Way of Life.* Translated by B. Alan and Vesna A Wallace, Ithaca NY: Snow Lion Publishers, 1997.

Sarton, May. *Journal of a Solitude.* NY: Norton and Co., 1973.

Sarvananda. *Solitude and Loneliness: A Buddhist View.* Cambridge UK: Windhorse Publishers, 2012.

Simpson, Joe. *Touching the Void.* London: Random House, 1997.

Sogyal, Rimpoche. The Tibetan Book of Living and Dying. San Francisco: Harper, 2002.

Sonam Rinchen, Geshe. *Eight Verses for Training the Mind.* Translated and edited by Ruth Sonam. Ithaca NY: Snow Lion Publishers, 2001.

Storr, Anthony. *Solitude: A Return to Self.* NY: Free Press Macmillan Publishers, 1988.

Suvajra, Dharmacari. *The Wheel and the Diamond: The Life of Dhardo Tulku.* Glasgow: Windhorse Publishers, 1991.

Suzuki, Shunryu. *Zen Mind, Beginners Mind.* NY: Weatherhill Publishing, 1970.

Suzuki, D.T. *An Introduction to Zen Buddhism.* London: Ridge &Co. 1949.

Tenzin Palmo, Jetsunma. *Into the Heart of Life.* Ithaca NY: Snow Lion Publishers, 2011.

Thoreau, Henry David. *Walden.* NY: Signet Classics, 1960.

――――. *The Journal of Henry David Thoreau, 1837 – 1861.* New York: NY Review Books Classics, 2009.

Tsangnyön, Heruka. *The Life of Milarepa.* Translated by Andrew Quintman. NY: Penguin Books, 2010.

Tsongkhapa. *Readings From The Refuge Tree of the Western Buddhist Order.* Edited by Lokabandhu and Cittapala. Cambridge, UK: Windhorse Publications, 1990.

Twichell, Chase. *The Snow Watcher.* Buffalo, NY: White Pine Press, 1998.

Walshe, Maurice (trans). *Thus Have I Heard: The Long Discourse of the Buddha- Digha Nikaya.* London: Wisdom Publications,1987.

Vajragupta. *Sailing the Worldly Winds: A Buddhist Way Through the Ups and Downs of Life*. Cambridge UK: Windhorse Publications, 2011.

Vishvapani. "The Four Reminders." *Madhyamavani* V, Spring 2003.

———, Blomfield. *Gautama Buddha: The Life and Teachings of the Awakened One*. London: 2011.

Watt. Alan W. *The Way of Zen*. NY: Pantheon Books, 1956.

Zopa, Lama Rinpoche. *Vajrasattva: Practice and Instruction for Retreat*. F.P.M.T. 2003.

Made in United States
North Haven, CT
04 March 2024

49551399R00232